Mennonites, Amish, and the
American Civil War

YOUNG CENTER BOOKS IN ANABAPTIST & PIETIST STUDIES

Donald B. Kraybill, *Series Editor*

Mennonites, Amish, and the American Civil War

James O. Lehman and Steven M. Nolt

THE JOHNS HOPKINS UNIVERSITY PRESS
Baltimore

The Johns Hopkins University Press
2715 North Charles Street
Baltimore, Maryland 21218-4363
www.press.jhu.edu

Library of Congress Cataloging-in-Publication Data

Lehman, James O.
Mennonites, Amish, and the American Civil War / James O. Lehman and Steven M. Nolt.
    p.   cm. — (Young Center books in Anabaptist and Pietist studies)
Includes bibliographical references and index.
ISBN 13: 978-0-8018-8672-0 (hardcover : alk. paper)
ISBN 10: 0-8018-8672-4 (hardcover : alk. paper)
1. Mennonites—United States—Social conditions—19th century. 2. Amish—United
States—Social conditions—19th century. 3. Anabaptists—United States—History—
19th century. 4. Pacifists—United States—History—19th century. 5. United States—
History—Civil War, 1861–1865—Religious aspects. 6. War—Religious aspects
—Christianity—History—19th century. 7. Mennonites—United States—Political
activity—History—19th century. 8. Amish—United States—Political activity—
History—19th century. 9. United States—Politics and government—1861–1865.
10. United States—History—Civil War, 1862–1865—Social aspects.
I. Nolt, Steven M., 1968– II. Title.
E184.M45L44 2007
973.7088'2897—dc22   2006101464

A catalog record for this book is available from the British Library.

Contents

APPENDIXES

Tables and Maps

Tables

Maps

Acknowledgments

The research for this volume rests on decades of work in dozens of libraries and archives, and has thereby incurred debts too numerous to mention. References in the notes and bibliography acknowledge the many resources on which we drew. Special thanks go to the Spruance Library of Bucks County, Pennsylvania, and the Montgomery County (Pa.) Historical Society Library at Norristown for full access to their collections and for their special efforts in digging deeply into, and making available, unprocessed materials. Other Pennsylvania depositories whose collections and staff aided this study include the Library Company of Philadelphia, Historical Society of Pennsylvania, and Union League Collection, all of Philadelphia; Schwenkfelder Library, Pennsburg, Pennsylvania; and Berks County Historical Society, Reading, Pennsylvania. Extensive newspaper research was possible at the fine newspaper collections of the Lancaster (Pa.) Public Library; Lancaster (Pa.) Historical Society; and Franklin and Marshall College Library, Lancaster, Pennsylvania. Further west, the United States Army Military History Institute at Carlisle, Pennsylvania, and Pennsylvania State Archives and Pennsylvania State Library at Harrisburg, along with the Franklin County (Pa.) Public Library were quite helpful, as was the Juniata College Library, Huntingdon, Pennsylvania. In Maryland, staff at the local history rooms of the Washington County Public Library provided warm assistance.

The Ohio Historical Center in Columbus provided significant materials and helpful collections of newspapers for counties with Mennonite and Amish communities. The Wayne County (Ohio) Public Library and its local history section, and Wayne County Courthouse records proved helpful, as did other county libraries or historical societies in Ohio, Indiana, Illinois, and Iowa, along with the Indiana and Illinois State Libraries and Archives. The staff of the Elkhart County (Ind.) Historical Society was exceptionally accommodating, even allowing research in one case during off-season hours when the archives was otherwise closed. In Virginia, the Virginia Historical Society provided very helpful lists of Mennonite men of conscience. Public libraries in Rockingham and Augusta counties furnished important material as well.

Mennonite historical libraries and archives were especially helpful: Mennonite Heritage Center, Harleysville, Pennsylvania; Lancaster (Pa.) Mennonite Historical Library; Menno Simons Historical Library and Archives, Harrisonburg, Virginia; and Archives of Mennonite Church USA and Mennonite Historical Library, both of Goshen, Indiana, were especially important collections, each managed by extraordinarily knowledgeable and helpful staff.

Individuals who provided access to private papers included Christian Kurtz and Wilmer Reinford in Pennsylvania; Alta Schrock and Roy Showalter in Maryland; and Leroy Beachy and Oscar R. Miller in Ohio. Miller's collection supplemented the Holmes County Public Library. Finally, we are grateful to the many individuals who shared diaries, letters, and other sources from their private and family connections.

Our respective academic institutions supported this project in various ways. Eastern Mennonite University provided time, including a 1979–80 sabbatical and other resources to James Lehman. The Inter-Library Loan office at Goshen's Harold and Wilma Good Library filled countless requests from Steven Nolt. A grant from Goshen College's Mininger Center and from the college's Plowshares program supplied key financial support. Craig A. Mast, a highly skilled Goshen College history major, performed excellent editorial work on the book's text, notes, and maps and compiled the bibliography.

Special thanks go to Edsel Burdge Jr., Theron F. Schlabach, Joseph C. Liechty, and two anonymous peer reviewers, who provided helpful comment and critique. Donald B. Kraybill, series editor for the Johns Hopkins University Press's Young Center Books in Anabaptist and Pietist Studies provided wonderful guidance. Acquisitions editor Claire McCabe Tamberino shepherded this project at the Press, and manuscript editor Elizabeth Yoder polished our prose. Finally, we wish to extend our deepest thanks to our families for their generous support and patience during the many years this project was underway.

Mennonites, Amish, and the
American Civil War

Religion, Religious Minorities, and the American Civil War

Tremendous Storm Brewing

Peter Hartman hurried home to his family's farm outside Harrison-burg, Virginia, carrying the *Rockingham Register*. It was November 1860, and Peter's father, David, had sent his son to town for a copy of the county's weekly paper. Like other families throughout the United States, the Hartmans were keeping a wary eye on political developments that year, especially during the fall months, when four major candidates battled to be the U.S. President.[1]

When Peter arrived home that evening, the rest of the Hartman household was waiting. He handed the paper to an older sister, who usually read it aloud to the rest of the family. "The first thing my sister read," Hartman recalled, "was that Lincoln was elected." The news "made us all weak" and "almost made the blood run cold." The Hartman family had clear unionist sympathies and did not object to Lincoln himself; rather, they understood that the Illinois Republican's election portended political instability at best, and political breakdown and civil strife at worst. Peter's thoughts ran to something he had overheard an old man telling his father: "There is a tremendous storm brewing in the South, and when that storm breaks with all its fury, it will shake the South to its very center."[2]

Rural Virginians who harbored political concerns, David and Eliza-beth (Burkholder) Hartman were also Mennonites, members of a thriv-

Mennonite Henry H. Derstine (1841–1900) of Bucks County, Pennsylvania, in
about 1860, shortly before he "skedaddled" to Ontario to avoid the military draft.
He later returned to eastern Pennsylvania, married, and raised a family.
Credit: Mennonite Heritage Center, Harleysville, Pa.

ing community of church folk in the Shenandoah Valley whose lives both
paralleled and diverged from those of their white neighbors. For example, the Mennonites generally took a dim view of disunion, as did most
yeomen (small-scale independent farmers) in this part of their state, who
tended to be skeptical of the political rhetoric that came from Richmond
and other Southern state capitals dominated by wealthy planters and pro-

fessional elites. But Mennonites were also opposed to slavery, a position that, if it did not make them entirely unique in the slave-based economy of the South, certainly placed them outside the mainstream. Moreover, they were committed to a Christian ethic of pacifist nonresistance, unwilling to fight when ordered by the government or even to defend their families with force, a stance that set them apart in a Southern culture that championed martial honor—and even apart from most Protestant evangelicals with whom Mennonites shared some affinity.[3]

Yet Mennonites as a group would not share a singular Civil War story in the months and years that followed. Even as Rockingham County church members like David Hartman continued to nurse unionist sentiments, Mennonite bishop Jacob Hildebrand of Augusta County, Virginia, noted in his diary on the following May 23, "I was at Waynesboro; votet for Seesetion [sic]."[4] Nor were Mennonites in the North, where 90 percent of their numbers lived, as did their spiritual cousins the Amish, always of one mind on how best to reject rebellion as peace people.[5] Pennsylvania Mennonites became a core constituency for Radical Republican congressman and war hawk Thaddeus Stevens, who protected their conscientious objector privilege. Meanwhile, in Ohio, Mennonite bishop John M. Brenneman discouraged such deals. Brenneman drafted a petition to Lincoln but then demurred, deciding that the president was "but a poor dying mortal like ourselves." To expect help from civil authorities was to "lean on a broken reed."[6] The intensity of the war and the issues it evoked sometimes sparked contrasting reactions even from close-knit ethnic sectarians. Like the Hartmans, other Mennonites sensed that they could not withdraw from the tremendous storm that was brewing; but how to construe their separation in such a situation was far from clear.

Religion and the American Civil War

The Civil War remains an epoch-defining event, staggering in its enormity. The national conflagration killed more than 620,000 soldiers in four years. Nearly one in five men of military age in the South, and one in sixteen in the North, died. It is no exaggeration to say that everyone knew someone who did not come home from the war, a situation without parallel in U.S. history. And tens of thousands of men who *did* return had lost arms or legs, so that well into the twentieth century Americans had graphic and bodily reminders of the war's nearly 1.1 million military casualties—not to mention civilians killed or maimed.[7]

Beyond the obvious death and destruction, the scale and scope of the war altered American society in profound ways, redefining gender roles, restructuring constitutional authority, laying a foundation for the federal welfare state and creating unprecedented wealth in some places while sinking others into long-term stagnation. The war also brought an abrupt end to the institution of slavery, surely the most significant single development in the nation's history. Nor did the struggle's effect end at Appomattox. The war's shadow continues to inform the country's politics, mythology, and tragic system of race even in the twenty-first century.[8]

Not surprisingly, more has been written on the struggle between the Union and the Confederacy than on any other aspect of the American experience. From traditional military scholarship to gender analyses and cultural critiques, historians have mined the primary sources for generations and explored a host of interpretations with a rich array of outcomes. Remarkably, however, until quite recently the subject of religion and the war has not attracted much attention, despite the fact that in the 1860s the war evoked ample religious language, imagery, and themes.[9]

Antebellum America—that is, America in the years before the war—had experienced a marked revival of religion in large portions of its majority Protestant population (a renewal movement often tagged as the Second Great Awakening), as well as the establishment of a larger and more vigorous Roman Catholic community. Unprecedented denominational diversity stemming from the influence of immigration and home-grown new religious movements added to the yeasty mix. Moreover, the market-like competition of religious claims in a political atmosphere that generally regarded religion as a necessary component in building and perfecting a republic added dynamism to the public functions of faith.[10]

This dynamism especially surrounded the institution of slavery—the hub around which all other aspects of mounting national conflict in some way turned.[11] Certainly African Americans, both the four million enslaved and the much smaller free population, had long seen their struggle in religious terms. And before the war, the largest white Protestant denominations—Methodists, Baptists, and, Presbyterians—had split over the question of slavery, raising sectional stakes and dissolving the few interregional

Gideon M. Nice (1844–1916) of Montgomery County, Pennsylvania, was reared
in a Mennonite home but donned a Union uniform. Nice saw combat at the Battle of
Gettysburg. Credit: Mennonite Heritage Center, Harleysville, Pa.

institutions the nation otherwise could claim. "If our religious men cannot
live together in peace, what can be expected of us politicians?" Episcopa-
lian Henry Clay asked a Presbyterian editor in 1852. Clay's own church
sundered after Fort Sumter.[12]

For the millions who marched on both sides—arguably the most Christian of any military forces fielded in North America—religion continued to

play a profound role. As horrendous casualty counts mounted, soldiers—already schooled in an antebellum spirituality that stressed concepts of providence and covenant—found consolation and meaning in a series of religious revivals that swept through army camps and in personal disciplines of Bible reading, confession, and prayer. An active chaplaincy corps and an interdenominational Christian Commission, formed to provide for troops' spiritual needs, offered moral interpretations of the conflict.[13]

At home, often far from the battles' sound and fury but close enough to their effects, pastors had to rethink explanations of death, suffering, and sacrifice. Wartime conditions also demanded more active participation from laywomen and a new theology to explain their move into once-masculine roles. Turning to sacred texts in times of social stress, white Southerners constructed new and more extensive biblical justifications for slavery as a divinely sanctioned way of life. Meanwhile, in the North, a sudden groundswell of support for emancipation on the part of ordinary white voters—a politically remarkable development—was largely promoted from Protestant pulpits.[14]

Religiously based arguments for and against slavery were part of a broader use of faith to justify and sustain both sides in a fratricidal war. Framers of the Confederate Constitution believed they had improved upon the Federal document of 1787 by including God in their 1861 preamble and by making *Deo Vindice* (God will vindicate) the motto on their nation's official seal. Partway into the war, the Union responded by adding "In God We Trust" to its coinage. Presidents Abraham Lincoln and Jefferson Davis called for public days of prayer and fasting to bolster morale, and political and military leaders on both sides invoked God's blessing for their holy causes and divine condemnation on their opponents. Spiritual arguments, in a nation so steeped in religious rhetoric, concepts, and convictions, provided the most plausible of rationales.[15]

But if a growing historical appreciation for religion's central place in the nation's preeminent crisis is a welcome development, it remains incomplete. Thus far, the picture of wartime religion—and Protestant Christianity, in particular—is one that demonstrates faith's ability to motivate war efforts, stem surrender sentiments, and make sense of crushing disappointment. That religion could accomplish such things for both sides adds complexity and curiosity to the story, but any role for religion in *resisting* nationalist war machines remains shrouded.[16] True, Christian pacifists (a twentieth-century term few in the 1860s used to describe themselves) comprised only a small part of America's population. Yet they were able to secure legal conscientious objection status in the midst of America's first modern war—in both Federal and Confederate conscription contexts— and thus to set important constitutional precedents.[17]

Attention to the experience of sectarians in the Civil War, moreover, actually advances the emerging larger story of faith's place in more mainstream religious traditions. If spiritual convictions could keep people from participating in a national crusade and not just lend justification, then religion legitimately becomes an independent variable in the interpretation of human choices that shaped the 1860s rather than a secondary measure of something else. Shorn of its dissenting traditions, religion can appear passive and complicit.[18]

Indeed, the limited scholarly attention that Christian peace churches in the Civil War have received has often served to undercut the explanatory significance of religion by employing an ironic interpretation of pacifist experience. In these tellings, peace church people became convinced that war was the only means through which they could achieve Christian ends, and they therefore shelved their nonviolent commitments. Antislavery Wesleyan Methodists, for example, upheld pacifism and abolitionism until popular political logic said that only war could end the curse of bondage, and thus the church had no choice but to encourage enlistment.[19] A dramatic version of this story unfolded among many Northern members of the Religious Society of Friends (Quakers), America's best known pacifists, who responded to the muster drum when the cause was abolition.[20] Such accounts imply that religious rhetoric and beliefs are easily co-opted and are best understood as windows onto other more basic motivations.

But an account of Mennonites and Amish in the Civil War does not support that conclusion. Although they refused to own slaves (by some measures they had clearer record on this point than the better-known Quakers), their beliefs also kept them out of activist abolitionist circles, and—again, for theological reasons—they seldom thought they had to choose between peace principles and political goals. Even in war societies that deployed religion to mobilize a common cause, large majorities of Mennonites and Amish found resources in their faith to resist complete identification with Union or Confederate causes.[21]

Yet even with regard to such resistance, the Mennonite and Amish story is distinctive. Although religiously linked resistance to oppression has been a theme in the history of slave communities and among others without access to traditional avenues of public power, nineteenth-century Mennonites and Amish were not legally shut out of politics.[22] Rather, they were finding their way through a thicket of adaptation. Often they were in cultural quarrels with America and with one another over how best to secure particularity. In their dissent, Mennonites and Amish searched for American idioms to express a sense of social separation (rather than integration). In doing so, they differed from Irish American Catholics, for whom the crucible of war provided a way to "beat back . . . bigotry by showing that Catholics would serve their country."[23] For Mennonites, the question of political engagement was quite complicated, given their desire to identify authentic American ways to stand apart from the sectional crusades.

Several other groups, notably the German Baptist Brethren (often termed "Dunkers" in the nineteenth century), might also expand our understanding of Civil War religion and politics. They deserve their own detailed description.[24] The chapters that follow explore the Mennonite and Amish story. Doing so, they document religious liberty precedents, deepen understandings of the role of religion in American wartime, and demonstrate a creative account of ethno-religious adaptation in a highly charged patriotic and cultural mix.

Who Were the Mennonites and Amish?

Mennonites and Amish were heirs of the so-called Radical Reformation, a movement begun in the 1520s to reestablish the New Testament church on its own terms. A radical movement inspired by and yet frustrated with Reformers like Luther, Zwingli, and Calvin, its adherents sought to be more thoroughgoing in their religious reforms by decoupling church membership and citizenship, marking the community of faith through voluntary adult baptism, avoiding civil oaths that allowed the state to capitalize on divine clout, and following an ethical standard that shunned violence and even self-defense. Civil and religious authorities believed that such practices subverted the prevailing social order and thus condemned the radicals as "Anabaptists" (re-baptizers), hounding them mercilessly. From the 1500s through 1614, Catholic and Protestant rulers executed perhaps as many as 2,500.[25]

Eventually driven into marginal mountain enclaves or surviving as lease-holders on the estates of tolerant nobles, the Anabaptists became known as innovative agriculturalists and as "the quiet in the land." Meanwhile, some authorities had begun to tag the groups with the labels "Mennist," "Mennonist," and "Mennonite"—from the name of an influential Dutch Anabaptist leader, Menno Simons.[26] About the time that Anabaptist-Mennonites began to emigrate from Europe in the late 1600s, a schism among Swiss and Alsatian Mennonites produced a new branch, the Amish (or Amish Mennonites)—named for leader Jakob Ammann. Mennonites and Amish disagreed over matters of church discipline and over what the details of daily discipleship should look like, with the Amish faction typically taking a more separatist and sectarian stance. Nevertheless, they did not differ much in basic theology, and from an outside perspective both groups probably appeared more alike than different. Similar patterns of immigration and of settlement in North America only confirmed such observations.[27]

Invited to settle in the Quaker colony of Pennsylvania, some 4,000 Rhine Valley Mennonites and 500 Amish were among approximately 80,000 German-speakers who came to William Penn's "Holy Experiment" before 1770. Concentrated at first in southeastern Pennsylvania, members of both groups moved westward in the eighteenth and early nineteenth centuries, forming a string of communities that, by 1860, stretched to Iowa and Missouri. Mennonites also moved into Virginia's Shenandoah Valley after 1727, and to Upper Canada (Ontario) after 1786. Then, in the first half of the 1800s, a fresh wave of European immigration brought more Amish (about 3,000) and Mennonites (some 800) to North America. These arrivals largely bypassed the older communities in Pennsylvania and moved directly to the Midwest, Ontario, and upstate New York.[28]

By 1860 perhaps 40,000 baptized Mennonites and Amish lived in the United States—although such figures are always somewhat speculative, given the groups' reluctance to enumerate membership.[29] By far the largest group of Mennonites was the branch known as the (Old) Mennonites (or, frequently, simply Mennonites, without any modifier). Constituting approximately 80 percent of those who claimed the Mennonite name in 1860, the (Old) Mennonites descended from the immigrant group that had come to Pennsylvania in the 1700s. In church matters, local Mennonite congregations of this body were organized into seven regional conferences, each with a cadre of ordained leaders who provided collective discipline and issued instructive, and sometimes binding, conference directives.[30]

In addition to the (Old) Mennonites, there were a number of smaller Mennonite branches, three of which appear with some frequency in this book.[31] Formed in 1860, the new *General Conference Mennonites* were an alliance of perhaps 1,500 progressive-minded folk committed to an activist agenda of formalized mission, education, and publishing concerns. Moreover, they were open to experimenting with more American ways of managing church life, such as incorporating special purpose groups and using more democratic decision-making processes—innovations about which most (Old) Mennonites held reservations. This General Conference branch brought together a group of one-time (Old) Mennonites in eastern Pennsylvania (expelled in 1847 for their more liberal leanings) and several congregations in Iowa and Illinois composed of recent arrivals from southern Germany whose churchly assumptions did not match the slower cultural rhythm of the (Old) Mennonite majority.[32]

A cohort of so-called *Swiss Mennonites* who settled during the 1820s to 1850s in northeastern and northwestern Ohio and in eastern Indiana were another group. They were newcomers, directly from Switzerland, who maintained a traditionalist outlook and strong ethnic sensibilities. In 1860 these roughly 650 Swiss Mennonite church members saw themselves as different both from the Mennonite majority who had been in America since the colonial era and from the similarly recent—but progressive-leaning—south German immigrants.[33]

The *Reformed Mennonites* constituted the third minor Mennonite branch, and one that was highly sectarian and thoroughly dismissive of other Mennonites. Having distinguished themselves in 1812 in Lancaster County, Pennsylvania, from the (Old) Mennonites, whom they considered reprobate, the Reformed Mennonites had perhaps 1,500 U.S. members in 1860. Like other Mennonites and Amish of the day, those in the Reformed branch were almost all farmers and rural artisans. But despite their remarkably sectarian impulse, the Reformed Mennonites also included a number of physicians, a situation otherwise atypical among their spiritual cousins.[34]

Oak Grove Amish Mennonite meetinghouse, near Smithville, Ohio, 1862. During the mid-1800s the Amish divided into tradition-minded (Old Order) and change-minded camps. Change-minded congregations, such as Oak Grove, built meetinghouses and otherwise adapted more readily to American ways than did the Old Orders.
Credit: Pauline Smucker

For their part, the Amish in 1860 were more difficult to categorize and count because their highly congregational polity led to a good deal of local variation. During the 1860s, however, a distinct divide was emerging between *change-minded Amish Mennonites* and *tradition-minded Old Order Amish*. About two-thirds (53) of the nation's seventy-four Amish congregations comprised the change-minded camp, while the rest upheld the Old Order.[35]

Old Orders stuck by well-worn ways of structuring local church life, symbolized by congregational worship in private homes rather than meetinghouses, shunning worldly entertainment, and wearing distinctively plain attire. Change-minded Amish were more open to the appeals of an emerging consumer culture and the popular allure of change. They tended to institutionalize church life by building church meetinghouses, establishing formal programs such as Sunday schools, and toning down the implications of church discipline and the range of issues for which the church would employ discipline. In the twentieth century, the change-minded Amish majority would merge with the Mennonites, while the Old Order Amish—by then rejecting cars and technological gadgetry—would come to define what the public considered to be "Amish." But in 1860 those developments lay in an unknown future, and the change-minded Amish Mennonites saw themselves as faithful interpreters of the Amish way and the Mennonites' closest kin.[36]

Finally, in addition to the Mennonites and Amish, a related group included in this study were the *River Brethren*. Growing out of a 1770s Wesleyan-inspired revival movement among (Old) Mennonites in the Susquehanna River Valley, the River Brethren wedded the warm spirituality of the Methodists with the disciplined ethic (including the pacifism) of the Mennonites. During the 1860s, many River Brethren adopted the name Brethren in Christ. At that time they numbered perhaps two thousand; almost all lived in Pennsylvania, but a few were scattered in the Midwest.[37]

In 1860 Mennonites, Amish, and River Brethren shared many characteristics. Except for the recent immigrants, all groups were becoming fluent in English but considered a German dialect their first language at home and in worship. Humility was an espoused virtue in nineteenth-century American Anabaptist circles, expressed in many ways, including deference to group dictates. Most also adhered to a plain aesthetic in personal appearance, architecture, and decorum—even if their clothing did not diverge from that of their neighbors as much as is the case of the Old Order Amish today.[38]

Local congregations had resident preachers and deacons. Bishops administered baptism and the Lord's Supper, conducted marriages, and handled matters of church discipline. The congregationally organized Amish had one bishop for each church, while Mennonite bishops often had charge of a circuit of congregations. In the 1860s, no ordained leaders in any branch received special training or payment for their church work. As self-supporting farmers or artisans, they were expected to model an Anabaptist life as much as to articulate theological dogma. Preaching drew especially on New Testament scriptures and on stories and observations from everyday life to encourage separation from "the world." What separation meant in practice varied somewhat from the more culturally separatist Swiss Mennonite immigrants to the more sophisticated General Conference Mennonites. But all Mennonites and Amish adhered to some version of a "two-kingdom" theology—the belief that the kingdom of God, manifest by the faithful church, was categorically different from worldly society, which either did not recognize, or refused to submit to, divine dictates. How to live in the tension of those two worlds posed ongoing challenges, but all along the Anabaptist spectrum there was a general sense that the church stood apart from society more than it was a part of society.

One of the outstanding features of the kingdom of God, Mennonites and Amish believed, was its *nonresistance*, or defenselessness (*Wehrlosigkeit*). Following the example of Jesus, who refused to defend himself and told his followers to return good for evil, nineteenth-century Anabaptists renounced self-defense and refused military participation. The most thoroughgoing among them even rejected posting no trespassing notices on private property, since such signage implied the possibility of coercive enforcement.[39] But if communal convictions anchored Anabaptist ideals, it was complicated by those same churches' practice of voluntary adult baptism. Those who appealed to conscience also knew that conscience could not be corralled and coerced. Unbaptized children did not always adhere to parental wishes. Moreover, military service typically targeted young men at the very age they were opting for or against church membership.

This book details the story of negotiating nonresistant citizenship. The political implications were complex—whether in conversation with the state or in relations with neighbors or fellow church members. The scale and scope of the Civil War only increased the intensity of such matters, reaffirming convictions while often reformulating the old approaches.

Mennonites and Amish in a Sectional Conflict

The American Civil War was a decidedly sectional conflict, notwithstanding regional variation within the Confederacy and the Union and the presence of Border States whose governments took ambiguous positions. The Mennonite and Amish experience also had regional flavors,

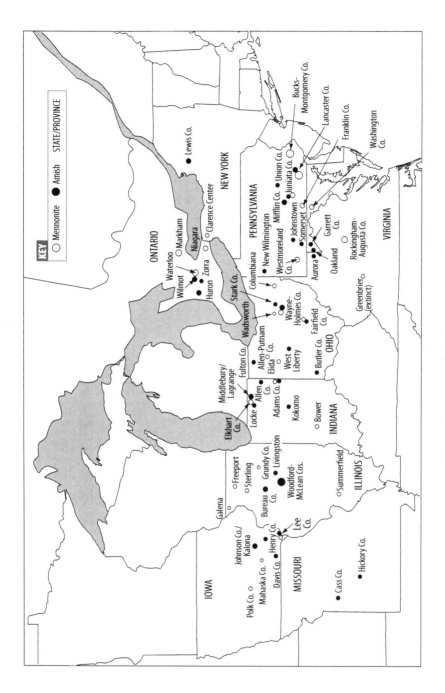

Mennonite and Amish Settlements, about 1860

owing to different contexts in which convictions took shape. For example, the large established communities in Pennsylvania differed in their history and political weight from the newer, smaller settlements in the Midwest, which were also more distant from the theaters of war. Meanwhile, the 350–400 Mennonite households in Virginia found themselves in the midst of the fighting, very often as unionists in a Confederacy where rejecting rebellion was seen as subversive.[40]

This book's story divides along chronological and regional lines. The opening chapters introduce the religious, cultural, and political issues that framed Mennonite and Amish people's Civil War experience, and describe their initial reactions to secession and the outbreak of hostilities. Three chapters then compare experiences of political pressure and the initial conscription acts of 1862 in Virginia, Pennsylvania, and the Midwest. Especially pivotal were the months from the fall of 1862 through summer 1863, for they brought significant political and ideological developments, not to mention major battlefield encounters. The fighting came home in dramatic ways for many Mennonites and Amish living in Pennsylvania and Union-occupied Maryland, and Lee's two northern incursions made matters of nonresistance more immediate. After recounting those events, we compare the different ways Northern Mennonites and Amish negotiated their wartime experiences—with many Pennsylvanians cultivating relationships with powerful political players, and many of their Midwestern counterparts articulating new sectarian arguments for apoliticism.

Then the account returns to Virginia, where the war had remained all too immediate and where civilians in the Shenandoah Valley suffered destruction regardless of political persuasion. Through it all, Mennonites in Rockingham County remained more resistant to Confederate coercion, while those in Augusta County continued to express some Southern sympathies until the bloody conflict ended in April 1865.

With the war's conclusion, competing schemes to reconstruct American society promised either to restore or to transform the young republic that had rent itself apart. The shortcomings of Reconstruction, especially for African Americans, were enormous. Yet in important ways the nation that emerged after 1865 was dramatically different. And perhaps more than they realized at the time, American Mennonites and Amish too had reconstructed their sense of peoplehood in the turmoil of the 1860s. Their new formulations, emerging from a war experience not shared by the thousands of new European Mennonite immigrants who began arriving after 1873 or by those who had lived in Canada, would mark the North American Mennonite and Amish world in important ways. Well into the twentieth century they would reaffirm regional and ethnic distinctions and produce powerful arguments for how to construe citizenship and peace.

Before the promises and perils of any reconstruction would surface, however, Mennonites and Amish shared in their nation's bloody travail. In 1864 (Old) Mennonite Christina Herr of Medina County, Ohio, wrote her cousin "the sorrowful news" that her "three oldest brothers went to war." It was very hard to see them go, she said, "but it cannot be helped." Someone must go, she decided, drawing on popular apprehensions, "or else we must lose our country." Worse yet, we might even "be treated like the slaves are." In the same letter her father, John Herr, poured out his own sorrow: "I little thought that wee was raising children to goo to war . . . but it realy now is so and I am often overcome that I can't keep back the tears when I think of the thousands which have already gone to an untimely grave." His wife Barbara "wept bitterly day and night," but "tries to bee resigned to [God's] will."[41]

The Herrs' letter expressed layers of pain and frustration, along with a certain ambivalence that the war brought on American Mennonites and Amish. Condemning rebellion but unwilling to suppress it with force, they struggled to make sense of their position as separatist citizens in a restless republic—and to interpret these experiences theologically and politically. Some of those raised in nonresistant homes put on uniforms, witnessed the carnage firsthand, and lost their lives. Other Mennonites and Amish suffered losses that did not show up in casualty counts but stemmed from the pain of rejected religious teaching and family schism. The Herr's sorrow, resignation, and weeping were both broadly American and particularly Mennonite.

Politics and Peoplehood in a Restless Republic

From Subjects to Citizens

In 1799 Thomas McKean, a Revolutionary War leader, won a contentious race to be Pennsylvania's governor, and soon the "Mennonist Society" of western Lancaster County addressed an open letter to the new executive in the German-language newspaper *Der Lancaster Correspondent*. The Mennonites began by complimenting the governor's character and wishing him good health, but then got to the point. As "a plain People" who spoke with "simplicity," Mennonites held "conscientious scruples against bearing arms." They understood that the "excellent [state] constitution" of 1790 guaranteed their opting out of direct militia service, but they wondered if McKean supported nonresistants' rights. "We profess ourselves to be friends of peace," the writers continued, "and hope not to be backward in our duties as citizens of a free state." For his part, McKean responded favorably, reaching out to the Mennonite constituency.[1]

This exchange between Mennonites and the governor highlighted three interrelated themes that became more important in the first half of the 1800s: citizenship, peace, and American politics. For Mennonites and Amish, citizenship was a relatively new reality, with implications for their peace convictions and their understanding of public life. They would still be sorting out these relationships in different parts of the young nation when, in the 1850s, the politics of slavery moved to center stage, radically restructuring national debates and setting up the crucial national election of 1860.

One of the most significant adjustments that nineteenth-century American Mennonites and Amish had to make was to citizenship. In Europe, Anabaptists had functioned politically as *subjects*—people who were not part of the state, but lived under rulers' authority. Subjects petitioned for privileges, which a government dispensed or took back as it saw fit. In the new American republic, however, Mennonites and Amish were *citizens*—people who by definition possessed rights without asking for them and had responsibilities whether they wanted them or not. Citizenship was, in theory at least, universal and equal in its protections and demands. Instead of the sharp distinction that separated subjects and their state, citizens themselves comprised the state, which did not exist apart from its people.

Already in the 1700s, Pennsylvania Mennonites had begun moving toward citizen-style participation in public life. No longer confined to being tenants and living under autocratic rule as they had been in Europe, Mennonites and Amish eagerly obtained land titles and worked with the provincial government to secure their property rights. Political involvement was easier because Pennsylvania's ruling party was heavily influenced by Quakers, who did not force militia duty on the colony's citizens. Moreover, citizenship was often cast in the form of preserving privileges that had been handed down by proprietor William Penn—so the language sounded familiar and subject-like, even as savvy politicians played out new forms of citizenship politics. In 1768, for example, well after religious Quakers had lost control of the legislature, Mennonites were still actively supporting the so-called Quaker Party. In September of that year, a prominent English official reported that "the head Men among the Mennonists have had a Meeting . . . and have fixed a new [election] Ticket," bearing their endorsement.[2]

The Revolutionary War temporarily put a damper on most Pennsylvania Mennonite voting, since Mennonites were among the state's "non-associators" (those who did not immediately recognize the new rebel government) and thus were barred from the ballot box after 1777.[3] Once the revolution was an accomplished fact, however, the new state constitution of 1790 welcomed all citizens—former rebels and loyalists alike—back to

the political process, and Mennonites obliged. The shape of that relationship would depend on at least two factors: the resilience of Anabaptist
convictions, such as peaceful nonresistance and a two-kingdom worldview; and an emerging democratic political culture that changed the flavor
of citizenship.[4]

Peace teaching ran deep in these circles, even if the tradition had not
produced many eloquent expositions of nonresistance. The posture of
peace was caught more than taught, but it came through encouragement
to imitate the meek Jesus and through stories in the massive Anabaptist
volume *Martyrs Mirror*, whose heroes had given, rather than defended,
their lives. Nonresistance had a host of practical implications for personal
relationships, but in relation to citizenship it meant that Mennonites and
Amish refused participation in state militias and typically avoided civic
roles that placed coercive power directly in their hands. What such a
stance meant politically was less clear. Politics might be a means to secure nonresistant citizenship; as the letter to governor McKean suggested,
political engagement could be in the service of separation. On the other
hand, politically active citizenship might seem to threaten claims to any
special nonresistant status.

At the same time, American Anabaptists rarely assumed that their own
conscientious scruples would ever be widely shared by others.[5] Unlike
pacifist Quakers, whose theology and social position allowed them to believe that their peace stance could become mainstream and should be politically influential beyond their own circles, Mennonites and Amish did
not expect that everyone would accept the ethical counsel of Christ, nor
did they question the necessity of state-sanctioned violence in a world
dominated by the worldly.[6]

Thus, Mennonite and Amish appraisals of government, citizenship,
and politics were rather ambiguous. On the one hand, Mennonites and
Amish were temperamentally oriented toward the church as their primary
community, and not the nation. Their two-kingdom theology encouraged
them to believe that the truly important developments in life took place in
the household of faith, not in legislative assemblies.[7] Yet they did live with
one foot in the kingdom of this world, and they were far from withdrawn,
participating in preserving orderly civic life to a greater degree than some
interpreters have assumed.

An understanding of conscience could connect life in these two kingdoms. Anabaptists did not believe that faith could be forced on an un-willing conscience, that "inner voice of God by which the Spirit of God speaks to men," in the words of progressive Mennonite reformer John H. Oberholtzer.[8] And a republic, as patriot leaders such as Thomas Jefferson explained, protected and respected personal conscience more than did other forms of government. A Bucks County, Pennsylvania, (Old) Mennonite minister Abraham Godschalk seems to have agreed; he prayed in the 1830s "for those who bear rule in our country, this glorious America, the people of which enjoy liberty of conscience and of worshipping God according to the dictates of their conscience."[9] Adding to this sense of appreciation was the fact that a good number of Amish and Mennonites, especially those who had immigrated after 1815, had come at least partly to avoid European military conscription. Nonresistance had helped bring them to an America that they believed would honor their convictions.

One of the ways Mennonites and Amish expressed their sense of citizenship was in their assumption that it was quite proper for the republic to require something of them. For example, as they publicly practiced nonresistance, they readily accepted *equivalency* for, rather than *exemption* from, militia demands. States allowed nonresistants to make cash payments in lieu of personal militia service.[10] Virginia's militia statute, for example, required men between the ages of 18 and 45 to spend four days annually in military drilling or to pay a small sum.[11] With few exceptions, Mennonites paid the equivalency fee after being enrolled. For example, in 1842 in Fairfield Township, Columbiana County, Ohio, as many as twenty-four Mennonites, two of them ministers, were named in the militia list.[12] In Chester County, Pennsylvania, in 1856, Amish land owner Abraham Kurtz paid a total of $86.36 in county, state, and militia taxes to tax collector John Plank. The following year John P. Mast was the collector when Kurtz paid. Here it seems that both taxpayer and tax collectors were Amish.[13]

American Mennonites and Amish had long served as tax collectors, county road supervisors, township trustees, and the like—offices that supported their interest in upholding orderly community life. But after about 1825, politics took on a different, more rough-and-tumble flavor. The rise of democracy was a second important factor in the shaping of Mennonite and Amish relationship to the public sphere. In a democracy, citizens no longer simply elected their social betters who then managed affairs on

everyone's behalf. Instead, male voters became players in a highly competitive game of power and persuasion that recognized no absolutes but
saw only constantly shifting majorities built on popularity and promises.
Some politicians now began asserting that voting for a candidate implied
complete support of, or even responsibility for, the candidate's subsequent
actions in office. Logic did not demand such a link, but some partisans
pressed the point as a way of cultivating party loyalty in this new world of
unstable coalitions. Such claims could unnerve Mennonite citizens, who
continued to see politics as a process that protected dissenters.

Convictions in Contexts

Whatever one's understanding, by the mid-1830s the meaningful avenues for political engagement had become the Democratic and the Whig
parties. Drawing on the ideas popularized by President Andrew Jackson
(1829–37), Democrats argued that the republic would thrive in an atmosphere of minimal government and local autonomy, so they denounced
large institutions such as Bank of the United States that wielded widespread influence. Democrats also championed the continual acquisition
of western land, insisting that political liberty ultimately depended on
an economic independence found only among land-owning farmers and
artisans.[14]

In contrast, the opposition Whigs argued that the young republic was
a fragile experiment that needed careful tending from knowledgeable ex-
perts. Rather than hasty development across space, which raised the specter of unruly people on an unmanaged frontier, Whigs spoke of development across time through the establishment of public schools, libraries,
and cultural institutions that could refine public opinion from generation
to generation. In the Whig scheme, entities like the Bank of the United
States were essential for orderly commerce. Whigs tended to be more
cautious when it came to appropriating Native American land or claiming territory from Mexico—actions that Democrats championed. At the
same time, Democrats often showed more tolerance for immigrant groups,
who were alienated by Whig efforts to impose Whig cultural values on
others.[15]

At first blush, Mennonites and Amish might have found attractive features in each of the national parties. The Whig emphasis on conservative

economics could appeal to generally well-to-do Anabaptists in established eastern communities who wanted to secure their children's financial futures. Amid tumultuous nineteenth-century economic upheaval, Whig policies on banking, taxation, and the sale of public land seemed prudent. For other Amish and Mennonites—especially recent arrivals from Europe who settled in the Midwest—the Democrats' pledge to allow local communities to remain unmolested by meddling outsiders sometimes seemed more appealing. Moreover, Whig reformers who promised to save society through civic temperance campaigns, Sabbath-keeping laws, and English-language public schools had limited appeal among two-kingdom Anabaptists, who believed moral renewal came through the gathered church.[16]

Although the national political environment set the stage for participatory citizenship, local relationships and regional contexts shaped Mennonite and Amish political engagement more than distant party platforms. Three broad regional patterns emerged by the 1850s, each of which had implications for civic life.

A Pennsylvania German Context

The Mennonites and Amish who settled in southeastern Pennsylvania during the 1700s were a small part of a much larger wave of German-speaking newcomers, nearly 80,000, mostly Lutheran or Reformed, who had come through the port of Philadelphia before the American Revolution.[17] Concentrated in southeastern Pennsylvania but with related settlements elsewhere in the state and in western Maryland, these people and their descendants formed communities marked by a distinct Pennsylvania German culture and dialect (sometimes also called Pennsylvania Dutch).[18] From architecture and clothing styles to folklore and food, Pennsylvania German cultural customs cut across denominational lines and set its adherents apart from their English, Scottish, Irish, and Welsh neighbors.

Although Mennonites comprised only a small portion of the Pennsylvania German subculture, they nevertheless lived as a part of it, for example, by marking special Pennsylvania German holidays. Pennsylvania German Mennonites sometimes intermarried with Lutheran and Reformed families, attended ethnic-dominated local schools, and shared burial grounds. Pennsylvania German religion prized pietist values, discouraged flashy dress, resisted innovation, and guarded local traditions.[19] In this region,

Lutheran and Reformed church-goers, no less than Mennonites, were often hesitant to endorse distant mission boards, tract societies, and Sunday school movements.

In such a context, Mennonite separation from society was not straightforward. In many ways, Mennonites found a comfortable ethnic niche, since Pennsylvania German culture could set them apart from the American mainstream without entirely isolating them. They could be different in the company of others.[20] True, Pennsylvania German Mennonites were rather distinct in their conscientious scruples; but even here, the cultural context provided something of a buffer for Mennonites and Amish who lived within its bounds. Nonresistance might seem more curious and less subversive when its adherents were part of a larger tradition known for being American in unusual ways.

Not surprisingly, Pennsylvania German Mennonites and Amish appear to have been more active in local and state politics than were their coreligionists in other parts of the country.[21] At the township level, Amish and Mennonites frequently held public posts, while Lancaster and a few other counties saw (Old) Mennonites elected as county commissioners. There were some Mennonite justices of the peace and a few legislators. In 1837 voters elected two Mennonites to the state constitutional convention: Mathias Pannebecker Jr. of Montgomery County, and Joseph Snively of Franklin County. Surviving evidence suggests that almost all Mennonites and Amish in Pennsylvania aligned with the Whig Party, and Whig leaders were said to have flattered Mifflin County Amish businessman and party stalwart Shem Zook by suggesting that he should run for governor.[22]

Of course, not every Pennsylvania German Anabaptist was politically active, and ordained ministers, in particular, typically saw their vocation as incompatible with holding public office.[23] Still, politics within the Pennsylvania German milieu could appear less a compromise with an evil world than an expression of participation in a friendly ethnic community.[24]

Life in the Shenandoah Valley

Pennsylvania Germans extended their ethnic enclaves beyond the borders of Pennsylvania itself. Moving into the backcountry of Virginia and the Carolinas, they created a small but discernable chain of communities that

"Farmer John" Landis (1785–1867) of Lancaster County, Pennsylvania, was a member of Mellinger Mennonite church and a prominent civic leader, bank president, county commissioner, and delegate to the 1848 Whig Party Convention that nominated Zachary Taylor for president. Credit: Lancaster (Pa.) Mennonite Historical Society

some historians have labeled "Greater Pennsylvania," where kinship and commercial connections to the Keystone State were strong.[25] The (Old) Mennonites in Rockingham and Augusta counties, Virginia, were part of this diaspora.

But despite their connection to the Pennsylvania German heartland, Mennonites in Virginia's Shenandoah Valley found themselves in a very different cultural context.[26] For one thing, the Pennsylvania German population was relatively small, and Virginia was overwhelmingly English in its orientation. Not surprisingly, Mennonites here were among the first to shift to the English language, even in internal church affairs. By 1850, 33-year-old Jacob Hildebrand, bishop for Virginia's Augusta County Mennonite churches, kept some congregational records in English.[27]

Then too, Virginia life was influenced by values rooted in both English cavalier society and rough-and-tumble backwoods life, both of which differed from specifically Anabaptist and broader Pennsylvania German orderly ideals. And even if yeomen farmers resented the influence of wealthy planters in eastern Virginia, they still lived with the results of such rule. Slavery became central to the state's economy, and a more hierarchical view of social relationships prevailed, transforming even the religion of common folk among evangelical Baptists and Methodists.[28] All of this made the Mennonites in the Shenandoah Valley distinct outsiders—generally tolerated or benefiting from benign neglect in the first half of the 1800s, but outsiders nonetheless. A few men of nonresistant background broke into the planter class and were accepted into the ruling Democratic Party. Mennonite-descended legislator and slave owner Samuel A. Coffman was such a figure, but his success in Virginia was possible only to the extent that he distanced himself from his heritage.[29]

Bereft of an influential Pennsylvania German subculture such as existed in Pennsylvania, Virginia Mennonites formed closer relations with the Valley's peace-church Dunkers and tended their ties to Mennonite communities in the North—relations and ties they would need when their Southern home became a war zone.

Amish and Mennonites in the Midwest

The Midwestern states from Ohio to Iowa offered a third cultural context for mid-nineteenth-century Amish and Mennonites. It included considerable variety but also common threads. The Amish and Mennonite population itself was more mixed here, a composite of easterners who had migrated west, plus recently arrived immigrants from Europe. Unlike the eastern Pennsylvanians, whose sizable Pennsylvania German neighborhood acted as a cultural buffer, or the Virginians, who might be ignored by the powerful in their area, Midwestern Mennonites and Amish generally lived in a region culturally dominated by New England Yankees set on reforming society and involving everyone in the process. In that sense, the Midwesterners were both isolated and exposed as Anabaptists.

In broad terms, such a setting could heighten minority sensibilities, or it could encourage assimilation.[30] Some Amish and Mennonites reacted by identifying with Democrats, who had staked a reputation on resisting Yankee efforts to legislate cultural conformity. Certain Amish and Mennonite settlements in Holmes and Wayne counties, Ohio, and around Berne, Indiana, seem to have moved in this direction, perhaps encouraged by the vocal Democratic newspaper editors in these places, as did the immigrant Hessian Amish in McLean County, Illinois.[31] Immigrant Amish preacher Christian Reeser Sr. of Woodford County, Illinois, was said to have voted Democratic in every presidential contest but two from 1844 to 1920; while Samuel Yoder, reared in Holmes County, Ohio, later reminisced about his and his siblings' Amish upbringing as "true, loyal Democrats."[32]

Meanwhile, other Midwestern Amish and Mennonites seemingly welcomed Yankee overtures and the political invitation into the mainstream. The rather eccentric McLean County, Illinois, Amish schoolteacher Joseph Joder was exceptional in the stridency with which he pushed the Republican platform and urged "every freedom-loving citizen" to go "to the ballot box and silently decide in favor of freedom"; but local historian Steven R. Estes has found broader, if quieter, Amish support for Whig and Republican politics in central Illinois as well as some local office-holding under their banner.[33] Amish preacher Christian Farni may even have gotten involved in some campaign activity. Entangled in 1857–58 in an embarrassing and costly fraudulent investment scheme, Farni engaged a local attorney named Abraham Lincoln to represent him and then wrote to Lincoln in 1859 that "when the political campaign will commence, I would like to have a hand in it, and I do readily believe that [we] can carry Woodford County in 1860."[34]

Democratic or Republican, the possibilities and challenges Midwesterners faced were different from those in the East or in the Shenandoah Valley.

The Politics of Free Soil

Of course, American Anabaptists were not the only people living with regional differences. As the nineteenth century wore on, such differences in the United States deepened into outright sectional rivalry. By the 1850s, sectionalism was producing intractable political conflict, almost all of it centering on the increasingly contentious issue of slavery and its place in the future of the American republic.

Relatively few white Americans living through the first half of the nineteenth century viewed slavery with the sort of moral clarity that those in the twenty-first century do. By the 1850s a sizable majority of Northerners had come to oppose slavery, but only a small number—committed abolitionists—did so because they cared very much about enslaved people themselves. Most antislavery sentiments were directed at the *institution* of slavery, which critics condemned on economic and political grounds. Slavery, it was said, gave slave owners an unfair competitive advantage, concentrated wealth, depressed wages, and retarded the growth of a free-market economy where workers were also free consumers. Opponents also charged that slavery undercut civic virtues such as political liberty and freedom of expression—but again, they were thinking of how freedom was diminished for whites. Most white opponents of slavery were concerned not so much with the plight of black slaves as with a fear that slavery limited economic opportunities and forced white workers into slavelike conditions.

In the 1850s this antislavery movement typically went by the name "Free Soil." Free-Soilers conceded that slavery could not quickly be abolished in the fifteen states where it was still legal, but they insisted that all western federal territories be closed to slavery and that any new land acquisition be reserved exclusively for a free-labor economy. Free Soil ideas provoked heated debate and began to divide the major parties. Would geographic expansion—one of the Democrats' central planks—increase acres available for slavery, as southern Democrats hoped, or for free labor, as many of the party's northern members wanted? Would Whig interest in reforming society endorse the antislavery activism of northern Whigs at the expense of the party's Southern wing?

Such questions became more acute in the wake of the Mexican War—a conflict that Democrats had provoked in 1845, only to disagree bitterly with one another over what to do with new territory the United States won. The historic Congressional Compromise of 1850 tried to settle matters between Free-Soilers and slavery promoters, only to leave both sides feeling as if they had been cheated. And a new Fugitive Slave Law that made Northerners complicit in the enforcement of slavery riled northern Whigs and Democrats alike. Suddenly, slavery was the unavoidable issue, eclipsing banking and taxation debates that had marked the political terrain for decades.[35]

Especially after 1854, when passage of the Kansas-Nebraska Territories Act made it appear that slavery would spread westward unchecked, northern Free-Soilers, who had been faithful Democrats and Whigs, broke with their respective parties and formed a new Republican Party, committed to Free Soil principles. The remnant northern Whig Party was crippled by the defection of its Free-Soilers, as were northern Democrats.[36]

In Pennsylvania, Mennonites were among the Whig constituents who transferred their allegiances to the new Republican camp.[37] In the Midwest, the picture was more complex, since loyal Democratic opinion remained strong in some places and the new Republican coalition in the Midwest was more closely tied to agendas suspicious of immigrants and religious minorities. Southern Ohio, Indiana, and Illinois were home to thousands of "Butternut voters"—Southerners who had moved north across the Ohio River and were cool to the moral claims of northern Republicans. Few Mennonites or Amish lived in Butternut territory, but the Butternut regions influenced Midwestern politics as a whole in a way that was not true in Pennsylvania.

Indeed, after the 1856 election, in which the Republicans fielded their first presidential candidate (who came in second), Mennonite Johannes Risser, an ardent Republican, was frustrated that so few fellow Midwestern immigrants saw eye-to-eye with him on political matters. Risser was an 1833 arrival from Friedelsheim in the German Palatinate. He settled in Ashland County, Ohio, then complained to relatives back in Europe about the country's German-language press, which he thought was in the pocket of the Democratic Party. German-born voters did not realize that voting Democratic meant voting "in favor of the spread of slavery," he groaned. To his astonishment, he had even heard that "nearly all our Mennonites in Iowa voted for the Democrats, that is, for the spread of slavery." By 1858 Risser was convinced that it was "the Christian duty of every citizen to work against slavery." "I would never cast a vote for the further spread of slavery, for I see in this affair a matter of conscience, as do all our children and relatives," he informed his sister and brother-in-law.[38] Risser later wrote several articles that questioned slavery's biblical justification and published two of them in *Das Christliche Volks-Blatt*, the new, Pennsylvania-based periodical of John H. Oberholtzer, a leader of the progressive General Conference Mennonite Church.[39]

Risser was highly unusual among Mennonites in his detailed condemnation of human bondage. Despite Oberholtzer's willingness to publish Risser's pieces, the *Volksblatt* itself never took a strong antislavery editorial stand. Oberholtzer was no friend of slavery, but in printing Risser's articles he may have acted mainly as a publisher reaching out to potential subscribers among recent immigrants. And by the late 1850s, Risser himself had only tenuous connections with other Mennonites, having aligned himself with a local "union church" that blended Lutheran and Reformed liturgies.[40]

Mennonites and Slavery

In the 1700s Mennonite and Amish arrivals in British North America had been part of a privileged minority, for they had come as free people able to control the terms and conditions of their work, a status that only about a quarter of the immigrants during those years enjoyed.[41] Nonetheless, once they arrived in Pennsylvania—or later moved to Maryland or Virginia— they would have had contact with enslaved Africans, since slavery was a legal part of British colonial life everywhere. In 1780 Pennsylvania enacted a gradual emancipation law, but it set a pace so slow that there were still a few slaves until 1847, and those in Pennsylvania German ethnic enclaves spoke that dialect.[42] Despite the presence of slavery in Mennonite and Amish neighborhoods, however, estate and census records yield virtually no suggestion that colonial and nineteenth-century Mennonites and Amish owned slaves.[43]

The silence of estate and census documents might seem weak evidence except that it matches the testimony of contemporary observers who pointed to Mennonite and Amish aversion to slave owning. When Quakers John Woolman and John Hunt tried to convince fellow members of the Society of Friends to reject slavery—until the later 1700s many Friends were slave owners or traders—they cited the Mennonites' consistent antislavery example.[44] In 1809 some Baptists in Page County, Virginia, also saw antislavery as a Mennonite distinctive. There, Baptist-style revivalism had appealed to a small Mennonite group under the leadership of one Martin Kauffman. Kauffman's people tried to affiliate with the Baptists, but the two sides could not make the union work because, in the Baptists' words, the Kauffman group "would keep no slaves, swear no oaths, nor bear arms in defence of their country."[45] Through the 1860s, Virginia Mennonites barred slaveholders from membership. As Mary Brenneman explained later, "There will be no slavery . . . in heaven, and ought to be none here."[46]

Puzzling is the case of Tobias Miller, perhaps a Mennonite, who lived near Leitersburg, Maryland, and whose 1820 census entry listed nine slaves. It is unclear how Miller came to own the slaves, six of whom were children. If he was indeed a Mennonite, did the church discipline him? Miller manumitted one of his slaves that summer, and two years later, when he died of typhoid fever, his clearly Mennonite heirs took steps immediately to free the rest. Since Maryland law prohibited the direct manumission of minors, some lived with members of the Miller clan as indentured servants until they came of age. Several were later buried in the Mennonite cemetery.[47]

Mennonite and Amish rejection of slavery likely drew on several roots. Perhaps the Anabaptist heritage of persecution made them wary of human trafficking. As three former Mennonites put it in a 1688 antislavery petition they helped draft, "In Europe there are many oppressed for Conscience sacke; and here there are those oppressed wch are of a black Colour."[48] Yet few Mennonite writers used these sorts of Christian humanitarianism arguments.

Instead, some historians have suggested that regional economic and ethnic contexts played a role in shaping Anabaptist attitudes on the matter. Relatively few Pennsylvania Germans of any religious affiliation owned slaves. Moreover, in rural southeastern Pennsylvania, slaves were not so much an economic asset as a status symbol.[49] For Mennonites and Amish, then, commitments to simplicity and relatively plain living also worked against their readiness to buy human property. In 1837, when Virginia bishop Peter Burkholder outlined what those who submit to the covenant of baptism "have to observe," he was clear that, since "all are free in Christ, they must take no part in slaveholding, or in trafficking with them in any wise." Moreover, he placed this prohibition in a discussion of Christian humility, in which no "members exalt themselves above the others, but in lowliness of mind . . . esteem other[s] better than themselves."[50]

As the 1800s wore on, geographic context no doubt also played a role in shaping Mennonite and Amish opinion. As late as 1860, many Pennsylvania Mennonites and Amish still would have had memories of slavery in their neighborhoods and were aware of fugitive slaves crossing the Mason-Dixon Line. One dramatic reminder was a bloody riot that erupted in 1851 in the Lancaster County village of Christiana when a Southern slave owner arrived to reclaim run-away "property."[51] Meanwhile, Mennonites in the Midwest lived in places where slavery had never existed and where the debate at times focused more abstractly on how the institution of slavery affected the economic equilibrium. Finally, for those in Maryland, Virginia, and Missouri, opposing slavery for any reason placed one on the sidelines.[52] None of this means that Mennonites' religious beliefs played no role in their antislavery attitudes. Rather, their beliefs emerged from a mix of motives and contexts that gave their rejection of slavery particular shapes.

Those shapes were almost never abolitionism, the political movement that sought to use state incentive or raw force to free all slaves currently held in bondage.[53] Given their two-kingdom worldview and typical disinterest in accepting responsibility for broader society, most Mennonites and Amish were not inclined to use the levers of government to reform society, even when they believed society was corrupted. In this respect they differed from Quakers, whose roots in the English Calvinist tradition primed them to proceed as if all of society could be brought into conformity with God's will if believers only took charge.[54] Mennonites agreed that divine purposes could be realized in the here-and-now, but only within the church. If keeping themselves pure seemed short-sighted to some critics, for Mennonites and Amish it was no simple burden.

But if few Anabaptists were abolitionist activists, many came indirectly to support government action against at least the spread of slavery. Even if the Whig-turned-Republican supporters among them were mainly voting their self-interest, their ballot box choices also produced decidedly antislavery public policy.[55] Harry Rexrode, a Virginia Mennonite who had moved to Elkhart County, Indiana, in the 1860s, might have been proud of the fact that "our church & the Amish did not preach negro in this county."[56] But the votes his fellow church members cast—especially in Pennsylvania, where a majority of Mennonites lived—wittingly or unwittingly did much to undercut slavery.

The Election of 1860

Harry Rexrode was not the only easterner who had migrated west with political convictions in tow. In 1857 an energetic 22-year-old (Old) Mennonite named John F. Funk moved from eastern Pennsylvania to Chicago.[57] A son of Jacob and Susanna (Fretz) Funk, of Bucks County, the young Funk followed a brother-in-law's call to join a thriving Midwestern lumber business. Although reared in a rural culture that knew little of city life, Funk dove into the urban scene, built up business connections, became friends with noted Sunday school promoter Dwight L. Moody, and followed with keen interest the fortunes of the young Republican Party. While the world of big-city contractors and evangelical activists was surely new for Funk, his political persuasions had been part of his eastern cultural baggage. Already he had gained some of his partisan principles from a politically oriented father and had picked up antislavery notions when he had been a student at Freeland Seminary, a relatively new Pennsylvania school begun by Mennonite-connected Abraham Hunsicker.[58]

By the time Funk went to Chicago, his people in Pennsylvania had transferred their loyalties to the new Republican Party, and Funk followed Republican fortunes from Illinois. His 1858 diary often recorded little else than political meetings.[59] He also sent copies of both the *Chicago Tribune* and the *Chicago Democrat* to his family back east until father Funk told John to stop mailing the *Democrat*—the Pennsylvania Funks only had time and interest to read the Republican-oriented *Tribune!*[60]

For his part, when the next presidential election rolled around in 1860, the Chicago-based Funk was well positioned to witness it, since two Illinoisans were among a crowded field of four candidates. Not only the number of contenders but also a set of sharply different agendas meant that the election was one of the most unusual and dramatic in U.S. history. After years of seeking to maintain its national base by skirting the issue of slavery's spread, the Democratic Party divided along sectional lines. Illinois Senator Stephen A. Douglas represented Northern Democrats who insisted that the federal government could neither encourage nor prohibit slavery in the western territories but had to leave the issue in the hands of local voters. In contrast, John C. Breckinridge, the sitting vice president and now presidential nominee for Southern Democrats, insisted that the federal government must guarantee slavery in all federal territories and strictly enforce the Fugitive Slave Law. On the other side of Douglas, Illinois Republican Abraham Lincoln argued that Congress had the authority to ban slavery from the western territories and should do so immediately. Finally, a small remnant of the old Whig Party backed former Tennessee Senator John Bell under the banner of a "Constitutional Union Party." They urged compromise on the matter of slavery but offered few specifics.

Satisfied with their status as a sectional party, Republicans did not try to run candidates in the South. Instead, slave-state voters typically chose between Breckinridge and Bell, while Lincoln and Douglas faced off in the North. An unusually dry summer in 1860, with poor harvests, added to a general anxiety and rancor. When John Funk sent a letter to his brother, Abraham K. Funk, in Pennsylvania, the Chicagoan used an envelope that bore a "lithograph" of Lincoln. Somewhere along the way a post office employee "bedaubed" the Lincoln image with ink, "done I suppose," A. K. Funk imagined, so "that he would then look like a *Black* Republican." The racist defacing only gave the Funks a new platform from which to wax eloquent about their candidate of choice: "Beneath that ink-stained brow," A. K. crowed, "we still can trace the sterling qualities of [Lincoln's] noble soul. He is in possession of a mind and heart that cannot be *corrupted*, a character that cannot be *stained*, and an integrity that cannot be *soiled* or *defamed*."[61]

One of John Funk's boyhood friends, F. R. Hunsicker, assured Funk that Bucks County had remained in the hands of "good *Republicans*." If it were up to the locals, Lincoln and his running mate, Maine's Hannibal Hamlin, "will walk into the capitol over their opponents." "There are, no doubt, some Douglas men in our midst, but *who* they are it is almost impossible to determine. They are so quiet that their 'silence may almost be heard.'" Everywhere people "have raised poles with large streamers bearing aloft and swing[ing] to the breeze the names Lincoln and Hamlin," including one with "a maul and four wedges, emblematic of 'rail splitting'" and "'honest old Abe.'"[62]

If Funk could assume common Republican commitments with his Pennsylvania kin, he must have stepped over a line when promoting Lincoln to some of his Midwestern business associates. At least one, William Thompson from Alexandria Bay, Michigan, upbraided the lumberman for advocating the Republican cause and castigated Funk as "a Black Republican of the darkest kind." Jumping to the conclusion that Lincoln was an abolitionist—a claim Lincoln himself had not made in 1860—Thompson warned Funk that massive social disorder would follow the freeing of slaves, disorder that did not comport with evangelical Christian virtues Thompson thought he and Funk both wanted. "An abolitionist is a combination of universalist and infidel—a man who in his own estimation thinks he knows more than his creator. It is impossible for a man to be an abolitionist and a Christian," Thompson insisted.[63]

Yet across the North, opinion was running against Thompson. When the balloting was over, Lincoln had garnered 54 percent of the popular vote in the free states (39 percent for the nation as a whole) and rolled up a solid Electoral College majority by carrying every Northern state. Southern Democrat Breckinridge came in second, claiming eleven slave states. Both Douglas and Bell—the candidates who had, in their own ways, suggested some sort of compromise—clearly lost.

The neighborhoods in which most Mennonites and Amish lived reflected some of the national mood. In Pennsylvania and some western locales, strong Lincoln support emerged; in other Midwestern settlements, Democratic sentiments prevailed. In slaveholding Maryland and Virginia, Mennonites lived where moderate voices were strong. Anabaptist voters may not have mirrored their neighbors' votes in every case, but there is little reason to believe that in 1860 they deviated dramatically from their local communities' patterns and preferences.[64]

Across the country, the election results were electrifying. Having won the presidency with only Northern votes, Lincoln symbolized to a great many Southern nationalists the end of their political power. And although not all white Southerners wanted secession—especially not the small,

Table 1.1. 1860 Presidential election returns in selected counties with significant Mennonite and Amish populations

State and county	Total votes	Lincoln (Republican) %	Douglas (Northern Democrat) %	Breckinridge (Southern Democrat) %	Bell (Constitutional Union) %
Pennsylvania					
Bucks	12,199	**53**	42	4	1
Franklin	7,364	**56**	34	9	1
Lancaster	19,656	**68**	26	4	2
Mifflin	3,009	**57**	40	3	1
Montgomery	12,615	**46**	44	4	6
Maryland					
Washington	5,420	2	5	46	**47**
Virginia					
Augusta	3,865	—	28	6	**66**
Rockingham	2,913	—	23	30	**47**
Ohio					
Allen	3,728	48	**51**	1	<1
Columbiana	5,401	**53**	39	6	2
Fulton	2,643	**62**	37	1	<1
Holmes	3,621	36	**63**	1	<1
Wayne	6,575	48	**49**	2	<1
Indiana					
Adams	1,552	41	**57**	1	1
Elkhart	4,437	**56**	44	<1	—
LaGrange	2,470	**69**	30	<1	1
Illinois					
McLean	6,181	**57**	42	<1	1
Tazewell	4,545	**52**	48	<1	<1
Woodford	2,706	46	**52**	<1	1
Iowa					
Johnson	3,389	**53**	43	1	3

Source: W. Dean Burnham, *Presidential Ballots, 1836–1892* (Baltimore: Johns Hopkins Press, 1955).

Note: Boldface numbers indicate winners.

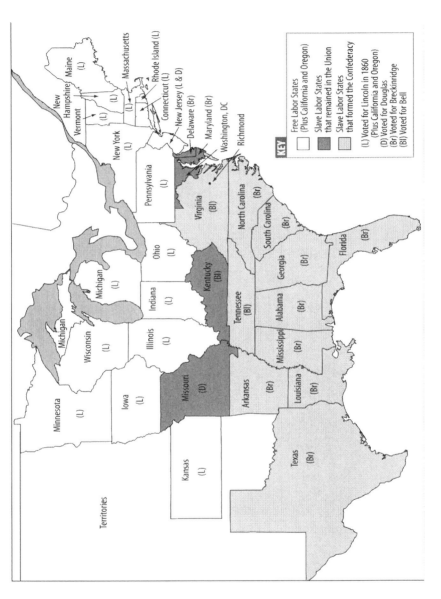

United States in 1861

KEY

Free Labor States
(Plus California and Oregon)

Slave Labor States
that remained in the Union

Slave Labor States
that formed the Confederacy

(L) Voted for Lincoln in 1860
(Plus California and Oregon)
(D) Voted for Douglas
(Br) Voted for Breckinridge
(Bl) Voted for Bell

Territories

Minnesota (L)

Kansas (L)

Iowa (L)

Wisconsin (L)

Michigan (L)

Michigan

Illinois (L)

Indiana (L)

Ohio (L)

Missouri (D)

Kentucky (Bl)

Tennessee (Bl)

Arkansas (Br)

Texas (Br)

Louisiana (Br)

Mississippi (Br)

Alabama (Br)

Georgia (Br)

Florida (Br)

South Carolina (Br)

North Carolina (Br)

Virginia (Bl)

Pennsylvania (L)

New York (L)

Vermont (L)

New Hampshire (L)

Maine (L)

Massachusetts (L)

Rhode Island (L)

Connecticut (L)

New Jersey (L & D)

Delaware (Br)

Maryland (Br)

Washington, DC

Richmond

non-slave-owning farmers and the large merchants with many Northern accounts—secessionists played on racial fears to pull yeomen and the business elite into a united white camp. The "North [intends] to free the negroes and force amalgamation between them and the children of the poor men of the South," one Alabama secessionist thundered, while a Georgian warned that, "ruled by Lincoln and his crew, in TEN years or less our CHILDREN will be the *slaves* of negroes."[65] Such arguments were more common in the Deep South than in Virginia, Maryland, or Kentucky, but they played strongly enough to set secession gears moving in more than a half-dozen states. On December 20, South Carolina voted to dissolve its ties to the United States, and six more states soon followed.

In Washington, outgoing President James Buchanan rejected the legitimacy of secession but had little power to do much else. Members of Congress quickly proposed as a compromise a set of constitutional amendments that would have ensured permanent federal support for the expansion of slavery. But president-elect Lincoln told fellow Republicans to "entertain no proposition for a compromise in regard to the *extension* of slavery," and they voted the measures down.[66] Perhaps Lincoln and other Northern leaders did not realize the depth of white Southern alienation or misjudged the strength of reaction that called for secession from the Union. Republicans may have hoped that conservative voices and wealthy Southern Whigs would prevail upon their fellows to remain within the Union for economic reasons. Yet those countercurrents never gained strength. Instead, delegates from seven states met in Montgomery, Alabama, to draft a constitution for a Confederate States of America and to choose Mississippi planter Jefferson Davis as provisional president.[67]

Meanwhile, seceding states had taken over federal property within their boundaries, but South Carolina's Fort Sumter remained in Union hands. In April, soon after his inauguration, Lincoln sent word to Jefferson Davis that unarmed supply ships were on their way to take provisions to the fort. In effect, Lincoln was forcing the new Confederacy to acknowledge federal sovereignty over the facility or else stop "a mission of humanity" and accept responsibility for provoking war. Davis decided to launch a preemptive strike and ordered Southern troops to force Fort Sumter's surrender. The ensuing bombardment on April 12 was militarily successful, but the Confederate attack aroused intense Northern support for the Union. Democrat Stephen Douglas, a fierce Lincoln foe just a few weeks earlier, went to the White House to declare his support for its Republican occupant. Returning to Chicago, Douglas summed up the emerging sentiment: "There are only two sides to the question. Every man must be for the United States or against it. There can be no neutrals in this war, *only patriots—or traitors.*"[68]

It was a starkly divided world in which Mennonite and Amish Americans found themselves in 1861.

§ CHAPTER 2 ℰ

Our Country Is at War

Chicago Patriot

On July 3, 1861, John F. Funk, the young Mennonite-reared lumber entrepreneur and Chicago Sunday school promoter, left home for an evening political rally. Less than three months earlier, South Carolina's attack on federal forces at Fort Sumter had sparked sharp reaction in both the North and the South, silencing calls for compromise and setting the stage for continued confrontation. Independence Day took on new significance in this context, and rallies mixed nationalist rhetoric and military recruitment speeches. With all the emotion energizing the events, perhaps it is no surprise that Funk stayed until three o'clock in the morning (on what was now July 4). Returning home, he went to bed for an hour, then rose at four, went out and "hoisted the flag, fired a salute of six shots with my revolver over it, went home and got breakfast," and then went to work.[1] The coming of war had heightened Funk's patriotic sensibilities.

The opening months of combat provoked varied responses among Mennonites and Amish in the North. Some men reacted like Funk, supporting the Union cause because they linked it to antislavery or because they instinctively resisted rebellion and political instability, but unwilling to enroll in any of the scores of volunteer regiments springing up across the country. At the same time, other men from Mennonite and Amish homes did respond to the muster call, and still others seem to have regarded the war as none of their business.

In Virginia, the weeks after Fort Sumter presented Mennonites with a very different situation. The fighting in South Carolina had produced a wave of popular sympathy for the Confederate cause and pushed the Old Dominion toward secession. In April 1861, delegates to a special state convention had approved a secession resolution and sent it to the voters for a referendum. Voting-age males, including the state's Mennonites, would have to take a public stand. Even if they abstained from voting, they would be signaling where they stood. Public pressure to rally around the emerging war colored experiences North and South, but in notably different ways.

For his part, Funk had reveled in the local excitement that accompanied Lincoln's call, following the fall of Fort Sumter, for 75,000 troops. Funk attended a "great Union meeting" and watched the first troops leaving for Washington, D.C. Everywhere, he noted, there were preparations for war, men enlisting, and banners flying "at almost every street corner," as secession sympathizers fell silent. On Sunday, April 21, Funk attended Sunday school and then went to the National Hall prayer meeting before watching the Light Artillery—including several of his friends—leave the city. That evening at Metropolitan Hall he heard a sermon on "Christian Patriotism" and witnessed many tender farewells as "brave fellows went to battle for the country." Two women with whom Funk spoke said that if he and his friends "wanted to be any kind [of] men at all they must go off to war." Five times that day, Funk helped sing "My Country, 'Tis of Thee."[2]

From his politically connected family in eastern Pennsylvania, Funk learned how the call to battle was stirring things there. Two weeks after war began, Father Jacob had written his son in Chicago and encouraged him to "make money and get rich." Was he telling his son to do two things at once—enhance his financial standing, but stay out of the military? Jacob also reported "much excitement" in Bucks and Montgomery counties because of the war. "Soldiers are marching to the seat of war daily and many would be glad to go but they are not wanted at present, so they must stay at home till further orders," father Funk reported, without indicating whether he was talking about men from Mennonite homes or non-Mennonite acquaintances.[3] He could have meant either one or both. It is clear that John F. Funk had many friends and a few relatives who enthusiastically went to war in those early days.

Lieut. Randolph M. Smith, boyhood friend of John F. Funk. Funk was
living in Chicago when he received this photo and news of Smith's joining the
91st Pennsylvania Volunteers. Credit: Mennonite Church USA Archives,
Goshen, Ind.

John's brother Abraham, still at home in Pennsylvania, reported in May that the stars and stripes were floating above all the surrounding villages and would do so as long as loyal Northerners rallied around the flag "under which our Forefathers fought, bled and died." His phrasing was curious, since Funk's Mennonite ancestors had stood aloof from the American Revolution.[4]

By June, Abraham wrote that the flags were getting tattered, the bottom had fallen out of the market, and times were dull. However, he did not blame the war or doubt the merits of the Northern cause. "We are for the war still and the Union forever," he insisted. Indeed, father Jacob observed that the war excitement was "verry Great," especially because there were "still traters Among the people in Buck County. But they Must keep vary quiet or Recive a Coat of tar and feathers."[5]

Secession Pressures

Presumably, then, Mennonites and others who did not partake of the war spirit in Pennsylvania or elsewhere in the North could remain quiet and not earn too much opprobrium. Developments in Virginia produced quite another story. In Chicago, John Funk's neighbors might support the Union cause or keep their opinions private. Virginia Mennonites had no such luxury.

A slave state with historic, economic, and cultural ties to the new Confederacy, Virginia nonetheless had initially resisted calls for disunion. Now, however, the federal use of force in responding to South Carolina shifted Virginia sentiment, and Mennonites in the Shenandoah Valley found themselves in the midst of a political debate about the merits of dissolving the Union. If a secession resolution came before the state's voters, nonresistants would have to declare their opinions at the ballot box.[6]

Already in February 1861, as public debates on secession were taking shape, the *Rockingham Register* had reported what most locals assumed: no people were more respectful of the rule of law than nonresistant Mennonites and Dunkers. "They carefully and promptly pay their taxes to support the government which protects the slave holders as well as themselves," the editor noted.[7]

The editor's comments about loyalty to established authority applied to Rockingham County Mennonites as well as to those in Augusta County, and in both places the subject of secession would be hotly debated. The prosperous Shenandoah Valley lay between Virginia's pro-secessionist strongholds, east of the Blue Ridge Mountains, and its anti-secessionists, concentrated in the Alleghenies to the west. At first the populations of Rockingham and Augusta had leaned heavily toward cooperating with the Union. Despite serious apprehensions about Lincoln's election, strong anti-secession feelings permeated the area. Most citizens saw remaining within the United States a lesser evil than the alternative of war. Repeated warnings appeared in local papers that civil strife would be disastrous, especially to Virginians, who would bear the brunt of Northern offensives into the South.[8]

In Augusta County, *Staunton Spectator* editorials at first reflected antisecessionism. In January the paper had described the state as being on the edge of a "fearful precipice," and cautioned readers to "look before we leap."[9] A week later the same paper called secession a "monster" that would victimize the "mother of States and Statesmen" and then followed the piece with testimonies from civic leaders who favored union. One prominent public figure, Alexander H. H. Stuart, warned that dissolution would bring frightful results. "Brother would be arrayed against brother, and the whole land would be drenched with blood," he worried. "Firesides and fields would be desolated by invading armies and the wail of the widow and the orphan would be heard in all our valleys."[10] The *Rockingham Register* carried similar sentiments. On February 4 its editor believed that conciliation was in the offing, since many politicians had gone to the "verge of a crumbling brink of an awful chasm" and backed off. The editor hoped the state convention called by the governor to consider secession would avoid the "terrible cup" of agony of Virginia's "dissolution and utter dismemberment."[11]

Days later, on February 12, the special secession convention gathered. Robert Y. Conrad of Winchester, in the lower Shenandoah Valley, served as chair of the Committee on Federal Relations, which would recommend for or against secession. For a long time a majority of delegates opposed separation, but a vocal minority kept a hot debate going. As more representatives began to lean toward secession, Conrad worked tirelessly and with great anguish to convince fellow delegates not to yield to the emotional crowds outside their meeting place in Richmond and who called for Virginia independence. Through early April, Conrad still had a majority in his committee against secession.[12] Meanwhile, on April 4, an Augusta County unionist, John B. Baldwin, met with President Lincoln in Washington to propose expedient federal recognition of the Confederacy that would create space for negotiation and allow tempers to cool, but Lincoln believed such compromise would make it harder to retain the integrity of the Union. Before Baldwin left, he warned Lincoln that if the federal government used military force against the states that had already voted to secede, Virginia "will be out in forty-eight hours."[13]

Eight days later, on April 12, South Carolina troops attacked and captured Fort Sumter, and Lincoln announced his intention to use all means to suppress insurrection. That news galvanized the North and electrified Virginians, many of whom now reacted sharply against the president's proposed show of force and denounced dictatorship from Washington. When news of the fort's fall reached Richmond on April 13, a large crowd gathered at the capitol to replace the American flag with the new colors of the Confederate States of America.[14] State convention delegate Conrad still hoped to convince those who were calling for war that residents of western Virginia would not stand to have the Union dissolved, but he was running out of time.

Lincoln's call on April 15 for 75,000 troops became a symbolic last straw, apparently demonstrating to wavering voters in the upper South— including many in the Shenandoah Valley—that the federal government had overreached its authority and provoked domestic war. Virginia Governor John Letcher bluntly refused to send Washington any troops. Two days later the state convention passed an "Ordinance of Secession" by a vote of eighty-eight to fifty-five and called all Virginia voters to ratify the decision on May 23. The counties of Rockingham and Augusta each had three representatives to the convention, all strong unionists when they went to Richmond. Five had refused to waver. Augusta's delegates—John Baldwin, Alexander H. H. Stuart, and George Baylor—voted against secession. So did two of the three in Rockingham, John F. Lewis and Algernon S. Gray; only Democrat Samuel A. Coffman voted in favor.[15]

The action of the secession convention and the impending popular referendum signaled a sea change in Shenandoah Valley public discourse. On April 16 the *Staunton Spectator* announced war and the formation of militia in Augusta County. The *Rockingham Register* published a piece entitled "War Commenced," along with various dispatches from the Confederate

War Department. The Rockingham paper also announced that the nonre-sistant Dunkers should not be afraid to hold their next annual meeting in Virginia, since hospitality was always to be found in the South. But, the paper warned, Southerners would not tolerate those who foolishly "med-dle" with the issue of slavery. "If some Christians are too conscientious to hold slaves or have anything to do with the institution of slavery," that may be their right. But should they preach against it, they can expect "ut-ter extermination of their peculiar views!"[16]

Within a few days, both newspapers had completed their editorial transformation. Now they unhesitatingly blamed Lincoln for provoking war, urged strong resistance "against usurpation, tyranny and military des-potism," and called on readers "to fight for our State, homes and firesides." "All is excitement, and there is not much calm reflection," admitted the Staunton paper in the run-up to the referendum.[17] Two days before the vote, the *Spectator* demanded unified support for secession: "Votes are now more precious than jewels, and none should be lost."[18] The Rockingham paper declared that only "demogogues and traitors" would consider voting against secession. The editor pleaded with German residents, likely with Mennonites and Dunkers in mind, having heard that some would vote against it or not vote at all. "We cannot believe this," the editor gasped. "They love their country and desire its peace and welfare too much to do this." Surely they know that if Lincoln were to march his armies over our land, he would point "his bayonets and loaded guns in our faces."[19]

For the moment, the Valley's Mennonites maintained a low profile. On April 18 bishop Jacob Hildebrand of Augusta County first noted in his diary the beginning of war, two days after the Staunton paper had announced it. Hildebrand went about his usual church business and a few days later baptized eight people in his home congregation. On April 17–18, 1861, the bishop and his congregation hosted the regular meeting of the Virginia Mennonite Conference at their meetinghouse. Remark-ably, the brief minutes indicate no discussion of the war or the impend-ing secession vote. Mennonites apparently were hesitant to bring discus-sion of politics into the church conference—or at least to record it in the minutes.[20]

For the next month, farmer-bishop Hildebrand was busy planting crops and carrying out his usual church work. He also went to Rocking-ham County to fill the temporary bishop vacancy in the Middle District.

In quick succession he held communion services at the Hildebrand meet-inghouse (38 communicants), Dry River Church in western Rockingham (220), Pike Church (110), and Brenneman Church (117). Hildebrand clearly had a great deal of social interchange with other Mennonites dur-ing this time, particularly with Rockingham County people. The topic of war and the secession referendum must have weighed in their conversa-tions, though it rarely appeared in his diary. On May 23, however, Hil-debrand voted for secession.[21]

The bishop had sided with the vast majority of his neighbors—Au-gusta County's vote was 3,130 in favor of secession and only 10 against. In Rockingham County the election outcome was similarly lopsided, 3,010 to 22. Fourteen of that county's nineteen voting districts had not a single vote against secession.[22]

Yet Hildebrand's choice was an uncommon one for Shenandoah Valley Mennonites, especially those in Rockingham County. Not that they failed to sense something of the dilemma that enfolded Hildebrand. Tradition-ally, Mennonites *had* advocated obedience to established government, provided it did not ask one to violate Christian conscience. But in a situ-ation of civil strife with competing claims of legitimacy, how was one to decide what constituted proper worldly authority? Hildebrand recorded no agony over such questions. Instead, like nearly all of his neighbors, he simply shifted his loyalties to the new Confederacy. On June 13, 1861, for example, the bishop convened a special church service for a "fast day and prayer proclaimed by the Preasdent"—Jefferson Davis.[23]

In Rockingham County, however, Mennonites were decidedly more Unionist in their sympathies and regarded secession as unholy rebellion.[24] Yet public pressure to cast supportive votes in the referendum was intense. Later testimony indicated that John Brunk; David Driver; Daniel P. Good; Abraham D., Gabriel D., and Simeon Heatwole; David E., Frederick S., and Henry L. Rhodes; Jacob Shank Jr.; Emanuel Suter; and Noah Wenger all voted in favor of secession.[25] Most claimed they had done so only after receiving death threats should they vote otherwise.[26] John Brunk declared that even the "most resolute" Union men of the area "were intimidated into voting" for secession. After the war, when applying to the federal government for reimbursement of property destroyed in the war, Brunk admitted voting under duress for secession, but he insisted that thereafter he had opposed the Confederacy and "did all I could to assist refugees and deserters from the rebel army to escape from the confederacy." As sexton for Weavers Mennonite Church, he "frequently concealed them" in the church building and accompanied fugitives "several miles in the night" as they made their escape.[27]

Despite the pressure, some Mennonites actually voted against secession or, more often, simply abstained. Jacob Wenger of Greenmount claimed he was one of eleven who voted against the secession resolution despite threats of hanging.[28] If Wenger is correct, upwards of half of the dissenting votes in Rockingham must have been acquaintances of Wenger, surely many of them Mennonites. Henry and Joseph Beery are known to have voted against it. Those who refused to vote included Samuel Shank, Abraham Shank, Samuel Coffman, Daniel J. Good, John Geil, Jacob Geil, Peter Blosser, and David C. Brenneman.[29] Jacob Geil of Edom heard "rumored threats" and "was closely watched."[30] Half the above men were church leaders. Minister Abraham Shank went to Timberville to vote for union, but there he met an uncle, "one of the strongest union men" in the county, who persuaded him it would be prudent to abstain. Shank's relative had decided that actively opposing session might do "some injury and it would not do any good."[31] Later, a witness deposed that minister Samuel Shank was a Union man who never did "anything for the rebel government." In fact, said the observer, at a conference of Mennonite ministers he heard Shank "declare publicly that he regarded the United States as his government, and that the other . . . was not a government at all but a rebellion."[32]

Defending Nonresistants in Pennsylvania

In the North, men with "conscientious scruples" attracted no editorial attention during the war's first weeks except in Pennsylvania's Lancaster County, where a sizable Mennonite population with significant political clout came in for criticism. On June 19 the *Daily Evening Express* printed a long article headed "Citizens of Lancaster County Opposing the War for the Union—The Mennonites Asserting the Higher Law of Conscience." Since "treason took up arms," the editor claimed, he had not heard of a single pulpit withholding support for the Union. But now he learned of a Mennonite "convention" near Strasburg that had decided to contribute neither men nor money to the cause. Such failure to support the war was all the more galling because "these Mennonites are among our richest farmers, and have, in this favored land, been happily free" from the persecution their forebears knew in Europe. "If there is a people in the world who ought to be grateful to a government, and willing to contribute substantially towards sustaining it in this righteous struggle," fumed the editor, "the Mennonite farmers owe this debt." How would slackers of this ilk feel if they had lived in Harpers Ferry, he asked? Would they rather have their fine horses taken by "rebel thieves" than have them used defending freedom? These "rich but close-fisted farmers" should expect no sympathy if Confederates overran Lancaster, he warned.[33]

Curiously, this attack appeared in a Republican newspaper, despite the fact that area Mennonites traditionally supported that party. Ironically, the Democratic *Lancaster Intelligencer* then came to the nonresistants' defense. Writer Andrew M. Frantz claimed to have long known the Mennonites, and he called the *Express* piece "unexampled malignity and lying." Frantz reminded readers that liberty of conscience was guaranteed by the federal constitution and that the Pennsylvania constitution clearly called for military exemption for men of conscience, provided they paid an equivalency fee. Some Mennonites might be rich, Frantz conceded, but their wealth came from "honest industry—not by printing papers and lying." The nonresistants were "as good and as loyal as the best of our citizens," he concluded.[34] The *Express* then retracted part of its original story and also added that its editor had heard troubling rumors that unnamed parties were harassing elderly Mennonites into contributing to a war fund.[35]

Had it not been for John F. Herr, the public discussion might have ended. In 1812 Herr's father had founded the sectarian Reformed Mennonite branch, but son John F. had not affiliated with that or any other Mennonite group, instead becoming something of a local political and religious gadfly. Now he entered this fray, announcing that slanderers were charging him with unscrupulously having "worked upon the weakness of an old and wealthy Mennonite" to obtain money for military purposes. A "plain unvarnished exposition of the facts," Herr insisted, was that he and others had formed a company of cavalry to protect Lancaster County against invasion and then decided to invite neighborhood farmers to contribute. They began by calling on a Reformed Mennonite minister who

declined to donate, but they next called on several men from the larger
(Old) Mennonite Conference and found more sympathetic ears; four men
each subscribed $100. There was nothing more to their solicitation.[36]

Labeling Herr's piece "foulest slander," a self-proclaimed "closed-fisted
farmer, a Mennonite" responded in the *Lancaster Examiner & Herald*. In
fact, the writer thundered, Herr and his company had used dishonorable
means to obtain their money. They had targeted an old man of more than
eighty years and spun exaggerated tales of rebels poised to take Washington, D.C., Philadelphia, and Lancaster. Herr and his friends then ha-
rangued the man until he made a donation. Next they went to "a very
influential Mennonite, as evenly spun as you find men anywhere, and
generally known to be cautious," and harassed him for some hours to get
a pledge of $100. Thereafter, using the names of these two reluctant but
respected donors, they convinced others to give.[37]

John F. Herr was livid at the "Close-Fisted Farmer's" charges, declaring
the writer "an unmitigated scoundrel" purveying base falsehoods. Under
the title "The Mennonite Question," Herr reiterated his story, denounced
unpatriotic Mennonites, and implied that unnamed Mennonites were
now using a lawyer to harass him.[38]

Coming to the rescue of Mennonites' civic reputation, the *Examiner &
Herald* printed the contents of several "cards" just then in public circulation, which included the names of Mennonites John Ranck, Jacob F. An-
drews, Christian Herr, and Rev. Jacob Andrew, and which stated Mennonites' refusal to assist in arming and equipping soldiers but willingness
to pay additional taxes. Another such "card" from Abram Groff attested
to having been frightened and unduly pressured by John F. Herr. A third,
from Henry Rohrer, recounted similar pressure but promised to "pay any
amount of tax" put upon him. These statements tended to discredit John F.
Herr, who issued a somewhat conciliatory piece, admitting that he had not
made himself clear enough and that his warnings about imminent rebel
invasion might have been taken too seriously.[39]

Significantly, the war of words ended when two county commissioners
weighed in on the exchange in the *Examiner & Herald*. As major Republican political figures in the area, they vouched for the loyalty and good
will of area Mennonites, assuring readers that Mennonites were contributing money toward the support of soldiers' families and that some had
furnished straw for the troops at Camp Johnston, near Lancaster.[40] For the

time being the public debate ceased, but it pointed to things sure to resurface in eastern Pennsylvania: resentment of peace church separatism and wealth, Mennonite offers of cash in lieu of bodily service, and the voices of Mennonites' powerful political defenders.

Marching to War

John F. Herr was hardly alone in raising volunteer troops in the heady days of 1861. Throughout the North, community leaders responded to the threatened dismemberment of the United States with wild enthusiasm for the president's call to arms. On the Sunday following the fall of Fort Sumter, "congregations of every religious denomination" listened to sermons summoning men to fight for the Lord. Religious periodicals called for soldiers, church buildings became centers for enlistment, and some clergy served as recruiting agents. Peace suddenly became unpopular. The American Peace Society suspended its lectures and collapsed. Civic leaders announced that a nation "degenerates when it becomes essentially nonmilitary," and peace "rusts the national character," causing the country to sink into "demoralization and decay."[41]

At least a few Northern young men with Mennonite or Amish connection got caught up in early war hysteria. At Norristown, Pennsylvania, on Monday evening, April 15, an excited crowd gathered at the courthouse to hear the news of Lincoln's summons to arms. After a local judge spoke, a band struck up "Yankee Doodle," and a handsome lawyer in his mid-twenties stepped forward and pledged to march and defend the Union. The volunteer was Charles Hunsicker, grandson of Mennonite bishop John Hunsicker of Skippack. "It is not time to talk," the young man reportedly said. "We want men—we want money. I shall go wherever called out by the Governor, and will not return unless honorably." By Saturday morning war fever had brought six hundred more men forward, one of them Hunsicker's older brother, Davis.[42]

Where did the Hunsickers learn their war language? Their father, Joseph, had cashed in on the lumber trade on the Schuylkill Canal and sent several sons to college. They, in turn, became attorneys, justices of the peace, and in one case, a sheriff. Joseph was an associate judge in Montgomery County, and although he had not forgotten his spiritual heritage, he no longer attended a Mennonite church. He visited and wrote letters to his sons in camp, but he was unable to communicate his lingering nonresistant misgivings. "Pap don't understand this war business," remarked son Davis. "It is new to him and contrary to his early teaching." Over a dozen common Mennonite surnames, such as Buckwalter, Clemmer, Detweiler, Kulp, and Moyer, appeared on the roster of six hundred volunteers comprising Charles Hunsicker's Montgomery County regiment, an indication that other men from Mennonite homes or heritage were going to war.[43]

Norristown became so "agog with patriotism" after Lincoln's call that within six days "more than one-third of the voting population" had enlisted. Six companies boarded the train and rushed to Camp Curtin at Harrisburg. After organizing into the Fourth Regiment, and still without uniforms, equipment, or training, raw recruits were on their way to Perryville, Maryland, to guard the crossing of the Susquehanna River.[44]

The pattern was repeated across the country, including counties with sizable Mennonite and Amish communities. Within a few days the Logan Guards of Mifflin County, Pennsylvania, were off to Harrisburg. So were the Doylestown Guards of Bucks County and the National Light Infantry of Pottsville. The Union and Lancaster Guards and Strasburg Cavalry in Lancaster County, Pennsylvania, were not far behind.[45] At Doylestown, young Henry Derstine watched the Ringgold Regiment gather but waited until his Mennonite father left for Philadelphia and then hurried to be "sworn in as an Artillery-man." When father Derstine returned, however, he forced Henry's discharge.[46]

Nor did it take long in the spring of 1861 in Wayne County, Ohio, to put together the Given Guards of Plain Township or the Smithville Home Guards.[47] On Sunday, April 28, in neighboring Holmes County, the McNulty Guards, with colors flying, formed a procession and attended the Evangelical Lutheran Church of Millersburg, where they heard Rev. U. J. Knisely preach a sermon especially for them. Drawing a parallel with the biblical Queen Esther, whose rise to power was providential, Rev. Knisely told the troops that, given the perilous times, who knows but that "you are come into the kingdom for such a time as this?" Go then to the war in "devotion to a righteous cause." That evening recruits attended the Methodist Church and heard a similar sermon.[48] Such rhetoric had its effect, appealing even to a young Ezra Yoder of Wayne County's Oak Grove Amish Mennonite congregation, who badly wanted to volunteer. But "my parents and my church being non-resistants," he remembered later, "I was held in check for a year in my patriotic aspirations." As soon as he turned 21, however, he enlisted.[49]

On October 21, William G. Bigelow raised the Belleville [Pennsylvania] Fencibles, which later became Company C of the state's 45th Volunteers. When they left for Washington, they took three men from Kishacoquillas Valley Amish families—Samuel A. Glick, Samuel M. Lantz, and David K. Zook—apparently the only Kishacoquillas Valley men of Amish background to join military ranks during the war. The story was different on the Juniata River side of the mountain, where eventually at least twenty-four enlistees bearing Amish surnames were found on military rolls—though most were from households estranged for several generations from the Amish church.[50]

Hastily called war meetings drummed up popular fervor. In a small village like Winesburg, Ohio, near a Mennonite congregation on the northern edge of Holmes County, and with many Amish living to the south, the "Union Meeting" of April 23 featured both English and German speakers. The newspaper reported that "one sentiment prevailed—that of maintaining the Union at all hazards." A committee appointed to raise funds and equip soldiers included Eli Hostetler, Esq., Stephen Troyer, and John M. Miller. Before adjourning, the gathering called for another meeting at Mount Eaton, a few miles north on the edge of a large Wayne County Swiss Mennonite community.[51]

Politicians encouraged grassroots enlistment efforts and eagerly worked to see that their states delivered the president's requested troops. Ohio's governor William Dennison boasted to Washington that his state would supply the "largest number you will receive." The *Holmes County Farmer*, whose editor watched many other newspapers, said that already by May 2, Ohio had some 40,000 volunteers, almost 30,000 more than initially had been requested from federal officials.[52] For his part, Indiana's governor, Oliver P. Morton, did not even ask how many troops Lincoln wanted. Instead, on April 15 he telegraphed a promise of 10,000 men "for the defense of the nation and to uphold the authority of the Government."[53] By early June, Ohio, New York, Indiana, and Illinois had successfully raised nearly a hundred regiments.[54]

Lincoln's initial request for 75,000 volunteers soon ballooned to 400,000. On July 4 he spoke to a special session of Congress and requested the "legal means for making this contest a short and decisive one" by authorizing additional troops and $400 million. "Let us renew our trust in God," the president intoned, "with manly hearts."[55]

Congress responded quickly. Thaddeus Stevens, the fiery Republican abolitionist whose district included a large number of Lancaster, Pennsylvania, Mennonites and Amish—constituents with whom he maintained cordial ties—was chair of the powerful Committee of Ways and Means. Stevens backed the White House request despite its unprecedented size, scope, and expansion of executive power. "I thought the time had come when the laws of war were to govern our action," Stevens remarked. Under his leadership, Congress promised more than the president had asked, authorizing a half-million troops and a half-billion dollars.[56]

"Noble Hearts Have Ceased Their Beating"

Back in Chicago, John Funk resumed making entries in his diary on August 10, still enamored with the Union cause and bemoaning the "traitors" who were working "for our defeat," but now also writing with a spirit tempered by the reality of Northern defeat at the early engagement at Bull Run (Manassas). "Our Country is at war," Funk wrote. "Hundreds of Brave men have fallen. Hundreds of stout and noble hearts have ceased their beating and died, wrapt in the mantle of Glory that clothes the patriot when he gives his Life for his Country's Good."[57]

From Pennsylvania, Abraham Funk kept his Chicago brother informed about acquaintances signing up for war, including boys whom John had once taught in school. Now they were fighting "the wicked and lawless Rebels." In November, John learned that his cousin, Samuel F. Geil, son of Mennonite parents Jacob and Anna (Funk) Geil, had enlisted in Ohio.[58]

Periodically, Funk received letters from friends who wondered if he had enlisted. One of them was from Jonathan Fly, an old friend from home who was now in Easton, Pennsylvania. Fly reported hundreds of men leaving town in response to the call of their country. He mused that sometimes he felt he should go too because of the sad spectacle of the dismemberment of "the latest and grandest experiment of democratic government." The result of the current struggle "will realize or dash forever the hopes of untold millions," Fly was sure, sounding the theme of America as a republican beacon in a benighted world. "We are in the crucible," he concluded.[59]

Apparently, Funk was feeling the crucible's heat himself. At least his diary through the fall of 1861 suggested his unsettledness. One September night, for example, unable to sleep because of the buzz of mosquitoes, Funk moved outside to try to make a bed on a lumber pile, only to be disturbed by the tramping boots of soldiers. With sleep eluding him because of "clouds, friends, and damp airs, and disturbed thoughts," he could not keep his mind off of enlistment or of the fact that the Union had not made short work of the Confederacy. At other times he noted that his head was "out of order" or that he was losing his temper at work. He even admitted to skipping his beloved Sunday school work to catch the latest war news at the post office.[60]

With no Mennonite church in Chicago, Funk attended services with one of several denominations, frequently the New England-based Congregationalists, who saw themselves as cultural custodians of Yankee America. At Thanksgiving he listened to a sermon about the "great national sin of slavery" that had precipitated the war. As a staunch antislavery man, Funk warmly approved the sermon and other pro-Union preaching he heard, but he was also anxious about slack Union fortunes.[61]

Like his friend and fellow Chicago Sunday school worker Dwight L. Moody, Funk supported the Union cause but could not bring himself to enlist. Moody, the future evangelist of international fame, reportedly explained, "There has never been a time in my life when I felt that I could take a gun and shoot down a fellow-being. In this respect I am a Quaker."[62] For Funk the ties to Christian nonresistance were closer and deeper, though it would be more than a year before Funk would publicly claim a Mennonite peace position as his own. Until then, he lived, as did a good number of Northern Mennonites and Amish during the war's opening months, between a genuine commitment to Union principles and church teaching that no cause could justify the taking of human life.

For other nonresistants, the war's rumble still seemed remote. From Wayne County, Ohio, Oak Grove Amish Mennonite Eli L. Yoder, a schoolteacher at Madisonburg, had written a letter to friends on August 15 describing school concerns, plowing, refreshing rains, and the prospects for sowing grain. As for the war, he wrote, "everything out here is comparatively quiet." Indeed, local concerns remained commercial. Nearby, the town of Wooster was to quarter a regiment for a few weeks, "which is expected to raise the market," Yoder reported. The government was calling for a thousand good cavalry horses, but unfortunately only paying $85 to $100 apiece. Nor was travel disrupted, and Eli advised his friend that this would be a fine time to visit.[63]

In the end, there is no way of knowing exactly how many Amish and Mennonite young men went to war in the conflict's early months, but it was likely not a large number. Parents often tried to hold their sons from enlisting, although they were not always successful. In early 1862, Jacob and Maria (Clemens) Landes of Montgomery County, Pennsylvania, reflecting on the war's first nine months, wrote to friends about the conflict's awful waste of money and how terrible it was that men created by God could become so hateful as to take each other's lives. Somehow they had seen letters from soldiers then in Kentucky and Maryland, and noted that "Many [young men] have left their parents and against their wishes have enlisted; others have left wife and children and gone to the field of battle." And some had already been brought home for burial. "We live in very critical times," the Landeses lamented.[64] Did the "many" young men refer to people from their Mennonite community? Perhaps a few were.

Yet judging from surviving evidence, most Mennonites and Amish resisted the call to arms. Certainly it is clear that when conscription began in 1862, significant numbers of these young men availed themselves of whatever legal and extralegal means they could to escape participating in a military system they had, to that point, voluntarily avoided.

In fact, the coming of conscription would pose a major challenge to nonresistants as the war moved into its second year. Though patriotic enthusiasts in both camps had assumed the struggle would not last long—each certain of their side's ability to find a quick and decisive military solution—by the end of 1861 a new realism had settled in. Things looked so bleak for the Union at the start of 1862 that Lincoln despaired, "The bottom is out of the tub." He dismissed his Secretary of War, replacing him with Edwin M. Stanton, and became more directly involved in daily war decisions.[65] Growing frustration and anxiety would increase public pressure on Mennonites in the North. In Virginia such dynamics were also at work, producing early calls for conscription.

Conscription, Combat, and Virginia's "War of Self-Defense"

Public Pressure on Peace People

Already by the summer of 1861 the pressure on Mennonite young men in Virginia to participate in the war had intensified. The Confederate victory at the first Battle of Manassas (Bull Run) buoyed Southern spirits, but the months that followed also made it clear that the federal government in Washington, D.C., was committed to crushing rebellion no matter how much time, money, or effort it took. And for Virginians, it became obvious that Northern strategy would focus, in large part, on subduing the Old Dominion. If Virginians soon learned they had less to fear from Union Maj. General George B. McClellan than they first believed, owing to McClellan's cautious military style, they also realized that the weight of war would press down especially upon them.

For Mennonites and other peace people in the Shenandoah Valley, this context proved critical. The mixture of anxiety and optimism heightened popular patriotism and eroded tolerance for those who dissented from the cause, even in the Shenandoah region where enthusiasm for the Confederacy had been tempered in the conflict's opening months and nonresistants might have hoped to receive a measure of sympathy.

Instead, men unwilling to fight found themselves in difficult straits, no longer able to be excused from the state's militia by way of the small fines that had gained them exemption in the early nineteenth century, when drilling with arms on militia day had been as much a social event as a civic duty. Now, three possibilities lay before them: accept forced service against conscience, face court-martial (and perhaps death) as deserters, or go into hiding.[1] Nor was there much time to reflect philosophically on their narrowing options. One Sunday morning in June, for example, as minister Samuel Coffman was preaching at the crowded Weavers Mennonite Church west of Harrisonburg, the sound of hoofbeats coming into the churchyard distracted the preacher. Two uniformed men entered the meetinghouse, and an officer strode to the front, sat down, and listened to the rest of the sermon. When Coffman finished and called for a closing hymn, the officer rose and ordered every man between the ages of 18 and 45 to report immediately for military training. The officer then marched out, leaving the shocked and soon sobbing congregation unable to sing the hymn the preacher had announced. Pale and shaken, Coffman himself could only rise and dismiss a group that was coming to realize more intensely the immediacy of war.[2]

Confederate officers were not the only ones issuing public directives to Virginia's peace churches. Only days later, the *Rockingham Register* carried a long piece addressed "To the Tunkers, Mennonites, and Others Opposed to War." The pseudonymous author, "Ne Qui Nimis," opened with professed respect for those who lived "orderly and honest lives" and admitted "the honest religious convictions of all men." But, he noted, Virginia had been forced into war. True, war is hardly consistent with the principles of Christianity, "Nimis" conceded, attempting to score rhetorical points with nonresistant readers. "All wars and fighting are opposed to the spirit of the gospel . . . [since] Christ is the prince of peace." But does the scripture prohibit defending oneself? No, "Nimis" insisted, asserting that the right of self-defense is the first law of nature, and one confirmed by the Bible. Yes, "Nimis" knew that Jesus talked about turning the other cheek, but that was "absurd" and was not to be taken literally. Moreover, if peace people really did intend to follow Jesus' directive and "go the second mile," then they should respond to state conscription by agreeing to twice the length of usual conscripted service. If the state drafts one son, the father ought to send a second son as a volunteer.[3]

Turning to political argument, the author contended, "In this war of self-defense, preaching peace weakens the hands of the very government you helped to put in place by your votes!"[4] At the least, said "Nimis," when

Virginia requests your service, "you ought to go and be *shot at*, even if you cannot conscientiously shoot."[5]

A month later, pseudonymous "Justice" replied with a defense of the nonresistants. Responding to the suggestion that those with "religious scruples" be taxed two or three dollars a day, "Justice" contended such a course of action would reduce "hundreds of farmers and others" to poverty, because the peace people of the Shenandoah Valley were hardly "fat farmers." Nor were these scruples of conscience obscure principles, but they were "part and parcel" of their faith. Like early Christians, these Mennonites and Brethren would rather "seal their faith with their blood" than fight. And history shows that persecution only makes the persecuted more zealous: "If kind reason cannot produce a change, harsh means never can." Moreover, no nation prospers while persecuting dissenters. "The right to worship God according to the dictates of our own conscience is a liberty above all others," continued "Justice." The South must not hand the enemy propaganda by allowing the North to accuse the Confederacy of maltreatment. "Beware that we provoke not the Majesty of Heaven to anger, and thereby cause Him to overwhelm us with swift destruction for our sins," the author concluded.[6]

In any case, before the end of July numerous Mennonite men found themselves forced into the state militia because there was no means of exemption. In Rockingham County a number of them stopped by the home of minister Samuel Coffman (just ordained bishop) to say goodbye and to give their pledge not to kill.[7] Among these forced into service was one Christian Good. After the first battle in which Good had been assigned to the front lines, his captain asked Good if he had fired his weapon. "No," Good replied, "I did not shoot." Later, when questioned again, he gave another negative answer. Incredulous, the officer asked if Good was unable to "see all those Yankees over there," to which Good was said to have replied, "No, they're people; we don't shoot people." Similarly, Jacob Wenger was only "in the militia about seven weeks" before ending up "in the guardhouse" because he "refused duty." Lewis "L. J." Heatwole, who was a teenager during the war, remembered that refusal to shoot brought threats "to the point of being court-martialed and shot" but that such coercion failed to dissuade, and apparently threatened court-martials never took place.[8]

Instead, certain commanding officers informally detailed some men of conscience to noncombatant tasks: Samuel Brunk received assignment to the Baltimore Railroad, Joseph Nisewander made shoes, Henry L. Rhodes was a teamster, and several others helped produce niter.[9] Noncombatants who remained in military camps gathered in the evening to sing hymns such as "Am I a Soldier of the Cross?" The hymn was surely familiar to the Baptists and Methodists among the soldiers, who were said to have listened appreciatively. But for the Mennonite and Dunker singers, the lyrics conveyed a set of loyalties that separated them from those in uniform.[10]

Unlike those who reluctantly reported when drafted in summer 1861 but then proved uncooperative, a few Mennonite men, such as Michael Shank, refused even to respond to their summonses. Apprehended and hauled by wagon some seventy miles down the valley to Fort Collins, near Winchester, Shank composed a poem of ten stanzas for his wife and children. The verses convey his anguish at being separated from them and his wish that "the rulers of our land" would "obey Jehovah's great command, and love their foes as well as friends." As summer gave way to fall, some who had been pressed into service began deserting. In some cases, officers allowed men to go home to help with harvest, and conscientious objectors never returned to camp.[11]

In Augusta County, further up the valley, young men from Mennonite homes ended up in military service too—a few voluntarily. Benjamin F. Hildebrand, son of church trustee Jacob R. Hildebrand, was 18 when he enlisted on July 9, 1861, in the 52nd Virginia. He remained with his regiment throughout the war and was present when General Robert E. Lee surrendered in April 1865.[12] Bishop Jacob Hildebrand lost two hired hands to military service in the spring and summer of 1861, both of them members of the Hildebrand Mennonite Church.[13] William Eavers had begun working for Hildebrand on April 1, but a mere six days later the bishop's diary noted—rather matter-of-factly—that Eavers "was going to muster."[14] Two weeks later (April 21), Eavers' name was listed with seven others who joined the bishop's church.[15]

Others from Augusta County Mennonite homes who eventually went to war included Joseph W. Grove, oldest son of Hildebrand Church minister Isaac Grove, who died on December 30, 1862.[16] Abraham J. Grove, probably the son of aged deacon John Grove, was "slain in the war" in 1864. At least ten Confederate veterans were buried in the Hildebrand meetinghouse cemetery, although several may not have been from Men-

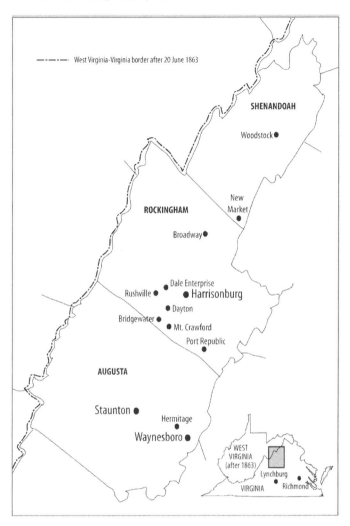

Augusta, Rockingham, and Shenandoah Counties, Virginia

nonite homes. Others, including David Kennedy, were church members, as was Gabriel Hildebrand, the brother of trustee Jacob R. Hildebrand.[17]

The Coming of Conscription

While relatively lax militia impressments and desertion marked the war's first winter, the coming of spring in 1862 brought renewed pressure for

men to go to war. Some soldiers had lost the easy optimism of the conflict's early days, and civilians were less eager to volunteer. "The romance
of the thing is entirely worn off," wrote one of Maj. General Thomas J.
"Stonewall" Jackson's soldiers posted in the Shenandoah Valley in January 1862.[18]

Key Confederate officials feared a manpower disaster. One-year enlistments—which comprised nearly half the troops—would soon expire, and
few of them seemed keen on reenrolling, leaving a severe shortage of soldiers just when the Yankees would be beginning their spring offensives.
Fifty-dollar bounties and sixty-day furloughs did not entice enough men.
In the face of such realities, General Lee urged a centralized Confederate conscription effort, even though such plans were deeply controversial
since they seemed to contravene some secessionists' commitment to states'
rights. Virginia's Governor John Letcher, for example, stoutly opposed
the idea of a Confederate draft, calling it the "most alarming stride towards
consolidation" of government power "that has ever occurred." Nevertheless, Southern nationalists such as President Jefferson Davis agreed with
Lee, and on March 28, 1862, Davis called on the Confederate Congress
to initiate conscription. Supporters of the measure prevailed, and even
Letcher conceded that "harmony, unity, and conciliation" were in such
short supply that only a national draft could ensure ongoing popular commitment to the cause.[19] Meanwhile, Virginia's own legislature was tight-
ening the terms of state service.

Thus, state and national conscription plans simultaneously moved forward that spring—and the politics of their provisions soon became entangled. For nonresistants, the coincidence of the two draft measures wind-
ing their way through Richmond halls of power would prove significant,
since members of the Confederate Congress nodded in the direction of
states' rights by appropriating nationally the bargain Virginia's state legislators had struck with their Mennonite and Dunker citizens. Perhaps
the observations of one of the South's preeminent generals, along with
Confederate capture of fleeing conscience objectors who then offered no
resistance, also played a role in shaping lawmakers' minds.

Virginia's plan for a draft was the first to move forward that spring.
For some months, Dunker elders John Kline and Benjamin F. Moomaw
had been in contact with Rockingham County legislators to plead for exemption for men of conscience. House delegates Algernon Gray and John

Hopkins agreed to introduce some commutation provision, and the law passed on March 29 exempted members of churches whose creeds prohibited bearing arms, provided each draftee paid $500 plus 2 percent of their assessed property value and took "an oath or affirmation that he will sustain the Confederate government." Those who became members later or could not afford the costs were to be assigned work not requiring "the actual bearing of arms."[20]

Perhaps the sentiments of Stonewall Jackson, commander of Valley forces, had influenced officials. On March 21, Jackson had communicated to S. Bassett French, aide-de-camp to Virginia's governor, that certain religious groups in his military district opposed war. Eighteen Dunker and Mennonite men had just been arrested trying to escape to the North, and Jackson hoped to "employ them in other ways than fighting." He understood that some would hire substitutes, while others would report for service but then refuse to shoot or deliberately take bad aim. So, continued Jackson, for the "greatest efficiency and securing loyal feelings and co-operation," and because the "non-combatants" were reliable teamsters, why not organize them into companies of one hundred and assign them to various staff departments without issuing them arms? If they did not have enough work, he could always make them drill, just in case "circumstances should justify" their being given arms. But Jackson, whose own sincere religious convictions were well known, was more inclined to believe that these "faithful laborers" who were "careful of property" would enable other Southern men to return to the front ranks, which would "save many valuable horses and other public property" as well as arms.[21]

Jackson was shrewd enough, aware that it took more than sharpshooters to win a campaign. No reply from Governor Letcher has survived, but ten days later Jackson wrote again, promising to make sure "the religionists who are opposed to fighting" but willing to serve as teamsters would be paid. He also issued orders to Lieut. Colonel J. R. Jones to "promptly" call out the militia of Rockingham County. But Jackson "authorized" Jones to tell "Tunkers and Mennonites" that Jackson "believes them to be sincere in their opposition" to war and therefore the general would assign them to noncombatant roles where "they can serve their state as well in such a capacity as if bearing arms."[22] Thereafter, a few Mennonites pressed into militia service did act as teamsters, but most seem to have remained unenthused and regarded such work as too directly tied to war.[23]

Debating Exemption

Back in Richmond, the Confederate Congress was debating its national conscription bill that would supersede those of the states, including Virginia. On April 16, 1862, with remarkably little political disagreement, more than two-thirds of the Confederate Congress passed what was the first comprehensive conscription act in American history. The legislation provided for drafting for three years service all able-bodied men from 18 to 35 in every state. The statute exempted several classes of men, including civil servants, railroad workers, teachers, clergy, and anyone providing a substitute. But the law made no allowance for conscientious scruples, and thus seemed to undermine Virginia's provision. North Carolina Quakers, especially, but also Virginia Dunkers and Mennonites, began searching for ways to have the law amended. Before such lobbying could prove fruitful, however, nonresistants received unexpected publicity when men of conscience, caught fleeing north, ended up in a Richmond prison.

In fact, during March and April, Confederates captured at least two groups of young men trying to escape ahead of conscription. One group of eighteen—the group Stonewall Jackson had mentioned—was brought to the Harrisonburg, Virginia, courthouse where the men lived for several weeks while performing forced commissary labor. Soon the detainees had to share their living quarters with three more men when, on April 5, officials arrested Gabriel Heatwole Sr., Joseph Beery, and John Kline— the first two Mennonite and the latter a Dunker elder—and clapped them into the same jail. In the neighboring county, the Staunton newspaper approvingly noted the arrests and labeled all three "men of influence."[24] Conditions in the makeshift prison soon produced illness. Dunker and Mennonite women brought provisions, and some family members feared the men might face execution.[25] With local sentiment running so strongly against men of conscience, it was easy to expect the worst. As a Rockingham County Confederate leader later admitted, it was a "perfect reign of terror" when "people had to do as they could and not as they would."[26]

Eventually, Virginia's $500 commutation fee became the detained men's means of release. Family and fellow church members scrambled to collect enough funds to have the men freed. By any measure, it was a tremendous amount of cash to secure at one time. Years later, Peter Hartman

Rockingham County Courthouse, Harrisonburg, Virginia, built in 1833. In 1862 its second floor jury room served as a prison for eighteen Dunker and Mennonite men whom Confederate pickets captured trying to flee the South. Credit: Harrisonburg-Rockingham County (Va.) Historical Society

recalled how his father, David, had solicited money, and "he never had money flow in like it did at that time."[27]

Meanwhile, a group of seventy-four men had tried to escape and made it over the Shenandoah Mountain, but two Confederate pickets captured them near Petersburg in what is now West Virginia, brought them back to the Valley, and placed them in the Staunton Courthouse jail. From there, officials put the men on a train to Richmond and Castle Thunder prison.[28] Curiously, Jacob R. Hildebrand, an Augusta County Mennonite farmer, noted in his journal on March 20, 1862, that at Staunton he "heard that five cavalrymen took 72 Reffugees on their way to the Yankees. They had 32 horses & 12000 in gold & silver" and were sent to Richmond. "They are from the lower end of this county and Rockingham."[29] Was he unaware that some in the group were fellow Mennonites?

On March 31, the prisoners received a visit from Sydney S. Baxter, a former Virginia attorney general, now acting as a "habeas corpus commissioner" for the Confederate War Department.[30] Baxter reported that the group consisted of Dunkers and Mennonites "from Rockingham and Augusta Counties." Baxter also said the men were "regular members in good standing" and that they "bear good characters as citizens and Christians." He noted that both denominations believed that God forbade shedding human blood. He did not doubt the sincerity of their declaration that they had "left home to avoid the draft of the militia" so as to not "violate their consciences." Baxter thought the men "intended to return home as soon as the draft was over." Some had made attempts to procure substitutes, others "had done much to support the families of volunteers," and some had also provided horses to Confederate cavalry. "All of them are friendly to the South," he concluded, and they express a willingness "to contribute all their property if necessary to establish our [Confederate] liberties."[31]

Baxter knew that the Confederate Congress might yet consider a commutation provision for objectors who provided "pecuniary compensation." When he mentioned this possibility to the prisoners, Baxter reported, the men assured him that they would "cheerfully pay this compensation" and that those who could not afford it would "cheerfully go into service as teamsters or in any employment in which they are not required to shed blood." On this basis, Baxter recommended they be discharged upon their "oath of allegiance" to submit to the laws of Virginia and the Confederate States "except taking arms in war."[32]

It seems Baxter overplayed the refugees' eagerness to cooperate. In any case, the men continued to sit in the Richmond prison. That did not mean they went unnoticed. In fact, Rockingham County civic leader Algernon S. Gray, who was in Richmond at the time, reportedly told a Dunker leader that the imprisoned objectors "did more to impress the members of the Congress than all the other influences together." The fact that two sentries captured some seventy men, who then demonstrated "quiet submission to authority all the way," dramatized their scruples against violence and self-defense.[33]

Still, the prisoners' example did not stand alone. Behind the scenes, North Carolina Friends had lobbied for conscientious objection, and Virginia Mennonites and Brethren had approached Rockingham County representative John B. Baldwin with similar requests. The Virginians could point to the legislation their state had passed in the spring, and they asked Baldwin if that law might provide a model for the Confederate Congress. Baldwin encouraged the Dunkers and Mennonites to prepare a petition making such a point, and leaders from the two groups did so on September 1. Although some "persons have preferred the charge of Disloyalty against our Churches," the petitioners began, Dunkers and Mennonites were in truth obedient citizens—a remarkable claim, given the accumulated record of unionist activity. Since March, "most of our members" liable for service in Virginia "have already payd the penalty of $500 & 2 per cent . . . and have complied with the law. We only ask Congress, so far to *respect our Rights, our Consciences, and the Act of the state of Virginia.*" This petition, along with those of the Quakers, the distribution of Quaker and Mennonite writings on peace, and the example of the Dunker and Mennonite prisoners stood behind the Confederate Congress's passage on October 11, 1862, of exemption from military service for members of "the Society of Friends, and the association of Dunkards, Nazarenes, and Mennonists," provided those liable furnished a substitute or paid a commutation fee of $500.[34]

Now nonresistants had an uneasy peace at a stiff price or the cost of a substitute. In addition, those who had not been baptized before passage of the act were not exempt. Nineteen-year-old Manasses Heatwole, for example, was ineligible for exemption and was forced into the 52nd Virginia Infantry, Company F. Curiously, that placed him in the same regiment (but a different company) as Benjamin F. Hildebrand, son of Mennonite diarist Jacob R. Hildebrand. Heatwole soon deserted but was again inducted and present at a number of battles, the last of which was Gettysburg. Then he escaped to Ohio.[35] A similar case was that of Melchiah Brenneman, who became a cavalryman and served over three years. On the day before Gettysburg, he was wounded. Eight months later he deserted and with three other men fled north. Brenneman went to Pennsylvania and later to Ohio, where he became a Mennonite deacon.[36] As such cases illustrate, ending up in a Southern uniform did not necessarily mean Mennonite-reared men had much commitment to the cause.

Hiring a substitute—a key provision of the Confederate draft legislation—was not uncommon for Virginia Mennonites but could be costly. Jacob Geil paid $600 for a six-month substitute before the $500 commutation provision was passed, and George Brunk paid $50 a month to a substitute from Page County. Henry L. Rhodes had a substitute furnished by his employer. John Brunk sent a substitute in the place of his son. Others, such as David C. Brenneman, Henry and John Geil, Jacob Shank Jr., Samuel Shank, and Isaac Wenger also supplied substitutes.[37] There is little evidence that Virginia Mennonites debated the merits of hiring substitutes or considered it a form of indirect participation in the same way they viewed noncombatant personal service.

Taking a different tack, Jacob Geil and Abraham Blosser won draft exemptions by becoming civil servants. Geil purchased the postmaster position at the village of Edom for $280, and Abraham Blosser purchased a mail route for $1,000 from a disabled Methodist preacher. But Geil soon gave up his position, and Blosser, when criticized, arranged to take an additional route and carried mail for nearly four years.[38]

No doubt the substitute provision in the South raised the wrath of many because wealthier men could buy their way out of the army. Or, if patriotism and honor meant little, a poor man could become rich by offering himself as a substitute, then deserting at the first opportunity and doing it all over again. By late 1863 the price of substitutes went as high as $6,000, the equivalent of three years' wages for a skilled workman. Abuse became so severe that the Confederate Congress abolished substitution by December 1863, though the $500 exemption for conscience remained for a time.[39]

Nevertheless, despite the commutation and short-lived substitute options, it seems that most Virginia Mennonite men sought to avoid any connection with the military, even though such a choice meant one eventually became a fugitive. Perhaps in this regard they followed the example of Samuel Coffman, the influential bishop who lived west of Harrisonburg and was a strong promoter of nonresistance. As a young man, Coffman had left the declining Mennonite settlement in Greenbrier County, a mountainous area in western Virginia. Emigration had caused the Greenbrier Mennonite community to dwindle, and most of Coffman's siblings who remained there had become Methodists and did not share his peace position.[40] Now, from his Rockingham County pulpit, Coffman denounced conscription, though he learned it could be dangerous to be too outspoken. Soon "a certain Colonel threatened to come with his regiment to take Bish.

Samuel Coffman (1822–1894), bishop of the Middle District of the Virginia
Mennonite Conference, beginning in May 1861. Credit: Menno Simons Historical
Library and Archives, Harrisonburg, Va.

Coffman and all the brethren capable of bearing arms into the army." By
May 1862 things had become so tense and the threats against his life so
serious, that Coffman fled to Pennsylvania for six weeks.[41]

Nor was Coffman alone in fleeing Rockingham County. Many young
men tried to leave because of the uncertainties in obtaining exemption.
The network of hiding places formed what was known as an "underground
railroad" to Union territory. Others simply hid locally, hoping to wait out
the end of the war. Simon Burkholder fixed a place in his barn where he

stayed hidden for eighteen months. Mennonite potter John Heatwole had been forced into the war in 1861 and was startled the next April to learn that his discharge had been nullified and he was to serve three more years. He stayed four months longer in the 33rd Virginia Infantry of the Stonewall Brigade and then deserted and went into hiding. The Harrisonburg provost marshal's office offered a reward for his capture and sent squads to hunt for him. The pressure "finally drove him into the mountains, where he built a lean-to in a remote hollow." Reputedly, Heatwole walked backwards up a mountain in the snow so as to baffle scouts on his trail.[42]

Daunting Challenges, Diverging Choices

The experiences of a trio of men—Philip Parret, Gabriel Shank, and Samuel Rhodes—illustrate different paths Virginia Mennonites took in the face of prevailing patriotism and conscription. Parret, whose father was Presbyterian and his mother Mennonite, grew up attending Cook's Creek Presbyterian Church west of Harrisonburg. He enlisted in Stonewall Jackson's Brigade early in the war but deserted in August 1862. A year later he rejoined his regiment, stayed for six months, and then deserted again in the spring of 1864. Thereupon, he immediately requested and received baptism in the Mennonite church and fled north to Franklin County, Pennsylvania. There he later became the first English-speaking Mennonite minister in the region.[43]

Gabriel Shank, son of David Shank and grandson of Virginia music publisher Joseph Funk, enlisted in the 10th Virginia and became his company's color bearer. In late 1862 Shank married a Presbyterian woman but remained in active duty and saw action at Gettysburg and in Maj. General Jubal Early's raid on Washington, D.C. Captured by Union forces on September 22, 1864, he died of smallpox the next March at Fort Delaware Prison and was buried at Salem, New Jersey.[44]

The third man, Samuel Rhodes, tried repeatedly to go north and kept a detailed journal of his "Traveling Adventures."[45] His story suggests the difficulties such a course entailed. Rhodes claimed that half the men between 18 and 45 among his relatives and friends had fled or gone into hiding. In mid-March 1862, Rhodes decided to head north. He traveled toward Muddy Creek and Rushville near the Bank Mennonite Church, where he learned of a company of fifty Mennonites and Dunkers trying to make their escape. When he failed to connect with that group, he waited until the next evening. By that time seven more men had shown up. They discussed strategy, collected rations, and at ten o'clock headed toward the mountains. At two in the morning, they arrived at the home of Union sympathizers, where they learned that another group of refugees had passed through only a short time before, heading for the Petersburg road in Hardy County (now West Virginia). After only two hours at this way station, Rhodes and his group—now having swelled to twelve—moved on, this time in the rain. All the next day they slogged through mud and fog as they tried to overtake the fugitives ahead of them.

Reaching the road to Petersburg on the South Branch of the Potomac River, they continued on, but the next night went the wrong direction and eventually found themselves heading toward Brocks Gap, west of Broadway, rather than Petersburg. Furthermore, they learned that the company of fifty ahead of them had been captured. Now Rhodes's little band knew it was in danger. To make matters worse, the next night they got lost again, provisions ran low, and they estimated they were only about twenty-five miles from home. After some discussion, they decided to return home, load up with provisions, and set out again. This time only seven men participated in the escape group, and one of them had the mumps. At Dry River they pulled off their boots to walk through icy water, then braced themselves with shots of whiskey and proceeded over several mountain ridges. Several more times their provisions ran low and Rhodes returned home for more. Finally, because of weather and fragile health, Rhodes decided to stay home and hide locally for a time, while the others scattered.

Rhodes stayed hidden for two weeks. Thereafter, he kept moving from place to place almost daily among relatives or friends. After six weeks of such movement, he decided to go north following the Union army after learning "delightful" reports that federal troops were at Harrisonburg. But that news faded quickly as Confederate forces arrived and chased them out. Rhodes had missed his opportunity.

In early May, Samuel Rhodes and a friend, A. J. Bowers, decided to try again. Three miles west of Harrisonburg at the home of Rhodes' brother, they ran into Confederate Colonel Turner Ashby's cavalry. The two climbed through a window, found no one home, and went to bed. The next afternoon Rhodes found his brother and family hiding in their barn, afraid of the Confederate troops in the area. That night Rhodes and Bowers started north again. At New Market they ran into several others who had been part of Rhodes's earlier escape group, but he and Bower headed for Winchester. Once on the way, they ended up in the home of a minister, who put them up for the night. But Rhodes discovered the man was a "rank Cesesh," who would have reported them at the first opportunity, so they hastened on the next morning. At Winchester the fugitives obtained Union passes for Martinsburg, and they finally made it to the Potomac, where they parted ways. Rhodes then met three other men of conscience from Rockingham County, and together they sought refuge in western Maryland.

By now it was mid-May, and Rhodes hired himself out by the day. He stayed in Maryland until December 1862, when he went to Lancaster and Altoona, Pennsylvania, where he worked as a carpenter until the "rebble arma" invaded Pennsylvania during the Gettysburg campaign and Altoona shops closed for ninety days while many of the men went off to war. Rhodes then headed for Iowa, but fell ill. He tried to return to Virginia, but he only got as far as Hagerstown, Maryland, where he died on April 26, 1864.

Mennonites and the Confederate Cause

Virginia Mennonites such as Rhodes believed they were giving their highest allegiance to God, although a sizable majority also indicated clear Unionist political sympathies. A significant exception was Mennonite Jacob R. Hildebrand of Augusta County, whose journal is full of pro-Confederate concerns.[46] In March 1862, with his oldest son Benjamin already in the 52nd Virginia Infantry for eight months, Hildebrand was concerned that war news was "rather disturbing" for the South. The next day he heard that Governor Letcher had called for 40,000 more men and wondered if he, at age 42, would be pressed into the militia reserve class. Hildebrand, a trustee of the Mennonite church, apparently never expected that he, his sons, relatives, or fellow church members would avoid military service by going into hiding. Indeed, he seems resigned to entering the state militia, noting, for example, on March 14, 1862:

"Today I have to Report in Staunton & from there to Winchester as the enemy are said to be there in large numbers. God only knows whether I shall ever return again. Yet one thing I know that I have committed all things into his hands knowing that he careth for us & that he is able to keep that which I have committed to him; now unto him that is able to keep us from falling be honor Dominion now & forever; Amen. This ends my journal for the present."

But the journal did not end, and the next day, "contrary to expectations," he returned from Staunton, unneeded. Still, the war news was bad. The Yankees were said to be south of Winchester and coming up the valley.

Jacob R. Hildebrand's journal reflected his general apprehension. His wife, Catherine (Rodefer) Hildebrand, became ill for ten days, and he bemoaned the "evil times" as war and death were "sweeping a great many off." Catherine had a dream on March 19 that intrigued Jacob, though he was unsure he should put much stock in dreams. Catherine had dreamt that someone's barn caught fire, causing great alarm. Before the fire was extinguished many shingles burned, but some remained and all the rafters stood upright without damage. Jacob wondered if the barn might represent the Confederacy, the rafters the Confederate states, and the shingles the people of the Southern states. Perhaps, he suggested in unusual Mennonite musings, the Confederacy would endure.

Within a week, Hildebrand appeared before the "Board of Exemption," and two doctors exempted him for "Disease of the Heart." No doubt that was a relief to Catherine and the three children at home, Gideon, Michael, and Mary Susan. In May Hildebrand and neighbor John Grove left for the army "to see our friends."[47] Hildebrand lamented the many dead and wounded but indicated he was happy that Rebels were chasing "the enemy" toward Pendleton County. Returning home, he reported to a "great many persons" who wanted firsthand news from the Confederate camp.

Hildebrand continued to reveal his sympathies in his journal, especially as he recorded the dramatic events of May 1862. That month Stonewall Jackson's famous Valley Campaign sent thousands of troops (including Benjamin Hildebrand) marching up and down the Shenandoah, attacking, eluding, and very often defeating Union forces in retreat and pursuit.[48] In the midst of these events, Hildebrand noted that President Jefferson Davis had designated Friday, May 16, 1862, "as a day of humiliation and

Prayer, for aid from the Allmighty in our strugle for Liberty & Indipendence." Hildebrand prayed, "Lord, Regard the Government under which we live" and may the "magistry of the land" be wise, "exemplary in conduct, & faithful to their trust." He hoped that people might be reformed and "not destroyed. Thus may we be holy, that we may be a happy people, whose God is the Lord."

Two days later, Hildebrand "felt a great deal concerned about our army. May God in his mercy save us from our enemys is my daily prayer." Then he went to visit son Benjamin, camped west of Harrisonburg. He slept in camp that night and the next day watched his son and the regiment "go down the valey with the army to drive out Abe Lincolns Hireling tools who are Invadeing our soil & desecrating our homes." For several weeks the fighting between Harrisonburg and Winchester filled his journal entries—except for May 25, which was communion Sunday at the Hildebrand Mennonite Church. Apparently, he suspended his Confederate loyalties in the face of churchly ritual priorities.

May 25 also turned out to be the day Jackson's forces struck a decisive blow against Union troops at Winchester, sending them fleeing northward. Jackson soon took his troops back up the Valley, and Hildebrand's journal returned to Confederate concerns. By the end of May, Hildebrand had became so uneasy about Benjamin's welfare that he went searching for him until he found him. A week later, he heard "heavy fireing" in the direction of Port Republic in eastern Rockingham County, but he was happy to hear that the Yankees had been "Repulsed." Indeed, the June 9 battle at Port Republic marked the end of major military maneuvers in the Valley that year and sealed Jackson's strategic Confederate victory. In the process, though, the fighting had taken the life of Jackson's key cavalry commander, Brig. General Turner Ashby, near Harrisonburg. In his diary, Hildebrand noted the general's death.[49]

The next day, down the valley in Rockingham County, the family of David and Elizabeth (Burkholder) Hartman learned of Ashby's death from Union soldiers who came to their house looking for breakfast. Fifteen-year-old Peter Hartman had heard "the wounded men scream" and "the cannon roar over on the side toward Harrisonburg," and a few days later Confederates commandeered him to take straw to Harrisonburg as bedding for the wounded. "I never want to see another sight like that," he confided later. "Men coming in, torn to pieces." A schoolmate who had been to New Market told Hartman of seeing "rows of men side by side on [a] barn floor" as "doctors were there taking off arms and limbs and they had quite a stack of them."[50]

To the west of Augusta and Rockingham counties lived two Whanger brothers, whose political sympathies seem to have been more like the Hildebrands than the Hartmans. The Whangers were members of an isolated and dwindling Mennonite community in Greenbrier County, a section of western Virginia with strong Confederate sympathies. There David and Joseph, sons of David C. and Amelia (Tipton) Whanger, joined Confederate forces in late 1862, before the western counties voted to become West Virginia. David, age 24, and Joseph, 22, signed on with the 26th Virginia Infantry on October 25 and November 26 at Lewisburg, near their home. Oral tradition says that the young men's father had been the last Mennonite minister for the small church that met for worship in private homes. But the elder Whanger, a farmer and blacksmith, had died on November 18, 1861, shortly after Federal soldiers had taken the family's horses.[51]

In late summer 1863, only ten days apart, both Whanger sons were captured by Union forces. After some months at Camp Chase, Ohio, both men ended up in January 1864 in a Rock Island, Illinois, federal prison, a place so unhealthy and overcrowded that hundreds of prisoners died from smallpox, pneumonia, and diarrhea. Yet both brothers survived. Like many prisoners, they agreed to take an oath of allegiance to the United States. In October, David enlisted in the U.S. Frontier Service; Joseph, despite the oath, was rejected and released—likely because of poor health—and ended up in Kansas.[52]

The experience of the Hildebrand and the Whanger families was unusual, however. Most Virginia Mennonites had opposed secession and remained cool to the Confederacy during the war's first months and years. Although most lived in the Shenandoah Valley, where a less-virulent strain of anti-Union feeling might have provided a more moderate political environment, the pressures engendered by battle on Virginia soil had turned the conflict into a struggle interpreted as self-defense, one in which dissenters and nonresistants were downright dangerous. State and national legislators in Richmond might extend exemption or noncombatant privileges to Mennonites and Dunkers, whose reputations had won them some grudging respect. But for the peace people themselves, noncombatancy often was unacceptable and exemption too costly. Hiding at home or attempting a fugitive trek to Pennsylvania became more common responses.

Nonresistants in Pennsylvania faced challenges too, but they were of a very different nature from those of their Virginia compatriots. In the Keystone State, Mennonites had more direct access to the halls of power, even as popular attitudes were in some respects more hostile and resentful.

Negotiation and Notoriety in Pennsylvania

"We Are Coming, Father Abraham"

In the summer of 1862, Union military fortunes in the East looked dismal. Maj. General George B. McClellan's slow drive in April and May toward the Confederate capital of Richmond—the so-called Peninsula Campaign—ended with high casualties and strategic failure in a late June series of engagements known as the Seven Days' Battles. For their part, Southern forces had also sustained heavy losses—and indeed, the Army of Northern Virginia's victory was narrower than most observers realized. Still, McClellan's retreat and the collapse of the large-scale Federal offensive on which so many Northerners had placed their hope sank morale to a new low. Moreover, Union troop strength sagged, and leaders began considering compulsory mobilization.[1]

The advent of conscription would push Northern Mennonites and Amish off the political sidelines. For those in Pennsylvania, the ensuing struggle for exemption drew on the distinct resources that their context offered. First, Pennsylvania constitutional law offered precedents for those with conscientious scruples, and a politically active Quaker population, centered in Philadelphia, was sure to remind leaders in Harrisburg of such legal traditions. Yet Mennonites did not always agree with Friends' approaches or assumptions and did not necessarily rely on these would-be allies. Instead, Mennonites in southeastern Pennsylvania spoke for themselves, worked with their own political patrons, and framed understandings of nonresistant citizenship in which civic participation legitimated civic privilege.

For both practical and political reasons, Northern state and federal officials had held off conscription.[2] Lincoln's 1861 calls for volunteers had resulted in heavy enlistments; in fact, this showing was so impressive that the new Secretary of War, Edwin M. Stanton, who took office in January 1862, had actually ordered all recruiting offices to close that spring. But now the North's precarious strategic position seemed to demand dramatically different action. To preserve the president's political clout and avoid the appearance of desperation in the wake of McClellan's defeat, Secretary of State William Seward arranged in midsummer for the influential governors of New York and Pennsylvania to publicly urge Lincoln to call up more men to "crush this rebellion." Party to the backstage plan, Lincoln responded by asking for 300,000 volunteers and signing a new revenue act levying a tax of 3 percent on incomes between $600 and $10,000 and 5 percent on those that were higher.[3] At about the same time, the president surprised most of his cabinet by presenting a draft of an Emancipation Proclamation that proposed freeing slaves in rebellious states by January 1, 1863. For Lincoln, the call for more men and money was related to a shift in his thinking about the scope of the war and the means needed to achieve an expanding set of aims.[4]

Despite a catchy new recruiting song, "We Are Coming, Father Abraham, Three Hundred Thousand More," the president's new plea was less successful than had been his call for volunteers after Fort Sumter. As a result, Congress began discussing some sort of national conscription scheme and on July 17 passed a new militia bill that empowered the president to call state militias into federal service for nine months. The War Department quickly followed up with a request for 300,000 nine-month militia men. This came on top of the president's July 2 call for volunteers.[5] Since most Northern state militia systems had long ago fallen into disarray, the new law was a complicated affair that involved enrolling all able-bodied men age 18 to 45 and then calling into service, via randomly selected names from those lists, enough men to complete the state quotas unfilled by volunteers. Lincoln signed the measure, and on August 9, 1862, the War Department issued orders on how to proceed with enrollment and the draft.[6]

To grease the process, the War Department began offering volunteers an advance of $25 on the $100 they otherwise would receive upon honorable discharge, and some local communities also offered bounties, hoping to increase volunteers and thus diminish the number of slots that would need to be filled via conscription. Indeed, in most places the system coaxed enough volunteers into the ranks, but large-scale conscription was necessary in several states, including Pennsylvania. A bevy of provost marshals made sure local troublemakers did not disrupt the draft, and eventually the system produced 421,000 three-year volunteers and 88,000 nine-month militia.[7]

In the meantime, the possibility of forced induction threw Pennsylvania Mennonites into action. Their approach differed from Quaker activists. For example, in April 1862, the Sadsbury Monthly Meeting, which covered Lancaster and Chester counties, had published a long "Address" in the Lancaster *Daily Evening Express*, apparently aimed at nonresistant readers. It called on "fellow workers in the cause of righteousness" to petition Congress, issue tracts, and otherwise work to abolish slavery. That kind of social reform and responsibility suited few Mennonites' understanding of the relationship of church and state. Yes, Mennonites had banned slavery from their homes, but only when the state sought directly to entangle Mennonites in affairs that contravened conscience would they actively oppose civil powers or seek to change public policy.

Conscription was such a direct entanglement, but even here, Mennonites sought exemption within a framework that recognized government's authority over them. Although the first draft was set for August 15, 1862, there were so many complications with the new system that it was October or November in many places until officials began to draw names. In the meantime, Mennonite lobbying efforts swung into action. Minister Jacob Beidler of Swamp Mennonite Church near Quakertown, in Bucks County, reported several different Mennonite delegations to Governor Andrew Curtin during the war, the first about this time. For his part, Beidler hoped "that the constitution would still be our protection," and he had confidence that the governor would rescue men of conscience, although the early draft directives, in English, were not always clear to German-speakers like Beidler, the preacher admitted.[8]

From Lancaster County, Mennonites sent noted preacher Amos Herr and layman John Shenk to see Governor Curtin and to explain their posi-

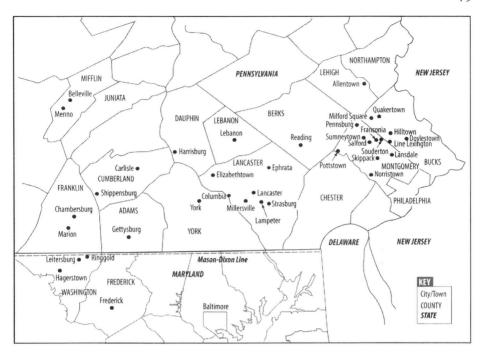

Southeastern Pennsylvania and Northern Maryland

tion. Memory preserved what Mennonites understood to be their working relationship with the state. When the governor asked, "Well, what do you people do for us? Do you vote?" Herr and Shenk answered affirmatively, and Curtin then promised, "We will do something for you."[9]

Curtin's plan turned out to be a process for obtaining conscientious objector status. Men of conscience would apply to local officials for certificates of exemption. Anyone signing such a certificate affirmed "that he conscientiously scruples to bear arms," whether in self-defense or in protecting his country. Furthermore, he affirmed that this belief had not "been formed lightly, but carefully, deliberately and conscientiously," and that it was of long standing and in relation to all wars. Those taking such a certificate were also obligated to pay an exemption fee—the amount to be determined by the legislature—"equivalent for personal service."[10]

Pennsylvania Mennonites were quite agreeable to this fee-in-lieu-of-service proposal, a potentially costly but accepted practice with a long history in Europe and North America. At Doylestown in the second week of

STATE OF PENNSYLVANIA,

Lancaster County, ss.

Before me, Commissioner to Superintend Drafting for said county, personally appeared *Jacob F. Harnish of E. Hempfield* who being duly *affirmed* did depose and say, that he conscientiously scruples to bear arms, believes it unlawful to do so, whether in self-defence or in defence of his country, or otherwise howsoever; that the scruples and belief above stated, have not been formed lightly, but carefully, deliberately and conscientiously, and are now declared and professed not for the purpose of evading the military service of his country in the present exigency, but because he solemnly and religiously holds and maintains them, and in his conscience believes that it is his bounden duty to act in accordance with them on all occasions, and under all circumstances.

Jacob F. Harnish

Affirmed and subscribed before me, this *25* day of *October* 1862.

James L. Reynold
COMMISSIONER.

Application for exemption filed by Jacob F. Harnish (1828–1917) of East Hempfield Township, Lancaster County, Pennsylvania, attesting to his "scruples" against bearing arms "whether in self-defense or in defense of his country." Harnish had a second cousin, also named Jacob Harnish, who joined the 31st Pennsylvania Volunteers and died in 1865 as a prisoner of war in North Carolina. Credit: Pennsylvania State Archives

September, an apprehensive crowd, estimated to number in the hundreds, came seeking exemptions. "I have never seen harder pressing and crowding in all the days of my life," wrote one Mennonite. "Everyone had to push with good earnest and all his might to get his name registered in the forenoon."[11] The newspaper listed those who had signed depositions for conscientious scruples; about two-thirds of the men in the list of 312 were Mennonites.[12]

The governor's remarkably sympathetic response to nonresistants did not calm all anxiety since in the end it was local officials who implemented the process, and not every neighborhood took kindly to Amish and Mennonite convictions. Controversy erupted in Montgomery County, for example, when Commissioner James Boyd issued very few of the exemption certificates that nonresistants were scrambling to obtain. By his own admission, Boyd asked applicants: "Would you stand by and see your wife or children murdered and not save them if you could do so by a resort to arms? Would you stand by and see your father or mother murdered and not save them if you could do so by a resort to arms?"[13] If Boyd did not like a particular answer, he refused to grant the certificate. Rumor had it that Boyd boasted he had "not allowed a single one [exemption] in Montgomery County."[14]

On September 24 two Mennonites from Skippack, Isaac Kulp and John Berge, complained to Governor Curtin about Boyd. They had learned that commissioners in neighboring counties grant exemptions "to nearly all who took the required oath," but "our commissioner" granted hardly any. "We would therefore, in the name of many praying hearts, ask you what to do under these trying circumstances, whether there is mercy at your hands," they wrote. William Clemmer believed that politics motivated Boyd's recalcitrance: Boyd was a Democrat and knew that men of conscience were almost all Republicans.[15]

Perhaps partisan appeal was enough to motivate Curtin and Secretary of the Commonwealth Eli Slifer. They launched an investigation that forced Boyd to defend himself. It was not true, Boyd claimed, that he refused to administer the affirmation of conscience, though it was correct that he "rejected all who . . . did not answer the questions satisfactorily." Furthermore, insisted Boyd, he had had only three applicants in the whole county—hardly a statement with any veracity. Boyd claimed that the "Menonites, Hereites [Reformed Mennonites], Swingfelters [Schwenkfelders], and Dunkards in the county" had decided that they could not honestly take the oath, so they "did not apply at all."[16] The problem, Boyd said, lay with the neighboring commissioners who were too lenient: "Everybody [in those places] gets off that wants to, particularly in Bucks Co." The governor was not impressed with Boyd's explanation, and on October 21, ordered Boyd to discontinue his "wanton harshness and disrespect" of nonresistants' "convictions."[17]

Although he did not live in Boyd's jurisdiction, Bucks County Mennonite preacher Jacob Beidler had found the situation troubling. Writing to his friend, businessman and deacon Jacob Nold Jr., of Columbiana, Ohio, Beidler complained that Commissioner Boyd "demanded more than was his right" and that "there was well nigh no escape" for nonresistant men. So "some of our preachers arose and again went to our governor and once more petitioned" that those caught in the draft "be released" from direct service, but not necessarily "released from paying a fine."[18] Churches such as Line Lexington collected money to cover the costs of the delegation, which included bishop Jacob Kulp of the Plains congregation and deacon Abraham M. Clemmer of the Franconia congregation, both in Montgomery County. Moritz Loeb, publisher of the Doylestown *Der Morgenstern*, a favorite German-language paper of area Mennonites, also went along. According to Beidler, Kulp's "earnest pleading and humble deportment" communicated effectively, and the governor acted to rein in Boyd.[19]

Other Mennonites saw divine chastisement, despite ample evidence of political goodwill from Harrisburg. "We have had very good harvests . . . this year," Bucks countians William and Samuel Gross wrote their Canadian cousins in September. "All that is wanting to make us blessed and happy is unity, love and peace throughout our country." But "at present everything looks dismal and gloomy, dark clouds are hanging over us and everything looks foreboding of gloom and despair for judgments have come." Every day brought "tears of sorrow and distress," confessed the Gross brothers, who interpreted the draft as a "visitation" from God to teach peace people new humility.[20]

John H. Oberholtzer, the progressive minister and chairman of the newly formed General Conference Mennonite Church, also believed the draft was a form of spiritual testing. Writing on October 29 from Milford Square, in Bucks County, in his paper, *Das Christliche Volks-Blatt*, Oberholtzer said that when news came of the draft, "we saw robust men shed tears and women begin to weep together." People ran to draft officials in hopes of learning that "the destroying angel had passed them by."[21]

Although (Old) Mennonites, such as the Gross brothers, and General Conference Mennonites, such as Oberholtzer, sometimes drew similar messages from current events, there were some substantial differences in the outlooks of the two groups. When leaders from the more tradition-minded and communally oriented church of William and Samuel Gross approached the state, they did so believing that they spoke for a disciplined body whose dissent from the war was an expression of collective conscience. Oberholtzer's progressive brand of Mennonitism, in contrast, put more of an accent on individual conscience—a source of authority that others could not easily judge. Not surprisingly, by fall 1863 Oberholtzer's group was unable to decide what to do "when members of our congregations bear arms" and determined only that "each congregation is to handle

General Conference Mennonite leader John H. Oberholtzer (1809–1895), of Milford Square, Pennsylvania, a progressive-minded minister who edited *Das Christliche Volks-Blatt*. Credit: Mennonite Heritage Center, Harleysville, Pa.

such brothers according to circumstances."[22] For (Old) Mennonites, bearing arms would have been a sure sign that the soldier no longer considered himself a brother.

Although differences between Mennonite groups were not insignificant, key similarities pointed to common convictions as well. A belief that Christians should submit to civil authority in everything that did not contravene conscience, for example, resulted generally in Mennonite and Amish acceptance of state demands for equivalency from nonresistant citizens—a position that separated even General Conference progressives from, say, Quaker activists, despite their seemingly common appreciation for individual conscience.[23]

Of course, one did not have to be nonresistant to resent the draft. A great many Americans objected to conscription, believing it was un-American. For many who tried to dodge the draft, religious conviction was hardly a factor. Thousands of eligible men disappeared, thereby becoming *skulk-ers*, who hid in the neighborhood, or *skedaddlers*, who headed for remote regions. Thousands fled to Canada, where papers reported a steady stream of "white fugitives from Uncle Sam's plantation," as the Chatham, Ontario, *Planet* put it.[24] Meanwhile, Democratic Party newspapers in the United States derided the draft as a loss of liberty and an enormous increase in federal power.[25]

Seeking to avoid politically unpopular drafting, states and municipalities increased bounties in the hope of filling quotas with volunteer enlistments. In Lower Salford Township, Montgomery County, Mennonites contributed money to raise such bounties. Michael Alderfer pledged $100, and his wealthy uncle, Abraham Alderfer, offered $125. Names such as Alderfer, Kratz, Delp, Hunsicker, Bergey, and Godshalk appeared on the subscription list.[26] No doubt these nonresistants believed that by donating they lessened the likelihood that their own sons would be subject to conscription.

Pennsylvania's Draft Wheels Begin to Roll

With enrollment lists finally assembled, the militia draft began on October 16 in areas that were short of enlistees.[27] In Norristown, Commissioner Boyd informed the crowd watching the proceedings that he needed 1,320 men to fill the quota. The cylindrical "wheel of tin," about six inches long and sixteen inches in diameter, carried the names of 7,734 enrolled men, each with his name written on a slip of paper that was tightly rolled and placed inside the wheel, which was turned to shuffle the papers. Everything was done in plain view so people could see the lottery proceed as a blindfolded person drew the names. Each person chosen received a draft notice and was given five days to appear at the Norristown Court House, bringing along clothing, shoes, and a blanket.[28]

Local newspapers published lists of those being drafted, as did the German-language paper of Pennsburg and Sumneytown, which also published a list of ninety-eight who were exempted because of conscientious scruples (*Wegen Gewissens-Skrupeln*), many of whom were Mennonites.[29] Actually, the paper's list was incomplete, since 194 Montgomery County men filed depositions of conscience between September 10 and November 1. From the large number of exemptions and from complaints appearing in the Norristown *Herald and Free Press*, it appears the county had some difficulty in meeting its draft quota, and more than three hundred men had "neglected or refused to answer the draft." Certainly not all of these were men of conscience, but such news hurt morale among the soldiers already in camp, the paper complained.[30]

Some local newspapers seemed surprised that so many Mennonites had registered scruples. Earlier, newspaper editors had taken one look at the exemption certificate and predicted that few men would agree to such absolutist wording. But the editors badly misjudged nonresistant convictions. Later, in fact, Commissioner of the Draft A. K. M'Clure reported that while numerous counties only had a few men of conscience, in jurisdictions where Mennonites, Amish, Dunkers, and Quakers lived, large numbers claimed that exemption. For a dozen counties the total was 2,628.[31]

Of all Pennsylvania's counties none came close to Lancaster's 667 exemption certificates. Bucks County had half that many with 367. Montgomery and Franklin, with considerable peace church populations, had nearly 200 each. Mifflin, York, Adams, and Somerset counties each had more than 100. Certainly some Mennonites and Amish in Pennsylvania joined military ranks; nor were all exemption certificates held by their young men. Nevertheless, it is clear that their most common response to the call to arms was a refusal to go to war.[32]

In central Pennsylvania, Mifflin County Amish responded collectively and consistently to the draft. Between September 8 and 16, officials issued 117 depositions, 88 of them signed by Amishmen.[33] Many took another precaution and contributed with "liberality" more than $2,800 for bounty money to entice volunteers. When the draft came to Mifflin County, only eleven slots needed to be filled.[34] Amish women also established neighborly goodwill by contributing fruit, vegetables, and bedding to a Ladies' Aid Association that served soldiers' families.[35]

In contrast to Mifflin County, Lancaster County's draft commissioner, James L. Reynolds, had to process a large draft. The *Examiner & Herald* claimed that 2,661 names had been drawn from the draft wheel, and that did not include Lancaster city.[36] Surviving enrollment lists carry many typical Mennonite, Amish, River Brethren, and Dunker names marked "conscientious" (tables 4.1 and 4.2). Nearly all of them were processed in late October.[37]

Table 4.1. Selected names listed as "Conscientious" in 1862 militia draft
Enrollment Book 2, Rapho Township, Lancaster County, Pennsylvania

Name	Age	Occupation	Church
Jacob Brubaker	25	Farmer	
John Brubaker	32	Farmer	
Joseph Bomberger	33	Farmer	
Jacob Cassel	44	Farmer	Old Mennonite
Noah Engle	28	Farmer	
John M. Engle	29	Farmer	
Simon J. Eby	30	Farmer	
Daniel Engle	35	Farmer	
Jacob M. Engle	38	Farmer	
Benjamin Engle	28	Farmer	
Abraham Horst	40	Farmer	
Benjamin Landes	25	Laborer	
Christ Gish	27	Miller	
Isaac Geib	33	Farmer's Son	Dunker
Henry Ginder	32	Blacksmith	Dunker
John Ginder	30	Farmer	Dunker
Samuel Hollinger	36	Farmer	Dunker
Benjamin Niseley	38	Farmer	Old Mennonite
Jacob Rohrer	32	Farmer's son	Old Mennonite
Joseph H. Rider	31	Farmer's son	Dunker
Isaac Zug	25	Farmer	Dunker
Benjamin Zug	25	Farmer	
Abraham Zug	18	Laborer	
Emanuel R. Zug	22	Laborer	
Samuel Zug	34	Farmer	Dunker and Justice

Note: Occasionally, the enroller listed church membership.

Berks and Lehigh counties also resorted to conscription but had relatively small Mennonite or Amish populations. Of the 2,328 men drafted
in Berks County or the hundreds of men drafted in Lehigh County, fine
print listings in local newspapers reveal only a few names suggesting
Mennonite connections.[38] York County officials required that a minister
or a respected man of the congregation accompany a man requesting ex-

Table 4.2. Men with Amish or Mennonite surnames listed as
"Conscientious" in the 1862 militia draft enrollment, Book No. 5, Leacock
Township, Lancaster County, Pennsylvania

Name	Age	Occupation	Name	Age	Occupation
Jacob Beiler	33	Farmer	David Martin	26	Farmer
Samuel Beiler	37	Farmer	Samuel Petersheim	33	Farmer
Christian Beiler	21	Laborer	John Renno	36	Farmer
John W. Beiler	37	Farmer	Jacob Swartz	27	Farmer
John Fisher	37	Farmer	Henry Stoltzfus	23	Farmer
Samuel Hertzler	39	Farmer	Jonathan Stoltzfus	29	Farmer
Abraham King	38	Farmer	Jacob Stoltzfus	21	Farmer
Jonathan Kauffman	35	Farmer	Noah Smoker	29	Farmer
John Kauffman	40	Farmer	John Snavely	33	Farmer
Michael Kauffman	27	Farmer	David Smoker	30	Farmer
Michael Lapp	31	Farmer	Jonathan Smoker	30	Farmer
Christian Lapp	21	Farmer	Samuel Smoker	21	Farmer
John R. Lapp	40	Farmer	Jacob Stultzfus	22	Laborer
Tobias Leaman	18	Farmer	Reuben Wenger	32	Farmer
Joshua Lapp	26	Farmer	Jonathan Wenger	34	Farmer
Elias Lapp	19	Farmer	Jonathan Zook	24	Farmer

Note: Occasionally, the enroller listed church membership.

emption.[39] A few Mennonites here entered the military, such as Daniel
Lehman Gehly of Windsor Township, who became a militia colonel.[40]

In Bucks and Montgomery counties, the draft scared a few conscientious men enough to "skedaddle" to Canada or western territory. Others
went to local justices of the peace and tried to secure physical disability
exemptions. Townships with considerable Mennonite populations had
many names on the physical infirmity lists (table 4.3).[41] Ministers were
exempted because of vocation, but even some Mennonite ministers pro-
cured disability affidavits, including John Walters, Henry B. Moyer, A. F.
Moyer, and Isaac Detweiler.

Groups of draft-age men also pooled funds into makeshift draft insur-
ance, pledging to give the necessary amounts to pay for substitutes for
those in the pool whom the draft might strike. Although the practice of
draftees paying substitutes to take their place may strike twenty-first-cen-

Table 4.3. Examples of disability exemptions circa August 20, 1862,
Bucks County, Pennsylvania

Name	Disability exemption
Samuel Souder	Becomes nervous when frightened or excited
Jacob Leatherman	Weakness of spine
John A. Detweiler	Lameness of right shoulder
Samuel Delp	Sick headaches and other problems
John Alderfer	Not sound about his lungs or liver
Isaac W. Moyer	Pleurisy, rheumatism
Abram F. Hunsberger	Dislocation of right shoulder
Jacob D. Rosenberger	Hernia for 15 years

tury moderns as curious, it had a long tradition in Anglo-American (and French) militia and citizen-soldier history.[42] Substitutes might step forward either from among those eligible for the draft but not chosen or from the ranks of the ineligible but willing, such as immigrants who had not yet declared their intent to naturalize. Indeed, public criticism of substitution usually centered, not on the concept itself, but on the system's inefficiency when substitutes collected their fees and then skedaddled themselves. In November 1862 a Harrisburg paper complained that "many, if not nearly all" substitutes failed to report.[43]

Despite its general social acceptability, substitution was ethically ambiguous for some peace people, who wondered if it represented too proximate a position with the military. In contrast to an exemption fee that might be used to fund the public good in any number of ways, substitution contributed directly to war-making ability. Family members recalled that, years after the war, John S. Stoltzfus of the Millwood Amish Church in Lancaster County still kept as a tragic reminder the uniform his draft substitute had worn before dying in battle.[44] On the other hand, for young men from Mennonite families who were not yet baptized church members and were thus not in a position to claim conscientious exemption status, hiring a substitute seemed an appealing option.

In any case, a hurried traffic in substitutes sprang up, with potential draftees paying $100 to $1,500. Mennonite Gideon Stover of Hilltown paid $600 for "a German" substitute, while Henry, Jacob, and Elias Koch each paid $160 for other men to go in their place.[45] Christian Myers of

Plumstead paid his substitute $1,000. Substitute brokers also emerged, arranging relationships and earning commissions. Wealthy Mennonite Michael Alderfer from Montgomery County even became a broker. Later tradition says he felt guilty for having done this, as did Frank Moyer, who paid $1,000 for his substitute and then was deeply shaken when the man was killed. Jacob S. Overholt of the Line Lexington congregation decided he did not want to be responsible for a substitute's life, so he reported for duty himself. (There, tradition holds, he met none other than President Lincoln, who, upon learning that Overholt was 46 and had twelve children at home, wrote an order for his release.[46])

Substitution was not uncommon among Mennonites in Cumberland and Franklin Counties. In Cumberland, with its eight congregations, three of which were of the highly sectarian Reformed Mennonite branch, eighty-three men, many of them Mennonites, obtained certificates of scruples.[47] A few of these Mennonites hired substitutes who also bore typical Mennonite names, including William Landis, Moses Horst, Nathaniel Martin, Abraham Hess, William Burkholder, George Weaver, and Christian B. Erb.[48] Perhaps young men who had not joined the church and were ineligible for exemption went as substitutes for older church members who were drafted. At least that was the practice of Mennonites who had moved in the 1830s from Cumberland County to Wayne County, Ohio, and continued to maintain contacts with kin in this Pennsylvania community.[49]

In Franklin County, 183 people received certificates of conscience, at least 53 of whom were Mennonites or Reformed Mennonites. (Many of the rest were River Brethren or Dunkers.) Some men from Mennonite homes were drafted, and some of them hired substitutes. Others entered armed service. The local 126th Regiment included likely Mennonites Samuel Showalter, John Grove, Jacob Bear, Henry Landis, John H. Lesher, and Jacob Shirk.[50] Although unbaptized sons followed the muster drum, it appears that only one baptized member from Franklin County did so: Samuel K. Snively, who joined the 2nd Pennsylvania Volunteers, was excommunicated from Falling Spring Reformed Mennonite Church. This strong record of nonparticipation resulted, the community's historians have argued, not because Franklin County Mennonites possessed unusually rational arguments for peace, but because the community "transmitted nonresistance teaching and attitudes in many informal ways, both verbal and nonverbal, as children witnessed the adults around them model lives of peacefulness."[51]

Beyond the Mennonite Pale

Elsewhere in Pennsylvania, Mennonite and Amish communities were often not large enough or stable enough to provide the kind of formative culture of peace for their people that the Franklin County settlement had for its members. Those who lived beyond the state's southeastern Mennonite and Amish pale also lacked the influence of their coreligionists in the east and attracted few political patrons. At the same time, since they were Pennsylvania residents, these more dispersed nonresistants still benefited from generous state policy due, in part, from the work of well-connected easterners.[52] Such a policy, however, could not make up for a shallow culture of conscientious conviction.

Several older Amish and Mennonite communities in southwestern Pennsylvania were, in the 1860s, declining if not dissolving, perhaps making it harder for their young men to resist wartime enlistment pressures. In Westmoreland County, small Mennonite populations in the West Overton and Jacobs Creek area were home to only a few men of conscience. Mennonites had thrived there in the early 1800s, but the settlements had suffered significant out-migration and defection to other denominations. At Jacobs Creek there was little hesitation about young men going off to war. At West Overton, patriarch Abraham Overholt and his son had grown wealthy from milling, distilling, and producing coke from coal.[53] Overholt had many descendants and other relatives in Union ranks.[54] Although nearly eighty years of age, Overholt "visited the seat of war twice . . . to encourage soldiers in the field with whom he was personally acquainted."[55]

In Somerset County a sizable number of Mennonite and Amish young men took up arms. In northern Somerset lay an old Amish settlement known as "Glades" in Brothersvalley Township. But by 1861 the church was nearly extinct, and oral sources later suggested that nonresistant convictions had waned and younger men did not hesitate to volunteer.[56] At least four members of the Yutzy family served in the military.[57] David Yoder, brother of the Glades church's last bishop, Abner Yoder, had three sons in the army—Tobias, Moses, and John—and a nephew, Jonas Yoder.[58]

Nor was military participation by Amish and Mennonites uncommon in other areas of Somerset County.[59] Christian Hostetler of near Meyersdale, Pennsylvania, a married member of the Amish church, enlisted. He was not immediately excommunicated, but when he returned from the war the bishop is said to have refused to serve him communion, so he moved his family to northern Somerset near Holsopple, where Amish apparently were more accommodating.[60] Jonas Keim from near Salisbury volunteered at age 17. Later he was active in the Springs, Pennsylvania, Mennonite Church, which allowed him a military funeral.[61] When Springs' deacon John Folk was drafted, he paid $500 for a substitute, though tradition holds that he received little church support.[62]

To be sure, peace teaching had not disappeared entirely, and depositions of conscience from Somerset County indicate some Amish and Mennonite surnames such as Yoder, Schrock, Beachy, Miller, Kauffman, Hochstetler, Blough, and Keim.[63] Elklick Township at the southern end of Somerset County had numerous Amish and Mennonite surnames among the twenty-six drafted, a few of whom were discharged upon receiving conscientious objector certificates.[64] But such men seem to have been in the minority within their churches.

In Cambria County, north of Somerset, several townships had Amish and Mennonite residents. In Yoder Township three men—Samuel Harshberger, Jacob Yoder, and David Yoder—each gave $100 to local bounty funds to entice other men to enlist. County histories also identify Civil War participants such as Jonas Kauffman, who enlisted in the 54th Pennsylvania, and his Mennonite brother-in-law, Daniel Kauffman, who served "with great bravery" in the 83rd.[65] Henry Blough, son of minister Jacob Blough, became captain.[66] Records also show that twenty-eight men from Cambria filed scruples in the fall of 1862.[67] That was enough for the Cambria Tribune to scold those who "took the conscientious-scruples oath, and swore themselves free from military duty" to a government that defended them. "We didn't think there were so many cowards among us!" the paper complained.[68] Critical sentiments were not absent from public debate back east, but what was missing in the Commonwealth's southwest were voices defending the nonresistants and converting their concerns into the political discourse.[69]

Political Notoriety

In fall 1862 public discourse around Mennonites and politics increased considerably in southeastern Pennsylvania. The October militia draft fell close to an autumn voting season, sharpening debate around the power, privileges, and limits of nonresistant citizenship. Already in September, the *Doylestown Democrat* had unloosed biting sarcasm at Mennonites' rush to obtain certificates of exemption from the draft. "The lame leaped as if they had been restored, the blind saw the door open half a mile distant," the editor complained, and the deaf who couldn't hear a cannon at their elbow, immediately heard the whisper when the draft officials were ready. Their behavior was "embarrassing in the extreme."[70]

If Mennonites and other nonresistants drew editorial attention, they had defenders as well as detractors. Given their close political ties to the ruling party, they became part of partisan debates. Editors unaware of the Mennonites' connections soon learned that they typically voted Republican and that a number of Mennonites even served on Republican "Committees of Vigilance" to help get out the vote. At Quakertown, for example, Daniel Landes, Isaac Groff, Andrew B. Shelly, Jacob Clymer, and Jacob Kauffman served as vice presidents or secretaries of such groups.[71] As a result, the Republican *Bucks County Intelligencer* praised "the non-resistant voters of Bucks County," who "turned out nobly" for the election, and held up these law-abiding people who are opposed to "warlike strife and bloodshed" yet do their part in supporting civic order and refuse to "sympathize with traitors." The paper quoted the Republican Lancaster County *Examiner*, which lionized "the non-resistant voters" for their noble "loyalty at the ballot box." The *Examiner* recognized that these people, "on account of religious scruples," could not go to the battlefields, yet "this large and influential class" certainly helped to uphold the government come election time.[72]

Of course, such contentions angered the *Doylestown Democrat*. Republican peace people were "unscrupulous" in advocating war while expecting other men to do the fighting, the paper growled. Although some progressive-leaning General Conference Mennonites, such as A. B. Shelly, Henry Detweiler, Jonas Benner, William H. Oberholtzer, and Elias B. Rosenberger, had provided relief for needy families whose men had been drafted, most of the "very conscientious" Mennonites were content to leave their communities vulnerable to violence "from the hands of the assassin or spoiler."[73]

In Lancaster County a similar line of criticism surfaced. The editor of the *Lancaster Intelligencer* rubbed his eyes in disbelief as he watched the draft proceed, labeling the event "one of the most disgraceful exhibitions we have ever seen." At the exemption proceedings, hundreds of "hale, stalwart young men from the country" came forward to claim they were "*conscientiously* opposed to bearing arms." It "beggared all description!" Compounding matters was the hypocrisy by which these same "*Patriots*" vote the Republican war ticket but do not object "to the shedding of blood by others in the defense of the Union." Mennonites must really be "*conscientiously* opposed" to risk having "their own veins opened by the enemy!"[74]

The *Intelligencer* went on to challenge the very idea of group exemptions for conscience. "Is it *right* to exonerate only those who belong to a particular denomination of Christians?" editor George Sanderson asked. The state constitution does not say "that Quakers, or Dunkers, or Mennonists, or Omishmen shall not be required to bear arms." Conscience was an *individual* matter. The editor thought the current system an "invidious distinction between sects or denominations." Such distinction was even more suspect because it is a "well-known fact that nearly the entire membership of the four denominations" belong to the "Abolition [Republican] party."[75]

Republican newspapers came to the nonresistants' defense. The *Lancaster Examiner and Herald* first assured its readers that the number of conscientious objectors was "comparatively small," and then reminded them that since this was a state militia draft, the longstanding state recognition of scruples was legitimate. However, the paper did acknowledge the criticism that too many men were seeking exemptions for physical reasons. How can it be that our "proverbially healthy county" had so many "halt, lame, ring-boned and spavined men?" the paper asked.[76]

Lancaster's *Daily Evening Express* also weighed in with comments. It explained that the genuineness of men's convictions was supposed to be tested by officials asking them "whether they would defend their wives and families from a murderer." Yet the *Express* admitted that some made "tender conscience a cloak for cowardice." In such cases, "strong able-bodied, high-charging last-cent parties swallowed at a single gulp, without choking or making a wry face" to obtain their certificates. These same men then take produce to market and have a reputation for having a sharp eye for business. Most certainly they would defend their chickens, pigs, and garden produce at market, even "with their lives if necessary." But, sighed the editor condescendingly, "we must remember and exercise charity to those who, from infancy, have been brought up with noncombatant principles."[77] Nevertheless, the editor rejected the argument that those who would not fight should also not vote. Certainly nonresistants have the right to vote, which is a "most sacred political duty," the Republican paper declared.[78]

To the northwest, in Mifflin County, newspapers drew connections between Amish nonresistants and partisan politics. When the local Republican *Lewistown Gazette* editor saw an August edition of a Lancaster County paper commenting on the state provision for men of conscience, he decided to do his own research, and on September 10 he published his findings regarding "The Omish and the Draft." His focus, though, turned out to be partisan criticism of "locofoco demagogues" (Democrats) who were at work among the Amish and others who held "religious scruples."[79] These politicos were telling the Amish that their votes for Lincoln in 1860 had brought on the draft and that now they would have to go to war "contrary to their creed," thus turning legitimate ethical anxiety into questionable electioneering for Democratic Party votes.[80]

In response, the other local paper, *The True Democrat*, pointed out that there was considerable negative local feeling about this "very large population of citizens." Yes, said the *Democrat*, the law may declare the Amish exempt from conscription, "but justice certainly would not." Indeed, men who vote should be forced to fight, the paper concluded.[81] Not so, the Republican editor responded, insisting that the Amish were misunderstood. They were ready to "bear the full burden of taxation and contribute liberally towards putting down the rebellion," but "deem it as wrong to furnish a substitute as to go themselves."[82]

The peace position in Mifflin County, Pennsylvania, quickly became a partisan football as the *Gazette* accused the *Democrat* of levying "slurs." Furthermore, advised the Republican paper, raising the specter of nonresistant political power, "Every Omish, Tunker, or other men of that stamp" ought to "repay this insult" by sending every man to the polls to give "the hypocritical patent democracy," as represented by the *Democrat*, a "taste of the ballot box." That would make "the whole gang howl."[83]

At least one person feared that nonresistants might take the *Gazette*'s challenge too seriously. The night before the election, someone scattered leaflets on the roads of Menno Township with the message:

> Take Notice
> All dutch that took the oath not to bare arms in defence of their country
> Is warned if they vote at this Election their buildings shel be laid in ashes
> So I Say take warning in time before it be too late
>   To be Drafted I am[84]

It is unclear whether the threat made any Amish stay away from the polls. Nor is it entirely clear that those who voted cast Republican ballots. The townships of Menno and Union, with heavy Amish populations, cast 112 votes for the Republican legislator and 95 for the Democrat, while in Union it was 103 Republican and 119 Democratic.[85]

The approaching election elicited further commentary on nonresistant political participation. For example, in Lancaster County the *Lancaster Express* contended that even those who do not fight retain the right to vote, which is a "most sacred political duty."[86] In Montgomery County the Republican *Herald and Free Press* hoped that the Mennonite-populated Franconia, Lower Salford, and Towamencin townships would carry the Party, "where the traitors [Democrats] thought to play upon the consciences of the voters."[87]

If Mennonite and Amish voices were properly discrete during this pre-election debate, those who spoke for them often defended the non-resistant stance by invoking the peace people's willingness to contribute to the public treasury or otherwise finance support for the suffering. A story that ran in the Lancaster *Daily Express* in late August and in the Allentown *Friedens-bote* in early October was a remarkable effort along these lines, simultaneously carving a legitimate public place for Mennonite pacifists while encouraging them to earn their acceptance.[88] The newspaper's story was said to have come from an old and respected Mennonite in West Hempfield Township, and it presented lore from two centuries ago among the "Anabaptists or non-resisting people of Holland." The Dutch were at war with Spain, so the story ran, and the treasury was running dry. In this hour of gloom a "plain farmer" made his way to Amsterdam, obtained an interview with a high-ranking official, and learned that the state needed

750,000 guilders. "You shall have the greater part in thirty days and the balance soon," the farmer said. In short order he had collected the sum from Dutch and even Swiss Mennonites, and enabled the Netherlands to win the war. Later, the Dutch government wished to repay with interest what it thought was a loan, but the Mennonites refused to be repaid, explaining that in Holland they had found liberty of conscience and freedom from persecution: "Your cause was our own and we have done no more than good Christians were bound to do." Then came the moral from the *Daily Express:* "Our Mennonites, Amish, and Dunkerds, are descendants of Holland and Switzerland, and profess to be as pious and loyal as their ancestors of old, and our Government being in the agonies of a death struggle to maintain a government which has fostered all, and under which nonresisting citizens have acquired wealth in abundance beyond a parallel in the country, will they not respond to the call of such a kind mother?" In fact, it seems Pennsylvania Mennonites and Amish were willing to make such contributions as part of a civic bargain to avoid bodily involvement. At least they repeatedly offered such philanthropy and implied a readiness to give to public coffers.

Given such willingness and the way in which the payment of exemption fees was central to the public defense of conscientious defenselessness, it is ironic that the Pennsylvania legislature never got around to setting a commutation fee for the 1862 state militia draft. In the end, men with scruples who took out exemption certificates did not have to pay anything, despite the wording on the certificate itself.

While one imagines that the Commonwealth's Mennonites and Amish accepted the unexpected waiver with some gratitude, they had remained ready to contribute. Indeed, such civic participation was at the heart of the relationship they had crafted with their neighbors over the course of more than a century. It shaped how others viewed them and how they saw themselves, presenting nonresistance as a legitimate—even if peculiar and politically charged—expression of citizenship.

Meanwhile, to the west, different patterns were emerging in contexts that combined sectarian sensibilities and community commitments in other ways.

CHAPTER 5

Patterns of Peace and Patriotism in the Midwest

Conscription and Equivalency

"Nearly all the dutch are consciencious," Eli J. Hochstedler complained in October 1862, referring to fellow Amish in his Howard County, Indiana, home. Hochstedler was writing to his cousin, Samuel S. Yoder, of Holmes County, Ohio, and although Yoder too was from an Amish family, neither man shared his parents' nonresistant convictions. "Woe unto the souls who cause the innocent blood to be shed of the patriots of our *free & beloved Country!!!*" Hochstedler cried. In his church near Kokomo, he knew of "but 2 besides myself who are not [opposed to joining the war effort]." To make matters worse, the patriotic Hochstedler fumed, such objection was just a cover for cowardice, and some men "never would have joined the Omish Church had it not been for [the draft]."[1]

Hochstedler's letter described wartime situations that seemed similar to those surfacing among Mennonites and Amish in Pennsylvania. Clearly, while most church members sought to separate themselves from personal participation in violence, a minority stood ready to join in the crusade. Yet the Midwestern context in which Yoder and Hochstedler lived gave particular shape to the experience of nonresistants in this region—and to those who rejected peace principles. First, Amish and Mennonite populations in Ohio, Indiana, and further west were more diverse than those in the East, since the Midwesterners represented several immigration and migration streams. Even in areas where they had concentrated to some degree, such as northeast Ohio, differences among themselves were as significant as their collective separation from worldly society.

Then too, Ohio and Indiana Mennonites and Amish lacked the political clout and connections of those in Pennsylvania. Midwesterners might petition their governors, but there is no evidence that chief executives noticed or responded—much less met with them. And when Amish and Mennonites here voted, they often seem to have supported local favorites but received little in exchange for their trouble. Local newspapers from neither party gave much attention to them. Patterns of peace and patriotic participation in the Midwest were more of a patchwork that reflected immigrant particularities and local politics. As notions of nonresistant citizenship evolved in Pennsylvania, Midwestern Mennonites and Amish often found themselves with starker alternatives: stand apart in sharply sectarian style or blend rather inconspicuously into the civic landscape.

By summer 1862, war was pressing Midwestern Mennonite and Amish communities in new ways, especially as they considered the looming prospect of the state militia draft. Some jurisdictions—including Illinois and Iowa—managed to fill with volunteers the quotas levied by Washington, but Ohio and Indiana failed to do so and made plans for an October draft.[2] Ohio's Governor David Tod (a Democrat-turned-Unionist Lincoln supporter) had pleaded for men to crush the Confederacy's "unholy rebellion."[3] But not enough willing souls responded.

No doubt nonresistants wondered whether they would be allowed to pay an "equivalency fee" in exchange for exemption, and apparently, so did a few of their neighbors. Someone from Berlin, in Ohio's Holmes County, wrote to Governor Tod on August 11 to suggest what might be done about those "calling themselves Amish" whose "religious tenets are opposed to war or fighting personally." Since the Amish "probably would not make very efficient soldiers," the writer suggested imposing a fine rather than forced induction. Yet the author also darkly warned that "a considerable number of the sect are however opposed to the Government and sympathize with the rebellion," and questioned "whether an exception or distinction should be made in their case."[4]

In the end, admitting that he was acting "without any well-defined authority," Governor Tod simply announced an equivalency fee of $200 for "members of religious denominations whose creed forbids taking up arms." On October 5 he wired Secretary of War Edwin Stanton that Ohio hoped to use the exemption money collecting in state coffers to hire draft substitutes and to care for sick and wounded soldiers. Tod hoped Stanton would offer some affirmation, but it is not clear that the Secretary did.[5]

Next door, Indiana's legislature "omitted to fix any equivalent" fee as they laid plans for a state draft, and on September 24, Republican Governor Oliver P. Morton appealed to Washington to set a price. The War Department's C. P. Buckingham, in turn, asked what Morton thought was fair. The governor wired back that it should be "not less than $200 per man," and the Department agreed.[6] Midwestern Quakers objected to the very idea of equivalency, and in Ohio they eventually extracted an exemption from the exemption fee itself. (At the same time, as many as a third of Midwestern Friends willingly joined the military to expunge the scourge of slavery from the nation.) Mennonites and Amish in Ohio never availed themselves of this Quaker-negotiated total exemption—perhaps never even knew about it—and throughout Ohio and Indiana, either paid the $200 equivalency or hired substitutes.

Petitioning Those in Power

As officers and civil servants developed war strategies and wired news between capitals, seventy-two Amish ministers from six states met in Wayne County, Ohio, for the first of what would become a series of national ministers' meetings called to discuss problems facing their church. Curiously, while the gathering's minutes detail dozens of discussions, they included almost no direct references to the war.[7] Enormous as the national conflict was, Americans of all sorts—including nonresistant Americans—also sought to cultivate normalcy in communities that they expected would outlast the current fighting. In 1862 in Wayne County, for example, two new church meetinghouses went up. Immigrant Swiss Mennonites in Sonnenberg replaced a log structure with a new frame building, while near Smithville, the Amish Mennonites of Oak Grove constructed their first meetinghouse.[8]

Yet war was never far in the background. Hardly had Sonnenberg Mennonites finished their new meetinghouse than they gathered in it to draft a resolution to state officials expressing their peace principles. Another

Swiss Mennonite group across the state did the same, and that same year an (Old) Mennonite bishop in Elida, Ohio, penned a petition to President Lincoln. These documents are important statements of Midwestern Mennonite nonresistance. But equally significant is the fact that the governor apparently ignored them and that the man who drafted the presidential petition did not send it and was unsure anyone should. In this part of the country, deep convictions often were matched by marginality that was ascribed or self-imposed.

Despite Wayne County, Ohio's significant Mennonite and Amish population, the *Wooster Republican* took no note of nonresistants as the draft went into motion. Instead, it called readers to "awake to the duties of the hour" and announced that "only the cowardly and the base" would shrink from duty.[9]

Twelve miles east of Wooster, Sonnenberg Mennonites felt differently. On Wednesday, August 6, members gathered to consider "the present sad state of the Country, and to deliberate upon the duties of all good and Loyal Citizens." Relatively recent (1819–1850s) immigrants, these Swiss appreciated the religious freedom and economic opportunity they found in the United States but hoped such liberty would not come at the price of their peace convictions—convictions that had played a large part in prompting their emigration from conscription-prone western Europe.[10]

The document the congregation presented to the Wayne County Military Committee, who in turn forwarded it to Governor Tod, presented a classic statement of Mennonite and Amish nonresistance and two-kingdom theology. The Sonnenberg Swiss would "support the Government in all things required of us which do not conflict with our confession of faith." They condemned "all rebellion and insurrection against the Government, as resistance against the Ordinance of God" and promised to obey government "as far as our Conscience will allow." Yet there also were "things in which we must obey God more than men," the church reported, so they would refuse "military service," which "conflicts with our confession of faith." Since that confession also enjoined them "to sacrifice property and all that we possess in case of necessity rather than to make use of the sword," they were willing to pay a commutation fee, but they stubbornly refused to "consent to violate our faith" by personally bearing arms.[11]

Signed only by "our ordained ministers of the Gospel," the document bore the names of aged bishop Ulrich Sommer and popular minister Christian Sommer—who in less than two months would unanimously be chosen by the church as assistant bishop to the older man. Yet the statement obviously had much broader support, since all men drafted from the congregation claimed exemption "on the ground of their religious belief in non-resistance."[12]

On the western side of the state, another Swiss Mennonite settlement, this one spanning Allen and Putnam Counties and including about one hundred households, also sent a petition to Columbus. It sounded themes similar to its Sonnenberg counterpart, citing its signatories' immigrant experience, willingness to pay "a reasonable fine," and the hint that in "a free country" the state should take scruples seriously.[13] There is no evidence that Tod responded to either of these petitions.

Meanwhile, Columbiana County, Ohio, businessman and (Old) Mennonite deacon Jacob Nold was also anxious about the possibility of the impending draft.[14] Along with a friend, Peter Basinger, Nold went to Medina County, Ohio, to see elderly Mennonite bishop Abraham Rohrer for advice. Rohrer was quite ill but managed to say that someone ought to prepare a petition and get a few ministers to take it to the White House.[15] Nold shared the idea with two other people, including John M. Brenneman, a bishop at Elida, Ohio. On August 19 Brenneman responded with a draft of a letter to Lincoln, but he insisted that he had no interest in delivering it.

In 1862 John Brenneman was no doubt the best known and most widely traveled (Old) Mennonite leader in the Midwest, noted for his deep spirituality and humility and for his connections to a great many congregations. Brenneman averred that "it would not be wrong to send a petition to the President," though he questioned the practical and spiritual wisdom of such a move. Did one need a military pass to get to the capital city? he wondered. Moreover, it would be more productive instead to petition "the ruler of the universe" on one's knees.[16] Yet Brenneman did not want to seem dismissive of Nold's plea, so the Elida bishop had penned the petition.

Writing in highly deferential language, Brenneman approached the president in the posture of a subject asking for privileges rather than of a citizen exercising rights. He "would humbly pray the President not to consider us too burdensome" in presenting "our weak and humble petition" that was prompted by "sore distress."[17]

Brenneman described Mennonites as a people who were now under intense pressure because they would not "take up arms." Lincoln "must not mistake us to be secessionists or rebels against the government," Brenneman hastened to add, as Mennonites "are entirely free from that guilt" and were "wellwishers" to the Union cause and abhorred rebellion "against so good a government as that of the United States." Indeed, the document declared, if any Mennonites should be found guilty of treason, then "let them be dealt with as rebels."[18] Brenneman recounted Mennonite understandings of the state as approved by God to "establish good policy, rules, and laws," and his people's obedience to civil authorities so long as they "do not militate against the Word of God."

Then, in a nimble turn of argument, he used the vulnerable and passively noncooperative image of the church, which he had just sketched, as ground for requesting public protection in the form of a presidential directive that Mennonites not "be forced or compelled to take up arms." Would the President issue "immediate orders" to the governors, the bishop suggested, "especially to the governor of Ohio, as the Mennonites in Ohio seem to be in the most danger."[19] Mennonites in the Confederacy had been harassed by their rulers, the petition noted. Surely Union leaders "are fully as kind and merciful (and we trust much more so) as they of the South."

Brenneman hastened to add that Mennonites did not "censure, judge, or condemn" other Christians who disagreed with them on this matter, since such judgment rested with God. Nor would they "murmur or complain at all" if the federal government imposed extra taxes on them. In any case, Brenneman was sure his church wished "to be liberal and charitable to those poor women and children whose husbands and fathers have gone to the army, if they are in needy circumstances."

Perhaps in the hands of a Pennsylvania Mennonite with political connections, the petition might have traveled to Washington via Congressman Thaddeus Stevens. But few such channels existed in Ohio. Moreover, even a leader as prominent as Brenneman was hesitant to approach the state, no matter how diffident the document. "What is the President?" Brenneman asked Nold, "but a poor dying mortal like ourselves, and if we lean entirely upon him for help, I fear we would lean on a broken reed."[20] No evidence exists that Brenneman's draft made it beyond Nold.

Patterns of Participation in Northeastern Ohio

Although Brenneman had written of Mennonites as if they were singular, Midwestern Mennonite and Amish opinions and practice did, in fact, vary. Some apparently sympathized with the "Copperheads"—adamantly anti-administration Democrats who denounced Lincoln's war strategy and emerging emancipation policies. Others were staunch Unionists, who decried the Confederacy and intuitively agreed that the North should crush rebellion on the way to restoring national fortunes. And while many were committed nonresistants, a noticeable minority were much less attuned to the peace principles Brenneman had outlined.

A collection of Amish and Mennonite communities in northeast Ohio's Wayne, Holmes, Stark, and Medina counties provide a vivid illustration of the varied reactions that the 1862 draft provoked. In a relatively small area that stretched some forty miles in either direction, settlements stemming from several immigration streams and Anabaptist branches existed in close proximity. The particular background and local context of each shaped their responses as much as any generalized theological conviction.

In the south, Holmes County's sizable Amish community, with roots in Somerset County, Pennsylvania, and Garrett County, Maryland, was composed largely of conservatively inclined members whose churchly conduct would soon earn them the label "Old Order." A sizable majority of young men there stayed out of war and did so by availing themselves of Ohio's $200 equivalency fee. Those who did not, such as the four sons of Yost and Anna (Hochstetler) Yoder of Winesburg, expressed little interest in their parents' faith or had already married non-Amish partners and distanced themselves from the church.[21] In any case, the Amish sense of separatism, nurtured in Appalachian valleys and the northeastern Ohio frontier, shaped men who clearly stood apart from the mainstream or decidedly rejected Amish identity in order to support the popular crusade— alternatives that had not seemed as stark to Mennonites in the East.[22] Table 5.1 lists the Amish drafted from Holmes County in 1862, revealing a pattern of their paying the $200 fee or very rarely hiring substitutes.[23]

Holmes County was also home to a small Mennonite congregation com-

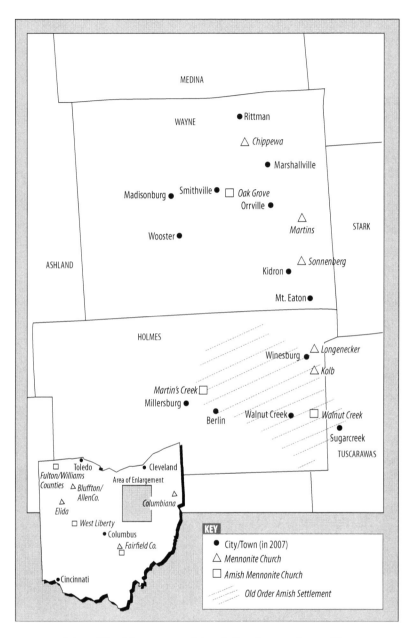

MEDINA

WAYNE

● Rittman

△ *Chippewa*

● Marshallville

Madisonburg ● Smithville ● □ *Oak Grove*
Orrville ●

△
Martins

STARK

ASHLAND

Wooster ●

△ *Sonnenberg*
Kidron ●

Mt. Eaton ●

HOLMES

△ *Longenecker*
Winesburg ●
△ *Kolb*

Martin's Creek □
Millersburg ●
Berlin ● Walnut Creek ● □ *Walnut Creek*
●
Sugarcreek ●

TUSCARAWAS

□ Toledo ● Cleveland
*Fulton/Williams
Counties* △ *Bluffton/
AllenCo.*
Area of Enlargement
△ Elida
△
Columbiana

□ *West Liberty*
● Columbus
△ *Fairfield Co.*
□

KEY

● City/Town (in 2007)
△ Mennonite Church
□ Amish Mennonite Church
//// Old Order Amish Settlement

● Cincinnati

Major Ohio Mennonite and Amish Populations, about 1862

Table 5.1. Mennonites and Amish on 1862 Militia Draft List, Holmes County, Ohio

Name	Age	Township	Church	Substitute	Paid $200	Other
Moses J. Beechy	44	German	Amish		X	
Christian Beechy	27	German			X	
Joseph Beechy	19	Walnutcreek	Amish		X	
Peter Berkey	28	Paint	Mennonite			Illegally drafted
Joseph J. Christner	26	German	Amish		X	
Michael Erb	24	German	Amish		X	
John J. Fry	24	German	[a]	Cyrus Garwell		
John Fry	44	Mechanic	[a]	Cyrus Darwell		
John M. Freed	28	Paint	Mennonite	John W. Snyder		
Christian Farnwalt	41	German	Amish		X	
Samuel Fry	35	Walnutcreek	Amish		X	
John C. Gingerich	23	German	Amish		X	
Benedict Gingerich	25	German	Amish		X	
Joseph Gingerich	35	Walnutcreek	Amish		X	
Jacob A. Garber	27	Walnutcreek	Amish		X	
Daniel Helmuth	19	German	Amish		X	
Amos Hochstetler	19	German	Amish		X	
John Helmuth	37	German	Amish		X	
Noah H. Hochstetler	38	German	Amish		X	
Gideon Hochstetler	27	German	Amish			Illegally drafted
Moses Harshberger	19	German	Amish		X	
Edward Hochstetler	24	German	Amish		X	
Moses G. Harshbarger	25	Berlin	Amish		X	
Peter P. Harsbarger	24	Walnutcreek	Amish		X	
Samuel Hochstetler	21	Paint	Amish	Joseph Keys		
Michael Immel	37	Walnutcreek	Amish	William Welch		
Abraham A. Kauffman	35	German			X	
Joseph Kuhns	25	Walnutcreek	Amish		X	
John Kendal	23	Walnutcreek	[b]	George W. Brandon		
Joseph Kuhns	25	Walnutcreek	Amish		X	
Elias Kuhns	27	Walnutcreek	Amish		X	
Jacob Kulp	28	Walnutcreek	Mennonite		X	

continued

Table 5.1. continued

Name	Age	Township	Church	Substitute	Paid $200	Other
Isaac Kulp	26	Walnutcreek	Mennonite			Mental incapacity
Jacob F. Miller	21	Berlin	Amish		X	
Eli D. Miller	27	Berlin			X	
Andrew Miller	20	Berlin	Amish		X	
David M. Miller	23	Berlin	Amish		X	
Joseph L. Most	21	Berlin	Amish	John Getz		
Abraham L. Most	23	Berlin	Amish		X	
Christian E. Miller	18	Walnutcreek	Amish		X	
Lewis E. Miller	18	Walnutcreek	Amish		X	
Ephraim Miller	25	Walnutcreek	Amish		X	
John J. Miller	26	Walnutcreek	Amish		X	
David J. Miller	30	Walnutcreek	Amish		X	
Jonathan Miller	35	Walnutcreek	Amish		X	
Emanuel J. Miller	22	Walnutcreek	Amish		X	
Andrew Mumaw	25	Paint	Mennonite	John McKnight		
Jeremiah Miller	24	Paint	Amish		X	
Samuel Moyer	22	Paint	Mennonite	E. M. Jones		
Peter Miller	43	Saltcreek	Amish		X	
Daniel D. Most	27	Saltcreek	Amish		X	
Abraham Neisley	37	German	Amish		X	
Henry Newcomer	26	Paint	[c]	Joseph Longnecker		
Peter Oswald	18	Mechanic	Amish		X	
Daniel Rober	31	German	Amish		X	
Daniel J. Slaubaugh	35	Berlin	Amish		X	
Daniel Stutzman	28	Berlin	Amish		X	
David Stutzman	34	Walnutcreek	Amish		X	
Elias Shrock	20	Walnutcreek	Amish		X	
Abraham Shrock	42	Walnutcreek	Amish		X	
Abraham Stutzman	36	Walnutcreek	Amish		X	
Jacob G. Stutzman	32	Walnutcreek	Amish		X	
Christian Stutzman	38	Walnutcreek	Amish		X	
Wilham Strahm	18	Paint	Mennonite	Went into 67th O.V.I.[d]		
Peter Strahm	26	Paint	Mennonite	No information		

Name	Age	Township	Church	Substitute	Paid $200	Other
George Shoup	18	Paint	Mennonite	Thomas Orr		
David J. Troyer	24	German	Amish		X	
Andrew Troyer	18	German	Amish		X	
Emanuel Troyer	23	German	Amish		X	
David Troyer	31	German	Amish		X	
Benjamin Troyer	23	German	Amish		X	
Eli D. Troyer	20	Berlin	Amish		X	
John Troyer	32	Walnutcreek	Amish		X	
Samuel Weaver	19	Walnutcreek	Amish		X	
Yost Weaver	20	Walnutcreek	Amish		X	
Benjamin Weaver	24	Walnutcreek	Amish		X	
Daniel Weaver	38	Paint	Amish		X	Physical discharge
Jonas Yoder	20	German	Amish	No information		
Daniel J. Yoder	26	Mechanic	Amish		X	
John Yoder	18	Berlin	Amish		X	
Christian Yoder	42	Berlin	Amish		X	
John Yoder Sr.	42	Berlin	Amish		X	
Jonathan Yoder	44	Walnutcreek	Amish		X	
John M. Yoder	37	Walnutcreek	Amish		X	
Daniel Yoder	23	Walnutcreek	Amish		X	
Moses Yoder	26	Walnutcreek	Amish		X	
Jacob Yoder		Saltcreek	Amish			Minister
Simon Yoder	19	Saltcreek	Amish			

[a] Uncertain whether Dunker or Amish.
[b] Uncertain whether Mennonite or Amish.
[c] Uncertain church membership.
[d] O.V.I., Ohio Volunteer Infantry.

posed of households with roots in eastern Pennsylvania's Bucks County. This Longenecker-Kolb group—known by the names of their two meetinghouses—had a much higher percentage of sons going off to war than did the Amish. From their eastern background they carried a sense that civic participation was compatible with Mennonite sensibilities. But in Ohio they lacked the political and social structures to mediate that participation in ways that still allowed them to be separate. Faced with a new choice between sectarianism or full engagement, many here chose military service. This small church produced more than a dozen soldiers, including the five sons and a nephew of prominent member Peter Longenecker Jr.[24] The small number of Mennonite objectors on the list here (see table 5.1) usually gained exemption by hiring a substitute. George Shoup, son of the Longenecker-Kolb minister Martin Shoup, paid his substitute $500.[25]

To the north, in Wayne County, another Mennonite church of eastern Pennsylvania background—this one from Lancaster County—cut a similar profile. Only a few men from families who worshiped at the Martins-Pleasant View meetinghouses sought exemption from military service by obtaining substitutes or paying exemption fees. Daniel R. Eberly, John Gardner, Jonas Huntsberger, Abraham Martin, and Daniel Weaver all enlisted in August 1862 before the draft. So did Daniel and Enos Buchwalter, whose mother, Anna (Hartman) Buchwalter, "kept a light burning in her bedroom every night from the time [they] left home" until Daniel returned (Enos had died in Louisiana). From the same church, Isaac D. Huntsberger, brother of Jonas, enlisted later, as did Isaac's brother-in-law, Benjamin F. Kurtz. In all, the small Martins–Pleasant View Mennonite group produced at least twenty veterans.[26]

Wayne County's Swiss Mennonite immigrant community, centered around Sonnenberg in southeastern Wayne County, responded quite differently than did the Pennsylvania-rooted churches to the northeast and southeast. As the Swiss had explained in their petition to the governor, they had come to America to escape forced European soldiering and were not about to accept military service here. At the same time, their Swiss heritage included the assumption that exemption carried a price. So while no men from the sizable Sonnenberg church entered the military, and almost all gained exemption by paying the $200 equivalency fee, a large majority of households also contributed money to the Wayne County Military Committee. No other Ohio Mennonite or Amish congregation contributed so heavily to such a fund.[27]

Sonnenberg schoolteacher Ulrich Welty also served on the Sugar Creek Township Committee that raised money for the "Volunteer Fund." By August 20, 1862, he had turned in $220, more than twice as much as any other committee member. Welty's name appeared again on August 21 with $478 he had raised from people on the "Menominete church list."

In the next several months some sixty members of the congregation contributed funds. Some, such as minister (and soon-to-be bishop) Christian
Sommer, gave twice. Minister Christian Schneck's name appears, as does
the younger deacon, Peter P. Lehman.[28] About a fourth of the families gave
small amounts of three or five dollars; most gave ten to twenty-five. The
total reached a remarkable $1,649.

Northwest of the Sonnenberg church, in the area around the village
of Smithville, was Wayne County's thriving Oak Grove Amish Mennonite congregation. Amish families from Pennsylvania and arrivals from the
French Alsace mingled congenially in the Oak Grove congregation, which
represented the change-minded wing of the Amish tradition in contrast
to the more tradition-minded Amish in Holmes County. Part of the progressive agenda at Oak Grove was a desire to adapt life and faith, to some
degree, to the general contours of American culture, confident that human society was improving and that Christian virtues added an element
of moral uplift. It is perhaps not surprising, then, that Oak Grove exhibited a decidedly mixed response to the war. Some men joined the national
crusade to rid the nation of slavery and uphold the progressive principles
of liberty and union. Others dissented from direct participation by hiring substitutes, while still others paid commutation fees. Remarkably,
however, the church gave few funds to the community military chest, recording only occasional and token contributions. No matter how the Oak
Grove Amish responded, they did so as progressive-minded individuals,
not in the Sonnenberg-style of a disciplined group.[29]

Northern Wayne County was home to several small Mennonite congregations—Chester Mennonite (a transplanted Pennsylvania church)
near New Pittsburg, the Chippewa Swiss Mennonites (related to the Sonnenberg immigrants) south of Rittman, and a highly sectarian Reformed
Mennonite church near Marshallville. In all three places, the number of
draft-eligible men was small enough that drawing definite conclusions is
difficult.[30] Two of the Chippewa Swiss bishop's sons, Daniel and John
Steiner, fled to Canada.[31] All told, numerous men from Wayne County
Mennonite and Amish congregations were snagged by the 1862 draft (see
table 5.2).[32]

To the north and east of the large Wayne-Holmes Amish and Mennonite population lay two Pennsylvania and Maryland–rooted churches in
Medina County and two Amish congregations in Stark County.[33] Medina

Table 5.2. Mennonites and Amish on 1862 Militia Draft List, Wayne County, Ohio

Name	Age	Township	Congregation	Substitute	Paid $200	Other
Peter Amstutz	28	Green	Crown Hill		X	
Jacob Amstutz	26	Milton	Crown Hill		X	
Jacob R. Brenneman	44	East Union	Martins			Physical discharge
Joseph Blough	33	Milton	Oak Grove		X	
Moses Blough	30	Milton	Oak Grove		X	
Abram Baumgardner	26	Paint	Sonnenberg		X	
Samuel Bowers	30	Paint	Longenecker	Rudolph Paul		
Jacob Conrad	40	Baughman	Oak Grove			Physical discharge
John Eckard[a]	30	Sugar Creek	Martins	Martin Stauffer		
Aaron Franks[b]	40	East Union	Martins	John H. Martin		
Matthias Garber	30	Sugar Creek	Sonnenberg		X	
Abraham Garber	28	Sugar Creek	Sonnenberg		X	
Joel Hartzler	39	Green	Oak Grove			No information given
Henry Hertman	20	Sugar Creek	Martins	Enlisted in 120th O.V.I.[c]		
David Hess	28	Sugar Creek	Martins	Israel Clippinger		
John Holdeman[d]	30	Chester				Minister of the Gospel
Christian Lehman[f]	23	East Union	Sonnenberg			No information given
Samuel Lehman[e]	21	East Union	Sonnenberg		X	
Michael Lantz	28	Plain	Oak Grove	Jacob C. Myers		
Daniel Loganbill	29	Sugar Creek	Sonnenberg	Joseph Parker		
Adam Martin	18	Baughman	Martins	Abraham Gift		
John Martin	42	Chester	Chester		X	
Daniel Martin	24	Chester	Chester	Samuel Everhart		
Abraham Moser	43	Sugar Creek	Sonnenberg		X	

Name	Age	Township	Congregation	Substitute	Paid $200	Other
Henry Plank	22	Green	Oak Grove	John Steel		
Jacob Plough	28	Green	Oak Grove		X	
Samuel D. Richards	31	Green	Oak Grove	John Henry		
Jonas Smoker	22	Green	Oak Grove		X	
Jacob Stoll	30	Chippewa	Reformed Mennonite	John Soner		
Daniel D. Stiner	26	Milton	Crown Hill			No information given
John M. Stiner	21	Milton	Crown Hill			No information given
Joseph Stuckey	25	Green	Oak Grove		X	
Samuel D. Stutzman	30	Green	Oak Grove			Physical discharge
Christian Schenck[g]	40	Sugar Creek	Sonnenberg			Discharged
John Yoder	40	Green	Oak Grove	Jacob Paul		
David P. Yoder	32	Milton	Oak Grove		X	
Solomon Zook	40	Green	Oak Grove			Minister of the Gospel

[a] Stauffer, the substitute, from Martins, but it is doubtful that Eckerd was.

[b] Martin, the substitute, believed to be from Martins, but no evidence that Franks was.

[c] O.V.I., Ohio Volunteer Infantry.

[d] Founder, in 1859, of the Church of God in Christ-Mennonite group.

[e] Brother of coauthor James O. Lehman's great-grandfather. It is not known what the disposal of his case was.

[f] Another brother of Lehman's great-grandfather. The family had only three sons, two of whom were hit by this draft.

[g] This is Christian Schneck, a minister at Sonnenberg.

County records are less certain, but a number of drafted men had names suggesting Mennonite connections: Berkey, Martin, Leatherman, Kindig, Kulp, Kreible, Kreider, Oberholzer, Rohrer, and Stauffer. Most obtained substitutes, something that was common among their kin back in Washington County, Maryland, and eastern Bucks County, Pennsylvania.[34]

Responses to the 1862 draft on the part of Stark County Amish are obscure.[35] Amish preacher Joseph Ramseyer, who was conservatively inclined, moved to Ontario, Canada, about 1862 to escape the draft. However, most of the Amish shared the progressive sentiments of the Oak Grove Amish Mennonites to the west and responded in a similarly mottled fashion. Some paid the $200 fee, upwards of twenty obtained substitutes, and a half-dozen men joined the 16th, 76th, or 115th Ohio Volunteers.[36]

If the Amish and Mennonites of northeast Ohio responded variously to the 1862 draft, they nevertheless shared a certain civic situation. That position was marked not so much by apoliticism as it was by the fact that their political involvements often did not distinguish them from their neighbors or earn them many favors. The situation in Holmes County provides one illustration. In mid-June 1862, Holmes County Amishman Samuel Mast received a letter from his brother-in-law, Samuel Hage, in Washington County, Iowa. Hage—who would soon be ordained a deacon in his Amish congregation—asked Mast if Holmes County had "eny democrat simpathisers" to the "rebellion." In Iowa there were "a few hipocrits here that smile at a union disaster but grone at the union victorys, but they have to keep it to them selves or they fare none of the best."[37]

Hage apparently knew little of Holmes County politics. Samuel Mast lived in a county where Democrats overwhelmed Republicans in phenomenal numbers, and the two townships with the most of the Amish—German and Walnut Creek—were among the most one-sided.[38] If the Amish voted—and the *Holmes County Republican* seems to confirm that some did—ballot results point to Amish participation in solid Democratic victories.[39] Moreover, the congressional (1860, 1862) and intervening gubernatorial (1861) contests only saw increasing Democratic majorities.[40] The county's two newspapers—the strong *Holmes County Farmer* and the weak *Holmes County Republican*—engaged in ferocious partisan rancor. The more extreme language came from the *Farmer*, which pressed the Midwestern Democratic line of Ohio party leader Clement L. Vallandigham, denounc-

ing Lincoln's handling of the war and using vicious racial slurs and bla-
tantly anti-African-American editorializing against abolitionists. When
only one person in German Township and one in Walnut Creek Township dared vote Republican in the fall of 1862, the *Farmer* dismissed the
first as illiterate and the other as "an abolition preacher."[41]

Nor were Democratic sympathies absent from Wayne County Mennonite and Amish communities. Townships with significant Mennonite
and Amish populations continued to return solid Democratic majorities.[42]
Sonnenberg memory holds that at least some Swiss Mennonites adopted
the Democrats' anti-abolition line, asking, "If the slaves help the Southern
people, why can't they have them?" and even wondering if the Confederacy was not partly justified in resisting meddlesome federal government
intrusion.[43]

Remarkably, however, neither Democratic nor Republican party estab-
lishments appealed to Amish or Mennonites, tried to win their votes, or
defended their honor. The nonresistants received no sympathy from the
Democrats, whom they apparently supported. True, in public gatherings
to drum up the vote prior to the 1862 election, Democratic congressional
candidate George Bliss sent German speakers to the townships of German, Walnut Creek, and Paint, while other rallies in the county had only
English speakers.[44] But both party papers condemned those who refused
military service. The *Republican* complained that "between seventy and
eighty Germans, members of religious societies whose articles of faith"
forbade their going to war, had paid $200 and were discharged from the
draft because of a "very unjust order from the War Department" exempting those with conscientious scruples. If these people "have been educated
to believe it a greater sin to take up arms in defense of their country than to
quietly submit to its destruction by traitors, let them at least be required to
furnish a substitute," the paper declared.[45]

For its part, the Democratic *Farmer* used the matter of scruples to tar the
paper's opponents—surely something that was far from flattering to the
area's nonresistants. The *Farmer* circulated a story that Republican candidate Martin Welker had sent "hirelings" among the "Amish and other religious denominations," proclaiming that he was responsible for the $200
exemption fee. Welker took umbrage at the charge and published a communication clearly distancing himself from the nonresistants. Meanwhile,
the Democratic *Farmer* groused that the "order from the War department

clears the Amish, Duncards, Quakers and other religious denominations opposed to fighting, from draft, on payment of $200 each." The $13,800 thus collected would buy "46 Niggers at $300 each—the Government price," the paper continued, suggesting that nonresistants ranked below slaves in social value.[46] If northeast Ohio Mennonites and Amish mirrored the region's anti-administration sentiment, they received nothing from the area's political powerbrokers in exchange for their support.

Elsewhere in the Midwest

Amish and Mennonite responses to the 1862 militia draft in other parts of the Midwest were variations on northwest Ohio themes. Young men responded variously to the call to arms, and newspapers castigated or ignored nonresistants. No one of influence came to their defense or courted their votes. In many parts of Ohio, Mennonites and Amish paid the equivalency fee, but in a few places, hiring substitutes was the norm.[47] In Jacob Nold's Columbiana and neighboring Mahoning counties, for example, the draft struck 200 and 350 men, respectively, a small number of whom were Mennonites, including Nold's son, Abraham. Mennonites there either hired substitutes or paid the $200 equivalency—though not everyone in the church could afford the fee. Furthermore, non-Mennonite neighbors who wished to hire substitutes but could not afford them became angry and threatened wealthy objectors. To keep the peace, some Mennonites had loaned money to non-Mennonites caught in the draft, Nold reported.[48]

At the same time, some Ohio counties raised enough volunteers to avoid having local conscription. The Swiss Mennonites of Allen County and the Amish Mennonites in Champaign and Logan counties, all northwest of Columbus, faced no state draft in 1862. Logan's radically Democratic *Mac-a-Cheek Press* listed names of Amish in the paper's circulation area who, though not facing the prospect of conscription, contributed to the volunteer funds for local regiments.[49] In Champaign County the *Urbana Citizen and Gazette* reported some twenty Amish contributing to the war fund.[50]

The 1862 draft in Putnam County, next door to Allen, was small, although it struck several Swiss Mennonites: Jacob Amstutz, Jacob Basenger, Daniel Basenger, John Sutter, and Christian Zimmerly, all of Riley

Table 5.3. Draftees with typical Mennonite surnames, 1862 Militia Draft, Columbiana and Mahoning Counties, Ohio

Name	Age	Sent Substitute	Paid Fee	Name	Age	Sent Substitute	Paid Fee
Noah Barkey	30	X		Aaron Weaver	28		X
Noah Bassinger	24		X	Samuel Witmer	32		X
Adam Detwiler	28	No infor-mation		David R. Witmer	23		X
Jacob Good	19	X		Joseph Witmer	23	X	
Christian Good	44	Discharged-over age		Jacob Witmer	43	X	
Christian Lehman	24		X	Peter Weaver	19	X	
Jacob Moyers	22	X		Abraham G. Yoder	31		X
Jacob Nola	28	X		John B. Yoder	40		X
Josiah B. Stouffer	25	X		Joseph Yoder	40	X	
John Jacob Snyder	26	X		Solomon Yoder	41	X	
Jacob Shank	30	No		Christian Zigler	26	X	
Abraham Nold	42		X	Christian Zigler	19	X	

Township. They responded as had their Sonnenberg Swiss compatriots on the other side of the state and paid the $200 equivalency.[51] Northwest Ohio's Fulton and Williams counties provided fewer volunteers, and each county had to draft about 225 men,[52] though limited records obscure a complete picture of the choices made by the area's Amish Mennonites, who had arrived not many years earlier from Europe. One local memory had Amish asking for exemption and then being told by neighbors, "You have drunken with us, and voted with us, now you can also fight with us."[53] Fulton County's 1862 Record of Drafted Militia reveals that substitution was common here, as it seems to have been in other immigrant Amish or Mennonite settlements. John Aeschbauker, John Guyman, Fred Greisser, Christ Kloffenstein, Christ Lauber, Peter and John Rupp, Joseph and Peter Roth, Christ Short, Michael Yoder, and Sol and Jacob Zimmerman all obtained substitutes.[54]

Substitution was also common in certain Indiana communities, such as the Yellow Creek (Old) Mennonite settlement in northern Indiana's Elkhart County and the Amish Mennonite settlements east and southwest of the county's seat at Goshen. For example, Jacob H. Wisler, son of Mennonite bishop Jacob and Mary (Hoover) Wisler, hired a Nelson Chamberlain from St. Joseph County to the west. Some other substitutes came from southern Michigan or from Indiana counties other than Elkhart, pointing to the possibility of substitute brokers working in the region.[55]

It seems that some men raised in Elkhart County Mennonite or Amish families volunteered for local Company E of the 74th Indiana Volunteers. The muster roll includes Moses V. Yoder, Eli Holdeman, David Ramer, Jacob C. Lehman, Daniel S. and John J. Witmer, and several men named Hess and Housouer.[56] However, records in the 1862 Elkhart County militia enrollment book suggest that large majorities of Mennonites, Amish, and Dunkers declared their opposition to participating in the war (table 5.4).[57]

In northern Indiana, as in northeast Ohio, neither political party adopted the nonresistants. The competing newspapers, both published in Goshen, regularly poured out vituperation against one another, but they agreed on criticizing religious objectors. The Republican *Goshen Times*, for example, sarcastically lashed out against those "with conscientious scruples against fighting an abolition war" and "against fighting for the perpetuation of slavery."[58]

Adams and Wells counties in eastern Indiana were home to a small Amish community and a good-sized group of Mennonites, both having come from Switzerland a decade or two before the war began.[59] Like their Swiss immigrant compatriots in Ohio, very few of the Indiana Swiss marched to war, though two are known to have enlisted. When Adams County had to resort to a draft in the fall of 1862, officials drew several Mennonite and Amish names from the wheel, but the *Decatur Eagle* and local militia enrollment books prepared in advance of the draft listed at least thirty-five men "conscientiously opposed to bearing arms."[60]

However, it is not clear when these and other Hoosier men of conscience actually paid the $200 fee, because on November 13 the *Eagle* carried a notice from Benjamin J. Rice, Provost Marshal of the county, that all such payments had "been postponed by the General Commissioner of the State until further order." Behind the scenes, an astonishing set of bureaucratic developments were unfolding.[61] State Commissioner of Drafting Jesse P. Siddall had set forth an unusual and complicated process for collecting the equivalency fee that had confused officials charged with the task.[62] As a

Table 5.4. Conscription figures for townships with significant Mennonite and Amish populations, 1862 Militia Draft, Elkhart County, Indiana

Township	Total Enrolled	Conscientious scruples	Volunteers
Elkhart[a]	265	34	60
Clinton	224	35	58
Harrison	271	42	26
Olive	165	14	96
Middlebury	239	21	153
Union	205	42	20
Locke	88	12	23

Source: Militia Enrollment Book, Elkhart County, 1862. Elkhart County Historical Society Archives, Bristol, Indiana.
[a] Excluding city of Goshen

result, only "some twenty-odd thousand dollars was collected," which, at $200 a draftee, suggested that only about 100 men had actually paid. To clear up the confusion, the state decided simply to return the equivalency fees that had been turned in![63]

Convoluted financial records were not the only problem in Indianapolis in 1862. In his final report, Adjutant General Terrell admitted that when the numbers were totaled, he discovered that Indiana actually had furnished 8,008 men "in *excess* of her quota, *on all calls* at the time the draft was made." In other words, by the time of the October draft, conscription would not have been necessary in Indiana, had Terrell only known the numbers more accurately.[64]

Patriotism at Home and on the Battlefield

Although Indiana refunded the commutation fee, there is no reason to believe the Mennonites and Amish there would not have willingly paid it. As their Amish compatriots in Holmes County, Ohio, had stated publicly in September: "We are religiously opposed to all wars, or fighting of whatever kind or nature . . . believing that the Gospel forbids us to take the sword. . . . [But] whatever the Government may demand of us in money, will be cheerfully and honestly paid," in gratitude for "the liberties and freedom of conscience we have so long enjoyed" in a country that is "an asylum for those that flee from the tyranny and oppression of the old country."[65]

Such words revealed a version of nonresistant patriotism that—recognized or not by editors and politicians who denounced men of conscience—characterized many Mennonites and Amish, even those who adopted anti-administration sentiments and found an American voice in Democratic Party idioms. Moreover, not a few young men from these communities had volunteered for military service, expressing a desire to identify personally with the national crusade, whether to fight for the principle of union or for a broader concept of freedom that included emancipation.[66]

Immigrants only recently arrived in the United States—Mennonites and Amish included—often identified with the Union cause that promised economic expansion. In Washington County, Iowa, German-born settler Samuel Hage, for example, worried that local land prices were in a slump due to the uprising of "king Jeff rebel," and hoped the South would soon tire of Jefferson Davis's effort to manipulate markets and "burn Coten down in rebel dom." Should Southerners fortunes begin to fade, he mused in the summer of 1862, he expected to see "better times again."[67]

Nor were all newcomers shy of the battlefield.[68] The small Summerfield, Illinois, Mennonite church, twenty miles east of St. Louis, was made up of Bavarians and aligned with the progressive General Conference Mennonite branch. There, young Samuel S. Haury, future missionary and church leader who had accompanied his parents to America in 1856, recalled "how enthusiastic he had been for President Lincoln and for the cause of freeing the slaves." Had he not been so young and small of stature, Haury might have run away from home to join the Union army, he thought.[69] From the same community, J. J. Krehbiel decided to support the Republican cause by means other than soldiering and is believed to have made wagons for the army.[70]

Even the "Swiss Mennonites"—recent arrivals with remarkable resistance to military service—produced a handful of volunteers. From Adams County, Indiana, John Jacob Baumgartner, step-son of minister Christian Baumgartner, joined the 44th Indiana, while Peter Stauffer, apparently having left home for the west, signed up with the (Union) Arkansas 4th Infantry. Neither man survived the war. Baumgartner was captured by

Confederates and sent to the infamous Andersonville, Georgia, prison, where he died, in June 1864, at age 24. A few months later, the 32-year-old Stauffer succumbed to dysentery after being taken prisoner by Confederate forces at Fort Smith, Arkansas, where his regiment was stationed.[71]

Midwestern Mennonite and Amish families whose ancestors had lived on North American soil for generations also supplied some willing soldiers. In August 1862, brothers Aaron and John Brubaker, two of Henry and Anna (Harnley) Brubaker's sons, joined the 108th Illinois and 86th Illinois, respectively. The Brubaker parents belonged to the Mennonite Church in Tazewell County, made up of households from Pennsylvania and Ohio. Two other sons, Daniel and Henry Jr., had enlisted in the early flush of volunteering the previous summer. In late April 1863, Aaron took sick and died as his regiment marched from Milliken's Bend, Louisiana, toward Port Gibson, Mississippi. Henry participated in the siege of Vicksburg and died in July 1864 of wounds sustained on the way to Memphis. Other Brubaker relatives were also in the Union army.[72]

In central Illinois, a significant number of young men from the progressive Amish Mennonite families of that area, most of whom had immigrated to the United States after 1830, joined Union ranks. Some, like Hessian J. Emile Strubhar of McLean County, joined the military in order to more quickly become a U.S. citizen when the war was over.[73] From the Partridge Creek (later Metamora) Amish Mennonite Church in Woodford County, Jacob Rediger, son of Joseph and Anna (Schmidt) Rediger, enlisted in August 1862 and served three years, as did 38-year-old Christian Gingerich, son of Partridge Creek's bishop Johannes and Barbara (Gerber) Gingerich.[74] Henry Detweiler, one-time member of the same congregation, piloted steamships on the Illinois and Mississippi rivers. In the spring of 1862, he offered his services to the government. A year later he had become master of the *Yankee* and "ran great hazards in his efforts to elude the enemy," sometimes disguising his ship as a gunboat.[75] From the Rock Creek Amish Mennonite community in McLean County, soldiers included Gideon Yoder, son of Joel and Lydia (Yoder) Yoder, who served from 1862 to 1865 in the 94th Illinois and participated in the siege of Vicksburg.[76]

Twenty-eight-year-old, Amish-reared Emanuel Hochstetler of Johnson County, Iowa, enlisted in 1862 in the 22nd Volunteer Infantry and also ended up at Vicksburg. Wounded there on May 22, 1863, he died shortly afterward in Memphis. Hochstetler was one of perhaps a half-dozen Iowa Amish and Mennonite men to join Union forces, the majority of whom did not survive the war.[77]

Indeed, the risk of suffering and death on the battlefield or in an army prison or hospital was well known to soldiers and those they left at home. Little wonder that some critics considered the conscientious to be cowards, or that they sometimes asserted patriotic claims in terms of masculinity.[78] Howard County, Indiana's Eli Hochstedler, for example, was incredulous that grown men would "give an oath that they would not defend themselves, their families or their property if armed robbers and murderers were to break in their houses." That was a "tough thing" to say, and objectors "took it without a wink." For his part, Hochstedler "would not have a wife that would not defend her rights," nor did he think the Amish nonresistants were being honest, as some "would as soon knock a fellow down as not" if they were crossed, he was sure.[79]

To the north, in Middlebury, Indiana, an Amishman who would stay out of the military nonetheless revealed some ambivalence about the adventure and intrigue army life could afford a young man. "If I was single yet," Levi Eash mused to his brother-in-law in Holmes County, Ohio, "I think I would [have] been gone myself before this time." But Eash, being a married man, had apparently joined the church and now seemingly was content with—though hardly adamant about—church teaching against war. His wife, Mary (Yoder) Eash, however, "mutch troubled her self when she heard that her Brothers had gone to war," Levi reported to one of those enlisting siblings. Was Mary more concerned out of familial fear that her brothers would be killed, or because, as an Amish woman, she believed they were rejecting God's will? For his part, Levi thought there was "badness" in going to war, since the scriptures command against it, but in a land of liberty "every one to his own notion."[80]

Correspondence among Mary Eash's four battlefield-bound brothers provides one window into the world of Amish sons who followed the muster drum.[81] By the time the war started, the Holmes County quartet of Noah, Samuel, Moses, and Jacob Yoder had all decided against Amish church membership, and Noah was married to a non-Amish woman named Catherine, who had attended the Grove Female Institute in Wooster, Wayne County.[82] Apparently the Yoders had grown up in a desperately

HON. S.S.YODER.

Congressman Samuel S. Yoder (1841–1921). Raised in a Holmes County, Ohio, Amish home, he joined the 128th Ohio in April 1862 and rose to lieutenant. A member of the U.S. House of Representatives 1887–1891, he is buried in Arlington National Cemetery. Credit: Courtesy of the Library of Congress

poor and cruel environment—perhaps one reason that the Amish community held little appeal for them. When Noah reminisced about his childhood, he recalled working terribly hard and seeing his brother Samuel "treated like a slave." All the while, their dear father had been "dishonored by the world" and "treated as the lowest of his race." Noah would never forget his mother's weeping for "wont of bread for her little ones." He could not erase from memory how "you [Samuel] and I and all our blood was dispised, abused and hated, because we were bourn poor" and how Noah had come home one evening to find his father dead and mother left with eleven "poverty stricken children."[83]

Noah and Moses were already in the military by 1861, and Noah had helped recruit "about 50 men."[84] He injected claims of masculine bravado into his letters, claiming that he had "not a drop of coward's blood" in his veins and boasting that he could "look death in the face like a lion." But both Noah and Moses became disenchanted with army life. Noah complained about incompetent officers and pointless marching orders that sapped soldiers' strength for no strategic purpose. It hardly helped that his wife Catherine reported that "folks at Berlin" thought Noah had turned out to be an abolitionist—a term of rank derision in that part of Ohio. She wished Noah would come home "and thrash the whole mess of them."[85] Meanwhile, Moses got stuck in the guardhouse for some infraction. Angry at his captain, he threatened to "send him to hell."[86] Samuel, a Holmes County schoolteacher, enlisted in 1862, as did Jacob—but not before trying to sell himself as a substitute.[87]

Only Samuel survived the war unscathed. Noah was shot through the left shoulder and had his left leg shattered and amputated at Murfreesboro, Tennessee, on January 2, 1863, after being left for dead for a day on the battlefield.[88] Jacob drowned at Milliken's Bend, Louisiana, in 1864. "If he could have died on the field of battle, I could have borne it," Noah cried when he learned of Jacob's death. But as it was, "O! God I cannot bear to think of it." Two weeks later, Noah heard that brother Moses had received a mortal hip wound at Kennesaw Mountain, Georgia: "What is wealth? What are honors? What is life to us! O! my good God! . . . I am grieved to death."[89]

Like Noah Yoder, hundreds of thousands of Americans received news of loved ones' deaths as the war dragged on. For many, such grim stories were mediated through letters that communicated the unimaginable grief that was now commonplace. For those in the North, unlike many in the Confederacy who saw suffering firsthand, the horrors at first remained many miles away. In late 1862 and 1863, however, the war came home to those living in Pennsylvania.

CHAPTER 6

The Fighting Comes North

Critical Months and Dramatic Developments

The Confederate military's successful counteroffensives in the spring and summer of 1862 provoked new optimism among Southern partisans and increasingly gloomy editorial comment in the North. As frustration and impatience mounted in his political backyard, Abraham Lincoln began discussing more openly his own sense that any Federal victory would have to include, in some way, the destruction of slavery. Restoring "the Union as it was" (which was becoming his Democratic rivals' rallying cry) was both too cautious a strategy and too modest a goal.[1]

On July 22, 1862, Lincoln informed his cabinet that he would soon issue some sort of emancipation order and thereby redirect the Northern cause toward abolition—a position he had privately embraced but now intended to make public.[2] In doing so, Lincoln would change the nature of the war, even as many of its military dimensions seemed at first unaltered. Although this shift in policy increased European regard for the United States and helped stave off diplomatic recognition for Richmond, emancipation was initially quite controversial at home and caused many Northerners—civilians and soldiers—to assess their commitment to the Union cause.[3] The new political and ideological debates that Lincoln opened, along with a series of critical battlefield encounters from Antietam to Gettysburg and Vicksburg, made the months from September 1862 to July 1863 especially critical ones.

For many Mennonites and Amish living in Union territory, events of late 1862 and 1863 were also pivotal, but for somewhat different reasons than those that their neighbors may have named. Unlike other Yankees, Mennonites and Amish seem not to have engaged the national debate over emancipation. At the same time, the other dramatically new development during these months—the presence of fierce fighting on Northern soil— did directly effect many nonresistants in Pennsylvania and Maryland, and pulled them into a series of shared experiences with others in their region.

Almost no surviving evidence points to Mennonite discussion of the president's plan to end slavery by force. Since very few nonresistants had ever taken a public role in the antebellum antislavery movement, the war- time silence is perhaps no surprise. Yet those living in heavily Republi- can territory must have understood that the matter was simmering at a new temperature; while those in places such as Holmes County, Ohio, or Adams County, Indiana, with their ardently anti-administration newspa- pers, certainly could not have missed vigorous denunciations of the "black Republican" plan to make abolition the centerpiece of the Union cause.[4]

Still, record of direct Mennonite discussion of emancipation is almost nonexistent, with a rare exception surfacing in northwest Ohio. In Janu- ary 1863, Henry Shank of Putnam County, Ohio, wondered aloud to his brother Frederick, in Washington County, Maryland, "Who would give his life to save a niggros?" Another brother, Jonas, bishop for the Putnam County Mennonites, later commented that he "would rather see slavery extended all over the creation than to had this curs [of war] upon our country." Elsewhere, the Shanks betrayed Unionist sympathies, but clearly they were not convinced of the merits of merging that cause with abolition. Perhaps Jonas, in particular, saw battlefield violence as a greater evil— and one that might even be prolonged by the president's proclamation.[5] Still the Shanks, in writing about these matters at all, were anomalies.

For their part, Amish leaders also steered clear of much direct discus- sion of the war during these months. Beginning in 1862 church leaders from across the United States met annually for three-day gatherings and left detailed minutes of their common concerns. Despite their coincid- ing with the darkest days of national division, the records of the Amish ministers' meetings reveal no references to the war, aside from two 1863 statements "that no church member should be allowed to serve in the war as a teamster" and that "during this time of war" it is "unseemly . . . to go to political meetings with a big mouth."[6] No doubt the minutes' silence on such matters points to the assumed authority of their nonresistant tradition; only currently contested matters such as the mode of baptism or the duties of deacons received extended attention. Yet, given the fact that some Amish men were marching to war, the nearly complete avoidance of the topic is notable, signaling the way Amish (and Mennonite) priorities and perspectives could remain outside the mainstream.

Yet that separatist stance, which had been possible in part because of the relative distance of the war from most Northern Mennonite and Amish everyday life, would be challenged in the span of nine months as Southern armies launched two dramatic invasions into Union territory. General Robert E. Lee's offensives in the fall of 1862 and summer of 1863 brought the war close to many in Maryland and Pennsylvania.

Until then, there had been something of a vicarious cast to the question of Northern Mennonite and Amish nonresistance. True, some young men had been required to declare or decline their intent to fight—and those who saw combat encountered its awful reality firsthand. But for nonresistant civilians outside of Virginia, violence and their relationship to it had remained somewhat academic during the war's first year and a half, mediated by newspaper accounts, high prices, and politically unpopular debates over conscription. "In the beginning of the war everything was pretty quiet so far as we were concerned," Catharine (Horst) Hunsecker, a teenager when the war began, later explained.[7] In 1861 she lived north of Chambersburg, Pennsylvania; beginning in September 1862, her community's quiet would be shattered.

For Mennonites and Amish living in or near these new Northern theaters of war, and for those in the Border State of Missouri, where violence also flared during these days, questions of self-defense and provisioning soldiers were suddenly immediate. Events and memories of these months suggest that when Mennonites and Amish in these places did have closer contact with the hard hand of war, they did not resort to violence to defend themselves or their possessions, but they frequently did employ stealth and savvy to protect their property. For some, the experience also seems to have evoked clearer Unionist sympathies, Rebel antipathies, and appreciation for civic order.[8]

Invasions in the Fall of 1862

"We have been left pretty much in peace," Mennonite Peter Eshleman of Washington County, Maryland, wrote to Ohio deacon Jacob Nold in the spring of 1862, adding somewhat cryptically, "We also take it for [wisdom] to hold ourselves quiet so we do not upset them as long as they leave us in peace."[9] Whether "them" and "they" referred to the Border State's Union or Confederate partisans is unclear, but whatever peace his people enjoyed came to a sudden end on September 4, as Lee took his army across the Potomac and into Maryland.

Buoyed by his August 29 victory at the Second Battle of Bull Run in northern Virginia, Lee decided to act quickly to take the war into Union territory, march through Maryland and into Pennsylvania, disrupt trade and communication with east coast cities, and threaten Washington, D.C. Hoping to stir latent Southern support, Lee forbade looting in Maryland and offered his "deepest sympathy [for] the wrongs that have been inflicted upon" residents by the "foreign yoke" of Yankee oppression—yet he found most people in the western part of the state cool to the Confederate cause. Nevertheless, Southern troops occupied without resistance the Maryland towns of Frederick and Hagerstown, and retook from Federal hands Virginia's Harper's Ferry and its critical rail and communication lines.[10]

Learning of these developments, Pennsylvanians panicked. When Jacob Stouffer Jr., member of the small Reformed Mennonite Church near Chambersburg, went to town on September 10, he discovered "Great excitement all over our neighborhood," the "town under martial law," and residents fleeing what they feared was an impending Confederate crossing into the Keystone State. The same day, Pennsylvania Governor Andrew Curtin issued a general order for "all able bodied men . . . to organize immediately." Some ten thousand hastily called militia were soon on hand to guard the border—and told to find their provender as they were able. Forty-five of them took at least two meals from Stouffer's kitchen.[11]

Even before Curtin had called for militia, newspapers had demanded self-defense. "We are asleep here in Pennsylvania," shouted the Lancaster *Express* on September 4, as Lee's forces entered Maryland. A few days later the paper claimed that in order for "this unrighteous rebellion" to be crushed, *"every man must become a soldier"* and spend three hours a day in musket practice; "he who doubts will be damned."[12] The editor castigated the rich—whom he had identified in earlier editorials as the area's nonresistants—for staying at home and letting poor working men fight to protect the property of the wealthy.[13] Back in southern Franklin County, not many miles from Lee's northernmost squads, farm families—including at least a few Mennonites—took a different tack. They packed their things and headed further north until the danger passed.[14]

But although a few Confederate scouts made it into Pennsylvania to steal horses (including three of Mennonite Andrew Lesher's), the expected large-scale Southern invasion of the state never materialized.[15] On September 13, Union soldiers in Washington County, Maryland, had found a copy of Lee's troop deployment orders lying in the grass, wrapped around three cigars, apparently dropped by a careless Confederate officer. With this remarkable piece of intelligence, Union Maj. General George McClellan was able to locate and corner Lee before his army made it across the Mason-Dixon Line. Although McClellan moved more slowly than Lincoln liked, by September 16, McClellan had closed in on Lee around the Maryland village of Sharpsburg, just east of Antietam Creek.

Already on the 14th, Pennsylvania Mennonites and others to the north of Sharpsburg, could hear "the roar of cannon all day from the southeast—from Maryland," as both armies moved into position for what would be a massive military contest on September 17.[16] Ironically, much of the fighting that day took place on farmland owned for several generations by nonresistant Dunker families, and the Dunker's modest Mumma meetinghouse ended up riddled with infantry and artillery shot.[17] When the carnage was over, the casualties totaled 23,000 (as many as 6,300 of whom died)—the bloodiest single day in U.S. military history.[18]

Back in Pennsylvania, Reformed Mennonite Jacob Stouffer noted the trains delivering more Northern reinforcements to McClellan, but on the ground at Antietam, the general was deciding not to press the attack another day. Lee's army limped back to Virginia, beginning September 19, leaving thousands of wounded soldiers behind. Union and Confederate injured ended up in makeshift hospitals in Maryland and Pennsylvania to be cared for by Hagerstown and Chambersburg citizens. Most of the maimed were soon moved elsewhere, but some eight hundred remained in

Some of the 6,300 men killed at Antietam (Sharpsburg). The battle-scarred Mumma
meetinghouse of the German Baptist Brethren (Dunkers) stands in the background.
Credit: U.S. Army Military Historical Institute, Carlisle, Pa.

the region for much longer. In early October Jacob Stouffer and his three
daughters visited "the Academy hospital to see the sick and wounded soldiers" and returned later with chickens and eggs.[19]

Less than a week later, on October 10, a Confederate raiding party was
back in Pennsylvania. Fifteen hundred cavalrymen under Maj. General
J. E. B. Stuart were on a mission to capture horses and destroy railroad
equipment and a key railroad bridge over the Conococheague Creek at
Scotland, Pennsylvania. Although they failed in this last assignment since
they did not have the explosives necessary to destroy an iron bridge, they
succeeded in burning locomotives and railroad buildings at Chambersburg and in requisitioning about 2,000 horses—including those from at
least twenty-two Mennonite farms—before slipping back into Virginia
two days later. Perhaps more importantly, they left southern Pennsylvanians jittery and ready to believe any rumor of invasion.[20]

In the wake of Stuart's raid, more Union soldiers moved into the greater

Chambersburg area, demanding food, wood, and other supplies from locals such as Jacob Stouffer's family. But if Mennonites readily provided such provisions to friendly forces, they were also quite ready to accept payment from the public treasury for the horses they had lost to the enemy and thus applied for monetary compensation from the Commonwealth. A nonresistant response to Southern soldiers could also, it seems, nudge Mennonites toward a closer identification with government.[21]

No Prospects for Peace

In Washington, D.C., Lincoln was disappointed with the military outcome at Antietam, since Lee's army had been allowed to escape. But Union troops had, at least, turned back the Confederate incursion, and the president decided to use the occasion to formally shift the Northern terms of war. Five days after the battle, he announced his Emancipation Proclamation. As commander-in-chief, Lincoln drew on his war powers to turn the Northern army into a tool of manumission. Beginning in January, federal forces would no longer recognize the institution of slavery in areas of rebellion. Although the Proclamation did not itself directly free any slaves, it fundamentally changed the war and made Union soldiers—regardless of their personal preferences—agents of abolition.[22]

This bold political move hardly brightened immediate Union prospects. In some regiments it initially provoked resentment. Moreover, embracing a new ideological cause did not appear to translate into battlefield success. After Antietam, Lincoln sacked McClellan in favor of Maj. General Ambrose E. Burnside. But in December, Burnside's leadership resulted in a disastrous Union defeat at Fredericksburg, Virginia. "It appears to me the Almighty is against us, and I can hardly see a ray of hope," Lincoln told an Illinois Senator and confidant later that month.[23] In all, prospects for ending the war appeared distant as 1863 dawned. Desertion spiked; in January several hundred Northern soldiers went missing daily.[24] Private John King, likely from a Mennonite home in eastern Pennsylvania, penned a January 24 letter in broken English to his friend John Gross that discussed the demoralization. Many in King's camp were sick, and others "are very dissatisfied here," he reported. Men "are kept worse than the niggers are." It was "disgraceful," he complained. "Here one might as well be in his grave."[25] The next major Union military action, in April 1863, also ended ignominiously as Lee surprised the Northern army and dealt it a severe blow at Chancellorsville, Virginia. And in the West, Federal efforts to take control of the Mississippi River seemed stalled around Vicksburg.

Yet the frustration, discouragement, and fear engendered by the war were not only products of major battles. For countless ordinary people, especially those in contested Border States or in areas around military theaters, the political instability and presence of organized violence had spawned a broader sort of lawlessness that injected unpredictability into daily life. Requisitioning of supplies, surprise appearance of army scouts or reconnaissance detachments, and uneasy relations among neighbors that could easily slide into vigilantism, all conspired to make life more sullen for many Americans in 1863. Such developments added to the ways that Border State Amish and Mennonites now encountered, more directly, the impact of war.

Oral tradition in the small Amish settlement that connected Oakland, Maryland, and Aurora, Virginia (later, West Virginia), provides one window onto the unnerving nature of civilian life. The presence of the Baltimore and Ohio Railroad through Oakland made the otherwise remote region a strategically significant place in 1863, with Confederate raiders and Union forces sparring and catching civilians in the process. Petersheim family lore holds that Southern supporters captured Christian Petersheim and forced him to haul supplies with his horses and wagon for weeks, while his family in Aurora wondered whether he was dead or alive.[26] A few miles away, near Red House, Maryland, dozens of Confederate troops stopped one morning at the home of Jacob and Elizabeth (Hershberger) Swartzentruber, ordered Elizabeth to provide buckwheat cakes for everyone, and then raided the family's pantry, pumped the well dry, slaughtered a milk cow, and left with bedding, clothing, and Jacob's watch.[27]

In the same community, on Sunday morning, April 26, 1863, bishop Daniel Beachy, accompanied by Christian Petersheim and Peter Schrock, were riding from Virginia into Maryland to hold church services for the Amish in the eastern end of the settlement when they encountered a Confederate scouting party. One jovial trooper rode up to the bishop and exchanged head gear, putting the Amish hat on his own head and placing his officer's cap on the bishop. After a round of laughter, the officer became serious and demanded Beachy give up his horse. The bishop's response, "Sir, I cannot give up my horse. I need it for farming," was met with curses, and the officer began forcibly unbuckling the saddle and pushing Beachy off. When Petersheim said they were on their way to church, the officer, apparently taken aback, desisted.[28] When the Amishmen made it to their Maryland meeting place, however, they learned that Confederate forces—a combination of Virginia cavalry and an irregular group known as John McNeill's Partisan Rangers—had taken control of Oakland and were engaged in destroying the town's rail station. After the morning preaching service concluded, Beachy and others fled to the woods and took circuitous routes home to Aurora, where their families, having learned that troop maneuvers were again afoot, feared the men had been captured. Elizabeth (Yoder) Beachy, Daniel's wife, had hidden cured meat and her dishes, and told her sons to drive the cattle into the woods. Such action saved supplies for the time being, but later, when the Southerners evacuated the area and Union troops moved in, the Federals confiscated much of the Beachys' food.[29]

Curiously, the Partisan Rangers, who had helped sack Oakland, had originally organized in Missouri, site of some of the war's most ruthless guerrilla warfare.[30] There vigilante groups of Confederate sympathizers battled frustrated Union troops unaccustomed to unconventional strategies that seemed to target some civilians while seeking cover from other noncombatants. Only a handful of Amish and no Mennonites lived in Missouri, but these families later recounted stories of violence and mayhem. Hickory County's Daniel Raber, a husband and father in his midthirties, apparently had to hide on more than one occasion to escape forced recruitment into one of the irregular groups that roamed the region. Troops from all sides helped themselves to the Raber's grain and animals, and by the end of the war the family had lost all their cattle. Especially traumatic was the experience of 15-year-old Christian Raber, who, while driving a wagon with another young man named Egly, was stopped by a drunken Union soldier. When Raber's companion argued with the soldier, the private shot and killed Egly. Deeply shaken, Raber then had to drive his friend's body twelve miles home.[31]

Different disruptions were said to have rattled the Solomon and Sarah (King) Yoder family, Amish who in 1860 had moved from West Liberty, Ohio, to Cass County, Missouri. Their Harrisonville farm near the Kansas border was located in a region that witnessed intense guerrilla warfare among competing groups aligned with the North and the South. The Yoders were not among the area's many civilian casualties, but on August 25, 1863, in an effort to stem such bloodletting, Union Brig. General Thomas Ewing issued an order evacuating civilian households from a three-and-a-half-county area.[32] Apparently, Solomon temporarily joined a Union state militia, thereby signaling loyalty and sparing his family immediate expulsion.[33] Meanwhile, Solomon's brother, Christian P. Yoder, heard of the family's plight and traveled by rail from Ohio to Missouri, but martial law prevented him from reaching them. Finally, family tradition reports, Sarah and the children were able to make it to Independence, Missouri, where they met Christian and went back to Ohio. After the war Solomon rejoined them, and when they returned to Missouri they found that their house and farm buildings had been burned.[34]

"The War is Upon Us!"

As skirmishing and marauding spread fear and uncertainty among civilians in the Border States and beyond, those living in what had become the corridors of conventional troop movement continued to bear the consequences of warfare. Lee's decision in 1863 to undertake another incursion into Northern territory brought the conflict home once again for Maryland and Pennsylvania Mennonites. Confederate forces crossed the Mason-Dixon Line, marched through Franklin County, and nearly invaded Lancaster County before what turned out to be a cataclysmic confrontation at Gettysburg.[35]

In advance of Lee's larger army, 1,600 Confederate cavalry under Brig. General Albert G. Jenkins moved through Maryland on June 15 and into Pennsylvania the next day, looking for horses and demanding ransom from the town of Chambersburg. "Jenkins Guerilla Brigade is in rule over us," Reformed Mennonite Jacob Stouffer wrote on June 17.[36] Stouffer was one of many in southern Franklin County to lose horses to Southern requisitioning. Thereafter, a steady stream of Confederate forces moved into western Maryland and Pennsylvania's Cumberland Valley. By happenstance, men from Lieut. General Richard S. Ewell's Second Corps, marching through Maryland during June 19–22, met Peter Heatwole, a Virginia Mennonite who had deserted the Confederate army and fled northward, finding refuge and employment among fellow church members northwest of Hagerstown. Apparently the troopers never guessed Heatwole's status, but he went into hiding for several days thereafter, nonetheless.[37]

For Cumberland Valley rural residents, Lee's march was devastating. Tearing down and often burning fences on both sides of the road so as to accommodate wider marching formations, the tens of thousands of soldiers left a swath of destruction simply by trampling planted fields and over-pasturing meadows.[38] Beyond that sort of basic destruction, soldiers also scavenged provisions and other supplies. Lee had issued orders against looting, telling soldiers they should pay for what they took—in Confederate currency.[39] Contemporary civilian reports and later memories suggest that Lee's order was both obeyed and ignored. Catherine Hunsecker, for example, remembered that her father exchanged food for worthless Richmond "blueback" bills.[40] In other cases, however, troops demanded food, tools, or cash, and looted what was not handed over. "They want everything—butter, milk, eggs, chickens, cheese, bread, etc.," Jacob Stouffer complained in his diary.[41] Confided Henry B. Hege to a relative in Lancaster County, "I tell you [the] greatest portion of them [Confederates] are nothing but thieves and robbers and some murderers." Hege had forfeited all his grain, oats, tools, and salt.[42]

Families lost not only foodstuffs but also money to Lee's men, who threatened violence if they were not given cash. One nonresistant Dunker was killed when he did not satisfy such demands.[43] Among area Mennonites, the most dramatic of such encounters involved Michael and Rebecca (Weaver) Hege's family, who lived near the village of Marion, Pennsylvania.[44] Mid-morning on June 27, three Confederate soldiers came into the Hege home, lined up Rebecca and the couple's two daughters against the wall at gunpoint, and demanded money. Michael turned over the family purse, but the soldiers were not satisfied and took him into a bedroom and demanded more. Opening a chest, Hege produced some additional money, and then two men began systematically to search other rooms while one trained a gun on Hege. Concluding their search, the Confederates reassembled in the bedroom and told Hege he would be shot. When Hege then turned his face, closed his eyes and prayed, one of the soldiers suddenly said, "Don't shoot," and the three marauders quickly exited, leaving the Hege household trembling.[45]

In stark contrast was an incident that supposedly had taken place on

Sunday, June 24, when a soldier stopped by the deserted home of Mennonite Sarah Kauffman. According to a Canadian visitor to Franklin County
the next year, Kauffman had found the following inscription in her hymn-
book when she returned that evening: "A rebel visited this house to-day,
and would have liked to found the residents at home; but such not being
the case, he leaves you his compliments written in this book, and hopes in
the future, you will be reasonable enough to stay at home. I have opened
your window to write this in this book but do not feel at all disposed to
injure your property."[46]

Given the evidence handed down in Mennonite families, it appears
Mennonites caught in the Pennsylvania war zone never used force to protect their property, but neither did they hesitate to be less than fully truth-
ful when concealing goods from Confederate requisition. For example,
Levi Horst, who lived north of Chambersburg, had sent his horses away
in advance of the approaching Southern army and then insisted that he
did not know what had happened to them; he also hid "the best of the
horse gears" but left "the older and less valuable harness . . . in the usual
place to avert suspicion that things were hidden away." Henry B. Hege hid
the wheels of his wagon and pretended not to know their whereabouts
when asked.[47] In general, Franklin County Mennonites appear to have
responded to Southern demands only grudgingly or by very reluctantly
handing over things they could not hide, whereas they were more forth-
coming—even generous, in some cases—when responding to Union troop
requests.[48] War zone pressures revealed dormant Union colors in some
Northern nonresistants.

Meanwhile, more Southern troops arrived into Pennsylvania, and Confederate commander Ewell took over a prominent piece of nonresistant
real estate—the Chambersburg Mennonite meetinghouse—to use as his
headquarters, sending correspondence and conducting four court-martials
from there.[49] In fact, it may well have been while Ewell was working out
of the meetinghouse that he issued his order to Maj. General Jubal Early
to march east and cross the Susquehanna River, cut the Pennsylvania Central Railroad, and attack Harrisburg and Lancaster.[50]

The continued Confederate offensive threw Pennsylvania's population
into a panic. As early as June 16, the New York Times had worried that
Harrisburg, the state's capital, was vulnerable. Now, with Southern forces
driving hard for the Susquehanna River's major crossing point at Wrights-

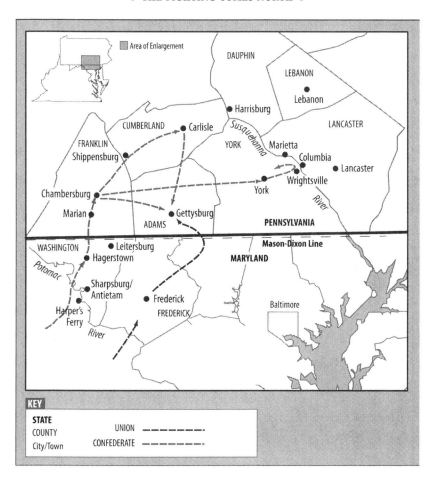

Military Movement in Pennsylvania and Maryland, 1863

ville, a frantic Governor Curtin telegraphed Secretary of War Stanton for federal help. "The War is Upon Us!" the Harrisburg *Daily Telegraph* cried, and trainloads of people and luggage fled north and east. At the state capitol, civil servants packed books, papers, and paintings for evacuation.[51]

In Lancaster as well, officials boxed courthouse records, shipped them to the rural village of Strasburg, and hid them under a bridge. Lancaster's mayor, George Sanderson, convened a public rally and implored "every citizen" to take up arms "in defense of our soil." Newspapers reported plans to guard the east bank of the Susquehanna River, suspend normal business in Lancaster city, and establish seven rendezvous points for informal militia composed of men bearing their own three-day rations and trench digging tools. Local colleges suspended classes so male students could join the defense, and newspaper headlines joined the chorus: "Defend Your Homes!" and "Maintain Your Honor!" Indeed, the governor had appealed to masculine honor in his effort to prod civil defense. Those without "the heart to defend their soil, their families, and their firesides," Curtin had declared, "are not worthy to be accounted men. Show yourselves what you are—a free, loyal, spirited, brave, vigorous race."[52]

Despite such language, contemporary accounts suggest that a remarkable number of men—including area Mennonites—did not rally to Curtin's call. If area nonresistants were not willing to take up arms for conscience sake, it seems they joined many of their non-pacifist neighbors in throwing energy into self-preservation. Some fled. Others focused on protecting property. For example, 16-year-old Christian F. Charles, son of a wealthy Mennonite family near Columbia (where Early's forces were expected to cross), went north to Lebanon County with his father's horses.[53] Also near Columbia, farmer John S. Nissley hid his cured hams in his haymow. Nissley did not leave the area, though some of his neighbors did.[54] Learning later of such choices, the *New York Times* was indignant. Had prosperity satiated Pennsylvania farmers to the point that they were "at an utter loss" what to do in the face of invasion except to rescue horses and pigs? Had it not occurred to them "to drive back the hostile invader?"[55] Worse yet, complained one of the men who did volunteer to defend Columbia, were those who tried to profit from the panic. He singled out an unnamed Mennonite family who, he claimed, were " 'conscientious' in everything except charging us full price for" the food they offered.[56]

Meanwhile, marching quickly eastward, Jubal Early's Confederate forces had reached the city of York on the morning of Sunday, June 28, and were demanding 1,500 pairs of shoes, 1,000 hats and pairs of socks, three days' rations, and $100,000 in cash. The town fathers came up with most of the supplies, but only $28,600. Early considered burning the town as punishment but then decided to act "in the spirit of humanity" and spare them.[57] He may also have wanted simply to avoid delay in reaching his primary goal: Wrightsville and its massive covered bridge.

Spanning the Susquehanna River, the massive Wrightsville-Columbia Bridge was a major transportation artery. Built in 1834 at a cost of

$128,726, the bridge was a mile and a quarter long and some forty feet wide. It never failed to impress visitors with the number of travelers it serviced, thanks to its railroad tracks, cartway, and two towpaths—all enclosed under one roof. Early dispatched troops under Brig. General J. B. Gordon to secure the strategic bridge.[58]

When members of Gordon's brigade reached Wrightsville later that afternoon, they encountered about twelve hundred Pennsylvania militiamen, who held the Southerners at bay for forty-five minutes before placing piles of lumber and a row of empty railroad cars in front of the bridge entrance and then retreating across it. As they retreated, the home guards readied the bridge for destruction in order to prevent Gordon's men from entering Lancaster County. The militia applied the torch, and "before the flames could be checked by the enemy, they had enveloped the entire span." All night crowds stood on both sides of the river, according to the Harrisburg *Daily Telegraph*, to gaze at "the conflagration" of "the entire length being on fire at once," a sight that evoked both relief and horror. The *York Gazette* reported that "the fire added to the orange of the sunset, and flames almost danced on the waters of the Susquehanna." Indeed, the enormous blaze was visible for miles, and burning timbers from the bridge, falling into the river and drifting downstream, looked like "infernal boats of hell."[59]

Foiled in their attempt to cross into Lancaster, Gordon and Early turned back to rejoin other Confederate forces now gathering around the town of Gettysburg. Lee had learned that the formidable Union Army of the Potomac, under Maj. General George G. Meade, was moving toward Lee, and in fact, on June 30 cavalry units from both armies clashed not far from Gettysburg. Home to a Lutheran Seminary and some minor industry, Gettysburg was situated at the intersection of important regional roads.[60]

The three days of blood-letting that began July 1 turned out to be the largest military engagement ever on North American soil. In Juniata County, some sixty miles to the north, 16-year-old Mennonite Sarah Graybill went into the house and told her father, Michael, that she heard an earthquake, not knowing that the low rumbling was that of the heavy Gettysburg cannonading.[61]

The first day's fighting, just north of Gettysburg, gave way on the second day to sustained but ineffective Confederate maneuvers against the east and west ends of Meade's defensive position south of town. Gam-

Fiery destruction of the Columbia-Wrightsville bridge on June 28, 1863, as portrayed in *Frank Leslie's Illustrated Newspaper* on July 18, 1863. Credit: Lancaster (Pa.) Mennonite Historical Society

bling on a massive strike at the center of the Union line on the third day, the Confederate offensive that came to be known as Pickett's Charge ended in crushing defeat.[62]

In all, some 23,000 Northerners and more than 25,000 of their Confederate counterparts were casualties at Gettysburg. The carnage was staggering. For example, the Union brigade commanded by Brig. General Samuel Kurtz Zook lost almost a third of its members: 49 killed, 227 wounded, and 82 missing.[63] The dead included Zook himself, who was fatally wounded on July 2 at the Gettysburg site known as The Wheatfield. Zook's great-grandfather, Amish immigrant Moritz Zug, had founded an Amish settlement in Chester County, Pennsylvania, and Samuel had grown up in that area, although his father had defected from the faith. Having moved to New York City with a telegraph company job before the war, Samuel had marched with the New York militia for three months after Fort Sumter and then returned to organize the 57th New York Volunteers. Now, as Zook's condition worsened the day after he had been hit, he reportedly insisted on knowing the Union army's fortunes. Told that Pickett's Charge was in retreat, Zook is said to have replied, "Then I am perfectly satisfied," and died.[64]

As Zook was dying, Lee was concluding that the only sane option he had was to withdraw to Virginia. Late on the night of July 3, in a heavy rain that turned roads to mud, the Army of Northern Virginia headed for the Potomac River, taking with them thousands of wounded men. General Meade, weary and not altogether certain what Lee's next move would be, was slow to pursue—earning the ire of President Lincoln, who believed yet another Union commander had allowed Lee to escape.[65]

Lee ordered Brig. General John D. Imboden to organize the transportation of as many as 10,000 wounded soldiers, while he took the rest of the army south by a different and faster route.[66] Even though the Confederates left behind 7,000 men who were too seriously hurt to be moved, Imboden's wagon train turned into an ordeal of prolonged pain and delayed death for many men as it slogged through mud in the same Franklin County, Pennsylvania, and Washington County, Maryland, communities that had witnessed these troops' invasion not many weeks before. Mennonite Henry B. Hege, who had seen the soldiers energetically pass his farm in June, described the July scene to a relative: "I was at the road when they retreated And i seen a nough Their wagon train was about 56 hours pasing And nearly all halling wounded some would groan at every jerk the wagon made all these that ware just Slightly wounded had to walk I seen some walking that was shot in the arms some sholders some in the face O it looked awful as their wounded were not dressed yet."[67] Twenty-seven wounded Confederates who were left at Ringgold, Maryland, perhaps suffering too much to continue on South, ended up in a makeshift hospital under the care of that community's Reformed Mennonite doctor, Benjamin Frantz.[68]

Meanwhile, a thousand miles to the southwest, Union Maj. General Ulysses S. Grant had wired Washington on July 4 that the Mississippi River city of Vicksburg had surrendered, giving Federal forces control of the western waterway and cutting the Confederacy in two. Coupled with Lee's defeat in the East, Grant's success in the West portended eventual Union victory.[69] Nevertheless, fighting would still rage for more than a year and a half and claim thousands of additional lives. Hereafter, however, battlefield confrontations would be on Southern soil, and Northern communities would be spared the direct havoc of war.

"We Heard the Cannon Plain"

Sixty-one year-old Mennonite minister Peter Nissley, who lived near Marietta, Pennsylvania, just up river from the Wrightsville-Columbia bridge, had not fled when Confederate invasion had seemed imminent in June. "We had some trying times," Nissley admitted in early August, about a month after Gettysburg. "The Rabels came [within] 6 miles from our place—that was at Writesville—on the Susquahanna River."[70]

Nissley's reflections included several themes that had emerged in bolder relief during the preceding year. First was the immediacy of wartime events—something civilian Mennonites and Amish outside of Virginia had not experienced during the conflict's first eighteen months. "We heard the cannon plain & saw the Fire of the burning bridge from my house," Nissley noted. "The Thursday following we heard the battle of Gettysburg quite plain—the cannonading soundet like distant Thunder but could hear Each separate report Distinctly, that is 35 mile from us . . . what awfull destruction of life and property this war has brought on us."

In his use of language, Nissley betrayed identification with the Union cause, even if he did not directly support its military means. "They tried

Mennonite minister Peter Nissley (1802–1890) of rural Marietta,
Lancaster County, Pennsylvania, in a photo from the 1850s. Credit: Lancaster (Pa.)
Mennonite Historical Society

to shell Columbia but could not reach it," he wrote of the Confederates,
but he then switched to first-person when describing the Union troops:
"Our few men that resisted them, retreated to, and Fired that magnificent
Bridge." He was thankful—and pleased—that the Southern soldiers had
been turned back.

Yet Nissley was not playing with common patriotism, and another theme he revealed was a nonresistant critique of the very legitimacy of violence. Ever since "the Lord spake onto Noah—he that sheddeth mans blood that blood shall be shed by man," lethal force had been forbidden the children of God, Nissley insisted. True, "we are engaged in a severe war-fare," the preacher averred, but it was a battle against the forces of pride and greed. "Christ expects all his followers to resemble him. . . . to abound in every good word and work, to be honest and Just in all our actions—to be charitable to the poor and needy—to visit the sick, feed the hungry, clothe the naked—in a word to love our neighbor as ourselves."

Peter Nissley wove these distinct themes together into a position that staked out a type of separatism within a political context that warranted a measure of appreciation and even identification—especially when the specter of invasion was on the horizon. If Nissley's people saw themselves as nonresistant citizens, the events of 1862 and 1863 confirmed such sensibilities.

The seasoned minister's thoughts on war and peace were included in a letter to John F. Funk, the young Mennonite entrepreneur in Chicago, whom Nissley had met not many weeks earlier while on a Midwestern trip. Funk, who until recently had been intensely politically minded, was in the midst of a theological and vocational conversion, and in the months to follow, he would begin articulating his own nonresistant response to the war, one that placed more of an accent on a distinct Christian ethic and less on a sense of civic identification. In the meantime, the complexity of impulses that Nissley's letter reflected was apparent in the evolving Mennonite relationship with Radical Republican war leader Thaddeus Stevens, the Congressman in whose district Nissley lived.

Thaddeus Stevens and Pennsylvania Mennonite Politics

Unlikely Allies

In June 1863, as the Army of Northern Virginia marched triumphantly into southern Pennsylvania, Lee's troops—otherwise under orders to limit their looting of Yankee property—took time to locate a Chambersburg ironworks owned by Thaddeus Stevens. The prominent Republican leader lived in Lancaster but happened to be visiting his Franklin County property at the time, and Southern soldiers just missed capturing him. "Upon the rumored approach of the Confederates," remembered Chambersburg businessman Jacob Hoke, locals "hurried [Stevens] away to Shippensburg by a byroad, much against his will and earnest protest." Failing to net the famous Congressman, the troops instead demanded "all the horses and mules belonging to the establishment" but promised not to burn the furnace. The Confederates made off with "about forty valuable animals" but returned a week later and set fire to the ironworks anyway. As they watched the plant "wholly consumed" by the flames, the soldiers must have known they were striking a blow at one of their most formidable political opponents.[1]

Thaddeus Stevens was a remarkable public figure, one whom both Republican friends and Southern foes had good reason to fear. Representing a district that included the city of Lancaster, Stevens was not averse to calling his most famous constituent—James Buchanan—a traitor.[2] Nor did he shy away from castigating his own party's leader, Abraham Lincoln, for the president's initially cautious endorsement of enrolling black troops. In fact, such direct criticism of Lincoln earned Stevens and his allies the label *Radical* Republicans. The Radicals saw the war as a clash between irreconcilable ways of life that could be resolved only with the destruction of the Southern plantation system, granting full civil rights to African Americans, and a thorough-going "reconstruction" of the Confederacy as "conquered territory."[3]

As a fervent idealist, Stevens could offer rousing and persuasive speeches on the necessity of abolition or the evil of secession. As a skilled politician, he possessed the shrewdness to build unlikely coalitions and achieve his goals. He had moved through Whig and anti-immigrant Know-Nothing circles before emerging in 1855 as a leader in the new Republican Party, along the way championing public schools, scapegoating Catholics, and advocating racial equality.

By 1863 Stevens' network of alliances included a close relationship with Pennsylvania's Mennonites. Democratic Party operatives were quick to call the pairing hypocritical, since Stevens was the most vocal prosecutor of a war his nonresistant supporters refused to fight.[4] Speaking on the House floor, however, the seasoned politico saw no contradiction in calling his conscientious objectors "our most loyal men"—a designation few public figures would have applied to those with scruples. Nor, it seems, did Mennonite voters mind being associated with "Old Thad." Especially as federal conscription lurched into motion, Stevens looked after "his Mennonites" as they engaged partisan politics to secure their separate status.

As 1863 opened, military manpower—a perennial problem for Union strategists—was again a challenge of major proportions.[5] The federally authorized state militia drafts of 1862 had solved a short-term need, but very soon the regiments consisting of two-year enlistees from 1861 and nine-month sign-ups from 1862, would be disbanding. There was little reason to believe these veterans would reenlist, but if the federal government enacted a new and permanent program of conscription, it might encourage seasoned soldiers to extend their service voluntarily. Frankly, Washington did not need to draft all that many men to have the threat of a draft prompt veterans to opt for reenlistment bonuses and sign up for another hitch. But in order for this "carrot and stick" system (as historian James McPherson

Republican Thaddeus Stevens (1792–1868) represented the Lancaster County,
Pennsylvania, district for thirteen years and cultivated connections with Mennonite
constituents. Credit: Lancaster County (Pa.) Historical Society

has called it) to work, any draft would have to be comprehensive and hold
the promise that anyone might be called.[6]

Thus, in late January 1863, Senator Henry Wilson of Massachusetts
introduced a bill calling for a National Guard of the United States. That
measure evolved into a national conscription bill. But any proposal to establish direct federal drafting was sure to be controversial since it represented an unprecedented expansion of federal prerogative and an intrusion
to traditional states' rights. Not surprisingly, heated discussion opened
with Democrats rallying to limit Washington's power and Republicans
arguing that the unusual circumstances trumped precedent. The bill also

became an occasion for debating the administration's general handling of the war. Even the severe winter storm that hit Washington on February 22 failed to cool tempers in the Capitol.[7]

Since conscription was contested, support or opposition hinged in part on the plan's apparent even-handedness in creating a "uniform system of drafting."[8] Thus, the issue of exemption from the draft became a lightning rod, attracting some of the most intense debate.[9] Purchasing a substitute to take one's place was a longstanding tradition in American military history, so that provision was included with little opposition. However, the possibility of allowing draftees simply to opt out with the payment of a commutation fee was controversial. According to proponents of cash commutation, such a fee actually made the draft more equitable by controlling the inflation of substitute prices to no more than the exemption charge. Thus, an exemption clause would work to keep the draft from becoming, in the notorious phrase, "a rich man's war and a poor man's fight," as had happened in the Confederacy, where substitute prices skyrocketed beyond reach of any but the well-heeled.[10]

But, Stevens argued in the midst of House debate, there was another reason "I do not and can not assent to" any version of the legislation that omitted provision for paying an exemption fee. That option provided an acceptable avenue of escape for a particular group of Unionists whose votes he valued. "There are in all countries exemptions for conscience sake," the Radical Republican intoned from the House floor, "and it is right that there should be." "In my own county a very large number of our best citizens, our most loyal men, are conscientiously opposed to bearing arms," he continued. "They are willing to pay taxes; they would be willing to pay this amount to procure substitutes; but I do not believe that they should be forced to violate their conscientious and religious scruples . . . which have descended to them from a venerable ancestry."[11] Although Stevens had a few Quakers in his district, he apparently was not referring to them, since they were petitioning Congress for complete exemption without any equivalency charge. Friends insisted that payment was "virtually an equivalent to personal service" and thus as unconscionable as bodily participation. They called on "the Heads of nearly all the Departments and left copies" of protests with the attorney general and each member of the House of Representatives.[12] Their argument won few supporters, not even Stevens.

On February 25, after maneuvering through twelve roll call votes, the House passed the Republican-authored Enrollment Act of 1863 along a near party-line vote.[13] It allowed any draftee to gain exemption by paying $300. Lincoln signed the bill, and the first federal military conscription became law in March. Soon Stevens was back home in Lancaster, proudly telling his Mennonite constituents about his efforts on behalf of men of conscience as well as his concern for those of modest means. He happily noted how the new law corrected the state militia draft of 1862, in which those with scruples had become victims of substitute brokers, paying as much as $800 or $1,200 for substitutes.[14]

The Federal Draft and Republican Reciprocity

Under the terms of the new legislation, the Provost Marshals Bureau in Washington, D.C., sent marshals or assistant marshals into each congressional district to enroll male citizens, and those applying for citizenship, between the ages of 20 and 45. The bureau would then use these lists to fill district quotas whenever the president called for troops, which Lincoln did four times. The first call, in July 1863, directed marshals to draw at random 20 percent of enrolled names.[15]

Despite the law's obvious provisions for objectors, some Amish and Mennonites found the prospect of federal drafting troubling. "No one had believed that things could get so bad," wrote Jacob and Maria (Clemens) Landes, from Montgomery County, Pennsylvania, to Canadian friends.[16] Indeed, young men from the Landes's neighborhood were heading for Canada to avoid conscription. Back in 1862 at least three Mennonites had been among those taking such a drastic step; now others followed them in 1863.[17]

On the whole, most late summer drafts in 1863 came off peacefully in Pennsylvania. When drafting occurred during July 9–21 in Lancaster County, however, residents were still reeling from the shock of the burning of the Columbia-Wrightsville Bridge and the carnage at Gettysburg. The wheel-shaped basket used for drawing names began rolling six days a week, and each day the newspapers reported the names drawn. Often the same page listed members of recently-organized regiments. Obviously, the draft did encourage volunteering, but it was much clumsier at putting the unwilling into uniform. National Archives records show that of the 3,362 men drafted in Lancaster County, 36 percent (1,214) paid the commutation fee, shelling out a total of $364,200. Only twenty-six men furnished substitutes. More than 42 percent (1,417) of men were discharged for physical or other reasons. That left 705 who went into the military.[18]

Large numbers of Mennonites and Amish paid the $300 fee in this draft, though it is impossible to determine exactly how many.[19] Critics complained that an inordinate number claimed physical disability. The *Daily Express* printed lists of names and reported infirmities. "We had always thought Lancaster county noted for the health and longevity of its inhabitants," the *Examiner and Herald* sarcastically reported, "but if the record of the Examining Board can be taken as evidence the reverse is the fact."[20] On July 28 the *Intelligencer* editorialized that with so many "diseased" and "incapacitated" people, "together with those who 'forked over' the $300," it seemed certain that few draftees "will trouble Uncle Sam for a new suit of clothes."[21]

In Mifflin County, with its significant Amish population, the *Lewistown Gazette* noted in July that "our community has been all excitement during the past week having meetings to raise enlistments." Thirty "responsible men" had stepped forward and promised $20,000 in order to provide $50 bounties to volunteers, hoping to gain enough willing soldiers to head off the need for a local draft. The promised money was to be "indemnified by bonds from the leading taxpayers of the county"—two of whom, in Union Township, were Amishmen Shem Zook and John Peachey. In Menno Township one of the three was Nicholas Hartzler.[22] Still, Amish in Bratton, Brown, Union, and Menno townships were drafted, but consistently they paid the commutation fee.[23]

On the Juniata River side of the mountain, numerous Amish surnames appeared on military rolls, but given the decline of Amish churches there prior to the war, very few of the men were church members. One exception was the family of William and Leah (Hartzler) Harshbarger family. Five sons paid commutation fees, but son Nicholas enlisted. He became a corporal and returned to Mifflin County to recruit more men—many of Amish descent—before he was killed in battle at Cold Harbor in May 1864.[24]

In Mifflin County, concerns about the draft merged with discussion of the 1863 election. On September 16 the Republican *Gazette*—apparently reflecting the fact that area Amish were Republicans—charged that Democratic "copperheads in Menno Township were beginning to make threats against the Omish in order to prevent them from going to the elections." After the election, the *Gazette* gloated that Democrats had been surprised by "a 15 inch bombshell from Menno" Township, which had caused "an awful scattering of wounded pigeons." Seemingly, Menno Township Amish had voted for Governor Andrew Curtin and the rest of the Republican slate. The *Gazette* admitted that "many Union men went to the polls who don't often go there, and this was especially the case in Menno and Oliver," townships heavily populated by the Amish.[25]

If Pennsylvania Republican leaders such as Stevens and Curtin took Mennonite and Amish concerns seriously, some of these constituents returned the favor beyond the ballot box in their support for Union Leagues that sprang up to rally the party faithful. Anti-war Democrats had earlier organized chapters of Knights of the Golden Circle, but Mennonites and Amish seem to have had no connection with the Knights. On the eastern edge of Lancaster County, Philip Huber tried to organize a chapter in Bowmansville and, on the porch of a local inn in plain sight of Bowmansville Mennonite Church, encouraged listeners to "evade the war by resisting the draft."[26] Nonresistants did not respond.

Meanwhile, Republicans hastily formed Union Leagues to counteract the Knights. "In this darkest hour of trial since our existence as a nation," said a speaker for a League being formed in Montgomery County, northwest of Philadelphia, we need "conscientious regard to loyalty."[27] During its first year the Philadelphia League mailed more than a million copies of seventy-one different publications, at least eight of which were in German.[28] At Bareville, in Lancaster County, the list of Union League officers and members included the names of Solomon C. Groff, Abraham Eby, John W. Buckwalter, Martin W. Kurtz, Abraham D. Graybill and Graybill G. Wenger—Mennonites or men with Mennonite family ties.[29] In Montgomery County a "Union County Committee" meeting on February 21, 1863, included representatives from various townships, among them Samuel Gehman from Franconia, Jonas C. Godshalk from Lower Salford, Henry R. and Daniel D. Hunsicker from Perkiomen East and West, and Isaac W. Kratz from Upper Salford.[30] Henry Hunsicker became president of the League at Trappe.[31] Progressive-minded Mennonites of the area, particularly those associated with the General Conference Mennonite Church or with Freeland Seminary at Trappe, championed the Union League.

In Lancaster city, the *Daily Evening Express* estimated that the Republican rally there in early October drew 30,000 people and included a seven-mile-long parade. A speaker read the names and addresses of 131 vice presidents and 23 secretaries of Committees of Vigilance, charged with promoting the party and getting out the vote. The list of leaders included an abundance of typical Mennonite and Amish surnames, particularly from townships with sizable church memberships.[32]

If some observers considered such activity unseemly for quiet plain people, Republican editors stood ready to defend their reputations. The October 7, 1863, Lancaster's *Examiner and Herald* condemned a "disgraceful" Democratic gathering at Manheim, where orator Isaac E. Hiester claimed that "The abolitionists [Republicans] have all the Dunkards and Mennonites to vote with them, who, good God! do not know that their Redeemer liveth." The editor was incensed at any such remarks that vilified "a class of Christians, so justly esteemed as the Mennonites and Dunkards." He further called on "the men thus virulently assailed" to go to the polls that fall and "vote as their conscience dictates." Historian Andrew Robertson's study on Mennonite voting patterns in Lancaster County confirms that Mennonites took the editor's advice.[33]

The same seems to have been true in Montgomery County to the east, where 1863 election results show that townships populated by Mennonites went heavily Republican. For example, Franconia voted Republican 265 to 100; Hatfield, 189 to 103; Lower Salford, 268 to 33; Perkiomen, 149 to 111; and Towamencin, 186 to 79.[34] In Bucks County the Republican "Committees of Vigilance" appear to have had a number of Mennonites or Mennonite-connected members, such as Isaac Tyson, Enos G. Moyer, S. W. Lapp, Abraham Ruth, Jacob Leatherman, J. W. Lapp, Enos F. Geil, Abraham Clymer, and more.[35] In Hilltown, Jacob Funk Jr., writing to his brother in Chicago, reported voting to reelect "our gallant and patriotic Governor [Curtin] . . . this truly great man," adding that it was unfortunate that Democrats had succeeded in putting "some of the meanest scamps of disloyalty" into local offices.[36]

Contesting the Commutation Fee

Meanwhile, federal conscription gears continued to grind. Draft legislation had successfully encouraged volunteering and stimulated reenlistment during the summer of 1863, but by early 1864 new inductees were again in short supply. On October 17, 1863, Lincoln had issued a call for 300,000 volunteers. Less than four months later, on February 1, 1864, he called for 200,000 more troops, and on March 14, another 200,000. Raising that much manpower required a new round of drafting, beginning in mid-April 1864. Then on July 18, the President called for another 500,000 men, which spurred a third draft that September. The final presidential troop proclamation came on December 19, 1864, and the fourth and final draft began February 20, 1865 and was still in motion when the war ended.[37]

With each new conscription, the number of men actually held for service was fewer. Already by fall 1863 it was clear that many men caught in the draft would apply for some exemption, usually availing themselves of the $300 commutation. That option quickly became a flash point, as critics chanted, "Three hundred dollars or your life."[38] In July 1863 anti-draft riots in New York City, the worst rioting in American history, had left 105 dead in a clash that revealed deep ethnic antagonism and class resentment.[39] While recent studies have shown that the image of a "poor man's war" was baseless—the Union army was economically representative of Northern society or perhaps even over-represented upper-middle-class Americans—the charge stuck.[40]

For eastern Pennsylvania Mennonites and Amish who used commutation as a legal means of expressing nonresistance, the matter of public perception was problematic, given their reputed wealth. The Lancaster *Intelligencer*, for example, claimed that the fee was no burden to the Mennonites who supported commutation champion Thaddeus Stevens.[41] Were his supporters as wealthy as the *Intelligencer* charged? Interestingly, evidence comes from records of the wartime income tax that Stevens, who chaired the House Ways and Means Committee, had pushed through Congress. The new income tax was progressive, Stevens had insisted, forcing "the rich . . . to contribute largely from the abundance of their means [while] . . . no burdens have been imposed on the industrious laborer and mechanic." The tax exempted the first $600 of income plus costs related to hired labor, insurance, interest on debts, repairs on buildings, other taxes paid, and the like.[42] As a result, most households, such as those of carpenters and laborers who often made only $400 a year, or modest merchants whose earnings might be over $600 but whose business expenses pulled them under the exemption threshold, paid no tax at all.

Thus, it is remarkable that when the Lancaster *Daily Express* listed the names and incomes of those liable, the list contained hundreds of typically Mennonite and Amish names—at least some, if not most of whom, were church members. Scores had incomes—even after the exemptions and deductions—over $1,000.[43] A few appear with $2,000–$4,000 and several are listed above $6,000. Clearly, Lancaster County Mennonites had more means at their disposal than many of their neighbors.[44] To be sure, some eastern Pennsylvania Mennonites were less well off, but they could rely on fellow members to obtain exemption funds.[45] In Plumstead Township, Bucks County, for example, a church committee examined each draftee's need and then solicited donations to cover costs.[46] In 1863 General Conference Mennonites north of Philadelphia declared it "a duty and not a charity to render [financial] assistance to the full extent . . . to those who have been called [in the draft]."[47]

Perhaps Lancaster Mennonites and Amish also tried to use their potentially embarrassing wealth as a way to gain their neighbors' good graces. At least their Republican apologists played up on their wartime charitable work. In early November 1862 the *Daily Evening Express* had featured the fact that local citizens were generous in supplying blankets for soldiers. They were not making an ostentatious display of it, said the editor, but it was worth noting that those engaged in doing this "are the Mennonites, the 'conscientious' men, upon whom so much unreasonable abuse has been visited, and who now show themselves more patriotic than the stay-at-home sensation-mongers who revile them."[48] From the published names it appears that Mennonites also served on the "Local Relief Committees" to aid financially the families of soldiers. And in January 1863 the "Amish Society, per Christian Beiler" had given $20 to the Ladies of the Dorcas Society of Lancaster for relief.[49] In Mifflin County, Republican newspapers praised Amish women for providing food and blankets for wounded soldiers and war widows.[50]

Such benevolence could not cool the growing controversy over commutation in general, which was, of course, a national concern much broader than that of the nonresistants alone. Congress was under pressure to tighten the draft, and objection to the commutation fee came from several quarters. On the one hand were the pacifist Quakers, who continued to argue for blanket exemption for nonresistants without any fee.[51] Secretary of War Stanton knew the Quaker position but feared that giving religious groups total exemptions would only raise more questions about a draft act that was already controversial.[52] Remarkably, in mid-December 1863 Stanton quietly sent a circular to regional provost marshals to place "on parole" Quakers with scruples, thus allowing them to be administratively forgotten and their fees uncollected.[53] Mennonites and Amish, however, seem generally to have been unaware of this option, in part because the provost marshals conveniently kept it quiet.[54]

A much larger number of voices calling for modification of conscription rules came from Democrats, who raised questions of cost and class, and from Republicans concerned with how those same matters affected war morale. Republican Senator Henry S. Lane of Indiana summed the feelings of many in Congress: "I am in favor of a conscription law, and would vote for it; but I will not vote for this most expensive, most cumbersome, and most demoralizing system."[55]

Petitions regarding the $300 clause went to Congress in January and February 1864 as that body debated amending the Enrolling Act, including two petitions from Bucks County Mennonites that included 221 signatures.[56] Remonstrating "against the repeal of the Commutation Clause," one list began with the name of Rev. Isaac Overholtzer, and the other with Jacob Leatherman. Some nonresistants in Overholtzer's and Leatherman's area adopted a different political tactic. Rather than petition Congress generally, they wrote directly to their congressional patron, Thaddeus Stevens, even though they did not live in Stevens' district. Isaac B. Tyson, of Mingo Mill in Montgomery County wrote Stevens in December 1863 and February 1864. Tyson had Mennonite relatives but was River Brethren—the Pennsylvania German revivalist group with Mennonite, pietist, and Wesleyan roots.[57] Tyson warned that removing the $300 clause would "make it very hard for the loyal people" in his church who wanted to obey government as far as conscience allowed. In fact, eliminating the exemption might sour his people on the governing party, and that is just what the "opposite party" (Democrats) wanted, he averred. Certainly Democrats "would sooner see the government destroyed than to give up their rotten party." Adopting a partisan tone—likely his own, but no doubt used with some effect on Stevens—Tyson declared that either the Democrats "must go down or the government will."[58]

If the government needed money, Tyson suggested levying a tax, which River Brethren and other nonresistant people—he admitted the Quakers might not be so sanguine—would gladly pay. During the summer 1863 invasion of Pennsylvania, many people said in Tyson's hearing that they would "give with all their hearts" if a tax were laid on them. Turning to a purely practical argument, Tyson explained that the government might as well collect a fee from "the many thousands of those harmless nonresisting people" since they "will not fight if they would be taken away by force and put in the army," so "they would be of no use to the government." Yet Tyson's personal convictions ran deeper than this pragmatic analysis; he would rather see death come in his family than a "draft with no way of escape."[59]

From within Thaddeus Steven's district, River Brethren minister Jacob S. Engel of Marietta wrote to the congressman in early January. Engel and his "nonresisting body" were deeply troubled to learn that the commutation fee might be repealed. Such a situation "would place us in a very difficult position, as we cannot conscientiously furnish a substitute, or personly serve in military service," Engel explained, suggesting that his church—like the Amish, but unlike most Mennonites—saw substitution as morally problematic. He pleaded with Stevens, as the "representative of our County to present & advocate our Case & if necessary give us an advice if you please how to proceed in behalf of our Church."[60] With Engel's missive went a letter from Barr Spangler, also of Marietta, attesting that Engle spoke "by instruction" of his church in Lancaster and Cumberland counties. If Stevens thought it would be helpful for the River Brethren to "remonstrate against the repeal of the commutation," Spangler would pen a petition and "circulate it for Signatures."[61]

Stevens also heard from Republicans who were not nonresistants but who knew the political clout eastern Pennsylvania peace people wielded. In December 1863, as Congress took up deliberation on commutation, a judge warned Stevens that "the dunkards, Mennonistes & other friends of the Union Cause who has conscientious scruples about bearing arms, would all or nearly all cease to support the administration" if commutation were not preserved. Politically, that "would be playing into the hands of the secessionists among us," he concluded.[62]

Nevertheless, as Congress opened debate many members shied away from blanket exemptions for religious groups. The Senate took fourteen votes related to the fee and increased it to $400, but when the bill reached the House, Stevens immediately moved to return it to $300. Stevens' allies, including Henry C. Deming, Republican of Connecticut, who chaired the committee that had drafted the House version, fell into line. Deming cited "the Mennonites," explaining that their "conscience tells them to take no oath, to do violence to no man, to take patiently the spoiling of their goods, to pray for their enemies, and to feed and refresh them when hungry or thirsty."[63]

The final version, signed by the president on February 24, 1864, included several changes to the original act approved the year earlier. A new Section 17 recognized members of "religious denomination" whose "articles of faith and practice" prohibit bearing arms and whose "deportment has been uniformly consistent with such declaration." Such people could pay the $300 commutation or accept assignment from the Secretary of War "to duty in the hospitals, or to the care of freedmen [former slaves]."[64] Many Friends were frustrated that the bill continued to place any demands at all on the conscientious, but Mennonites, Amish, and River Brethren were happy to have retained the monetary exemption, and there is no evidence that they pursued hospital or Freedmen's Bureau work.[65]

Despite the modest modifications in other parts of the draft law, those charged with administering conscription quickly complained that it still contained too many loopholes. Captain George Eyster, provost marshal for Adams, Bedford, Franklin, Fulton, and Somerset counties in Pennsylvania, found it no easier to raise troops under the amended law, as his statistics for Franklin County illustrate. Out of a total of 192 men examined June 6–11, 1864, 92 paid the commutation fee, 3 provided substitutes, 69 were exempt due to disability, and 10 were given other exemptions. Thus only 18 of the men drafted were actually held.[66] Holding few men each round meant that Eyster had to conduct more frequent drafts to achieve his conscription quotas. In such a context, substitution became more appealing, since hiring a substitute covered one's obligation for the length of the service being substituted, while the commutation fee did so only until the next round of drafting. In Somerset County, for example, John I. Kaufman, son of Amish parents Isaac and Polly (Lehman) Kaufman, was drafted twice. The first time he paid the commutation fee, but the second time he furnished a substitute.[67]

By June 1864, national Provost Marshal James B. Fry informed Secretary of War Stanton that of 14,471 recently drawn names, 5,050 paid the exemption fee. As long as the $300 commutation clause remained, Fry believed the draft was pointless. Stanton agreed, and Lincoln sent a message to Congress endorsing the commutation's removal.[68] In response, Dayton, Ohio, Republican Robert C. Schenck introduced a bill to eliminate the provision, and the measure became law on July 4, 1864. Read quickly, the legislation seemed to abolish exemption entirely. However, Thaddeus Stevens had again rescued his clients by inserting a critical phrase into section ten: "Nothing contained in this act shall be construed to alter or in any way affect the provisions of the seventeenth section" of the amended Enrollment Act. That section had defined conscientious objectors; the $300 exemption had disappeared for all draftees *except* nonresistants.[69]

Thereafter, grumbling about exemption focused solely on those registering scruples. Captain Eyster, still busy holding draft after draft in south central Pennsylvania and garnering only a few uniformed men each time, was concerned about reports from Cambria County that "persons reared in the faith and practice of certain non-combatant churches were allowed to pay the commutation." If that continued, warned Eyster, "able bodied men will become rapidly conscientious" so as to "escape their share of public obligations." By now his board held "a supreme disgust for this wretched doctrine."[70]

Eyster was not alone. Draftee I. M. Hay, of Salisbury, Pennsylvania, in Somerset County, complained bitterly about the exemption of his Amish neighbors who "are the strongest advocates of the war and have all along done their best to get others to go." Hay believed that "there is a bad feeling existing among neighbors in our community on account of this conscientious business."[71] Very late in the war, Cambria County's *Johnstown Democrat* registered its objection to those who "are conscientiously opposed to fighting, though they encourage their neighbors to fight." "How very conscientious some men are in these times of draft," the paper said sarcastically, particularly those who voted for Lincoln. "They either ignored their scruples in voting, or their oaths smell very rank . . . of cowardice."[72]

Already in July 1864, Lancaster's Democratic *Intelligencer* had voiced similar charges and criticized the revised conscription law as "one of the foulest outrages" for allowing certain religious groups the benefit of the $300 commutation clause denied to the general population. That was a blow to common laborers whom the *Intelligencer* championed. Of course, the legislation favored "the wealthy German farmers of Lancaster and other counties, who happen to belong to the Mennonitsh or similar Christian denominations." They only have to pay a "paltry" commutation fee. "And for this boon they are mainly indebted to THADDEUS STEVENS who wants their votes this fall to re-elect him to Congress." A week later the *Intelligencer* was still ranting about Mennonites. Why do they "vote for the war candidates?" the paper asked. If they think war is wrong "why do they vote for the candidates pledged to its continuance?"[73]

"Inconsistencies of the Mennonites [and] Omish"

As the 1864 elections approached, Mennonites stood ready to reaffirm their affection to "Old Thad." If the previous two years had demonstrated Stevens' commitment to them, the ballot box provided an opportunity for payback—and an occasion for opposition criticism. By now Democrats were certain they knew where Mennonite loyalties lay, and editors at Lancaster's *Intelligencer* were ready. The 1864 election saw all House seats—including Stevens'—up for grabs, as well as the presidency. Running for reelection in the midst of a war that had dragged on too long, Lincoln believed he might well lose. The Democrats had nominated Maj. General George B. McClellan, the one-time Union commander who had secured few victories but who remained popular with many soldiers and who offered an experienced alternative to voters wanting a shift in war policy. What such a shift might mean remained unclear, however, since McClellan made reunion a condition for ending hostilities, while his Democratic Party's "peace platform" called for immediate truce and negotiations.[74]

In September, as the election approached, the *Intelligencer* printed a sharp attack on "The Inconsistencies of the Mennonites [and] Omish," which have become "grave and religiously offensive in these deplorable war times."[75] Pseudonymous author "Union" claimed that the groups were "scrupulously exact" when it comes to being "harmless and defenceless," but when "it comes to voting for candidates for office who are for war," their consciences suddenly are not so tender. The writer quoted from Anabaptist articles of faith and then asked how such professors will "appear before God, their Judge, when at the next elections they roll up thousands of votes for the Abolition war ticket." In reelecting Stevens, he said, the Mennonites and Amish only help continue war. Moreover, after their votes for Lincoln in 1860 helped "to destroy the Union" in the first place, these people "placidly wash their hands" of blood. The only consistent thing for Mennonites to do, the essayist said, was to follow the example of the small Reformed Mennonite group whose members did not vote.[76]

A month later, right before the election, and under the signature of "Your Friend," a long and tedious piece appeared in the *Intelligencer*, addressed to "Members of the Menonite, Dunker, Ommish and Friends Persuasions." The author declared that he also believed in the peace that Jesus taught but wondered how members of these churches could vote for a president who would take "every man and every dollar at his command." If nonresistants wanted peace, they should vote for McClellan, who would "order a cessation of hostilities" and hold a convention of the States to end the bloodshed.[77]

Shifting the argument, the author pointed to the plight of "brothers belonging to your denominations living in the South, particularly in Shenandoah Valley in Virginia, who are just as loyal as any of you." These church members have suffered greatly at the hands of Union armies that have recently "destroyed all hay and grain together with all their farming implements" that "will 'starve out' and turn houseless more Union men, *women and children.*" How "can you then vote for a man who, if elected, will call upon you and your neighbors to go and kill your brothers, and devastate their properties?" the paper asked. "Will you do the fighting? If not, then in God's name do not elect him."[78]

Once more the *Intelligencer* questioned the Mennonite-Republican alliance, this time in a piece by a "Descendant of the Mennonites."[79] "If I have not been misinformed," the writer began, some Mennonite leaders of the area had advised that their people could vote Republican "without violating" their consciences. If that is true, then "Descendant" had a few questions. If it is wrong to draw the sword, why place that sword in Lincoln's hand? "Do not those of you who work or vote for the re-election of Mr. Lincoln stand in the position of the supposed disobedient disciple?"

Surely it must be clear that a vote for Lincoln means war "in which brother is killing brother." Mennonite suffering in the Shenandoah Valley at the hands of Union troops only illustrated the biblical truth that "those that take the sword shall perish by the sword."

"For your vote you are clearly answerable only to God and your conscience," the writer continued, but if as "non-resisting Christians" you realize that you cannot give your vote to Republicans who "will continue to use the sword and torch," consider voting for McClellan. The "cannon, sword and torch" are devastating "some of the fairest portions of our land, sweeping thousands of human souls unprepared into eternity, burning houses over the heads of helpless and unoffending women and children." Where is "the voice of Christian moderation and forbearance"? McClellan promised peace and prosperity as "a national man, a Christian, and not a politician like Mr. Lincoln!"[80]

Did such public criticism change or limit the Mennonite or Amish vote? Perhaps it contributed to conservative-minded Weaverland Mennonite minister John B. Weber's tortured conscience when he wrote from Spring Grove in Lancaster County about the war, "that all of us have heaped wood upon this fire."[81] Maybe it even prompted some Republican leaders to redouble their efforts in retaining the nonresistants. In mid-October, Elizabethtown's John Naille wrote Congressman Stevens suggesting how to shore up support "among the dunkers & Menonistes" in the face of "immediate peace" claims on the part of McClellan Democrats. Naille urged Stevens to find "men who can talk plain & simple" to these people.[82] In any case, the election results suggest that Lancaster's nonresistant voters came through for Stevens and Lincoln as the opposition feared they would.[83] By a sizable majority (13,466 to 7,987), Lancaster County backed Lincoln and Stevens, with support in Mennonite and Amish populated sections especially strong.[84]

There was one publicly dissenting Lancaster Mennonite voice in the run-up to the electoral contest. The exceptionally talented Reformed Mennonite polemicist and physician Daniel Musser, of Lampeter, published a 74-page pair of essays under the title *Non-Resistance Asserted*. The style and contents were not unsophisticated and suggested twin audiences. On the one hand, Musser sought to convince Just War Tradition readers and patriots who claimed the Christian mantle that "the kingdom of Christ is founded on the principle of love, forbearance, patience and passive submission to injustice and wrong, or evil in any shape." The truly converted received enough grace to bear persecution and to surrender the material goods of this world that violence was calculated to defend. Moreover, from a practical standpoint, human knowledge of the will of God was too clouded for Christians to choose sides in life-and-death battles.[85]

Simultaneously, Musser directed his argument to "those who profess the principle" of nonresistance but do not "correctly understand it, act inconsistently, and thereby bring the profession into disrepute and contempt." Should it be any surprise that patriotic soldiers sacrificing for "their country and Government, should feel some jealousy" toward Mennonites who participate in party politics but not on the battlefield? Musser asked. Revealing the highly sectarian underpinnings of his Reformed Mennonite theology, Musser argued: "There is but one way in which non-resistance can be consistent. That is, by entirely separating the kingdom of Christ and that of this world. . . . [so] that those who constitute the Church do not take any part in, or exert any influence over the Government, either individually or collectively."[86]

In 1862, Musser reminded readers, "Thaddeus Stevens was the avowed war candidate for Congress from this county, pledged to support the Administration in a vigorous prosecution of the war." Many men who professed nonresistance voted for him, knowing his position, but afterward "came forward and affirmed that they were conscientious, and could not fight!" The next year the pattern repeated when "very large numbers of these 'non-resistants,' both young and old, voted for Governor Curtin" and then refused his call to arms. "Those who cast their suffrage for the President placed him in office," Musser continued, "and put the sword into his hands; and I do not see how anyone can contend that it is sin for him to use it, and not for them to give him power to do so!"[87]

Musser backed his argument with a radically democratic political theory that had no place for minority voices and committed all participants to the course set by the majority. Such theorizing was fine with him, since true Christians were bound to be outsiders in any case: "They live in the kingdom of the world by tolerance only. . . . They do not feel concerned about the laws or institutions of the country wherein they are strangers." Using a metaphor that would have resonated with the era's nativists, Musser likened Christians in this world to immigrant aliens in the United States, who must not influence the government in any way and

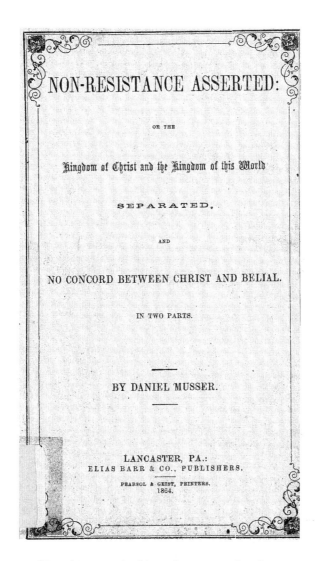

NON-RESISTANCE ASSERTED:

OR THE

𝔎𝔦𝔫𝔤𝔡𝔬𝔪 𝔬𝔣 ℭ𝔥𝔯𝔦𝔰𝔱 𝔞𝔫𝔡 𝔱𝔥𝔢 𝔎𝔦𝔫𝔤𝔡𝔬𝔪 𝔬𝔣 𝔱𝔥𝔦𝔰 𝔚𝔬𝔯𝔩𝔡

SEPARATED,

AND

NO CONCORD BETWEEN CHRIST AND BELIAL.

IN TWO PARTS.

BY DANIEL MUSSER.

LANCASTER, PA.:
ELIAS BARR & CO., PUBLISHERS.

PEARSOL & GEIST, PRINTERS.
1864.

Title page of Daniel Musser's booklet outlining an apolitical nonresistance.
Credit: Mennonite Historical Library, Goshen, Ind.

who should never forget that they are momentarily tolerated guests making use of other people's property.[88] Similarly, believers must stand ready to surrender their property to the state—typically in the form of taxes, and now too as draft exemption fees. Hiring conscription substitutes, however, was not acceptable since it compromised separation, as did voting, office holding, and petitioning.[89] In short, the truly converted nonresistant Christian was apolitical, condemning neither Republican nor Democrat, judging neither North or South, but humbly submitting to God's sovereign will and living faithfully in a parallel universe that was the kingdom of God.[90] If public criticism of nonresistant political participation was suddenly popular in the context of the draft, for Musser it merely brought to light a fundamental inconsistency that had been there all along.

Musser's rational argument presented a simple dichotomy in anything but simplistic terms. Several decades later his booklet fell into the hands of Russian novelist Leo Tolstoy, who cited it favorably, attracted to its highly sectarian and world-denying message.[91] But among eastern Pennsylvania Mennonites, Musser was in the minority. Perhaps the still-sore relations between his Reformed Mennonites group and the larger (Old) Mennonite church, stemming from the schism between the two, prevented most Mennonites from taking Musser seriously or even reading his essays. But even if, or when, they had read it, Musser's highly sectarian sensibilities did not square with their wartime experience in which the state, in the shape of "Old Thad" Stevens, could be a benevolent distributor of privileges and a genuine listening ear, and in which the ballot box was a vehicle for majorities to secure minority privileges. For Stevens' Mennonites, political engagement was critical to obtaining distinctive status as a separate people, not antithetical to it. In the Midwest, however, views that were much closer to Musser's were becoming the Mennonite mainstream.

﹦ CHAPTER 8 ﹦

Did Jesus Christ Teach Men to War?

Equal Burdens?

Deacon Jacob Nold was frustrated with his fellow Columbiana County, Ohio, Mennonites. Federal conscription had been in place for several months, but it was proving difficult to organize a mutual aid plan to help draftees cover their exemption fees. Writing in October 1863 to his minister friend Johannes Gross in eastern Pennsylvania's Bucks County, Nold admitted that the trouble had surfaced already the year before. "The [state] draft when it was placed in our community [in 1862] also hit a few persons who were poor brothers, and we thought about having a tax on the church to help them," Nold explained, "but we could not bring that much together." Now, a year later, Nold made a new appeal that the cost of commutation be "an equal burden to the rich and the poor." At first "the entire church was agreed," but then "a few brothers who have a lot of wealth, but . . . have no son in the draft . . . opposed it rather hard, so that it fell through again."[1]

As a successful businessman and a deacon responsible for the welfare of his congregation, Nold had hoped that each member would give "according to his means" and "regretted that in this troubled time things are so unequal." As relative newcomers to the region, perhaps his people were less well established than those in eastern Pennsylvania, whose wealth often outpaced their neighbors. Yet Nold believed that at least a few Columbiana nonresistants were reaping "profit from the war," which added to his chagrin. Some "must suffer and pay much, while others are making more money than in peace times," he was sure. More troubling, Nold heard of "heathenish carrying on in the name of politics" among some Mennonites. Thankfully, partisan activity was not common in his congregation, but "the party spirit is hard to keep out of the churches."[2]

Holmes County, Ohio, native Joseph Longenecker, son of Mennonites Peter and Elizabeth (Shank) Longenecker, was also disappointed with attitudes that the draft revealed in his home community, but for reasons quite different from Nold's. Longenecker was in Union uniform at Murfreesboro, Tennessee, when he wrote home in June 1863. He had just witnessed the execution of an accused deserter, describing the grim ritual in some detail. But what troubled Longenecker more was the news he was getting from Holmes County. Could it really be true, as he had learned from a recent newspaper account, that hundreds of Holmes countians would resist the draft? Longenecker found the possibility offensive. "One who is too much of a coward to fight for his home is also too big a coward to let himself be shot by resisting," he declared.[3]

Jacob Nold and Joseph Longenecker sounded some of the divergent themes that marked Midwestern Mennonite and Amish experiences in the later years of the war. Like Longenecker, federal troops were becoming impatient with the Midwest's vocal war critics—critics whose views permeated the secular newspapers serving some key Mennonite and Amish communities.[4] Such partisanship, in turn, had apparently pushed some nonresistants into the Democratic "Copperhead" camp, while attaching others more firmly to the Republican administration. Yet any political identification bothered Nold, who believed it compromised church integrity. Indeed, his sense of civic separatism illustrated a thread of Mennonite and Amish thought that was coming to mark the weave of theology among these groups west of the Alleghenies. Its articulation by new and influential Midwestern voices would prove to be a crucial legacy of the war.

In 1863 the federal draft was often a focus of emotional rhetoric, and communities debated the war's wisdom and the limits of loyalty and dissent. That spring, Mennonite-reared John Longenecker of the Ohio 102nd wrote that men in his camp would like "every rebel sympathizer in the North [to be] drafted and compelled to fight or be shot. I do hope the conscription law will force every enemy to the Government into the field."[5] At about the same time, in Wells County, Indiana, home to a portion of the

Swiss Mennonite and Amish immigrant community in the eastern part of that state, the *Bluffton Banner* ran an editorial surrounded by a thick black band of the sort typically used to frame an obituary, openly criticizing conscription. "If old Abe says 'fight for the nigger,' (as he will) the only alternative left is to go and fight, or be hunted down as a rebel," the paper charged.[6] Enrollment for the draft here even sparked a case of violent resistance when two men assaulted an enroller and tore up his lists.[7] Perhaps Mennonite and Amish readers in the region were more taken with the protest that came in the form of a pious poem printed in a March 1864 issue of the Decatur, Indiana, *Eagle*. Entitled "The Conscientious Objector," the anonymous stanzas asked:

> *Did Jesus Christ teach men to war?*
> *To fight, to slay, and kill?*
> *Oh no, he taught more peaceful truths—*
> *He taught his Father's will.*
> > *Put up thy sword into his place,*
> > *Now Peter I command—*
> > *Who takes the sword must die by it*
> > *Mine is a peaceful band.*
> *My kingdom is not of this world,*
> *Else would my servants fight!*[8]

While politically inspired resentment of the draft was common in many of the areas where Midwestern nonresistants lived, actual conscription in such places was far from systematic. In that sense the draft was hardly "an equal burden," to use Jacob Nold's term in a different sense. Many communities in Ohio, Indiana, Illinois, and Iowa did not conduct a draft in 1863, their quotas initially covered by volunteers enticed by the rising price of bounties. In Ohio, for example, the average enlistment bounty in 1862 was $25; in 1863 it was $100; in 1864, $400; and very late in the war, $500 to $800.[9] Other enlistees were motivated by news of the "rebel hordes" invading neighboring Pennsylvania in 1863, or by the Confederate guerilla cavalry known as Morgan's Raiders, who rode across southern Indiana and Ohio before being captured in Salem (near the Columbiana County Mennonite community) by local vigilantes. Indeed, such threats pushed the Ohio legislature to increase state militia pay to $1 a day or $2 for a day and night—much better pay than federal privates received—and the state troops that move produced also counted toward Ohio's federal draft quotas.[10]

Still, in the Ohio counties of Mahoning and Columbiana, several townships with Mennonite populations did not produce enough volunteers and needed to draft seventy or eighty men in the fall of 1863.[11] To the west, in the state's 14th District that included Wayne, Holmes, Medina, Ashland, and Lorain counties, brisk enlistment initially postponed a draft. In early 1864 the *Wooster Republican* proudly noted that every township in Wayne County (except Wooster!) had again filled its quota and that no draft would be needed. It also pointed out that the previous winter "about 13 meetings" had been held to raise money for bounties.[12] In Wayne County's Green Township a few men were drafted on May 17, 1864, including John W. Miller and John J. Zook, both of whom paid the commutation fee. Wooster Township's sixty-three draftees likely included a number of Amish and Mennonites.[13] The rest of Wayne County again met its quota through volunteers. By September 1864, however, Wayne County needed to draw 352 names for the draft, quite a number of them apparently Amish or Mennonites (see table 8.1).

To the south, in Berlin Township, Holmes County, six were drafted in May 1864, including Amishmen Daniel D. Mast, Martin S. Weaver, and Moses J. Yoder. Mast and Weaver paid the commutation fee, and Yoder was discharged for health reasons. The following month a small supplemental draft snagged Samuel S. Mast and John Christner from Berlin Township, both of whom paid the commutation fee. In German Township eleven were drafted, the majority of whom appear to have been Amish.[14]

Adding to the conscription mix in Ohio was a March 31, 1864, reorganization of the state militia. All men age 18 to 45 now had to obtain a physical disability certificate, join a volunteer company, or pay an annual state militia commutation fee of $4. It is not clear exactly how the law's provisions fit with concurrent federal conscription. In any case, the first deadline was August 15, and men not in compliance would be assessed a 30 percent penalty on their $4 fee. Furthermore, should a draft be ordered to fill any organized company, it was to be made first from those who had not paid the fee.[15] The *Holmes County Farmer* was indignant at yet another military exemption charge. "Only *four dollars*, gentlemen, and no backing out," sneered the editor. "It is cheap—cheap as greenbacks! Walk up—pay

Table 8.1 Likely Mennonite and Amish draftees, Wayne County, Ohio, September 1864

Green Township	Age	County Where Born	Occupation	Remarks
Elias Hartzler	40	Wayne	Farmer	Conscientious, paid fee
Jonas Smooker	24	Wayne	Farmer	Conscientious, paid fee
David Hostetler	25	Wayne	Farmer	Conscientious, paid fee
John Weaver	21	Wayne	Laborer	Held to service[a]
Eli Winger				Failed to report
Adam K. Kurtz	21	Mifflin[b]	Farmer	Held to service, furnished a substitute for 1 year
Jacob Y. Kurtz	36	Mifflin[b]	Carpenter	Conscientious, paid fee
Christian King	26	Wayne	Farmer	Conscientious, paid fee
David Kauffman				Failed to report
Christian Schrock	25	Wayne	Teacher	Conscientious, paid fee
Samuel Schrock	44	Somerset[a]	Farmer	Conscientious, paid fee Discharged, non-residence
David Hooley	34	Mifflin[b]	Farmer	Conscientious, paid fee
Jonas Yoder	38	Centre[b]	Farmer	Conscientious, paid fee
Stephen Yoder				Failed to report
Solomon Hartzler	35	Wayne	Farmer	Conscientious, paid fee
David King				Failed to report
Moses Yoder			Farmer	Failed to report; said to be Pennsylvania resident
David Amstutz	24	Wayne	Farmer	Furnished substitute for 1 yr.
Moses Yoder	36	Centre[b]	Laborer	Conscientious, paid fee
Saml. Hoover	41	Lancaster[b]	Wagonmaker	Held to service[b]
Daniel Hooley				Deserted after 100 days service
Gideon Plank	23	Wayne	Carpenter	Conscientious, paid fee
Jacob D. Yoder	22	Centre[b]	Tobacconist	Held to service
Aaron Stutzman	23	Wayne	Teacher	Left side hernia
John Miller	42	Centre[b]	Saddler	Impaired vision

continued

Table 8.1 continued

Paint Township	Age	County Where Born	Occupation	Remarks
Samuel Amstutz	29	[d]	Farmer	Conscientious, paid fee
Martin Buckwalter	28	Wayne	Farmer	Held to service
John Raber	32	Berks[b]	Shoemaker	Loss of teeth

Source: Record Group 110, #4837 - "Proceedings of the Board of Enrollment May 1863–Jan. 1865, and #4840 - "Descriptive Book of Drafted Men, May–Oct. 1864," Part VI, Ohio and Indiana, 14th District, Ohio, National Archives; Wooster Republican, Oct. 6, 1864. Samuel Amstutz from Paint Township was the brother of coauthor James O.Lehman's great-grandfather.

Note: These names believed to be Mennonite or Amish. The Oak Grove Amish congregation of Green Township was heavily hit in this draft. David Amstutz was from the Chippewa Swiss (later Crown Hill) Mennonite Church.

[a] Additional note in different handwriting—"Dischg. Quota full"

[b] Pennsylvania.

[c] In large handwriting up and down page "Discharged Quota filled by volunteers," but then no information is given on Samuel Amstutz and others who had paid the fee, as to whether the fee was refunded.

[d] Born in Switzerland.

up, and get your receipt! No questions! No grumbling!"[16] Records of this fee in Fulton County, in the state's northwest corner, demonstrate Amish nonparticipation in the militia there. In German Township, home to a sizable Amish Mennonite immigrant community, the list of men paying the $4 militia commutation fee ran to seventy-five names[17] (see table 8.2).

Heavy volunteer enlistments in northern Indiana cancelled the 1863 draft there. Until that fact became clear, however, the *Goshen Times* and *Goshen Democrat*, along with Elkhart papers, kept local people informed that a draft might be necessary.[18] The next year locals tried again to avert conscription by enticing volunteers with handsome bounties. John E. "Hansi" Borntreger, an Amishman from LaGrange County, wrote in his diary on September 4, 1864, that he had attended a "war meeting to raise bounty to buy recruits." He had done so three times that year and had contributed a total of $42.10.[19] At the time, the tradition-minded Borntreger was siding with the Old Order wing of his church, although other con-

Table 8.2 Men paying the $4 militia commutation, German Township, Fulton County, Ohio, 1864

Jacob Bender	Christian King	Joseph Nofziger
Peter Burkholder	Joseph King	Peter Nofziger
John Burkholder	John Hartzler	Valentine Nofziger
Christian Burkholder	Nicholas King Jr.	John F. Nofziger
Peter Beck	Christian King Jr.	David Nofziger
Jacob Fry	Samuel King Sr.	John B. Nofziger
Joseph Garrick	Joseph Kloppenstein	Joseph C. Nofziger
Jacob J. Griser	Benedict Kloppenstein	Joseph Nofziger[d]
Frederick Griser	Daniel Grieser	Peter Nofziger[d]
Christian Garrick	Eli Graber	Christian Nofziger Sr.
Christian J. Eicher	Peter Nofziger	Joseph Lichty
Peter Eicher	Jacob Nofziger	Levi Lantz
John Rupp Jr.	Jacob Rupp	Jacob Ruppe[e]
Christian Rupp Jr.	Peter Rupp	John Rufenacht
Joseph Roth	Christian Rupp Sr.	Christian Roth Jr.
John Rupp[a]	Daniel Short	Benedict Short
Christian Short	John Schad	Christian Schad
Joseph Schad	Joseph Schad[b]	Levi Neusbaum
Daniel Rupp	Christian Rupp[c]	Joseph F. Roth
Peter Roth	John Rupp Jr.	Peter Schad Jr.
John Schwartz	Joel Schmucker	John S. Stutsman
Moses Stutsman	John F. Wyse	John Wyse
Peter Wyse	Simeon Wyse	Jeptha Wyse
John Weaver	Jacob Weaver	Christian Wyse
Daniel Yoder	Jacob Zimmerman	Jacob Zimmerman Jr.

Source: Fulton Co. Militia Records, 1864, located at Northwest Ohio—Great Lakes Research Center, Bowling Green State University, Bowling Green, Ohio.

[a] Son of Joseph.
[b] Wagonmaker.
[c] Son of John.
[d] Son of Joseph.
[e] Son of Jacob.

servative Amish typically favored draftees paying the commutation fee instead of buying substitutes or providing bounty money to entice volunteers.

In June 1863 in eastern Indiana's Adams County, the *Decatur Eagle*, possibly with reference to the area's Swiss Anabaptist immigrants, noted that enrollment did not include those who had not taken out citizenship papers. Recognizing "that there is a large class of such in this county," the editor wanted them to know their rights.[20] Amish minister Henry Egly, from near the Adams County village of Geneva, was a progressive-minded immigrant who, according to tradition, was drafted and paid the commutation fee.[21] Egly's interest in evangelical revivalism had led to his parting ways with most other Amish leaders in 1865, but he was not joining the popular Protestant war cause.

Enlistments in Illinois and Iowa districts with Mennonite and Amish settlements generally were active enough in 1863 so that drafts did not materialize. In both of these states as well as in Indiana, some pockets of resistance to enrollment and the threat of a draft erupted. Most frequently such resistance occurred in counties where Democratic editors and politicians had strong influence. More than two-thirds of counties with disturbances had below average per capita wealth, suggesting class resentments on the part of poor citizens. In the central Illinois counties of Bureau, Putnam, Woodford, Tazewell, McLean, and Livingston (districts five and eight), where six Amish congregations were clustered, things were generally peaceful, though farther south two other districts experienced unrest.[22]

In the summer of 1864, after the repeal of the commutation clause for the general public, the only exemption possibility for men who could not claim conscience was to buy substitutes. As a result, the price rose dramatically, affecting drafted Amish and Mennonite sons who had not joined the church in time to qualify for conscientious objector status.[23] David Burkholder, of Locke (now Nappanee), Indiana, was one such draftee who ended up paying $600 for a substitute. A year later he was baptized into the (Old) Mennonite Church, and he eventually became a leading bishop.[24] In southeastern Iowa only one person connected to the Davis County Amish congregation, Christian Baughman, was drafted. That occurred late in the war, and tradition says he had to sell his 80-acre farm to afford a substitute.[25]

Church members had to provide proof of religious standing to qualify for the $300 conscientious commutation option. Thus in 1864 the Partridge Creek, Illinois, Amish bishop, Andrew Baughman, accompanied men from his Woodford County church to Springfield to affirm that they were members in good standing.[26] Early the next year, Swiss immigrant Amish bishop Peter Graber Sr., of Allen County, Indiana, witnessed a formal document attesting to the fact that his son had "been for more than five years past a true and active member" of the "Anabaptist faith and religion." Two other ministers and five lay members also signed the statement, which Bishop Graber then had notarized on January 20, 1865, in nearby Fort Wayne.[27]

Although Iowa Amishman Samuel D. Guengerich had been a church member for ten years at the time he was drafted, he could not easily call on his bishop to testify on his behalf. Guengerich's situation was unusual because he was drafted in his place of birth, Somerset County, Pennsylvania, even though he had been a child when his family had left there and moved west. Guengerich had returned briefly to Somerset County to marry Barbara Beachy when a federal marshal notified Guengerich that on March 11, 1865, his name had been enrolled and chosen to fill the southwestern Pennsylvania quota. Separated from his church in Johnson County, Iowa, but among people who knew him and remembered his family, Guengerich filed a "solemn affirmation" of scruples and had local Somerset County citizens certify that his "deportment has been consistent with his above declaration [of conscience]."[28]

Although the revised federal draft included provision for doing hospital work in lieu of paying the $300 commutation fee, there is no evidence of Mennonites or Amish availing themselves of the option except in the small southern Indiana Bower Mennonite congregation, whose members lived in Clay and Owen counties. There, member George Funk reported that bishop Jacob Bower baptized six men in the fall of 1864. Four of them—including two with families—had been drafted. But because they were baptized after being drafted, Funk said they were "compelled to go" but "were permitted to go into the hospitals and wait on the sick, which we believe is not contrary to the dictates of our consciences, and no violation of the Gospel or the principles of our church."[29]

The Politics of Resistance

Northern Mennonites and Amish who refused military cooperation typically did so through legal channels of exemption, though family lore has passed on a few stories of furtive noncompliance. For example, Amishman Christian Eash of Howard County, Indiana, is said to have hidden his three drafted sons, Daniel, Christian Jr., and Noah. The young men apparently were not church members and, drafted late in the war, were ineligible to pay the commutation fee. Father Eash surreptitiously placed a basket of food for them "at a stated place every evening" until the danger passed.[30] In northern Wayne County, Ohio, Daniel and Magdalena (Basinger) Steiner of the Swiss Chippewa congregation engaged in civil disobedience when they hid their one-time hired hand, Pete Veney, who was not a Mennonite, after he deserted from the army.[31]

More dramatic resistance to conscription, along with public opposition to the Lincoln administration, was common in some areas where Midwestern Amish and Mennonites lived. Whether or not nonresistants participated in such protest, vocal dissent was a public part of their neighborhoods. In the sizeable immigrant Swiss Mennonite and Amish community in Adams and Wells counties in eastern Indiana, the Democratic newspapers—the *Decatur Eagle* and the *Bluffton Banner*—reported sharp local criticism of the government. At the mass rally in Adams County's Jefferson Township in late March 1863, residents adopted resolutions calling for the cessation of hostilities, ending conscription, and discouraging abolition.[32] Elsewhere in Indiana, residents killed two enrolling officers and wounded several others.[33]

In Holmes County, Ohio, the *Farmer* mocked "Abolitionists" who were "prompted by Hell's blackest minions to secure the freedom of the negroes." When President Lincoln called for a day of prayer and fasting, the *Farmer* averred that if anyone "this side of perdition" needed prayer, "it is the sinners now at the head of Government—A. Lincoln & Co."[34] Then, in early June 1863, Holmes County experienced its own "draft riot" after someone heaved a stone at a draft enroller, sparking several arrests.[35] An armed group of about seventy men then "violently rescued" four of those imprisoned. The acting assistant provost marshal reported the number of "insurgents" as seven to nine hundred, and called in troops. The 15th Ohio

Infantry arrived, but not before disgruntled citizens drove enrollment officers out of two townships. Soldiers fired on one group of insurgents, captured a few, and sent them to Cleveland. In the meantime, reporters showed up at the "seat of war"—later dubbed "Fort Fizzle"—and the resistance made the *New York Times*. Even Mennonites in eastern Pennsylvania could read all about it in the German *Neutralist und Allgemeine Neuigkeits-Bote* of Skippack.[36]

All the events centered in Richland Township, in the western part of Holmes County, some distance from the Amish and Mennonite population concentrated to the east. It does not appear that members of nonresistant churches became involved in the fracas, although at about the same time, Abraham Rohrer, bishop of the Medina County Mennonites forty miles north, wrote that he was "deeply troubled" about "the great trouble or wrong-doing that is said to have taken place in Holmes County." He had taken pains to teach that Mennonites "desire to be peaceable and loyal to the government" and "would expel any transgressor publicly before the entire congregation" who did not "submit to the government in the paying of toll, tax and fees."[37]

Clearly, some Mennonites were uncomfortable with sharp anti-Republican rhetoric and supported the administration. Mennonite bishop Jonas Shank, from Putnam County, Ohio, wrote his Maryland brother that the war "will leave a Stain upon america as long as the world Remains." But equally troubling were the many Copperhead Democrats in his county who were making "heavy threats of resistens against the draft." Unfortunately, Shank explained, most good Union men were gone to war, leaving the troublesome Democrats "sticking at home" to stir things up.[38]

Yet election results suggest that some Amish and Mennonites were casting votes for the opposition. The unusual 1863 gubernatorial election in Ohio pitted John Brough (who had replaced incumbent Governor Tod) on the Republican ballot, against the nominee of the opposition "Peace Democrats," Clement L. Vallandigham, an outspoken war critic. A Congressman since 1858, Vallandigham had been gerrymandered out of office by Republicans prior to the fall 1862 elections, and he thereafter denounced the administration and openly courted arrest with arguably treasonous speeches that eventually got him convicted. Not wanting to make a political martyr of Vallandigham, President Lincoln commuted his sentence and banished him to Canada, whereupon Vallandigham campaigned for governor from Ontario.[39] The resulting contest could not have been a starker referendum on the Republican program for the war.

Although Brough handily won the statewide election by 61,752 votes, areas with heavy Mennonite and Amish populations often supported Vallandigham. The *Farmer* crowed about "Glorious Little Holmes" County chalking up a substantial 1,428-vote majority for Vallandigham.[40] And the results were even more dramatic in detail. In the heavily Amish townships of German and Walnut Creek, the vote was 248 to 25 and 180 to 13 in favor of Vallandigham. Holmes County's Paint Township voted 220 to 70 for the Democrat, while in Wayne County's Paint Township, it was 203 to 71. Also in Wayne County, Sugar Creek Township, where many Swiss Mennonites lived, voted 233 to 160 in favor of Vallandigham; and Green Township, with numerous Mennonites and Amish, tallied 172 to 23 in favor of the Democrat. In Wayne County as a whole, Vallandigham barely won, making his larger majorities in Mennonite and Amish townships even more striking.[41] Vallandigham also did well in Allen and Putnam counties, home to immigrant Swiss and (Old) Mennonite communities.[42] Of course, the numbers provide no proof of how particular Amish and Mennonites voted, but they suggest support for Vallandigham and a local political context in which partisan activity was sharply critical of the war.[43]

"Do Not Interfere with Political Affairs"

Late in the summer of 1864, returning to his Elida, Ohio, home from a preaching mission in Illinois, (Old) Mennonite bishop John M. Brenneman noted that farmers in the places he had visited were getting rich as crops did well that summer and war-inflated prices were high. For rural economies, that combination might seem providential, but for Brenneman, it was a sure path to perdition: "As riches increase, Pride and forgetfulness of God also increases." Meanwhile, the bishop noted a number of Mennonite sons from his circle of friends who had joined the army. All of this pointed to larger drama underway. "I think this Bloody war will be the means more propperly to Sift or Sepperate the truly Conscientious from the worldly minded," he remarked. "Theas two opposite kingdoms have been too much Blended & mingled together."[44] Delineating those realms—the peaceful church and the violent world—was a task Brenneman and other Midwestern leaders had taken up.

Indeed, in this context, a number of influential voices emerged in Mennonite and Amish circles that collectively articulated a fresh consensus on the meaning of nonresistance and its social and political implications. In highly sectarian style, this approach asserted a sharp distinction between the ethics of the church and those of the world as represented by the government. So incompatible were these worlds that Christian integrity seemed to require a sort of civic withdrawal, since voluntary personal involvement in governmental affairs implicated one in all the wicked ways of the state. Twin publications issued in the latter part of 1863 by young John F. Funk in Chicago and seasoned bishop Brenneman of western Ohio were notable new statements in this regard, but church conference minutes and correspondence echoed such sentiments. Moreover, in 1864 Funk launched a bimonthly periodical for (Old) Mennonites and Amish Mennonites—a first of its kind—that ensured wider dissemination of these convictions.

An enthusiastic patriot at the time of Fort Sumter's fall, Funk had by 1863 undergone a dramatic ideological evolution.[45] Early in the war, his lively letters to *Das Christliche Volks-Blatt*, the magazine issued by progressive General Conference Mennonite leader John H. Oberholtzer of Milford Square, Pennsylvania, revealed some of Funk's growing ambivalence about the war. Funk documented Chicago's intense war fever and his own anxiety when Union forces fared poorly on the battlefield.[46] He hesitated to go as a soldier, though in 1862 his reasoning was ambiguous. Believing that the state militia would soon be called, he noted in his diary that he "would go just as willingly as do anything else, if my faith and belief in the justice of violent measures at any time and in any case allowed me to do so. It would be wrong for me to go before my government compels me to do it."[47]

Funk's feelings about war began to shift in October 1862, after he traveled from Chicago to Elkhart County, Indiana, to attend the annual conference of Mennonite ministers from that state and from Ohio. There he heard the powerful preacher and bishop John M. Brenneman, who expressed concern for how peace principles were playing out among Mennonites. Funk was impressed as he watched forty-six "new converts" baptized and as he sensed the piety present among those gathered for the occasion.[48] Funk had been baptized in Pennsylvania, but living in Chicago without any Mennonite church to attend, he had been moving in evangelical Protestant circles. The Elkhart conference made an impression on Funk, and at Christmastime 1862, he went to visit his Bucks County, Pennsylvania, home with a new interest in Mennonite faith.

On Sunday morning Funk went to the Line Lexington meetinghouse that he had attended as a boy. There he listened to a sermon by the church's venerable preacher, 84-year-old John Geil, whose six-foot height and shoulder-length white hair contributed to his striking patriarchal pose. Perhaps the emotion associated with a return home enhanced the sermon for Funk, but he found it a "sacred feast" for the soul. After the service, Geil made his way to the meetinghouse stove to light his pipe and converse with congregants. There he met Funk. Geil, whose own grandson had gone off to war, asked the sophisticated Chicagoan, "Have they made a soldier of you?" "No," Funk responded, "I would make a poor soldier—I would not fight." "Yes," the old minister replied, "that has always been our privilege and we shall probably always retain it."[49] What the exchange may have meant for Funk at the time is unclear, but it was an encounter he later noted as significant.

Funk returned to his business engagements and Sunday school evangelism in the Windy City and mulled the fact that "so many of our Mennonite boys had already and were still enlisting," apparently no longer entertaining any possibility of military participation himself.[50] Then, in May 1863, he received an unexpected visit. Ohio's bishop John Brenneman and Lancaster County, Pennsylvania, minister Peter Nissley stopped in Chicago on their way from visiting a young Mennonite settlement in Sterling, Illinois.[51] Brenneman knocked on Funk's door on a Sunday morning, then went along with Funk to Third Presbyterian Church, where Funk often attended. Funk was unsure how the two men would respond to the idea of going along to his afternoon Sunday school commitment, given (Old) Mennonite reticence to bless such ecumenical endeavors. But they agreed to accompany him to the Milwaukee Depot Mission, where Funk was superintendent, and were astonished at the school's vitality and the enthusiasm with which the children repeated Christ's words: "Love your enemies, bless them that curse you."[52]

That evening Brenneman and Funk had a long talk. The young man showed Brenneman a partially finished manuscript entitled *Warfare: Its*

Chicago Mennonite businessman John F. Funk (1835–1930) with several of his
Sunday school pupils. Credit: Mennonite Church USA Archives, Goshen, Ind.

Evils, Our Duty. Brenneman was startled by Funk's straightforward pre-
sentation, even wondering if publishing such a plainly anti-war tract
would put Funk in personal danger, but he encouraged Funk to finish it
and have it printed. Funk immediately did so, and by July 22, 1863, he
had 1,000 copies.[53]

Boldly addressing the "Mennonite Churches throughout the United

States and Canada," Funk used stark language and vivid imagery. If his turn toward peace teaching had been sparked in part by the reserved piety at the Line Lexington meetinghouse, he cast his concerns with a dramatic flair more akin to his Chicago context. Indeed, parts of Funk's 16-page tract did not rely on explicitly religious rationale, but instead used graphic word images to portray the senselessness and inhumanity of killing. Funk described "the military hero" who "comes to us with garments red with human gore," and the "thousands" who "have been maimed and cut . . . limb from limb." Yet the essay also developed an unmistakable theological center around Jesus, who provided the message and model for peaceable living. The categorical commands of Christ (which turned into the "duty" of the essay's title) seem impossible, Funk admitted, but "trust in God, he will give you strength" to bless enemies, submit to wrong, and resist retaliation.[54]

Meanwhile, Funk had encouraged John Brenneman to write a book on nonresistance, with Funk promising to see it published. The Ohio bishop agreed, driven by his growing sense that peace teaching was too thin in the scattered and often isolated Mennonite communities of the Midwest that he tried to support. Back in 1855, eleven years after he was ordained, Brenneman had moved from Fairfield County, Ohio, near Columbus, to Allen County on the western side of the state.[55] Both were smaller (Old) Mennonite communities, and Brenneman kept up contacts with similar settlements as well as with larger Mennonite and Amish population centers. In fact, until the late nineteenth century, no Mennonite leader traveled more extensively or spoke more widely. As he visited Midwestern churches during the 1860s, he believed he saw too many defections, and in his own community he was troubled that so many Mennonite men had taken up arms. There was Christian B. Lehman, son of Christian and Elizabeth (Bookwalter) Lehman, who enlisted in 1861 in the Ohio 81st. Or Daniel Stemen, grandson of bishop Henry and Rachel (Beery) Stemen, who enlisted in October 1862 and died at Corinth, Mississippi. Daniel's sister Barbara was married to a Joseph Baker, who left Barbara and their four children for three years of marching. And there were others.[56]

Brenneman drew on his pastoral experience in composing his peace manuscript, and by August 1863 he had it to Funk.[57] On October 20 the printer delivered 2,000 copies of *Christianity and War*, which was three times the length of Funk's booklet.[58] Brenneman's piece began with the wider question of the essence of Christianity. Indeed, it was not until page eighteen that Brenneman got to "the all-important question . . . Can a Christian take up the weapons of death?" For Brenneman, nonresistance was also about following Jesus, but less in the style of obeying directives and more in the vein of having one's personality transformed into that of the meek, selfless Christ, so that violence was a practical impossibility. He wrote at length about the nature of repentance and selfless contrition that led believers to "deny ourselves, to take up our cross." Abandoning ambition was initially difficult, which is why Jesus said, "Narrow is the way which leadeth unto life." But ultimately, "a Christian, who is a partaker of Christ's Spirit and nature," becomes "a harmless and defenseless lamb" for whom the question of war is senseless.[59]

True Christian humility was so alien to the ways of the unregenerate world that there was no point in expecting understanding or accommodation. "Stand aloof!" Brenneman exhorted. "Is it not enough for us to be Christians?" he asked. "Or must we also be called, or call ourselves, after a worldly name—a Democrat or a Republican? Surely we ought to guard against this evil." Politics was an "inconsistency," and anyone who professes and then votes "acts in opposition to the non-resistant principles of their profession." "Therefore, be separate," Brenneman concluded, and "run not with others. . . . let us not be entangled with the trifles and follies of this present evil world."[60]

Perhaps the fact that *Christianity and War* appeared anonymously was a reflection of Brenneman's own deeply formed habit of humility and an effort to deflect public credit for his work. But anonymity may also have stemmed from fear that a pro-war public would not take kindly to the book's contents. Brenneman was "almost certain" that in western Ohio Funk would have been "arrested and imprisoned" for distributing his earlier pamphlet on peace. (Chicagoans must be "more quiet and peaceable" than locals in tiny Elida, Brenneman mused!) The unpopularity of nonresistance translated into "prejudiced toward the Mennonites" that confirmed outsiderhood.[61]

While neighbors may have found Funk's and Brenneman's brand of apolitical nonresistance foreign, if not offensive, for Midwestern (Old) Mennonites and Amish such logic was becoming mainstream. In October 1864, when Indiana and Ohio (Old) Mennonite ministers met for their autumn conference session in Elkhart County, Indiana, the discussion of nonresistance was tied to the question of voting. Since we cannot go and fight, "it is inconsistent for us to vote for worldly officers," the leaders concluded. Voting means that "we would make ourselves liable also even by force to defend and sustain those whom we elect." The assembly "earnestly recommended and enjoined that the brethren do not interfere with political affairs, nor take part in elections." Perhaps such an appeal implied a certain level of participation already taking place, and the conference was aware that some members thought voting was a civic responsibility. But they countered that the "the higher powers would suffer no loss" if Mennonites did not vote. Moreover, the church would have more "union, peace and love."[62]

Some months later, the national Amish ministers' meeting—the annual gathering that had begun in 1862 as a forum for Amish leaders to share matters of mutual concern—heard the testimony of aged bishop Jacob Schwartzendruber of Johnson County, Iowa. In poor health, Schwartzendruber was unable to attend that year's gathering in Wayne County, Ohio, so he sent a letter summarizing his thinking.[63] All violence is forbidden for Christians, declared Schwartzendruber. Instead, they must imitate the humble Christ who taught love for enemies. Articulating an apparently common Amish conviction, the bishop opposed hiring of draft substitutes but approved paying the $300 commutation. The fee was a legitimate tax, but substitution implicated one in mortal combat.

Indeed, personal political participation of any kind was problematic. "Are we doing right in voluntarily supporting the war with money or votes for those who want to wage war?" Schwartzendruber asked. "Our people should all keep themselves apart from all party matters in political things where brother votes against brother, and father against son." Why do "we want to help to rule the world, we who are chosen out of the world by God?" he asked. No, "we are strangers in the world for we are the children of God." Thus, the Iowan insisted, "let the world rule itself," but submit to the state and be "subject in all things that are not contrary to the Word of God."[64]

Schwartzendruber was a tradition-minded leader, but change-minded Amish and (Old) Mennonites soon had another voice—or collection of voices—promoting a similar stance. Shortly after John Funk published his booklet on war, and with the strong encouragement of John M. Brenneman, Funk launched a monthly magazine for Mennonite and Amish readers.

Produced in Chicago beginning in January 1864, the *Herald of Truth* disseminated nonresistant opinion that concurred with editor Funk's thinking. Each issue appeared in English and German companion editions.[65]

Brenneman had suggested that the paper be titled "Advocate of Peace," but Funk thought that name a little too strong, given the tenor of the times. Yet Funk did not shy away from pressing nonresistance of a civic separatist stripe. Nothing is "so wicked and so corrupt and so detrimental to . . . pure Christianity" as a "secular or political paper," the editor explained in the *Herald*'s first issue—a remarkable statement from Funk, who only three years before had eagerly swapped newspaper accounts with his brother in Pennsylvania. In a companion piece, Brenneman promised that the *Herald* would "be free from all . . . political matters." In the same inaugural issue, Brenneman contributed the essay "Peace be with You All that are in Christ Jesus," emphasizing the link between peace with God and peaceful living with others.[66] Both of Brenneman's articles appeared in the German and English issues, but Funk did not try to translate from the German the 12-stanza poem Brenneman had written. Entitled "Kriegs-Lied" (War Song), the poem presented the Civil War as a dire warning.[67]

Ach Menschen wachet auf,	*Oh people, wake up,*
Beschauet doch den Lauf,	*Just observe the course*
Von dieser Zeit,	*Of these times,*
Wo Krieg und Kriegsgeschrei,	*Where war and the cry of war,*
Wo Plagen mancherlei,	*And where many calamities,*
Das Land endzweit.	*Torment the land.*

"How horribly the terrible weapons, so cleverly invented, are cracking, bringing swift death and disaster," one verse intoned. "Neither blood, nor life, nor goods and property are spared. Many are fighting to suppress the enemy with violence, and many struggle for money, fame and honor." Jesus had warned of such times and calls people to repent before the day of judgment.

The new *Herald of Truth* quickly became an unofficial but authoritative churchly voice on the war. In May 1864, Brenneman chided Mennonites and Amish who "are conscientiously opposed, with the arm of flesh to do battle for the kingdom of this world," and yet go to the polls and vote. Unfortunately, but predictably, those who electioneer disagree on matters of party politics and then gather at the communion table on Sundays. "Is this the way to 'let our light shine before men?'" asked Brenneman.[68] Soon Funk chimed in that "the man who would be excused from military service for conscience sake, must always abide by his conscientious principles both in times of war and in times of peace."[69] Funk also noted Reformed Mennonite Daniel Musser's new pamphlet outlining a highly sectarian stripe of nonresistance.[70] Although Funk would later tangle with Musser on other doctrinal matters, the *Herald* editor approved Musser's ideas on peace and politics.

The *Herald* also began raising questions about the ethics of hiring draft substitutes, a practice typically frowned on by the Amish but more common in Mennonite circles. Funk did not equivocate. Purchasing the service of a substitute was inconsistent "before the eyes of the world." Contributing to local bounty funds was "a much disputed subject," he admitted, but then explained why doing so improperly crossed the line between passively rendering due taxes and participating in the worldly practices of the state. Certainly, nonresistants should give "freely and heartily" to relieve the suffering of orphans, widows, and the sick, even if they be veterans, but that was a different matter.[71]

Two months later the *Herald* printed a strong statement from Mennonite minister John M. Christophel, of Elkhart County, Indiana, on providing volunteer bounties as a means of "Preventing the Draft." Christophel feared some Mennonites had been "induced" to "unite with the world in preventing a draft, as they call it." They refused to admit that there is a crucial difference between "what I do voluntarily, and what I am compelled to do." Christophel was puzzled by Mennonites who said they wanted to avert a draft because their adult sons who were not yet church members might then be called into service. If men are old enough to be drafted, the minister said, they are old enough to be church members and should have been baptized already. Christophel had no time for religious identities blurred by parental faithfulness or ethnic attachment. The church and the world were sharply divided, yielding no middle ground.[72] Given these worlds, the nonresistant Christian understood the civic sphere, not as a site where legitimate separation from evil might be won, but as an alien place from which to withdraw.

Funk's *Herald* eventually gained circulation beyond Brenneman's network of Midwestern Mennonites and Amish. A few eastern Pennsylvanians began subscribing, and knowledge of the new paper may even have made its way across the battle lines to Mennonites in Virginia.[73] Late in the war, the *Herald* would publish correspondence from refugees from the Shenandoah Valley now living north of the Mason-Dixon line.[74] Those letters described the suffering the war had visited upon their region. Indeed, Mennonites residing in the South were living in a distinctly different regional context, one that was feeling more than its share of pain.

CHAPTER 9

Resistance and Revenge in Virginia

Confederate Context

The first months of 1863 offered several encouraging signs to those who yearned for Southern success. Confederate troops scored symbolic—if strategically limited—victories, recapturing Galveston, Texas, in January and foiling a Union attack on Charleston, South Carolina, in April. A month later, in Virginia, outnumbered soldiers under General Robert E. Lee decisively defeated Federal forces at the crossroads of Chancellorsville (though the death of key Confederate commander Stonewall Jackson soured the victory). At the same time, other signs portended trouble for the Southern Republic. Runaway inflation had devastated what was left of the economy, and the spring of 1863 saw a series of so-called bread riots in a dozen cities—Richmond's, on April 2, was the largest—in which hundreds of war wives and widows marched into stores and took supplies they deemed immorally overpriced.[1]

Although Mennonites living in Virginia's Shenandoah Valley "breadbasket" were spared such hunger, they felt the army's renewed efforts to commandeer food and supplies. Given the effect of inflation, Richmond was now collecting foodstuffs through a "tax-in-kind" of one-tenth of farm production—a strategy that netted more value than collecting traditional taxes paid in Confederate dollars. In Augusta County, Mennonite church trustee Jacob R. Hildebrand returned home from worship one Sunday to find an impressments officer taking corn. Suspecting the government "Press master" would come for more, Hildebrand rose at 3:00 a.m. the next morning and hid twenty-five bushels. The agent did, in fact, return the next day and took the remaining fifteen bushels.[2] In Rockingham County, Confederate commissary agents pressed many horses into service, including four that belonged to John Rhodes and some from David Brenneman.[3] Aware of regional food shortages, some Harrisonburg-area Mennonites chose to sell their produce to the poor, apparently at prices reasonable enough to earn some thanks from the *Rockingham Register*.[4]

Almost everywhere, diminishing supplies, hunger, and a general increase in civil disorder and even lawlessness marked Southern society. Whatever the Confederate battlefield triumphs in early 1863 may have been, the South's basic building blocks remained precariously stacked. Adding to the bleak picture were the two devastating military losses that July—at Gettysburg, in the east, and at Vicksburg, in the west—matched by the final collapse of possible international recognition from Britain and France. The accumulating bad news only increased the social and political pressure on Virginia's nonresistants, who had won military exemption in 1862 but who now found themselves under fresh popular scrutiny.[5]

Rockingham Resistance

Since the start of the war, the response of the Mennonites in Rockingham County had been largely one of passive resistance to the Confederacy and active refusal to participate in its armed forces. Not only had many Mennonites not endorsed secession, they had used both legal and extralegal means to escape military induction. True, a number of young men from Mennonite homes, including a few who were church members, were in the army either by choice or as a result of forced induction early in the war, but some of these latter ones had quickly deserted. And with the establishment of formal provision for men of scruples, the enrollment books show large numbers having obtained exemption by October 1, 1863. The "Roll of Exempts" for Rockingham County indicated Mennonites and Dunkers by church affiliation.[6] Appendix B reproduces lists from two books, the first enumerating all exemptions from December 1862 until January of 1864, and the second those who were exempt by virtue of church affiliation in May, July, and August 1864. Dunkers outnumbered the Mennonites in the first list, since Rockingham had a larger population of Dunkers than Mennonites. In the second book, the number of Dunkers and Mennonites is more nearly equal. A number of Mennonites and numerous Dunkers also appear to have obtained substitutes who were in service on October 1, 1863. Many names listed in the second book were also listed in the first.

While some men had escaped to the North before Confederate provisions had been enacted for those with scruples, the passage in 1862 of conscientious privileges had given Mennonites some confidence that their position was taken seriously in Richmond. Indeed, in January 1863, when the Confederate Congress considered a revised conscription bill that made no mention of religious objectors, the *Richmond Daily Examiner* asked sympathetically whether it was "the purpose of Congress to annul its [1862] contract with these men and drag them into service." But a few months later, after the disaster at Gettysburg, leaders were less sure there was any political value in exempting classes of potential soldiers, and nonresistants wondered if their status was in jeopardy. Virginia's Governor John Letcher recommended to a special session of the state's House of Delegates the abolition of exemption on religious grounds.[7] By December, President Jefferson Davis told the opening session of the second Confederate Congress that he needed more troops "to add largely to our effective force as promptly as possible" and that fresh soldiers "are to be found by restoring to the Army all who are improperly absent, putting an end to substitution, modifying the exemption law, [and] restricting details."[8] In response, on December 28, 1863, the national legislature in Richmond abolished the substitution system and the following February expanded conscription to include all men ages 17 to 50 (instead of 18 to 35). Remarkably, though, it retained the conscientious objector provision.[9]

Despite the Confederacy's continued formal acknowledgement of conscience, there is evidence that Rockingham County Mennonites were increasingly concerned about their place in the Old Dominion.[10] More men went into hiding or left for the North in late 1863 and 1864. Despite inflated dollars, some may have been unable to pay the $500 conscientious commutation fee—especially after the number of men tagged for service expanded to include those up to age 50. Moreover, a good number of the 17-year-olds now liable for induction were likely not yet church members and thus unable to qualify for religious exemption. Having lost the possibility of substitution, skedaddling was their only avenue of escape.

As 1864 wore on, Reuben J. Heatwole recalled, the church community was drained of draft-age men: "Sunday congregations were composed of only a few old men, little boys, and the women."[11] In May 1864 Heatwole himself accompanied his brother-in-law, Henry G. Brunk, and a group of fifteen 17-year-olds, in fleeing to the North. In 1862 Brunk had been among the seventy would-be escapees who were captured by Confederate scouts and imprisoned in Richmond. That time, Brunk was released on the condition that he take up noncombatant work. Quickly deserting, he had gone into hiding for almost two-and-a-half years, coming out only occasionally, such as when he stood at a distance at the November 1862 funeral of his young son and then slipped away before the last hymn. Now Brunk was on the road again, and this time his group was successful, making its way to Clarksburg, West Virginia, where they all affirmed allegiance to the Union. From there, Heatwole and Brunk went to Williamsport, Maryland, and then boarded a train to Hagerstown, where they met more Virginia Mennonite refugees, including Heatwole's brother-in-law, Charles Rogers. Rogers was working for Washington County, Maryland, Mennonite minister Michael Horst, and Rogers helped the newcomers find jobs too. Brunk took up leather working and shoe repair in Hagerstown.[12]

Brunk now sent word to his wife, Susanna (Heatwole), that she should meet him in Maryland. The spunky Susanna, who had managed well during her husband's many months as a fugitive and had endured their son's burial alone, packed baby Sarah and a few provisions in a one-horse wagon and left, accompanied by her sister. Details handed down by family who heard Susanna recount the adventure later paint a picture of a harrowing trip. At one point, the story goes, Confederate soldiers tried to take her horses. Ordered to follow, she retorted, "I'll do no such thing!" and headed in the other direction. Later, discovering that the bridge was burned at Harper's Ferry, she took the advice of a local miller and simply drove her wagon across the challenging waters. Arriving in Hagerstown, she located Henry through a seemingly miraculous set of circumstances, and their reunited household remained there for several months before starting a new life in Geneseo, Illinois, and raising a family whose members would play prominent roles in (Old) Mennonite circles in the Midwest and back in Virginia.[13]

Beyond stories of escape, records of Virginia Mennonites' formal response to evolving war conditions are slim. The minutes of the spring

Susanna Heatwole Brunk (1839–1909). Credit: Mennonite Church USA Archives, Goshen, Ind.

1864 church conference session, for example, were sparse and contain no direct references to the hostilities. Perhaps the unpopularity of their peace position made discretion the better part of valor when recording discussion of the war. Significantly, the conference did reaffirm its prohibition of owning or trafficking slaves, and it continued to forbid members to hire neighbors' slaves unless masters allowed those slaves to retain their own wages. The only exceptions the ministers permitted were cases involving the neighborly exchange of farm labor; in such situations, Mennonites could accept slaves' work as part of a pattern of informal reciprocity.[14]

Certainly the bulk of the conference membership, who lived in Rockingham County, must have been aware of their neighbors' increasing impatience with nonresistants' weak support for the war effort. Editorials in the winter and spring of 1864 in the *Rockingham Register* raised critical questions about the loyalty of Mennonites and Dunkers. In February the *Register* "heard it stated that some of them did not intend to raise more upon their farms than will be necessary to pay their taxes"—suggesting they were giving only minimal moral support to the Confederate economy. If this were true, the *Register* declared, Congress should put them in the army and force them to participate.[15]

A week later, in early March, the charge resurfaced. "Some of our German friends who have been exempted from military duty" are not going to plant extensive acreage this spring, the paper asserted. If the editor learned who these "unpatriotic" individuals were, he would publish their names and forward them to the Secretary of War, apparently to request that their draft exemptions be revoked. "Men who will not serve the great cause. . . . ought to be put in the front ranks of our armies and if possible made food for gun powder," the *Register* declared. The charges were more serious, given the Confederacy's increasingly unstable economy, hyperinflation, and dwindling commodities. In fact, Richmond's adoption of a 10 percent agricultural tax-in-kind in 1863 had been an attempt to secure desperately needed resources from planters and small farmers slow to hand them over for questionable government credits. Within a month, the Rockingham paper received some responses defending the nonresistants and claiming that they grew enough foodstuffs to share with the poor—though the paper's editor was not convinced.[16]

Anti-nonresistant sentiment peaked in mid-June 1864, when Confederate partisans assassinated Dunker elder John Kline of Broadway. Well known for his anti-slavery and anti-secessionist views, Kline had continued to attend national Brethren annual meetings, which involved his crossing enemy lines, and was rumored to be assisting draft-eligible men from his church fleeing to the North. Kline was returning from visiting a sick neighbor when vigilantes ambushed and murdered him.[17] The *Rockingham Record* printed a tepid rebuke of the assailants, calling their action "lawless" and a "tragedy" but also criticizing "the erroneous views which [Kline] entertained" and his "antagonism . . . to the Confederacy."[18] Indeed, as the Confederacy weakened, loyalists lost patience with Unionist nonresistants. And when Rockingham County Mennonites and Dunkers responded to such pressures by continuing to seek draft exemptions or

escape to the North, this only confirmed the suspicions of Southern sympathizers.

Augusta County Perspectives

Among Mennonites in Virginia Conference's Southern District, the response to the draft and the Confederacy was somewhat different. There,
in Augusta County, the smaller church body of just more than fifty members worshipped in two meetinghouses and lived among English or
Scots-Irish neighbors, many of whom were Presbyterians.[19] The District's
bishop, Jacob Hildebrand, was respected by these neighbors as well as by
his own Mennonite people. Energetic and well-off, Hildebrand owned a
thousand acres in the Madrid area of Augusta County.[20]

Yet bishop Hildebrand was seemingly less attuned to the opinions of
fellow Mennonites in Rockingham County. When the Confederacy introduced the $500 exemption fee for men of conscience, Hildebrand
wrote the young bishop, Samuel Coffman, of the Middle District in Rockingham County, that the Augusta County Mennonites intended "to set
apart a day for thanksgiving to God and our government for the privilege
and kindness granted to us defenseless followers of our meek and lowly
Saviour to be exempt from the army by paying a small fine." He expected
to observe January 28, 1863, as a time to note "this great blessing" and to
"pray earnestly for our government." Hildebrand wondered if the Rockingham County churches in bishop Coffman's charge would join in this
day of thanksgiving, and if Coffman would ask bishop John Geil of the
Northern District to join, too.[21]

Coffman's answer has not survived, but it must have been decidedly
negative, given the tone of Hildebrand's subsequent apology for even raising the possibility. The larger Virginia Mennonite body had little use for
the Confederacy, and praying for divine blessing on Richmond was apparently more than they could stomach. Again, bishop Hildebrand wrote
to Coffman in Rockingham County, "sorry and sick to the very bottom of
my heart. . . . that I have again in my great weakness offended some of my
beloved Brethren and Sisters whom I so deeply love." A Dunker preacher
had suggested the day of prayer, bishop Hildebrand explained, and among
Mennonites in the Southern District "there was not one single objection
made but all seemed to be in favor of it." Elsewhere in the letter, the bishop

referred to the $500 exemption charge as a "small fine," suggesting both his financial situation and his genuine thankfulness that "us defenseless Christians . . . can get off from bearing arms." He apparently had not realized the response he would engender in Rockingham County.[22]

Indeed, although Hildebrand and other Augusta County Mennonites exhibited clear Confederate sympathies and a number of young men (including some church members) from Southern District families donned gray uniforms, there is no evidence that the bishop directly discouraged the church's nonresistant stance. In fact, bishop Hildebrand's commitments seem clear when he pled with his son Samuel to stay out of the military. In January 1863, as his father was preparing to conduct the special thanksgiving and prayer service, Samuel was in the far western part of Virginia, deep in the mountains at Cowpasture River in Alleghany County, employed on the railroad.[23] Father Hildebrand wrote Samuel on March 19 that he was "hoping and trus[t]ing that the Lord will have mercy upon you all and bless you with good health." After noting an acquaintance who got sick in the army and had come home to die, Hildebrand reminded his son "how important it is to be prepaired to meet Death," though he hoped this would not be on a battlefield. "I hope the war will end before long," the bishop confessed. "Try and be a good Boy so that you can ceep out of the Army and I will reward you well for your Hardships." Father Hildebrand understood that Samuel had a difficult supervisor and that his job was unpleasant but begged him to remember that life in the army "wold be a great [d]eal wors and harder and you wold not get a chance to come home for a hole year."[24]

The Augusta County bishop also feared his son joining the so-called Home Guards, or Raid Guards, local defense forces raised by voluntary enlistment.[25] On September 22, 1863, only a few weeks after a son of Hildebrand's cousin joined the Home Guard, the bishop wrote Samuel, "I want you to be ware and dont suffer your self to be perswaded to join the home gard for I beleve it is just a way they have to get men into the Army." Please obey me, the father enjoined, and "I will reward you well; and the Lord will Bless you for it. I often pray to God for you," and you must also "pray to God that he will still gard you and ceep you from eavel." Samuel apparently heeded his father's advice; at least he stayed out of the military.[26]

Although Samuel did not take up arms, other Augusta County Mennonites did, including members of Jacob R. Hildebrand's household. A first cousin of bishop Hildebrand, Jacob R. Hildebrand was a prominent farmer, church trustee, and soon-to-be deacon. Jacob R. Hildebrand—whose son Benjamin had joined the 52nd Virginia Infantry back in 1861—frequently went to Staunton to get war news or to listen to a morale-boosting Confederate speech.[27] Clearly, he identified with the Confederacy, and in his journal, he recorded uncritically propaganda from Richmond such as reports that Yankees were surrendering because "they Refused to fight any longer for the Nig." On August 25, 1863, Jacob R. and Catherine Hildebrand even hosted two Confederate army engineers for dinner.[28]

Yet Jacob R. Hildebrand did not glory in death and destruction, and he seemingly found the war's violence troubling. On the way to visit his son Benjamin in October, just after the battle of Bristoe Station, father Hildebrand passed the area where "our men first skermished with the enemy" and sadly recalled how people had once "hailed with joy the firing of the first gun." Now it was desolate countryside. Returning home past the Port Republic battlefield, he saw that hogs had rooted out bodies from Yankee graves and scattered the bones. Soon thereafter, he confided to his journal that he felt despondent, supposing that "the cause of it is that I have not lived close enough to God in my walk and conversation."[29]

Doubtless that conversation included more frequent talk of war, since in the fall of 1863 his second son, Gideon, had became involved in fighting. Not a church member, Gideon was unsuccessful in obtaining a substitute, and on September 5, 1863, at a meeting in Fishersville, he had joined an Augusta County Home Guard company. By the end of the year, the Home Guard was engaged in helping "Run the Enemy below" New Market.[30] Hildebrand's journal never suggested that hiding or fleeing to the North were options that conscripted Augusta County Mennonites took seriously, despite the importance of such moves among their counterparts in Rockingham County.

On Christmas day 1863, trustee Jacob R. Hildebrand was ordained one of two new deacons for the Virginia Mennonites' Southern District. Earlier, the bishop had ridden his horse to the home of each church member and received nominations for the open leadership posts.[31] The bishop informed the eight nominees—including Jacob R.—of their candidacy on Christmas Eve, and the next day the men drew lots to determine divine selection.[32] Interestingly, the new deacon did not directly mention his own ordination in his diary entry for the day. Instead, he reflected philosophically, "This is Christmas day there are maney who were alive one year ago who are now in their graves maney of whom died of disease others were killed in battle & were denied buriel, in this most unrightous & desolating war & we don't know what God has laid up in store in the Impenetrable council of his wisdom for us, yet we mus say that he has been our help in times past & is our hope in years to come."[33]

As a deacon, Jacob R. Hildebrand now attended the semiannual gatherings of the Virginia Mennonite Conference, and at the spring 1864 session the group immediately chose him to be the secretary, suggesting their respect for him. Yet Hildebrand himself was having a difficult spring. Unseasonably cold weather, bothersome grand jury duty (including a case that involved "trading with slaves"), and high taxes brought on another bout of melancholy, though his journal also reported several "Impressive Sermons" that buoyed his spirit, including one his cousin preached on April 8, when the Augusta Mennonites again obliged Jefferson Davis's call for a state-sponsored special day of "Humiliation & prayer."[34]

Perhaps the deacon was increasingly anxious for the safety of his sons, although his journal entries reveal little about how he and Catherine felt regarding their boys' military service. In mid-February 1864, Gideon transferred from the Home Guard to the 1st Virginia Cavalry, prompting his father to pray, "May God still continue to watch over him and bring him safe through this war." The same month, Benjamin turned 21, and his father hoped he would become "a good citizen & a devout Christian." But if the Confederacy now had two Hildebrand boys in uniform, it otherwise had too few men under arms, causing the Confederate Congress to expand conscription to men as old as 50. The 44-year-old Augusta County deacon then dutifully reported to Staunton to be enrolled, and later returned "to pay my fine of $500 to Exempt me from Military duty." In both modest and more intrusive ways, the war was closing in on the Shenandoah Valley.[35]

Escalating War of Revenge

Union military strategy took a more aggressive turn in the spring of 1864, when Lieut. General Ulysses S. Grant transferred from his Mississippi Valley post to a position as commanding general based in Virginia. Grant's plans for the war in the east, which included taking Atlanta, Georgia, and pressing in on Richmond, Virginia, also involved coordinated attacks in related regions, such as the Shenandoah Valley. But not everything went as planned. Already in May, Federal forces from West Virginia had tried to take the Shenandoah town of Staunton, only to be defeated at New Market. A month later another Union foray into the Valley plundered Lexington before dissolving into retreat across the western Allegheny Mountains. Rockingham County Mennonite Peter S. Hartman, a Union sympathizer, was nonetheless sharply critical of the conduct of the retreating Yankees. "Those men acted the worst of any men I ever heard of in my life," he declared. "They riddled feather ticks and pillows. This was a matter of revenge, for they had been utterly defeated in battle."[36]

But the rounds of revenge would not stop here. In the wake of these abortive Union invasions, the Confederate commander in the Shenandoah, Lieut. General Jubal Early, was able to operate freely in the Valley and use it as a base from which to raid into Maryland and Pennsylvania, where several communities paid the price for Lexington's suffering. Marching swiftly, Early's forces crossed the Potomac at Williamsport on July 6, sending Maryland and Pennsylvania into panic. Early's ultimate goal was to threaten Washington, D.C., but along the way cavalry under Brig. General John McCausland commandeered civilian property and extorted ransom from unwitting towns. Washington County, Maryland, Mennonite Davis S. Lesher reported having "a great deal of trouble here this summer with our horses on account of the rebels" who were rounding them up and riding away with them.[37]

Assuming that the Confederates were planning to march into Pennsylvania as they had the summer before, residents of the state's Cumberland Valley, which had provided a convenient invasion route, grew understandably anxious. "[T]his Evening is pretty much of an excitement it is rumored the Rebs is coming," wrote Reformed Mennonite housewife Anna Mellinger on July 3. Mellinger, who lived east of Chambersburg, filled her diary with snatches of news regarding troop movement and speculation on where the soldiers might turn up next.[38] Three days later, things had gotten tense enough for Levi and Anna (Lehman) Horst's family, Mennonites who lived west of Chambersburg, that they "loaded the large covered emigrant wagon with bedding, necessary furniture, and supplies" and headed "about seven or eight miles to . . . grandfather's near Shippensburg." After an eventless week, the Horsts moved back home but remained apprehensive.[39]

Ruins of Chambersburg, Pennsylvania, after McCausland's July 1864 raid. Credit: U.S. Army Military Historical Institute, Carlisle, Pa.

For the time being, McCausland's men stayed in Maryland, harassing prominent Union sympathizers—such as relatives of Postmaster General Montgomery Blair—and forcing payments of $20,000 from the residents of Hagerstown, and $200,000 from those in Frederick. Then, on July 30, Confederate cavalry crossed into Pennsylvania and rode into Chambersburg with a demand for $500,000 within two hours or the town would be put to the torch. Perhaps Chambersburg civic leaders could collect funds from their rural hinterland, the Southern soldiers suggested. But there was hardly time to see what the country folk, including the area's many Mennonites, could contribute. Already before the two hours were up, some of the invaders, stoked with liquor, got busy with their burning.[40]

By one o'clock in the afternoon most of the town was on fire, "an inferno of blazing houses, with several thousand numbed or crying men, women and children cowering in vacant lots and in the town's cemetery." Southern officer Fielder C. Slingluff later reported that his men remembered how Federal troops had destroyed civilian homes in Virginia, and saw the destruction of Chambersburg as the North's comeuppance. But not all Confederate soldiers obeyed the orders to burn, and some even helped protect property and furnishings.[41]

The Chambersburg Mennonite Church, one mile to the north, escaped the conflagration, but rural Mennonites soon realized that something terrible was happening in town. Nineteen-year-old Catherine Horst and her family, recently returned from their brief flight toward Shippensburg, "stood out in the yard and watched the flames and smoke of the burning town. We knew many of the people in town and naturally were anxious to know what would become of them." Fear spread that Confederates would fan out and "burn out the whole valley and that no one would be safe." However, troops torched only a few farm buildings very near Chambersburg, and none belonged to Mennonites.[42]

The next day was Sunday, and the Horsts ventured out to survey the ruins. They could hardly recognize familiar stores and buildings, but the human toll was all too easy to see. "Some of our friends were in need of bedclothes and other things. We helped them in such ways as we could," remembered Catherine many years later.[43] The Horsts were among a number of area (Old) Mennonites and Reformed Mennonites who came into town with supplies or who offered lodging to neighbors whose homes had gone up in smoke. From farther east, in Bucks County, Pennsylvania, the General Conference Mennonite's East Swamp congregation sent a special August offering collection to help the Chambersburg homeless.[44]

As the town of Chambersburg smoldered, Early's army halted its northern incursion and pulled back into Virginia. To be sure, his bold advance had taken Northern leaders by surprise, and a round of Federal finger-pointing distributed blame for the invasion's startling success. But Washington, D.C., had been too heavily fortified, and Union troop strength in eastern Virginia too strong, to allow Early to remain outside the protection of the Shenandoah Valley for long. Indeed, Union strategists decided that the Valley itself should become the focus of a reenergized Northern campaign. To that end, Lincoln approved the formation of a new Army of the Shenandoah, and Grant appointed an ambitious young officer named Philip H. Sheridan at its head.[45] For Mennonites in the Shenandoah Valley—and all their neighbors—it would prove a fateful step in a new round of revenge.

CHAPTER 10

Burning the Shenandoah Valley

The Advent of Hard War

On Tuesday, June 7, 1864, Gideon Hildebrand stopped at the Augusta County, Virginia, home of his parents, deacon Jacob R. and Catherine Hildebrand. Gideon was in the area on a fifteen-day "horse detail" from the 1st Virginia Cavalry, which he had joined in February. But military maneuvers closed in on the area, and Gideon's opportunity for rest and family was short-lived. The next day he and three other Confederates were sent out scouting. Surprised by several Yankees, Gideon "shot one of them." In the melee that followed, Hildebrand lost his horse and pistol, but escaped with his life.[1]

Father Jacob described these events in his journal but left the outcome of the encounter ambiguous: Did Gideon kill the Union trooper, or merely wound him? Or was Gideon himself unsure of what happened to his opponent? Although the deacon's diary was filled with war news, never had an entry been this dramatic or immediate. Yet if Gideon's lethal actions at close range troubled father Hildebrand, the journal did not reveal it. Perhaps by now the tangled web of war that involved so many of Hildebrand's kin and community had broadened his approval of the means needed to defend the Confederate cause. In any case, his son's skirmish was only the first in an accelerating series of incidents soon to engulf the area. Death and destruction would press even closer on the Mennonites of the Shenandoah Valley, especially during the Union's campaign of indiscriminate burning in the autumn of 1864. For those in the Valley, the events would be a nightmare long seared into their memories.

The series of failed Union raids into the Valley during the spring of 1864 had left Confederate forces there in complete control. Lieut. General Jubal Early was able to move freely and use the Shenandoah's shelter as a staging ground for a surprising thrust into Maryland and Pennsylvania, including the burning of Chambersburg. Early's July incursion into the North frustrated Union commander Grant. His own march through the Wilderness, Spotsylvania, Cold Harbor, and Petersburg—a Virginia campaign he had promised to finish "if it takes all summer"—was getting bogged down, as was the Union drive toward Atlanta, further South.[2] Confederate claim to the Shenandoah Valley only added to the Federals' burgeoning morale problem. By mid-summer the best-selling sheet music in the North was the wistful "When This Cruel War Is Over." Then too, national elections were looming, and if Union leaders did not produce some decisive military results, ballot box prospects for the Republican administration were dim.[3]

With all this in mind, the Union's commanding general created a new Army of the Shenandoah, with the goal of following Early "to the death" and taking control of the Valley.[4] More specifically, on July 14, 1864, Grant dispatched a message to Washington, D.C., promising to "eat out Virginia clear and clean as far as they go [into the Shenandoah Valley], so that crows flying over it for the balance of the season will have to carry their provender with them."[5] "I do not mean that houses should be burned," Grant clarified the next day, but stressed that the Valley should nonetheless be made "a desert" and "all provisions and stock should be removed, and the people notified to move out."[6] To carry out the project, Grant selected an enterprising and enthusiastic young officer, Maj. General Philip H. Sheridan, to lead the campaign. Sheridan saw his chance to become famous and wasted no time in setting about the task of decimating the "breadbasket" of the Confederacy.[7]

As much as twenty-five miles wide, the Valley and its fertile fields comprised the northern portion of the so-called Great Valley of Virginia. Angling northeastward for 125 miles toward the Potomac River, the Shenandoah was bounded on the east by the Blue Ridge Mountains and on the west by the Alleghenies, with the maverick Massanutten Mountain range boldly puncturing the valley from Harrisonburg to Front Royal.

Throughout the war the Valley had contributed a great deal to Virginia's economy and had directly and indirectly supplied Southern armies.

In one sense, the Valley's peace church population of Dunkers and Mennonites had only strengthened the region's productive possibilities, since the nonresistants' opting out of military service (even if at some personal cost) kept a more stable labor force at home and operating many of the area's productive farms. During the war at least one Mennonite businessman, the wealthy hog farmer and miller Isaac Wenger, had regularly taken his cured pork and bacon to the Confederate capital, where he cultivated a clientele willing to pay in gold rather than Confederate currency. Wenger kept up his Rockingham County-to-Richmond business even when the presence of Union troops forced him to travel at night or ride lookout while his hired hands drove the pork-laden wagons.[8]

Despite the area's productivity, violence had been no stranger to the Valley—notably, during the 1862 Valley Campaign of "Stonewall" Jackson—and thousands of soldiers from both sides had trudged back and forth across its lush landscapes. But while towns and farms had suffered occasional pillaging, there had been little systematic destruction of civilian property. Now, as the autumn of 1864 approached, however, neither side hesitated to make noncombatants' lives miserable. Early's men had burned Chambersburg, and Northern strategists were desperate to force a Southern surrender. Behind the scenes, Union leaders had begun implementing a policy of "hard war" that targeted Southern economic resources and sought to demoralize civilians by destroying their livelihoods. An advocate of hard war, Grant now authorized its use against the strategically valuable Shenandoah Valley.[9] In a military operation that lasted from August to December 1864, Sheridan attacked the Valley's economic base in an effort to cripple the Confederacy, leaving "a legacy of blackened ruin that served as a graphic counterpoint to the storied lushness of the area."[10]

Along with their neighbors, Virginia Mennonites suffered the trauma of the Union burning. Never before—or since—had Mennonites in the United States experienced such collective property destruction. During that fearsome fall, many Shenandoah residents—including most of the region's nonresistants—protested that their loyalties had long lain with the Union, so Federal troops should spare their properties. "To this," Mennonite Peter Hartman recalled, "Sheridan answered that all was Union now."[11]

Sheridan's ride through the Shenandoah Valley, as sketched by contemporary artist J. E. Taylor. Credit: Western Reserve Historical Society Library, Cleveland, Ohio

Not so, of course, with Jacob R. Hildebrand, the Augusta County deacon who seems to have retained some sympathies for Richmond. His journal provides a window into the anxious and deteriorating nature of civilian life in the Shenandoah Valley even before Sheridan arrived. On Sunday afternoon, May 22, after Jacob R. had enjoyed "an Impressive sermon" from his cousin, bishop Jacob Hildebrand, in the Mennonite meeting-house near his home, the deacon heard the sound of cannon fire "in the Direction of Richmond"—a reminder of the conflict pressing in on Valley residents. Then, early in June, Abraham J. Grove, a young man likely from the Hildebrand congregation, was killed in battle. Shortly thereafter, on June 7, deacon Hildebrand went to the battleground to help bury "our dead" after a skirmish near Staunton.[12]

Two days later Hildebrand reported "All Excitement" due to another skirmish close at hand between Fishersville and Waynesboro. The "Enemy lost 6 killed & some wounded," he wrote, while "none of our men killed but several wounded." A month later Hildebrand noted that "Providence it appears still favors us," as "2 squadrons of our men Repulsed 4,000 of the Enemy" along the Charles City Courthouse Road. Hildebrand's journal now frequently reported Confederate military fortunes in sympathetic and first-person style. Yet on July 29, 1864, Jacob paid $500 to ensure his exemption from the draft.[13]

Within several weeks Hildebrand had gone to visit both sons' encampment (Benjamin had been with the 52nd Virginia Infantry since 1861) and found them "both well Thank God." On the way home, on August 19, Hildebrand noticed burning barns and observed the Yankees "burning Every barn they come across that has either hay or grain in it." As the deacon traveled up the Valley Pike, he saw "a good many" smoldering barns. Sheridan's troops had begun pursuing their assignment of havoc.[14]

The Burning

Jacob R. Hildebrand was seeing the effects of the first six weeks of Sheridan's campaign—a month-and-a-half period of rather irregular and unsystematic engagement with Confederate forces during which the Union army geared up for a major assault. On August 26 Grant sent word to Sheridan, underscoring the importance of the destructive task at hand. If the war should last another year, Grant thought, "we want the Shenandoah Valley to remain a barren waste."[15] Sheridan apparently understood his orders, for already on August 16 he had informed his cavalry commander, Brig. General A. T. A. Torbert, that, although "no houses will be burned," the "officers in charge of this delicate but necessary duty, must inform the people that the object is to make the Valley untenable for the raiding parties of the Rebel Army."[16] As though the order demanded repeating, on September 28, James W. Forsyth, chief of staff of the Union forces' Middle Military Division, sent a message from Harrisonburg to the commander of the First Cavalry Division, telling him to "destroy all mills, all grain and forage" and to drive off or kill all stock. Forsyth also reminded him to avoid burning "private houses."[17]

Perhaps the message regarding the destruction of homes did need to be underscored, since it did not take long for Union troops to become careless. On September 29 the soldiers were in Port Republic and burned part of the town. [18] The following day Jacob R. Hildebrand reported in his journal that the Yankees in northern Augusta County and southern Rockingham County were making "a General burning of barns" and "also some houses."[19]

Meanwhile, on September 19, Sheridan's 39,000-man Army of the

Shenandoah had defeated Jubal Early's forces at Winchester—the town had now changed hands seventy-three times during the war—and the following day, after fast pursuit, beat the Confederates again near Strasburg, twenty miles further south.[20] Sheridan's success drew praise from Lincoln and Grant, although he failed to report the 4,500 Union casualties at Winchester, more than twice the number his forces inflicted on Early.[21]

Sheridan became adept at surprise and daring recklessness, but he soon found that chasing Early was not a simple matter. The Confederates knew the terrain, where and how to hide in the Blue Ridge Mountains, and when to strike.[22] The result was a series of skirmishes. From Augusta County, deacon Hildebrand nervously watched the approaching Union troops. In late August he went north to Rockingham County to attend the annual Virginia Mennonite Conference held at Weavers Church, west of Harrisonburg. Wryly, he reported that "nothing of much Importance transpired there." Undoubtedly, Hildebrand's mind was on his two sons engaged in fighting Federal forces. Returning home, the deacon was relieved to find Gideon back for a visit and well. Four days later, on September 2, Hildebrand's diary reported the sad news that his sister's son, Samuel Martin Miller, had been fired upon while on picket duty. The 21-year-old had tried to flee, but his horse fell and in the process broke Samuel's neck and killed him. "How unsearchable are thy Judgements oh Lord & thy ways past finding out," concluded Hildebrand, mixing grief and resignation.[23]

In late September, Port Republic, Staunton, and Waynesboro were some of the last places Confederates yielded to Union troops in Rockingham and Augusta counties. That brought fighting very close to the Hildebrands. On September 25, Jacob R. observed refugees fleeing over the mountain, apparently afraid that battle lines were moving near. Two days later Hildebrand noted that the Yankees had taken Staunton the night before. That day he also watched his friend J. H. Coiner's haystacks go up in flames, along with others in the neighborhood, victims of the Union plan to destroy foodstuffs. All this was not far from Hildebrand's own two farms. Remarkably, the deacon's buildings escaped torching on the 29th when Yankee troops were in the area.[24]

From the perspective of Union soldier Henry Kauffman of the 110th Ohio Volunteers, decisive Northern victory hinged on destroying the Valley's productive potential. Writing on October 2 from Harrisonburg,

Kauffman reported that "our cavalry is scouting around the country gathering up the cattle, horses and sheep and bringing them in for the benefit of the Army. They have gathered up 4,500 beefs." That would "help pay" for what the Confederates had done farther north in Union territory, Kauffman thought. Like his commanders, Kauffman was combining a logic of reprisal with a shift in strategy that was transforming civilian resources into acceptable military targets.[25]

A day earlier, also in Harrisonburg, Sheridan had sent two dispatches to Lieut. General Grant and one to Maj. Gen. Henry Halleck. Sheridan reported that his men had thrown the iron bridge into the South River at Waynesboro as well as the bridge at Christians Creek and had destroyed the railroad from Staunton to Waynesboro. Their destruction of mills, grain, forage, and foundries between Staunton and Mt. Crawford was "very great." His troops had also collected 3,000 cattle and sheep. "What we have destroyed and can destroy in this Valley is worth millions of dollars to the rebel Government," he concluded, and his plan was to continue levying such devastation.[26]

By one report, "Union cavalry stretched a cordon across the Valley floor and systematically fired barns and herded away animals." One trooper counted 167 barns burning simultaneously.[27] Other sources do not describe quite such systematic destruction, and Union forces actually failed to penetrate all of the Valley's small back roads. Yet Sheridan was reputed to have said that "the people must be left nothing but their eyes to weep with over the war."[28] In any case, the general believed that his strategy was working. As early as October 7, Sheridan could report that "the whole country from the Blue Ridge to the North Mountains has been made untenable for a rebel army" and conclude that "the people here are getting sick of the war."[29] Much later, when Sheridan wrote his memoirs, he philosophized on the significance of private property in people's lives. He considered war a struggle that involved more than uniformed combatants. Those back home expected soldiers to die; but it was quite another matter to bring suffering and deprivation to civilians themselves, and especially to deprive them of their property. Death on the battlefield was not the maximum punishment of war, thought Sheridan. Reducing civilians to poverty "brings prayers for peace more surely and more quickly than does the destruction of human life."[30]

"Holocaust of Fire"

To this point, the destruction in the Valley had seemed devastating enough, but in early October Sheridan "unleashed a firestorm of devastating proportions" upon the region's residents, including area Mennonites.[31] On Monday, October 3, Sheridan's chief engineer, Lieutenant John R. Meigs, and two other men working on maps of the Harrisonburg area were returning to headquarters in a drizzling rain. On the way they met three men dressed in oilcloths who turned out to be Confederate scouts. At first, all involved concealed their weapons and intentions, but soon the Southerners ordered Meigs to surrender. Meigs answered by shooting Confederate George Martin through the groin. More shots followed, and Meigs was killed.[32]

Learning of Meigs's death, Sheridan flew into a rage and declared it murder, not an act of war. Calling in Brig. General George A. Custer, an officer who already had distinguished himself in burning barns and mills, Sheridan announced his plans to avenge the death.[33] After their meeting, Custer "vaulted into his saddle" and exclaimed, "Look out for smoke!"[34]

Sheridan had barked out orders to burn the town of Dayton along with all houses in the surrounding area. Custer's cavalry were to destroy the outlying region, while the soldiers of the 116th Ohio were assigned to burn Dayton itself. Many of the Ohioans were troubled by the order, having come to know Dayton's residents even in the short time they had been there. Nevertheless, on the morning of October 4 they went from house to house and "informed them that the town was to be destroyed that evening." The inhabitants pleaded for mercy but also prepared to leave. The surrounding area marked for destruction reached south to Bridgewater, east to the Valley Pike, north to Harrisonburg and the Rawley Springs Turnpike, and westward to the area called Rushville.[35] All told, it encompassed quite a number of Mennonite farms.

Some soldiers relished their orders, recalling the Confederate burning of Chambersburg. Others apparently felt revulsion; one, when asked about the burning, replied, "It is not civilized war." Major James Comly of the 23rd Ohio Volunteers demanded written orders before believing his men were to carry out such burning. After he received confirmation of Sheridan's intentions, he executed them "as carefully and tenderly as possible" but insisted it was not "soldierly work."[36] For his part, Commissary Sergeant William T. Patterson of the 116th Ohio was outraged when he heard of the order. Late in the evening, before Dayton itself had been struck but after the outlying region had been put to the torch, he saw the whole countryside "wrapped in flames, the heavens are aglow with the light thereof." Never had he seen "such mourning, such lamentations, such crying and pleading for mercy."[37]

Patterson's commander, Lt. Colonel Thomas F. Wildes, shared Patterson's distress. He "begged and prayed Sheridan to revoke the order." Sheridan, who respected Wildes, then rescinded the order to burn Dayton, five minutes before the flames were to be applied. When an officer announced the news, "there was louder cheering than there ever was when we made a bayonet charge."[38] Truly, "war is cruelty," concluded Patterson. If this were farther down the valley, where locals had aided Confederate raids into the North, the destruction might have been justified, Patterson wrote in his diary. "But this place is the most loyal or at least most innocent of any I have seen in the Valley."[39]

Dayton may have been saved, but not the farms in the surrounding countryside. When those lighting fires got to Mennonite Reuben Swope's farm, the Swopes' pleas for mercy went unheeded. Family memory holds that one of Custer's men asked Swope's 20-year-old daughter Susan if she thought women of the Valley would ever forgive the Northern soldiers for this deed. "Do you think if it were Southern soldiers burning the houses of your mothers and sisters they would be forgiven?" she is said to have retorted. When the family had gathered what they could from the house, the soldiers set fires in each of the downstairs rooms, then left with a warning that they would shoot the Swopes if the soldiers returned and found the flames extinguished. The Swopes put the fires out anyway. Later, as they surveyed all the other burned buildings in the neighborhood, Reuben reconsidered. Fearing the Federals would make good on their threat of execution, he re-lit the house and allowed it to burn down.[40]

Near Mole Hill lived Gabriel and Margaret (Swank) Heatwole, whose large family were all Mennonites, although one grandson, Henry Heatwole, had gone to war. "Old Doc Gabe" saw Reuben Swope's buildings on fire and expected that Union troops would soon be at his place. His extensive property included a mill, a cooper shop, a barn, storage buildings, bar-

rels, and stockpiled lumber, all of which were burned. The house, however, was spared. Gabriel's son, John G. Heatwole, and his wife, Elizabeth
(Rhodes), lived on the east side of Mole Hill. When Sheridan's men tried
to set that barn on fire, Elizabeth grabbed a rake and pulled apart the small
fire on the barn floor. The soldiers tried twice more, but the determined
woman chased the men off.[41]

A short distance to the north lived bishop Samuel and Frances (Weaver)
Coffman. For several days soldiers carried off the Coffmans' grain and hay.
Finally, the officer in charge told Frances Coffman that she had half an
hour to remove what she could from the house. After Frances and her
daughter exhausted themselves hurriedly getting most things out, the officer announced that he had changed his mind and they could return their
things.[42] The road by the Coffman home, it turned out, was the boundary
for the burning of dwellings. The Coffmans lived on the north side of the
road, and on that side houses were spared unless they accidentally caught
fire. A little east of the Coffmans lived Frances Coffman's parents, Samuel
and Elizabeth (Rhodes) Weaver, whose home was on the south side of
the road, across from the Weavers Mennonite Church meetinghouse.[43]
In preceding days soldiers had stripped the farm bare, and now all the
buildings were burned. A bit west of the meetinghouse, on the north side
of the road, stood a large log house that the Weavers also owned; it was
spared.[44]

No matter where their loyalties lay, Mennonite families, along with
their neighbors in the area, were burned out as Custer's forces went to
work on October 4. One of the first places targeted had been the 135-acre
farm of Noah C. and Sarah (Basinger) Wenger, very near the spot where
Meigs was killed. The Wengers packed up and went to the Valley Pike to
join refugees heading north, taking advantage of Sheridan's offer of travel
protection for Union sympathizers who wished to flee. After Union soldiers set fire to the abandoned Wenger home, Andrew Thompson, a 13-
year-old neighbor, managed to douse the flames and save the house, which
the Wengers found when they returned in spring 1866.[45] For his part,
young Mennonite minister David Landis also took up Sheridan's offer of
protection to go north. His family loaded the wagon, hooked a six-mule
team, and went in search of the refugee camp. Having to wait a few days
for the refugee train to assemble and leave, David went home to look in on
his farm, only to discover all the buildings consumed by flames.[46]

Benjamin Wenger, a Mennonite deacon and successful farmer had just recently built a new house in anticipation of conveying his original residence to his son Abraham. Within a few hours of the Yankees' arrival in the area, both homes and the barn were on fire. Shattered at the sudden loss of everything, the Wengers went to Sheridan's Harrisonburg headquarters to apply for passes to leave for Union territory.[47] Some 200 yards north of the Pike Mennonite meetinghouse lived the Michael Shank family. They also decided to pack quickly, "leaving behind nearly all . . . household and kitchen furniture," while their five children stood crying in a driving rain. Soon after their escape, the Shanks' house, barn, and outbuildings "were entirely consumed" by fire.[48]

It was a fearsome time to be living in the Shenandoah Valley. Margaret Rhodes was given fifteen minutes to leave her house, but then her house was spared. Teenager L. J. Heatwole—later a prominent Rockingham County Mennonite bishop—watched what he called the "holocaust of fire" as Northern soldiers applied the torch to all the mills and barns and a number of houses from Dayton west to Coakleytown and north to Dale Enterprise. It was, Heatwole said, "a sum of destruction that baffles the pen to describe." Nearly all families in this section spent the night out in the open, with great fires raging upon every side.[49] Loyalties, conscience, nonresistance—none of that mattered as those setting fires pursued their orders.

Young Peter Hartman later remembered that they had no sleep the night before Sheridan's troops came through. The dogs in the neighborhood anxiously barked until morning. The next day was Sunday, but no worship service was held. Hartman went to visit a neighbor near Weavers Church. From that vantage point they could see the army coming up the pike and spreading all over the country. Hartman decided he had better get home. Arriving back at his family's farm, he found it overrun with soldiers shooting the livestock. All thirty hogs were killed (or so they thought until two weeks later they found one still alive) as well as the chickens and sheep. The Union troops confiscated the Hartmans' horses, but spared several cows.[50]

South of Broadway, 34-year-old Mennonite minister Samuel Shank and his wife, Sarah, watched in horror as soldiers set fire to their barn and outbuildings. The conflagration soon ignited their recently built house, which stood near the barn. Shank had insulated the home with sawdust—an innovation that now proved tremendously destructive as the structure burned exceptionally hot and fast. The Shanks managed to save a few things from the ferocious blaze, but soldiers held them back from reentering.[51]

Occasionally, Union men disobeyed orders to burn barns if they believed a barn was too close to a house, and one squad helped an old woman remove her furniture from the house, then left without setting it on fire. But these were exceptions to a pattern of indiscriminate destruction.[52] In fact, Grant wanted Sheridan to go over the mountains toward Richmond and export the "sort of hellishness" he had "patented" in the Valley.[53] Sheridan, however, insisted on continuing northward down the Valley to complete his destruction in that direction, and Grant acquiesced.

Writing from Woodstock, Sheridan reported to Grant that from Staunton north and from the Blue Ridge Mountains to North Mountain on the western side of the valley, his troops had destroyed more than two thousand barns and seventy mills, along with their stores of wheat, hay, flour, and equipment. The burning included the main part of the Valley, the Luray Valley east of the Massanutten Mountain, and the Little Fort Valley nestled in the Massanutten range. Sheridan also explained that Lieutenant Meigs had been killed and that "for this atrocious act all the houses within an area of five miles were burned."[54] If Grant objected to Sheridan's act of revenge, his rebuke has been lost.

Destruction of civilian homes pushed the boundaries—but not the spirit—of the North's hard war strategy.[55] Indeed, Sheridan's exploits received largely approving press in the North, and a grateful Congress in February 1865 passed a resolution of thanks for "the gallantry, military skill and courage displayed in the brilliant series of victories achieved in the Valley of the Shenandoah."[56] Not surprisingly, Confederate voices were outraged at what Sheridan had done. The influential *Richmond Whig* proposed retaliation, asserting that since the North had chosen to "substitute the torch for the sword" the Confederacy should send arsonists to burn Northern cities.[57]

Refugee Flight

Sheridan's public promise of protection for those wanting to go North engendered a sizable response. L. J. Heatwole later recalled the morning

"Getting Passes to go North . . . Oct 2 1864," sketched by J. E. Taylor, showing refugees receiving permission to join Sheridan's supply train that was heading north. Credit: Western Reserve Historical Society Library, Cleveland, Ohio

Sheridan's caravan began evacuating the Valley. Federal troops "were everywhere in motion driving livestock northward and applying the torch to barns and mills that remained from the day before." Sometimes skirmishing occurred, and "minnie balls whistled sharply overhead and cavalry men were seen galloping at top speed northward along the roads and over the fields."[58] Sheridan proudly reported to Grant that from the Harrisonburg vicinity alone "over 400 wagon loads of refugees" left for Martinsburg, West Virginia, and that he thought "most of these people were Dunkers." Actually, quite a number were Mennonites. Refugee Peter Hartman believed the wagon train was sixteen miles long.[59]

Hartman and six friends—including bishop Samuel Coffman's son, John S.—decided they had best go north too and went to Sheridan's headquarters, where they watched as the general and his colonels wrote out their passes. Apparently most of the 16- and 17-year-old nonresistants still in the Valley left at this time to avoid the possibility of future conscription. At night when the caravan stopped to camp, these teens sang, and Hartman later said that Union soldiers were intrigued by the hymns and even began asking them each day "if they would sing that night."[60]

The possibility of leaving the Shenandoah Valley with other refugees afforded Harrisonburg-area Mennonite potter Emanuel Suter the occasion to get his family out. Suter's diary records their October 5 departure amid anxiety over Sheridan's campaign of burning. At Martinsburg, the provost marshal required solemn allegiance from all Virginia refugees of their loyalty to the constitution and government of the United States of America.[61] After making such assurances, the refugees had to make their own way farther north. Peter Hartman, fortunate enough to have his own horse, made his way to fellow Mennonites near Hagerstown, Maryland, where he worked for bishop Peter Eshleman. Later, in February 1865, Hartman took the train to Cumberland County, Pennsylvania.[62]

The news of the Virginians' suffering soon spread to the large Mennonite communities in eastern Pennsylvania. The *Daily Evening Express* of Lancaster published a long piece on "Refugees," noting that five families of Mennonites had just arrived from the Shenandoah Valley. Not surprisingly, some of the facts were twisted, and the piece served a political purpose. Union forces were "obliged" to engage in such "wholesale destruction," the paper claimed, in the name of "self protection" since the Valley had furnished "large supplies to the rebel armies" and been a "hiding place for guerrillas" who "murder" Northern citizens. By destroying everything in the Harrisonburg region and sending every honest resident fleeing, only "guerrillas and robbers will be found there!"[63]

Two weeks later, on November 1, the *Doylestown Democrat* also reported on Sheridan's activity and the fact that Virginians were seeking refuge in Pennsylvania. Its editor stressed the suffering of Shenandoah civilians at the hands of Federal troops. Alluding to the impending presidential contest in which Lincoln was standing for reelection, the paper—with more than a touch of sarcasm—added that it was doubly sad that the Mennonites in the Confederacy were disenfranchised and "cannot vote for a President that carries on a war with so little regard to Christian principles." The *Democrat* contended that it had nothing but sympathy for "this denomination of Christians" that has been severely punished by the present administration—a remarkable turn, considering how little sympathy Democratic editors had for Pennsylvania Mennonites during the war.[64] Other papers picked up on the story. In Montgomery County, in the town of Skippack, the German *Neutralist* printed a long article on "Mennoniten Fluchtlinge" (Mennonite Refugees) that it reprinted from the *Lancaster*

Volksfreund.[65] Outside the Pennsylvania German pale, however, interest was practically nonexistent.[66]

Meanwhile, Sheridan's destruction continued. On November 11, the *Rockingham Register* summarized the severity of the damage in the local area, citing:

Dwellings burned	30
Barns burned	450
Mills burned	31
Miles of fencing destroyed	100
Wheat in bushels	100,000
Corn in bushels	50,000
Tons of hay	6,233
Cattle driven off	1,750
Horses carried away	1,750
Sheep carried away	4,200
Hogs carried away	3,350[67]

In the North, published reports of Sheridan's victory in the Valley, coupled with news of the Union capture of Atlanta earlier in the fall, were critical factors in Lincoln's November reelection.[68]

On November 19 the general himself sent word to his officers requesting accurate information regarding "material destroyed and property taken" so he could compute "the amount of damage done in the Valley." His report to superiors on November 24 covered destruction from August 10 to November 16 and included a great deal of military hardware (e.g., 94 artillery pieces, 1,061,000 rounds of small-arm ammunition, 19,230 small arms); 1,200 barns; 71 flour mills; 435,802 bushels of wheat; and more than 10,000 head each of beef cattle, sheep, and swine.[69] Even without a report of the number of civilian homes burned, the suffering obviously was severe.

On Christmas day Sheridan asked permission of Chief of Staff Halleck in Washington, D.C., whether he might "issue rations to people of the country between Winchester and Staunton." Halleck submitted the request to the Secretary of War, who answered that disloyal citizens should be sent south "to feed upon the enemy," but that "loyal refugees" could be "temporarily assisted and sent North, where they can earn a liveli-hood."[70]

War Trauma in Augusta County

The property destruction unleashed in the Valley certainly was severe enough, but it hardly compared with the personal pain many Virginians experienced as the war killed family and friends—a tragedy that Augusta County deacon Jacob R. and Catherine Hildebrand experienced during the conflict's closing months. In October 1864, Jacob's younger brother, Gabriel, left for Richmond to join the 52nd Regiment. He now had few options—pay the $500 fee, go into hiding, or enlist—and he chose the army. That same fall, deacon Hildebrand's son Benjamin returned home wounded, the ball still embedded in his arm. Then son Gideon came home, reporting that his horse had taken a nonfatal "shot through the head near the neck." Deacon Jacob thanked God that it was no worse. Gideon soon returned to service with a fresh horse, and father Jacob, as usual, committed him into God's care. Soon Gideon had a much closer call. This time a bullet passed through his horse's heart and then struck Gideon's leg above the ankle. Now deacon Hildebrand had two sons nursing wounds at home, though both rejoined their units by mid-December.[71]

On New Year's Day 1865, the 1st Virginia Cavalry disbanded for ten days, and Gideon came home for another short visit. At the end of the month, the deacon's third and youngest son, Michael, at 17, enlisted and went with Company E of the 1st Virginia Cavalry. "May God in his mercy watch over him & keep him from the wickedness of the prevailing vices, & also keep him safe from his Enemys," father Hildebrand penned in his journal. Then, on the first of February, amid rumors of a possible truce, Jacob and Catherine sent provisions to son Benjamin and brother Gabriel.[72] Rumors circulated that federal commissioners had proposed a ceasefire to Jefferson Davis. Lincoln promised generous terms, even sug-gesting the possibility of compensating slave owners. But no agreement materialized, for Davis insisted on independence for the Confederacy, and Lincoln demanded reunion and emancipation.[73]

So the war continued, amid sinking Southern fortunes and a growing sense of the inevitability of Union victory—an impending outcome that turned the final desperate months' of struggle into a sort of bitter and sense-

Deacon Jacob R. Hildebrand (1819–1908), of Augusta County, Virginia, late in life.
Credit: John R. Hildebrand

less endgame for many Confederate combatants such as the Hildebrands. Gideon and Michael were home for a brief visit in mid-February. Then Sheridan's cavalry and mounted infantry returned again to Waynesboro, looking for lingering resistance, and overwhelmed Early's now decimated forces. On March 2, referring to Southern armed forces with first-person familiarity, deacon Hildebrand noted in his journal, "We had about 1600 men" but "lost about 1000 privates in prisoners & 70 officers," and the rest "scattered to the four winds of the Earth."[74] It was the last time the Valley saw Sheridan.

Gideon and Michael Hildebrand managed to get home again briefly in early March, but on the tenth left to go with the 1st Virginia Cavalry. As usual, deacon Hildebrand wrote a prayer in his journal: "May God still watch over them & keep them from sin & dainger I commit them into his care & keeping." Then on April 7, James Irvine of Company E brought Gideon's horse home with the bad news that on the previous Saturday,

Gideon had been accidentally shot and badly hurt in the hip "by one of our own men." Gideon's brother Michael was able to stay with him for a day, but then fled in order to avoid capture by the Yankees; Gideon was unable to escape.[75]

It was becoming too late for the Confederacy as well. Even before the first of April, General Lee knew that he must abandon Petersburg in order to avoid being encircled by Grant's Union forces. However, pulling back from Petersburg would mean the fall of the capital, Richmond. Early Sunday morning, April 2, Union forces punched through the Confederate lines at several places near Petersburg. While the pastor at St. Paul's Episcopal Church in Richmond offered a prayer for the Confederacy, a messenger quietly handed worshiper Jefferson Davis a telegram from Lee stating that Richmond could no longer be defended. Ashen-faced, Davis got up and left church. Later that day, Davis and other government officials, carrying gold and archival records, boarded trains for Danville, Virginia, to the west. Other Richmond residents also fled, but not before torching most things of military or industrial promise. Mobs formed, and Southerners burned more of their own capitol than the Yankees had burned of Atlanta. On Monday morning Union forces occupied Richmond, restored order, and put out fires. Forty hours after Davis had left his office, Abraham Lincoln, who had wanted so much to see Richmond, sat at Jefferson Davis's desk on East Clay Street and surveyed the damage.[76]

Barely had Jacob and Catherine Hildebrand gotten the news of Gideon's hip injury when they learned that Lee had surrendered at Appomattox Court House, ending the fighting in Virginia. Later they would learn that their son Benjamin had been present at Appomattox. In the meantime, they still had no certain word of the whereabouts of wounded son Gideon. On April 17 deacon Hildebrand started for Fords Depot "to look after my son." He arrived on the 20th, only to learn that Gideon had died on April 2, the day Richmond had fallen, and that he had been buried without a coffin. "I took him up & made one for him & Intered him again," wrote his father, stunned by the loss to "friendly fire" of his son, so few days before the conflict's end.[77]

Later, in a letter from a "sorrowful friend," W. G. Shaver, the Hildebrand parents learned more details about Gideon's last moments. About an hour after Gideon's brother Michael fled the approaching Yankees, onlookers moved Gideon into a house to care for him. Shortly thereafter "he seemed to faint away or rather fall asleep." To those around him, Gideon "seemed to be prepared to meet his God" and was "conscious of having done his duty." To Shaver's surprise, Gideon died quickly, and Shaver did not "wish to interrupt him with talk." He gave Gideon's boots to a barefoot man. Shaver sympathized with the Hildebrands' loss but felt that "our loss is his eternal gain." Shaver apologized that he "could not have a coffin made for him but done the best I could under circumstances."[78]

On May 1, deacon Hildebrand, accompanied by Peter Reese, again headed for Fords Depot to fetch "the body of my Dear Son Gideon Peter Hildebrand who died of a wound the 2nd of Aprile. Got home the 10th & on the 11th we buryed him in the Graveyard at the Menonite Church near Hermitage augusta county Va." Bishop Jacob Hildebrand and another minister conducted the funeral, using the text from 1 Corinthians 15:55–57: "O death, where is thy sting? O grave, where is thy victory? ... But thanks be to God, which giveth us the victory through our Lord Jesus Christ."[79]

"Oh my son my son how I miss you," Jacob R. Hildebrand cried. "May God in his mercy grant us Grace that we may meet you in Heaven where there will be no more war & blood shed & where the wicked cease from troubling & the weary are at Rest."[80] This cruel war that the Mennonite deacon seemed in some ways to have supported, had finally ended.

CHAPTER 11

Reconstructed Nation,
Reconstructed Peoplehood

Glorious News and Uncertain Futures

Thursday, April 13, 1865, was a bright and sunny day in Johnson County, Iowa, when 52-year-old Daniel P. Guengerich, an Amish farmer who had emigrated from Waldeck, Germany, in 1833, went to town on business. There he learned "the glorious news of the surrender of Gen. Lee and his army." Back home, Guengerich's nearly 22-year-old son, Jacob, eagerly embraced those words, recording them with enthusiasm in a diary otherwise filled with more mundane details of weather and work. Five days later the worldly information that jarred Jacob's journal was startlingly more sober: "Got the shocking news of the assassination of A. Lincoln, a sorrowful event indeed."[1] Even for immigrant Amish living on a remote frontier, the president's violent death struck close to home, and their response was a modest sign of their attachment to the American nation.

The assassination sparked an abrupt and wrenching shift in emotion for the nation as collective relief at the close of four years of bloodshed suddenly turned to anxiety. Not only did the killing foreshadow the violence and lawlessness that would continue, despite the formal conclusion of hostilities, but it provoked an alarming sense of uncertainty about the future. While Lee's surrender marked the beginning of the end of Confederate rebellion, it was far from clear what the nature of the surviving

Union would be in the war's wake. With a million casualties, much of the South in ruins, and the profound social and political implications of the emancipation of four million slaves all standing between 1861 and 1865, no simple return to the prewar world was possible.

Among other things, the war had transformed the federal government, giving it remarkable new powers and prestige. With state governments in disarray in the former Confederacy, Washington for the first time stepped into welfare roles in the South, while in Northern states the extensive veterans' pension plan developed into the country's first old age social security system. Throughout the North and the West, the industrial and transportation capacities that war spending had generated were already transforming those regions. Cities mushroomed, and institutions, from corporations to universities, drew on the organizational lessons of the Union army to coordinate and consolidate power and influence.[2] Meanwhile, European immigrants had begun flocking to the United States by the millions, radically reshaping the country's cultural profile. Rather than stability, the end of the war revealed a disorienting flux.

Only a month before Lincoln's assassination, the president's second inaugural address had called for binding up the nation's wounds "with malice toward none" and "with charity for all." Yet no one really knew how Lincoln would have approached the enormity of national reconciliation and the aftermath of emancipation. And now his sudden death made all the unknowns of the war's complicated legacy seem more immediate— and unnerving.

As a state funeral train took Lincoln's body back to Springfield, Illinois, retracing the northern path the president-elect had traveled in the spring of 1861, throngs assembled at rail depots to watch it pass or to view the bier in larger cities where the entourage stopped. Two Amish boys, 11-year-old Jacob Stoltzfus and 9-year-old C. M. Stoltzfus, went to the station at Gap, Pennsylvania. "The train was draped in mourning crepe a yard wide and long hanging down from the windows," Jacob later recalled in vivid detail, and there was "crepe hanging across the R.R. . . . from telegraph pole to pole."[3]

In Harrisburg, the president's casket briefly lay in the state capitol building. John S. Coffman and Peter S. Hartman, Virginia Mennonite refugees who had fled north to avoid Confederate conscription, were working on a nearby farm and went with their employer and 45,000 other people to brave heavy rain and wait in long lines to pay their respects. The men remained in town until evening, when a six-horse hearse returned the body to the train while five bands played "O Come and Let Us Worship."[4] Even Democratic newspapers, such as the Lancaster, Pennsylvania, *Intelligencer* and the Holmes County, Ohio, *Farmer*, published glowing eulogies of the late leader. Lincoln had become a martyr whose death was interpreted religiously as atonement for national sin.[5]

From Chicago, Mennonite editor John F. Funk, who five years earlier had been deeply involved in Lincoln's campaign, used his *Herald of Truth* to note briefly "the sad event [that] has caused great mourning all over the land." The president's assassination, coming as it did on the heels of the war's conclusion, illustrated for Funk that killing was not confined to the battlefield. Funk urged his readers to "labor and pray" so that "the Prince of peace might have dominion . . . and that universal love might be the ruling principle in every heart."[6]

Reconstructing the Nation

Back in Washington, D.C., Andrew Johnson, who had been Lincoln's running mate in 1864 and had served only a few weeks as vice president, entered the White House. Republicans had placed Johnson, a Tennessee Democrat who had opposed secession, on Lincoln's ticket as a political gesture to those alienated by the administration's war policies. But Johnson's ideas about how to reunite the nation stood at odds with those of congressional Republicans. Claiming to be acting with Lincoln's magnanimous spirit, Johnson pursued policies that quickly allowed former Confederate leaders back into power and sharply limited the civil rights and economic opportunities of former slaves. Although Johnson had opposed the institution of slavery, he was committed to white supremacy and rejected almost all efforts to improve the lot of African Americans.[7]

Distrustful of Johnson, the so-called Radical Republicans—often led by the fiery Thaddeus Stevens, who was handily reelected by Lancaster voters every two years until his death in 1868—insisted that Reconstruction policy be placed in the hands of Congress. Stevens and his allies sought to bar former Confederates from power and guarantee African-American civil rights. Seeing to such rights would require ongoing military occupation of the South and heavy federal involvement in what had previously

Lincoln's funeral train at Harrisburg, Pennsylvania. John S. Coffman and
Peter S. Hartman, Virginia Mennonites who had fled north, viewed the president's
body here. Credit: The Lincoln Museum, Fort Wayne, Ind. #990

been state and local affairs, but the Radicals saw such innovations as a
small price to pay in the quest to complete a second American revolution.
The struggle between the president and Congress grew more intense, especially after November 1866, when Northern voters handed Republicans a decisive victory. Hoping to sideline Johnson completely, the Radicals in the House, again led by Stevens, impeached the president (though
the Senate acquitted him).[8]

The political battles in Washington had important implications for postwar life, but in many ways local and regional desires drove the stories that
played out in the North, South, and West. In the former Confederacy and
in the Border State of Missouri, campaigns of violence against one-time
slaves and a general atmosphere of lawlessness that intimidated white and
black reformers ushered in an era of social and economic conservatism that
would make any substantial or sustained social change elusive.[9] For a few
years, though, an alliance of federal officials, black community leaders, and
idealistic Northern white young adults invested remarkable energy into

Jacob E. Yoder (1838–1905) and an unidentified fellow teacher with their students at a Freedmen's Bureau School in Lynchburg, Virginia. Credit: Samuel L. Horst Collection of Papers Relating to Jacob Eshbach Yoder, Jones Memorial Library, Lynchburg, Va.

rebuilding the South on terms friendly to former slaves, or "freedmen." Combining forces with the federal Freedmen's Bureau, private groups such as the Quaker-organized Freedmen's Relief Association established schools and employment offices in Southern cities.[10]

One of the two thousand volunteer white teachers who went south was Jacob E. Yoder, a Mennonite from the Berks County, Pennsylvania, community of Boyertown.[11] Back in 1860, Yoder had enrolled at the new Millersville Normal School near Lancaster to prepare for a career in teaching. Millersville's noted professor James P. Wickersham was an advocate for freedpeople's schooling, and he encouraged his students and alumni to join the national cause linking formal education and civil rights.[12]

In March 1866 Yoder arrived in Lynchburg, Virginia, a city of almost 7,000 that had been relatively untouched by the war and was becoming a magnet for the region's rural freedpeople, who were property-less and often unemployed. Yoder taught in a makeshift school set up at Camp Jefferson Davis, an abandoned Confederate army base on the city's south side. As principal, Yoder oversaw a small corps of teachers, a group of 24 teachers-in-training, and some 345 African-American students enrolled in daytime and evening classes.[13]

The freedpeople's community spirit and determination impressed Yoder. Attending the anniversary celebration of Lynchburg's independent black Sunday school movement in June 1866, Yoder noted a banner that proclaimed, "We are Free." "So short time ago," Yoder mused in his diary, "a people pressed down by a proud aristocracy now rejoices in their freedom for which, as an old man tremblingly said today, 'I have prayed sixty years.' They naturally love freedom. Many of them have a more proper appreciation of the boon of liberty than tens of thousands of Pennsylvanians have."[14]

Like many of the volunteers who went South with a mix of idealism and Northern prejudice, Yoder was instinctively critical of Southern whites. "It is too plain that this people still love Slavery with some blind madness," he wrote shortly after arriving. "They have only accepted the result of this war, because they must. Many hate every measure that is intended to elevate them [African Americans]. Education is their [the freedpeople's] only passport to distinction. Therefore the whites so bitterly oppose it." At the same time, he seemed unsure of the transforming power of education among former slaves who were so "immensely poor;

profoundly ignorant; [and] remarkably vicious." Generations of bondage had corrupted black character, he decided, and it would take years to undo the damage.[15]

Yoder went home after one term of teaching, apparently expecting to be back in Lynchburg that fall. For reasons that remain unclear, he was unable to return until 1868. In the meantime, he kept up his Lynchburg contacts, including corresponding with Samuel Kelso, a noted African-American teacher and politician. In his diary, Yoder also followed Reconstruction's political twists and turns, blaming Andrew Johnson for shortcomings in meaningful Southern reform. When Yoder made it back to Lynchburg, he became administrator of a system of twenty-four primary schools in six counties, all serving African-American children, and he taught in the small Lynchburg high school established for freedpeople.[16]

Funding public education for both white and black students quickly became bogged down in Reconstruction wrangling. Only in 1871 did Virginia—rather than the federal government or Northern charities—begin supporting schools for black students. At that point, Yoder became a state employee, and he spent the rest of his life in Lynchburg, championing public education for African Americans in a political system increasingly unresponsive to the needs of its black citizens.[17]

Jacob Yoder's focused concern for former slaves made him highly unusual among postwar Mennonites. Judging by the sources that have survived, few Mennonites understood the war primarily in terms of abolition or its legacy in the freedpeople's future. To be sure, by 1900 a number of Mennonites who had adopted a more outward-looking theological posture and absorbed the evangelical spirit of the age would begin "industrial missions" in some black communities and would eventually invite converts to join their church. (In the twenty-first century the largest congregation in Mennonite Church USA would be a predominately African-American church in Hampton, Virginia.) But for a long time, such work and attitudes would be exceptional. For the most part, Mennonites in Virginia—and a handful of northern ones who later moved into the Deep South in search of affordable farmland—did not question the region's segregationist climate. And with few exceptions, the vast majority who remained in the North were far from the forefront of the twentieth-century's racial revolution.[18]

In this respect, Mennonites fit the pattern provocatively portrayed by historian David W. Blight, who charted the eclipse of African-American concerns in the aftermath of the Civil War. The story of national reunion framed the war's memory and meaning in a way that rendered the role of race in the conflict's origins and legacy invisible. Groups of white veterans decided that their fighting had been about heroism, not ideological differences. Politicians preaching economic advancement presented the war as an unfortunate detour rather than a redefining event. Black Americans did not figure in such memories.[19]

For many Americans—including, no doubt, many Mennonites and Amish—such remembering was linked to a strong desire to repair personal relationships disrupted by the war and to avoid new conflicts. In June 1865, when Emanuel and Elizabeth (Swope) Suter returned to the Rockingham County, Virginia, farmstead they had fled some months before, they discovered that resentful Confederate neighbors had "commenced carrying off the [family's] property" and otherwise seemed hostile to those who had opposed secession. Neighborliness was deeply damaged, Emanuel admitted, and yet he desperately wanted to believe that the lingering antagonism would blow over. Seeking signs of hope in white Reconstruction politics, he wrote optimistically to his father, still in Northern exile, that many former rebels had "taken the oth to the United States Government." Indeed, Suter claimed, "the Conffederacy is forgotten."[20]

Memory and War

Suter was certainly too sanguine in his assessment. The experiences of the Civil War remained keen memory and, in fact, shaped memories that transformed group and personal identities in profound ways—including perceptions of peoplehood carried by Mennonite and Amish Americans.[21] In the years that followed Appomattox, virtually no one could avoid confronting some memory of the war—whether in the bodily reminders afforded by thousands of veteran amputees who returned to communities across the nation, or in the stone monuments erected in many towns, silently presenting patriotic Union and Confederate accounts of the war.[22] Some of these markers included the names of the local fallen, ensuring that Mennonite and Amish sons who had gone to war and not returned would be publicly and permanently part of the local landscape for both their families and surviving comrades.[23]

Lancaster, Pennsylvania's Civil War monument, dedicated 1874, in Penn Square. Many towns erected prominent memorials, fixing public memory of patriotic sacrifice. Credit: Lancaster County (Pa.) Historical Society

But none of these public memories had a place for nonresistants—although some of them might have. Discarded muskets collected in the aftermath of Civil War battles revealed that as many as half were loaded multiple times, suggesting to some military analysts that many soldiers went through the motions of loading and firing, but could not actually bring themselves to shoot at fellow humans. Reticence to kill may have been much more widespread than Mennonites, Dunkers, and Quakers at the time realized, and their own practice may not have been as odd as they imagined. "War, when you are at it, is horrible and dull," Union veteran and future Supreme Court Justice Oliver Wendell Holmes Jr. said in 1884. "It is only when time has passed that you see that its message was divine."[24] It was this memory of divine war that prevailed in the decades that followed 1865.

Mennonite and Amish communities preserved or acknowledged few such memories. Near Danvers, Illinois, Hessian Amish immigrant Valentine Nafziger, who had enlisted and served in Alabama, Louisiana, and Texas, came home and joined the Grand Army of the Republic veterans post at Bloomington, where, presumably, he joined fellow members in recounting war stories. He did not join the Amish church.[25] Near Bluffton, Ohio, when Mennonite-reared Abraham Schneck, who had enlisted in 1862, returned home, fellow Swiss Mennonites ostracized and derided him as "Krieg Schneck" (War Schneck); he joined the Reformed Church.[26] Apparently few of the Mennonite or Amish-reared men who joined the military ever went back to their families' faith communities. Some, like Samuel S. Yoder, were alienated from their Amish upbringing even before they enlisted. Yoder became a probate judge and two-term Democratic Congressman who requested burial in Arlington National Cemetery.[27] Those who did connect to nonresistant congregations may have had to manage their memories carefully. After almost three years at war, Daniel Buchwalter joined Martins Mennonite Church near Orrville, Ohio, where, into his old age, he publicly promoted the congregation's peace stance. At home, however, he would "parade his grandchildren around the living room table to the tune of 'Marching through Georgia,'" and he happily posed for family pictures with his army-issued rifle.[28]

In contrast to such private reminiscences, a particular cluster—or clusters—of nonresistant war memories emerged publicly among American Anabaptists. Many of these memories bolstered convictions that differentiated them from their non-pacifist neighbors, while others separated them from one another and perhaps even anchored some more firmly to local ethnic contexts. In certain regions, suffering was a dominant theme; in other places, it was thankfulness or repentance.

With the fading of substitution as an acceptable alternative to personal military service, some stories emphasized for a new generation the moral dilemmas of the substitution system. Near Lancaster, Pennsylvania, Amishman John S. Stoltzfus, who had hired a draft substitute, was remembered as being reticent to discuss his wartime choice. His replacement did not survive the war, and Stoltzfus kept the man's uniform, occasionally taking it out in private to look at and contemplate.[29] Widely known in General Conference Mennonite Church circles was the story of Christian Krehbiel, whose family had immigrated in 1851 from Bavaria to Summerfield, Illinois, in large part to avoid military service. Drafted in his new country in 1864, Krehbiel followed conventional European practice and hired a substitute. Family accounts, however, stressed the emotional toll on Krehbiel when the substitute, an immigrant miner named Remigius Mantele, left for war. After Mantele contracted "camp fever" and returned to Illinois "looking like a skeleton," the Krehbiels assumed financial responsibility for him for the rest of his life.[30]

More straightforward in their nonresistant teaching were stories from Virginia of Mennonites, conscripted against their will, who shot over the heads of enemy troops and explained to indignant officers that fellow humans were not acceptable targets.[31] In a somewhat different vein was the story of Jacob M. Herr, son of a Mennonite minister near Carlisle, Pennsylvania, who joined the Union army and served for three years. When he returned from the war, apparently disillusioned with military life, he confessed error and united with his parents' church, only to be ordained eight years later to fill his father's office. Herr did not detail his time in uniform but said he "took comfort in the hope that he had never taken a life, or injured a fellow mortal."[32]

Such stories stressed the psychic toll of the war on men with scruples who faced the prospect of conscription, but a wider circle of memories focused the war's meaning in suffering and included the experiences of men and women of many ages. Published in church periodicals or passed orally along family lines and sometimes included in genealogies, the suffering motif that interpreted the war as a time of testing was especially prominent in Virginia or other places where the war raged close to Amish and Mennonite homes. Lost property, the toll on families (not just on drafted men), and the flight of those liable to be drafted or those assisting with draft resistance, figured prominently.

Among Virginia Mennonites the memory of wartime suffering took on a formal character after 1871, when households who had withheld support from the Confederacy and yet had lost property to Federal troop foraging could apply for reimbursement from Washington. The heart of this process, overseen by the congressionally established Southern Claims Commission, involved claimants publicly testifying, and bringing forward corroborating witnesses, to their anti-Confederate sentiments and the conditions under which they had lost assets.[33] Evidence of Union loyalty might include having voted against secession, refusing to sell to the Rebel army, resisting conscription, or being labeled as disloyal by neighbors who supported the South. The procedure increased local tensions in the 1870s as white Southerners, frustrated with six years of federally dictated Reconstruction, heard again the stories of dissent, loss, and betrayal. In Rockingham County, Virginia, more than 85 percent of claims were Dunker or Mennonite.[34]

In the end, only a minority of the Mennonite claims were allowed, since the Commission set a high standard for determining loyalty to the United States and establishing evidence of lost property.[35] But many claims were not allowed because Shenandoah Valley Mennonites—despite their overwhelming opposition to the Confederacy—*had* often tacitly recognized the authorities under which they lived. Apparently many did accept Confederate currency when Southern troops commandeered commodities, and some voted for secession or enlisted under extreme duress. In addition, because nonresistants did not carry out guerilla warfare against Richmond, they may not have fit the Commission's image of Union loyalists.[36]

Hog farmer Isaac Wenger was one Mennonite claimant whose petition for $1,765.60 the Commission rejected. Although Wenger produced evidence of loyalty and a string of witnesses to back him, the Commission noted that he had "furnished a substitute" to the Confederate army and "rendered aid and comfort to the enemy" by accepting payment for "supplies to maintain the [Confederate] army in the field."[37]

One of the striking things that emerges from the stories Mennonites and their witnesses told the Claims Commission is the prevalence of coordinated civil disobedience, no doubt the largest collective act of defiance ever carried out by American Mennonites. Frequently and consistently, Mennonites described assisting draft evaders—both Mennonites and non-Mennonites—to hide or to flee the Shenandoah Valley. Abraham D. and Magdalenah (Rodes) Heatwole were among those who ran "a sort of headquarters" for such activity, despite the "constant danger from having so many coming to our place for concealment and refuge while getting ready to go north." Just west of Harrisonburg, Daniel P. Good and David Hartman apparently assisted in the flight of more than a hundred men. John Brunk, sexton of the Weavers Mennonite Church, hid fugitives in the meetinghouse. Margaret (Heatwole) Rhodes, a woman in her mid-thirties, concealed draft resisters and acted as a "postmaster" for Unionists, transporting correspondence between family members and fugitives, going "a distance of 6 miles myself to deliver letters sometimes, leaving my

5 children with my mother in law." The boldness with which these and a great many others acted may have aroused suspicion, but only a few were ever caught. Fannie (Bowman) Rodes testified that neighbors suspected her participation in this Unionist underground railroad, at one point telling her son "they would blow his G_d D_mn brains out" and calling the family "lower than niggers." But Rodes was undeterred.[38]

Curiously, over time the memory of collective civil disobedience receded. Perhaps such blatant anti-Confederate activity became too unpopular to recount as the postwar myth of a noble Southern Lost Cause gained clout in the closing years of the nineteenth century. Perhaps too, Mennonites' sense that the Confederacy had always lacked legitimacy did not allow them to see their actions as radical protests, but as signs of orderly submission to the properly constituted (Union) government in Washington. In any case, stories of suffering, property loss, and personal flight eventually became the stuff of Virginia Mennonite Civil War memories.[39]

Postwar Peoplehood

Suffering was not the only legacy of the Civil War for Mennonites and Amish, especially in the North. In the land of the victors, joyful relief associated with the coming of peace might occasionally take on overtones of triumph. McLean County, Illinois, tradition preserves a postwar ditty that Amish mothers sang to their children, participating in broader Northern parody of Jefferson Davis:

> Oh ladies, have you seen Jeff Davis,
> He's changed his name of late,
> He ran away the other day
> From old Virginia state.[40]

And although parts of south central Pennsylvania still bore battle scars in 1865, the war had generated much new wealth in the North, for example, transforming John Funk's Chicago into the unrivaled commercial hub of the Midwest. In Pennsylvania, Mennonite-reared Levi Rutt Sensenig used the fortune he had made selling cattle to the Union army to create the Lancaster Stockyards, the largest animal trading center anywhere east of Chicago.[41] The war years had not been synonymous everywhere with suffering.

But Northern memories of the war did not uniformly suggest how Mennonites should relate to this new Northern culture of confident growth and consumption. Politically—and, to some degree, socially—the experience of the 1860s confirmed for eastern Pennsylvania Mennonites that being a separate people did not depend on civic disengagement. Indeed, neighbors would make a place for nonresistants if peace people participated in the political sphere. In 1912 a Lancaster County (Old) Mennonite penned an essay entitled "How about voting?"—with the inquiring title setting up a defense of the practice. The author's central example was a Civil War–era story that circulated among his people, a tale in which Lancaster Mennonites—including an esteemed minister—had visited Governor Andrew Curtin "to see in regard to getting Mennonites free from military service." The governor listened patiently, then asked if the petitioners voted. Learning that they did, the governor was said to have replied "Then we will do something for you."[42]

This notion that civic participation legitimated civic privilege was one of the war's legacies for Pennsylvania Mennonites, who practiced a sort of sectarian ecumenicity. The same essay on voting, for example, gently asserted that while the non-Mennonite world included corruption, it did not follow that the entire public square was profane. The biblical prophet Elijah "thought that he was the only righteous man in all Israel," the author reminded readers. "Then he found out that there were over 7000 that served the true God." The same was true today, the piece concluded, if one recognized gracious allies.[43]

Very soon some Pennsylvania Mennonites would be putting this Civil War lesson to use in the context of World War I. Working closely with their Republican congressman, W. W. Greist, they would avoid the harassment that befell pacifists in other parts of the country. More than a shrewd bargain, this understanding represented a democratic social contract in which participation entitled minorities to a measure of respect. In 1923, while many nonresistant Christians in the Midwest were still living under the shadow of the Great War, a majority of the general voters elected (Old) Mennonite Samuel G. Zimmerman as Lancaster County Commissioner. Republican leaders symbolically reaffirmed the relationship in 1926 when they made a donation toward the construction of the Weaverland Mennonite meetinghouse—home to one of the state's largest and most influential (Old) Mennonite congregations.[44]

But it was in its classically Midwestern form that the Civil War's legacy would prove most influential for American Mennonites and Amish. There the war had, for the most part, created a sharper sense of "outsiderhood" than it had in eastern Pennsylvania. Although Midwestern communities did not suffer the sorts of direct persecution that their fellow believers in Virginia did, the harassment in the Shenandoah Valley had come from Confederate authorities that lacked power after 1865. Mennonites in the Midwest, in contrast, had felt alienated from the political structures with which they would continue to live. Their war memories suggested that democracy had little room for minority voices and that those who would not help defend majority will with majority means should forfeit their place in the civic arena. Given such lessons, nonresistant people with any integrity needed to think about the possibility of cultural self-suffi-ciency.

Among the Old Order Amish, who emerged as self-conscious groups during the war years, this understanding of separation hinging on with-drawal was especially clear. But it also played a crucial role in the much larger bodies of (Old) Mennonites, change-minded Amish Mennonites, and so-called Swiss Mennonite communities. It helped that Midwestern Mennonites and Amish were blessed with articulate spokespeople such as Ohio's John M. Brenneman, Iowa's Jacob Schwartzendruber, and es-pecially Chicagoan John F. Funk (who was soon to move to Elkhart, Indi-ana). Beginning in 1864 Funk's *Herald of Truth* had begun speaking for a Mennonitism that offered an alternative to the world, and not just a par-ticular place to stand within that world.

Already in the spring of 1865, Funk had challenged other formulations of Mennonite identity. An April 1865 secular news story entitled "Pa-triotism Among the Mennonites" had described a set of resolutions passed by the Mennonite-linked Trinity Christian Society that met at German-town, Pennsylvania. That tiny group applauded the "success of our arms on sea and land," deemed the war a holy "struggle between truth and er-ror, right and wrong, freedom and bondage," and urged "every Christian patriot to pray . . . for the success of our armies." "He who, in the hour of his country's travail," the statement concluded, "stands not up manfully to vindicate her cause . . . is recreant to God and . . . unworthy of the name of an American citizen."[45] To be sure, the splinter group behind the resolu-tions deviated greatly from historic Anabaptist practices, having adopting infant baptism, for example.[46] Nevertheless, Funk's vigorous effort to set the record straight and his rebuttal to the tone and content of the resolutions that a secular newspaper erroneously touted as the Mennonite mainstream illustrated his convictions and the direction that his energy would take him in the years to come. Mennonites respected government, Funk insisted, but they stood apart from political entanglements since such relationships compromised their ability to take a consistent nonresistant stance worthy of Anabaptist two-kingdom theology.[47]

Yet Funk and the emerging Midwestern consensus on such matters was not mainly reactionary. In fact, Funk's editorial argument with the Trinity Christian group was a minor diversion from his larger, more positive project of constructing a Mennonite institutional world that could bind together large and small communities, established and frontier churches, wealthy and poorer Mennonites, into closer unity. The war had demonstrated the lack of consensus, coordination, and systematic communication among Mennonite and Amish Americans. Local sensibilities and informal correspondence networks had left scattered members of the faith—such as Funk in Chicago—adrift, and had isolated suffering coreligionists behind Confederate lines. If the war had not formally divided Mennonites and Amish (as it had Methodists, Baptists, Presbyterians, and Episcopalians), perhaps it was because there was too little real unity to begin with.

Into this organizational vacuum the entrepreneurial Funk brought his periodical, with regional synodical reports, editorial prodding, and letters from scattered readers—including correspondence from Virginia Mennonites such as Augusta County bishop Jacob Hildebrand, who longed for contact with Northern friends.[48] In addition, the *Herald* promoted a growing number of semi-official church boards and committees that promised to forge a clear and activist Mennonite identity that transcended place and tradition. These efforts would cast peoplehood in more clearly theological and ideological terms. Mission work, publishing concerns, and charitable homes for orphans, to name a few of the activities emanating from the industrious circle of Funk and his supporters, would offer Mennonites and progressive Amish Mennonites a purpose that paralleled projects in wider American society without making Mennonites party to those worldly plans.

In general, Midwestern (Old) Mennonites and Amish Mennonites warmly embraced this new theological and denominational vision, some to the point of remembering the years before the Civil War as a sort of "dark ages" of compromised faithfulness. It is too much to say that the Civil War experience was a singular turning point for American Mennonites in this regard, but the way Mennonites in this region experienced the war, and then remembered that experience, confirmed a sort of activist sectarian sensibility that strove to legitimate itself on its own terms. Well into the twentieth century, this formulation of Mennonitism would prove resilient and powerful, and it extended its influence into regions that had not immediately taken to it. Furthermore, this new expression of Mennonite identity fit the expectations of those outside the Anabaptist fold. Theologian H. Richard Niebuhr's characterization of Mennonites as representing "Christ against culture" drew especially on this pattern of peoplehood.[49]

The Civil War's significance in shaping Mennonite identity was also notable in its absence. In the 1870s, as Reconstruction was drawing to a close, some 18,000 Mennonite immigrants from the Russian empire arrived in North America, dramatically altering the face of North American Mennonitism. The Russians carried cultures and customs that distinguished them from Mennonites whose North American roots went generations deep. But just as significantly, the newcomers did *not* carry Civil War memories or the lessons those recent and traumatic experiences provided about how to relate to their new national homes. Not surprisingly, Russian Mennonites in America were less inclined to see as self-evident the apolitical logic of the postwar Midwestern (Old) Mennonite and Amish social posture.[50] Then too, almost half of these Russian arrivals settled in Canada, where they substantially augmented the Mennonite presence that had existed in that country since 1786. Mennonite cross-border connections had always rested on historical ties, but the frightful Civil War in the United States had had no equivalent for nonresistants to the north (except to the degree that a few Mennonite "skedaddlers" had settled in Ontario). That absence would contribute to an emerging continental divide among coreligionists, marked in part by Canadian Mennonites' less suspicious stance toward the state.[51]

For Mennonites and Amish in the United States, the war and the memories of war had acted as both lens and prism, focusing and distinguishing peoplehood along lines that would influence for generations their religious, regional, and ethnic sensibilities and their churches' interaction with American society. A two-kingdom people in a world of multiple identities, Mennonites and Amish faced the challenges of faithfulness and relevance, and formulated divergent responses to that tension.

A hundred years later, in the summer of 1962, Vincent Harding, the African-American historian and, at that time, Mennonite pastor in Atlanta, mused on the place of peace people in an American society still saddled, consciously or not, with the legacy of the events and choices made a century earlier. Mixing language that would have seemed both foreign and familiar to nineteenth-century Mennonites and Amish, Harding recalled "our persecuted Anabaptist forefathers," who "were a minority, forever in danger of their lives, always threatened with swift destruction of their property." Yet he wondered: Had the American descendants of those martyrs, prosperous and free from the immediate affliction of war for several generations and drawing on increasingly distant memories of marginalization, "forgotten what it is to rejoice in suffering for Christ's sake, forgotten our comradeship with the outcasts, forgotten how it was to be fools for Christ's sake?" Without such a lively historical memory, could any people hope "to be ministers of reconciliation, wherever there is conflict and strife?"[52]

The heirs of those who fought and those who refused to fight in the 1860s, along with all who probe the moral dimensions of human conflict, still live with such questions.

The Sonnenberg Petition

Shortly before the 1862 federally authorized state militia draft went into effect, the Sonnenberg Mennonite Church of Wayne County, Ohio, convened a special meeting to discuss their collective response to the war. That gathering produced a remarkably articulate petition, which the church presented to the Wayne County Military Committee, who in turn forwarded it to Governor David Tod. There is no record of any other Mennonite or Amish congregation holding such a gathering during the war.

The petition is a clear statement of nineteenth-century Mennonite and Amish understandings of the church and its limited obligations to state demands. The Swiss petitioners had emigrated from Europe, beginning in 1819, in part to escape pressure to participate directly in military affairs—background that surely informed this petition.

The document was signed by Ulrich Sommer (1792–1880), an 1824 immigrant, who had been ordained to the ministry in 1827 and elected to the office of bishop in 1842; and Christian Sommer (1811–1891), an 1819 immigrant who had been ordained minister in 1838. Two months after the meeting to draft the petition, the Sonnenberg church elected Christian Sommer bishop. See chapter 5 for additional context.

The petition is located in David Tod Papers, 1862–1864, Collection 306, Library/Archives Division, Ohio Historical Society, Columbus, Ohio.

The Members of the Mennonite Church at Sugar Creek and East Union townships Wayne County, Ohio, Assembled in Public Meeting on the 6th day of August 1862, for the purpose of Considering the present Sad State of the Country, and to deliberate upon the duties of all good and Loyal Citizens, agreed upon the following address and Resolutions, as defining their position in relation to the Affairs of the Country.

Whereas it is well known that during the period of two or three centuries our ancestors were persecuted by the Governments of different States of Europe, because of our Confession of Faith, which forbids us among other Articles to use Arms against, or to make war against our fellowmen under all circumstances.

And whereas we have for many years enjoyed the blessings of Religious liberty in this Country unlimited and unmolested, we hope that the same spirit of tolerance may still prevail and protection [will continue for us] as peaceful and inoffensive citizens in our hitherto enjoyed liberties.

But at the same time we deem it as our duty to define our views and express our willingness to support the Government in all things required of us which do not conflict with our confession of faith, therefore it is,

Resolved: that we offer thanks to our Government for privileges, liberties and protection we have hitherto enjoyed, and that we recognize it ordained of God as the government of our Country, therefore we condemn all rebellion and insurrection against the Government, as resistance against the Ordinance of God.

Resolved that we owe tribute to whom tribute is due, custom to whom custom, fear to whom fear, honor to whom honor,—therefore we are willing and deem it as our duty to obey the laws of our Country, and to support our Government by all means in our power, as far as our Conscience will allow.

Resolved: that there are things in which we must obey God more than men, and that to do military service conflicts with our confession of faith, as a matter of conscience we cannot consent to violate our faith if by any possible means we can prevent it, therefore we are willing to assist in aiding the cause of our country in any other way that may be required of us, in contributions of money or other requisites as much as [is] in our power to do, our confession bidding us to sacrifice property and all that we possess in case of necessity rather than to make use of the sword,—

We shall endeavour by all possible means to do our duty towards God and our Government, and hope that we will not be compelled to do any thing which to avoid we would, and are resolved to suffer the penalty of the law rather than to violate our faith, but that we will be allowed to satisfy the demands of Government by a Commutation instead of doing Military Service.

Signed by our ordained Ministers of the Gospel
Ulrich Sommer
Christian Sommer

Mennonites Identified on Roll of Exemptions, Rockingham County, Virginia, 1862–1864

Volume 1 of the enrollment books lists the following men "Exempt as of October 1, 1863."

Date of Exemption	Name	Age	Height	Complexion	Hair	Eyes	Occupation	Church
12-5-62	Christian Shank	24	5′6″	fair	light	hazel	farmer	Mennonite
12-10-62	Simeon Hildebrand	19	5′6″	fair	brown	gray	farmer	Mennonite
12-10-62	Emanual Suter	29	5′10½″	fair	dark	gray	farmer	Mennonite
12-10-62	Abram D. Heatwole	33	5′7¾″	fair	light	gray	farmer	Mennonite
12-10-62	George Brunk	31	5′8″	dark	dark	brown	shoemaker	Mennonite
12-10-62	Jacob Guile	34	5′9¾″	fair	dark	gray	farmer	Mennonite
12-11-62	Peter Blosser	30	5′11½″	dark	black	brown	farmer	Mennonite
12-11-62	Abram Wenger	37	5′8¼″	fair	dark	gray	farmer	Mennonite
12-15-62	Samuel Landes	27	5′9¼″	fair	dark	brown	farmer	Mennonite
12-29-62	Henry A. Rhodes	34	5′7¼″	dark	dark	blue	farmer	Mennonite
12-30-62	Abram B. Wenger	23	5′8¼″	dark	dark	blue	farmer	Mennonite
1-1-63	Jacob Early	38	5′8″	dark	dark	brown	farmer	Mennonite
1-19-63	Samuel J. Shenk	32	5′6¼″	fair	brown	gray	farmer	Mennonite
1-26-63	David A. Heatwole	35	6′½″	fair	brown	gray	farmer	Mennonite
1-28-63	David Suter	33	5′7½″	dark	dark	brown	farmer	Mennonite
1-31-63	Michael Showalter	31	5′7¼″	dark	dark	gray	farmer	Mennonite
2-14-63	Daniel Brunk	39	5′9¼″	dark	brown	gray	farmer	Mennonite

continued

Date of Exemption	Name	Age	Height	Complexion	Hair	Eyes	Occupation	Church
2-14-63	Jacob Fifer	27	5′8″	fair	brown	gray	farmer	Mennonite
2-16-63	H. A. Brunk	31	5′10½″	fair	light	blue	carpenter	Mennonite
2-16-63	D. C. Brannaman	26	5′9½″	fair	brown	gray	farmer	Mennonite
2-16-63	Daniel J. Crower	29	6′¼″	fair	brown	gray	laborer	Mennonite
2-16-63	Henry Good	31	5′8″	dark	brown	gray	farmer	Mennonite
2-16-63	Christian Good	20	5′8″	fair	brown	gray	farmer	Mennonite
2-16-63	Daniel H. Good	19	5′4¾″	fair	light	gray	farmer	Mennonite
2-16-63	Jacob Heatwole	38	5′9½″	fair	brown	gray	farmer	Mennonite
2-16-63	P. O. Heatwole	35	5′8¼″	fair	brown	gray	farmer	Mennonite
2-16-63	Simeon Heatwole	31	5′9″	fair	brown	gray	farmer	Mennonite
2-16-63	G. D. Heatwole	28	5′10″	fair	brown	gray	farmer	Mennonite
2-16-63	Henry E. Rhodes	29	5′8″	dark	black	brown	farmer	Mennonite
2-16-63	Anthony Showalter	32	5′10¼″	dark	black	brown	farmer	Mennonite
6-20-63	Jacob Wenger	34	5′4½″	fair	light brown	blue	farmer	Mennonite
8-13-63	Samuel Carpenter	42	5′10″	fair	dark	brown	farmer	Mennonite
9-21-63	Samuel Shank	35	5′10″	dark	dark	gray	farmer	Mennonite
9-23-63	Isaac Wenger	40	5′9¼″	fair	dark	gray	farmer	Mennonite
9-23-63	Martin Brannaman	37	5′11″	fair	light	gray	farmer	Mennonite
1-11-64	David E. Rhodes	25	5′11″	fair	brown	blue	farmer	Mennonite

Also listed in volume 1 are some Mennonites who had substitutes in service on October 1, 1863, but whose church affiliations were not given. The following may have been Mennonite: Abraham Swartz, Isaac Showalter, Frederick Rhodes, N. M. Burkholder, John Brunk, David B. Rhodes, Samuel A. Coffman, Isaac Wanger, Samuel Shank, David Shank, Lewis Driver, Samel F. Showalter, Samuel Brunk, George N. Showalter, Martin Brannaman, John T. Showalter, Abram Brannaman, Peter Wenger, J. M. Weaver, Henry A. Heatwole, Anthony Rhodes, and M. Brunk.

Volume 2 of the enrollment books again list numerous Mennonites who were "Exempt as Mennonite" from May to August 1864. Those identified as Mennonites:

Date of Exemption	Name	Age	Height	Complexion	Hair	Eyes	Occupation	Church
5-27-64	D. C. Breneman	26	5′9½″	fair	brown	gray	farmer	Mennonite
5-27-64	Henry Good	31	5′8″	dark	brown	gray	farmer	Mennonite
5-27-64	Jacob Wenger	34	5′4½″	fair	brown	blue	farmer	Mennonite
5-27-64	D. Showalter	23	5′8½″	fair	brown	gray	farmer	Mennonite
5-27-64	Michael Showalter	31	5′7¼″	dark	dark	gray	farmer	Mennonite

Date of Exemption	Name	Age	Height	Complexion	Hair	Eyes	Occupation	Church
5-27-64	Christian Shank	24	5'6"	fair	light	hazel	farmer	Mennonite
5-27-64	Jacob Guile	34	5'9¾"	fair	dark	gray	farmer	Mennonite
5-27-64	Daniel Brunk	39	5'9¼"	dark	brown	gray	farmer	Mennonite
5-27-64	George Brunk	31	5'8"	dark	dark	brown	farmer	Mennonite
5-27-64	John Rhodes	42	5'6"	dark	light	blue	farmer	Mennonite
7-20-64	John Guile	33	5'8"	dark	dark	gray	farmer	Mennonite
7-20-64	Joseph Blosser	37	5'8½"	dark	dark	hazel	farmer	Mennonite
7-20-64	Joseph B. Trissell	40	5'4"	dark	dark	brown	farmer	Mennonite
7-20-64	Lewis Driver	36	5'11"	fair	dark	hazel	farmer	Mennonite
7-20-64	David Burkholder	31	5'6"	fair	brown	brown	farmer	Mennonite
7-20-64	David Fry	38	5'7½"	fair	brown	gray	farmer	Mennonite
7-20-64	Samuel Landes	27	5'9¼"	fair	dark	brown	farmer	Mennonite
7-20-64	Abraham D. Heatwole	33	5'7¼"	fair	light	gray	farmer	Mennonite
7-20-64	David E. Rhodes	25	5'11"	fair	brown	blue	farmer	Mennonite
7-20-64	A. C. Layman	40	5'9"	fair	dark	gray	farmer	Mennonite
7-20-64	Benjamin Burkholder	25	5'10"	fair	dark	brown	farmer	Mennonite
7-20-64	H. A. Brunk	31	5'10½"	fair	light	gray	farmer	Mennonite
7-20-64	D. H. Weaver	26	5'10"	dark	dark	gray	farmer	Mennonite
7-20-64	Simeon Heatwole	31	5'9"	fair	brown	gray	farmer	Mennonite
7-20-64	H. Burkholder	27	6'3"	dark	dark	dark	farmer	Mennonite
7-20-64	Samuel Burkholder	21	5'10¾"	dark	dark	brown	farmer	Mennonite
7-20-64	Samuel J. Shank	32	5'6¼"	fair	brown	gray	farmer	Mennonite
7-20-64	H. L. Rhodes	26	5'11½"	fair	brown	gray	farmer	Mennonite
7-20-64	John Showalter	34	5'7"	fair	brown	gray	farmer	Mennonite
7-20-64	Jacob Heatwole	38	5'9½"	fair	brown	gray	farmer	Mennonite
7-20-64	Samuel Brunk	20	5'6¼"	fair	dark	gray	shoemaker	Mennonite
7-20-64	G. D. Heatwole	29	5'10"	fair	brown	gray	farmer	Mennonite
7-20-64	Daniel H. Good	19	5'4¾"	fair	light	gray	farmer	Mennonite
7-20-64	Jacob Brunk	43	5'9½"	dark	dark	gray	farmer	Mennonite
7-20-64	John Brunk	44	5'8"	dark	dark	blue	farmer	Mennonite
7-20-64	Henry E. Rhodes	29	5'8"	dark	black	brown	farmer	Mennonite
7-20-64	Jacob Early	38	5'8"	dark	dark	brown	farmer	Mennonite
7-20-64	Henry Heatwole	35	5'5½"	fair	brown	gray	farmer	Mennonite
7-20-64	Emanuel Suter	29	5'10"	fair	dark	gray	farmer	Mennonite

continued

Date of Exemption	Name	Age	Height	Complexion	Hair	Eyes	Occupation	Church
7-20-64	A. Showalter	32	5'10"	dark	dark	dark	farmer	Mennonite
7-20-64	P. O. Heatwole	35	5'9½"	fair	brown	gray	farmer	Mennonite
	Daniel Landes	32	6'2"	fair	brown	gray		Mennonite
7-23-64	Rudolph Keagy	30	5'7"	dark	dark	dark gray	farmer	Mennonite
7-23-64	Peter Blosser	30	5'11½"	dark	black	brown	farmer	Mennonite
7-23-64	A. C. Fishback	35	5'9½"	fair	black	gray	black-smith	Mennonite
7-27-64	Christian Good	26	5'8"	fair	brown	gray	farmer	Mennonite
7-27-64	David A. Heatwole	35	6'½"	fair	brown	gray	farmer	Mennonite
7-27-64	Noah C. Wenger	27	5'9¼"	fair	dark	gray	farmer	Mennonite
7-27-64	Simeon Hiltabrand	19	5'10"	fair	brown	gray	farmer	Mennonite
7-27-64	D. J. Crower	29	6'¼"	fair	light	gray	farmer	Mennonite
7-27-64	Henry Guile	31	5'11"	fair	brown	gray	farmer	Mennonite
7-27-64	Shem S. Heatwole	33	5'7¼"	fair	brown	gray	farmer	Mennonite
7-27-64	David Suter	33	5'9½"	dark	dark	brown	farmer	Mennonite
8-1-64	Jacob Fifer	27	5'8"	fair	light	gray	farmer	Mennonite
8-1-64	Martin Breneman	37	5'11"	fair	light	gray	farmer	Mennonite
8-1-64	John P. Good	44	5'7"	dark	dark	blue	farmer	Mennonite
8-1-64	Daniel Wenger	43	5'10"	dark	dark	blue	farmer	Mennonite
8-1-64	Isaac Niswander	30	5'9"	fair	dark	brown	farmer	Mennonite
8-1-64	Henry A. Rhodes	34	5'7½"	dark	dark	blue	farmer	Mennonite
8-1-64	Abraham Swartz	24	5'8½"	fair	dark	gray	farmer	Mennonite
8-1-64	M. Shank	33	5'8"	dark	brown	gray	farmer	Mennonite
8-1-64	Benjamin Wenger	21	5'6½"	fair	brown	gray	farmer	Mennonite
8-1-64	John Wenger	44	5'8¼"	fair	black	blue	farmer	Mennonite

Source: Mss4, R5915b, Rockingham Co., Va. Enrolling Books, 1862–1864, Vols. 1 and 2, Virginia Historical Society, Richmond, Va.

Note: A few surprises occur in terms of names. Several named as Mennonite are doubtful, and some named as Dunker may have been Mennonite. It is not surprising if officials were not altogether accurate in identifying denominations.

Abbreviations

AGR	Adjutant General Records, Department of Military and Veterans Affairs, Pennsylvania State Archives, Harrisburg, Pa.
BCI	*Bucks County Intelligencer*, Doylestown, Pa.
COD-1862	Conscientious Objector Depositions, 1862, Series 19.15, AGR, Pennsylvania State Archives, Harrisburg, Pa.
CVB	*Das Christliche Volks-Blatt*, Milford Square, Pa.
DD	*Doylestown Democrat*, Doylestown, Pa.
DE	*Decatur Eagle*, Decatur, Ind.
FB	*Friedens-Bote*, Allentown, Pa.
FRT	*Franklin Repository and Transcript*, Chambersburg, Pa.
GD	*Goshen Democrat*, Goshen, Ind.
GH	*Gospel Herald*, Scottdale, Pa.
GT	*Goshen Times*, Goshen, Ind.
HCF	*Holmes County Farmer*, Millersburg, Ohio
HCR	*Holmes County Republican*, Millersburg, Ohio
HFP	*Herald and Free Press*, Norristown, Pa.
HT	*Herald of Truth*, Chicago
JFFC	John F. Funk Collection, Hist. Mss. 1-1, Mennonite Church USA Archives, Goshen, Ind.
JHC	[Bishop] Jacob Hildebrand Collection, I-MS-3, Menno Simons Historical Library and Archives, Eastern Mennonite University, Harrisonburg, Va.
LDEE	*Lancaster Daily Evening Express*, Lancaster, Pa.
LEH	*Lancaster Examiner & Herald*, Lancaster, Pa.
LG	*Lewistown Gazette*, Lewistown, Pa.
LI	*Lancaster Intelligencer*, Lancaster, Pa.

MCA-G	Mennonite Church USA Archives, Goshen, Ind.
ME	*Mennonite Encyclopedia*, vols. 1–4, 1955–59; vol. 5, 1990
MHACV	Mennonite Historical Association of the Cumberland Valley, Chambersburg, Pa.
MHB	*Mennonite Historical Bulletin*
MQR	*Mennonite Quarterly Review*
MSHLA	Menno Simons Historical Library and Archives, Eastern Mennonite University, Harrisonburg, Va.
ND	*National Defender*, Norristown, Pa.
NR	*Norristown Republican*, Norristown, Pa.
NTH	*Norristown Times Herald*, Norristown, Pa.
OR	*War of the Rebellion: A Compilation of the Official Records of the Union and Confederate Armies*, 128 vols. Washington D.C.: Government Printing Office, 1880–1901
PAU	*Patriot & Union*, Harrisburg, Pa.
PDT	*Pennsylvania Daily Telegraph*, Harrisburg, Pa.
PMH	*Pennsylvania Mennonite Heritage*
RDMO	Record of Drafted Militia in Ohio, 1862, Series 89, Ohio Historical Center, Columbus, Ohio
RR	*Rockingham Register*, Harrisonburg, Va.
SS	*Staunton Spectator*, Staunton, Va.
SSYP	Samuel S. Yoder Papers, Manuscript Division, Library of Congress, Washington, D.C.
UCWE	*Unionists and the Civil War Experience in the Shenandoah Valley*, 3 vols. Comp. by Norman R. Wenger and David S. Rodes, and ed. by Emmert F. Bittinger. Harrisonburg, Va.: Valley Brethren-Mennonite Heritage Center and The Valley Research Associates, 2003–2005
WCD	*Wayne County Democrat*, Wooster, Ohio
WR	*Wooster Republican*, Wooster, Ohio

Notes

Introduction: Religion, Religious Minorities and the American Civil War

1. Brunk, ed., *Life of Peter S. Hartman*, 48.

2. Ibid., 49.

3. Virtually all leaders in major Protestant denominations who opposed slavery had left the slaveholding South by 1860, rendering churchly objection to the "peculiar institution" in that region all but voiceless; see Chesebrough, *Clergy Dissent in the Old South*, 72–79, 114–15; and Longenecker, *Shenandoah Religion*, 129–35, 142–50. On the relationship between evangelicalism and martial cultures of honor, which was tenuous in 1800 but entrenched by 1860, see Heyrman, *Southern Cross*, 242–49.

4. Bishop Jacob Hildebrand's diaries for 1861 and 1867 are located in JHC. Here and throughout the book we have retained original spelling.

5. Some 350 to 400 Mennonite households lived behind Confederate lines in the Shenandoah Valley, Virginia, counties of Rockingham and Augusta, but a few Amish also lived in the part of western Virginia that became West Virginia in 1863. As for the Border States, Mennonites and Amish lived in western Maryland, and a handful of Amish were in Missouri. The large majority of both groups were in Union territory, especially in Pennsylvania, but also in Ohio, Indiana, Illinois, Iowa, and New York.

6. John M. Brenneman to Jacob Nold, 21 Aug. 1862, Jacob Nold Collection, Hist. Mss. 1-873, MCA-G.

7. For statistics, see E. B. Long, with Barbara Long, *Civil War, Day by Day*, 700–28. On reasons behind the high casualty rates in this particular war, see the new interpretation in Nosworthy, *Bloody Crucible of Courage*.

8. See, e.g., Blight, *Race and Reunion*, or Goldfield, *Still Fighting the Civil War*.

9. For historiographic commentary, see the Introduction (by the editors) and Afterward (by James M. McPherson) in Miller, Stout, and Wilson, eds., *Religion and the American Civil War*. The entire collection is essential, but see esp. the overview by Paludan, "Religion and the American Civil War," 21–40. See also Noll, *Civil War as a Theological Crisis*, 1–16.

10. Hatch, *Democratization of American Christianity*; Butler, *Awash in a Sea of Faith*, 225–96; Noll, *America's God*, 53–364; Carwardine, *Evangelicals and Politics in Antebellum America*; Curtis D. Johnson, *Redeeming America*.

11. On slavery as central to the war, see Foner, *Slavery, the Civil War, and Reconstruction*; Levine, *Half Slave and Half Free*; and Holt, *The Fate of Their Country*. Although religion and the Civil War has not garnered extensive historical attention, the relationship between antebellum slavery and Christianity has generated a sizeable literature. Representative examples include Raboteau, *Slave Religion*; Haynes, *Noah's Curse*; Noll, *Civil War as a Theological Crisis*, 31–74; Elizabeth Fox-Genovese and Eugene D. Genovese, "The Divine Sanction of Social Order"; McKivigan, *The War Against Proslavery Religion*; and McKivigan and Snay, eds., *Religion and the Antebellum Debate over Slavery*.

12. Goen, *Broken Churches, Broken Nation*; Carwardine, *Evangelicals and Politics*, esp. 279–323; and Snay, *Gospel of Disunion*. An insightful and detailed case study is Carwardine, "Methodists, Politics and the Coming of the Civil War," 309–42. The Clay quote is from Goen, *Broken Churches*, 106.

13. Woodworth, *While God Is Marching On*; Faust, "Christian Soldiers: The Meaning of Revivalism in the Confederate Army"; Mitchell, "Christian Soldiers? Perfecting the Confederacy"; Paludan, *"A People's Contest": The Union and the Civil War*, 339–74; McPherson, *For Cause and Comrades*, 62–76; and Shattuck, *A Shield and a Hiding Place*. Armstrong, *For Courageous Fighting and Confident Dying*, shows that Northern chaplains preached abolition and helped convince Federal troops of the righteousness of emancipation.

14. Chesebrough, *"God Ordained This War"*; Moorehead, *American Apocalypse*; Faust, *Creation of Confederate Nationalism*; Mitchell, *Vacant Chair*; Faust, *Mothers of Invention*, on religion, esp. 181–87; Fredrickson, "The Coming of the Lord: Northern Protestant Clergy and the Civil War Crisis"; and Aamodt, *Righteous Armies, Holy Causes*.

15. Stout, *Upon the Altar of the Nation*; and Noll, *Civil War as a Theological Crisis*.

16. Few histories mention those who had "conscientious scruples," and those that do give them little space. The major source remains Wright, *Conscientious Objectors in the Civil War*. Three overviews by Peter Brock, *Pacifism in the United States* (1968); *Freedom from War* (1991); and *Freedom from Violence* (1991), each give limited space to the Civil War era. Curran, *Soldiers of Peace* details the perfectionist

pacifism of Alfred H. Love, a religiously inspired humanitarian pacifist who was not affiliated with any church. Although they are otherwise excellent treatments of the role of religion in the war, neither Stout, *Upon the Altar of the Nation*, nor Noll, *Civil War as a Theological Crisis*, give attention to religious pacifism. One text that directly introduces peace church voices into the interpretation of the war is Juhnke and Hunter, *The Missing Peace*; see chap. 5, "The Crossroads of Our Being: The Civil War."

17. Friedman, "Conscription and the Constitution"; Russell, "Development of Conscientious Objector Recognition in the United States"; Russo, "The Conscientious Objector in American Law"; and, from the government's perspective, Wherry, *Conscientious Objection*, 1:1–3, 29–48. According to the *Oxford English Dictionary*, the term "conscientious objectors" gained currency only around the time of World War I; however, during the Civil War related terminology also drew on the language of conscience, with terms such as "conscientious scruples," "conscience' sake," and "conscientiously opposed."

18. On the multivalent character of religious belief, see Kselman, ed., *Belief in History*.

19. Chamberlain, "First Pure, Then Peaceable"; and Hill, "Religion and the Results of the Civil War," 360, 372, 375–77. For a similar account and interpretation of the Adventist tradition in the Civil War era, see Knight, "Adventism and Military Service."

20. Nelson, *Indiana Quakers Confront the Civil War*; Hamm, *The Transformation of American Quakerism*, 66–69, 108; and Currey, "The Devolution of Quaker Pacifism." See also comments by Paludan, "Religion and the American Civil War," 27, and Hill, "Religion and the Results of the Civil War," 360–61, 378–79, both in *Religion and the American Civil War*. An important work with an international scope, Brock, *The Quaker Peace Testimony*, gives limited attention to the U.S. Civil War (166–83), but mostly provides information regarding leaders' negotiations with government rather than actual Quaker practice.

21. Freehling, *The South vs. the South*, provides an important account of dissent, but one that explores only geo-political and class roots and expressions, not religion. Chesebrough, *Clergy Dissent in the Old South*, focuses on mainline denominations, whose antislavery clergy simply left the South. Many North Carolina Quakers also moved, usually to Indiana.

22. The role of religion in sustaining dissent among antebellum African Americans shut out of political power and barred from assimilating into the dominant culture is explored, among other places, in Hughes, *Myths America Lives By*. See also R. Laurence Moore, *Religious Outsiders and the Making of Americans*.

23. Randall M. Miller, "Catholic Religion, Irish Ethnicity, and the Civil War," 261–96, and "Introduction," 14, in *Religion and the American Civil War*. See

also a similar theme in American Jewish history in Diner, *A Time for Gathering*, 156–60.

24. On the German Baptist Brethren (the main body of which, since 1908, has been called the Church of the Brethren), see Durnbaugh, *Fruit of the Vine*; and the three-volume *Brethren Encyclopedia*, especially its Civil War entry. Other important, though dated, works include Sanger and Hays, *The Olive Branch of Peace and Good Will to Men*, a study that does not really include the Mennonites, despite its subtitle; D. H. Zigler, *A History of the Brethren in Virginia*; and Bowman, *The Church of the Brethren and War*. A dramatic wartime event for Dunkers in the Shenandoah Valley was the assassination of Elder John Kline of Rockingham County, Virginia, on account of his peace principles. See Benjamin Funk, *Life and Labors of Elder John Kline*.

25. Surveys of the Anabaptist movement include Snyder, *Anabaptist History and Theology*; and J. Denny Weaver, *Becoming Anabaptist*.

26. Swiss and South German Anabaptists did not use the term *Mennonite* as a self-designation until they began describing themselves to English neighbors in North America.

27. Nolt, *A History of the Amish*, rev. ed., 27–95. As Continental immigrants, Mennonites and Amish were not a part of the Anglo-American religious establishment that included Episcopalians, Congregationalists, Presbyterians, and even, to some extent, Quakers. But with roots in the Reformation and with a conversionist theology, they also fit somewhat within the United States' broadly understood evangelical Protestant framework—in contrast, say, to English Catholics, who were linguistic and cultural insiders but religious outsiders.

28. For solid overviews of eighteenth- and nineteenth-century Mennonite history, see MacMaster, *Land, Piety, Peoplehood*; and Theron F. Schlabach, *Peace, Faith, Nation*.

29. Although church membership was very important for nineteenth-century Mennonites and Amish, church leaders did not typically publish membership lists, in part because they were not oriented toward a bureaucratic-administrative style of leadership, and in part because their theology of humility militated against the possibility of boasting in numeric growth. (A few even cited as reason to avoid churchly enumeration the example of divine judgment that fell on biblical King David for having counted the Israelites.) As a result, no one knows exactly how many baptized Mennonite or Amish members there were in 1860. One contemporary estimate appeared in the Mennonite-published *Herald of Truth*, where I. Daniel Rupp ["I. D.R."], the noted German Reformed historian who also kept tabs on other denominations, estimated that "in all America" there were "between fifty and sixty thousand members"; see HT 2 (Extra to Issue No. 21, September 1865), 78. In 1848 Baptist David Benedict had stated that there were 58,000 Mennonites in North

America, but there is no indication of the basis of his estimate—on which Rupp may have been drawing (see Benedict's *A General History of the Baptist Denomination*, 598). The 1890 U.S. Census—the first to include religious enumeration—showed approximately 35,000 baptized Mennonites and Amish among the groups that would have been present in 1860 (i.e., not counting churches and communities known to have immigrated to the U.S. after 1860): more than 17,000 (Old) Mennonites; 13,200 Amish Mennonites of all sorts; 1,655 Reformed Mennonites; and about 2,500 General Conference [GC] Mennonites (again, not counting the GC Mennonite communities whose members immigrated after the Civil War).

The relative sizes of the groups in the 1890 Census seem accurate, but we believe that the actual numbers for almost all groups in the 1890 Census was too low, due to known missed churches (especially west of the Appalachians) and church leader reticence to provide numbers. However, in 1887, Lancaster County, Pennsylvania, Mennonite leader Isaac Eby "estimated that they had about 5,000 members in Lancaster Co. This includes only those who have joined the church on profession of faith; and does not include the children." Eby's number compares favorably with the 1890 Census, which showed 5,365 baptized Lancaster Conference members living in Lancaster County itself. Also in 1887, minister Amos Herr told Quaker Joseph Walton that "the no. of their [Lancaster Mennonite Conference] members had more than doubled in Lancaster Co., in the last 30 years." (Quotations citing Eby and Herr come from Joseph Walton, Diary, vol. 14, pp. 9, 26, Quaker Collection, Haverford College, Haverford, Pa., transcript supplied by Edsel Burdge Jr.) If Eby and Herr are to be believed, then Rupp's and Benedict's numbers seem too high. We have chosen 40,000 as a rough but reasonable estimate of the baptized membership of Mennonites and Amish in 1860. Yet given large family size, attested in numerous published Mennonite and Amish genealogies, 120,000 or more may be a fair estimate for a *total population* figure for Mennonites and Amish (i.e., both baptized adults and unbaptized dependants) in 1860.

30. For an overview, see relevant sections in Theron F. Schlabach, *Peace, Faith, Nation*, 28–116, 141–58. The seven autonomous but cooperating (Old) Mennonite district conferences were Franconia (centered in Bucks and Montgomery counties, Pennsylvania, north of Philadelphia); Lancaster (centered in Lancaster County, Pennsylvania, west of Philadelphia, but in 1860 also taking in a number of central and western Pennsylvania settlements); Washington-Franklin (centered in the two Cumberland Valley counties of western Maryland and south central Pennsylvania); Virginia; Ontario; Ohio; and, beginning in 1864, Indiana (which also included members west of Indiana). Until 1864 (Old) Mennonites west of Ohio were included in Ohio Conference.

31. There were several other Mennonite groups, each very small in 1860, and for which little Civil War-era documentation exists. These include the highly con-

servative Stauffer-Pike (Old Order) Mennonite group near Lancaster, Pennsylvania (formed in 1845 by Jacob Stauffer at the Pike meetinghouse); the broadly ecumenical Trinity Christian Society (formed in 1851 by Abraham Hunsicker and reorganized 1863), near Philadelphia; the revivalist-oriented Evangelical Mennonite Society (formed in 1858 by William Gehman) in Lehigh County, Pennsylvania; and the Church of God in Christ (organized in 1859 by John Holdeman) in Wayne County, Ohio.

32. A summary of General Conference origins is Theron F. Schlabach, *Peace, Faith, Nation*, 118−40. After 1874 GC Mennonite ranks would swell as they began absorbing thousands of new Mennonite immigrant arrivals from the Russian empire, but in 1860 the General Conference was still a small group and represented a minority Mennonite point of view.

33. Gratz, *Bernese Anabaptists and their American Descendants*, 128−56, 173−84. The four settlements were at Sonnenberg (1819) and Chippewa (1825) in Wayne County, Ohio (later known as the Kidron and Crown Hill communities); Putnam County, Ohio (1833) (later known as the Bluffton-Pandora community); and Adams and Wells counties, Indiana (1838) (later known as the Berne community). Eventually, in the late nineteenth and early twentieth centuries, the Swiss Mennonites in these places did affiliate with either the General Conference Mennonite branch or with an (Old) Mennonite district conference. Co-author James O. Lehman has written congregational histories of several of the Ohio "Swiss Mennonite" churches that grew out of this immigrant group, including *Sonnenberg, A Haven and a Heritage* (1969); *Crosswinds* (1975); *Salem's First Century* (1986); and *A Century of Grace* (2004).

34. Scott, *An Introduction to Old Order and Conservative Mennonite Groups*, 105−19. Membership estimate is the consensus of the authors and historians Edsel Burdge Jr. and Stephen E. Scott.

35. Yoder and Estes, trans. and eds., *Proceedings of the Amish Ministers' Meetings, 1862-1878*, 388−99, lists the American Amish churches in existence at this time (plus those in Ontario and a few founded after the Civil War). Estimates of the number of change-minded Amish Mennonite churches versus nascent Old Order Amish churches come from an analysis of this list. Note that some of the most recently founded Amish settlements, such as those in Missouri, did not have fully organized churches in 1860.

36. Paton Yoder, *Tradition and Transition*.

37. Wittlinger, *Quest for Piety and Obedience*, 1−34, esp. 27, and 106, 129−42. Around 1855, two small subgroups separated from the main body, eventually taking the names Old Order River Brethren and United Zion Church. Noted Brethren in Christ historian E. Morris Sider estimates that "a figure of approximately 2000 would rather accurately describe the membership [in 1860] of the three groups

(River Brethren, United Zion, Old Order River Brethren) combined" (e-mail from Sider to Steven M. Nolt, 15 June 2005). A few River Brethren also lived in Ontario, where they received the nickname "Tunker" because of their practice of baptism by stream immersion. (The Canadian label for the River Brethren should not be confused with the U.S. nickname "Dunker" for the German Baptist Brethren, a different group.)

38. Theron F. Schlabach, *Peace, Faith, Nation*, details the similarities (and differences). For a contemporary example, see HCF, 4 Sept. 1862.

39. See chapter 1 for more discussion of Mennonite and Amish understandings of nonresistance. Almost all North American Mennonites and all Amish in 1860 subscribed to the so-called Dordrecht Confession of 1632, a Dutch-authored Mennonite (and later, Amish) statement of faith. Article 14 addressed nonresistance thus: "With regard to revenge and resistance to enemies with the sword, we believe and confess that our Lord Christ as well as his disciples and followers have forbidden and taught against all revenge. We have been commanded to recompense no man with evil for evil, not to return curse for cursing, but to put the sword into its sheath, or in the words of the prophet beat the swords into plowshares. From this we understand that following the example, life, and doctrine of Christ, we may not cause offense or suffering but should instead seek to promote the welfare and happiness of others. If necessary for the Lord's sake, we should flee from one city or country to another; we should suffer the loss of goods rather than bring harm to another. If we are slapped, we should turn the other cheek rather than take revenge or strike back. In addition, we should pray for our enemies and, if they are hungry or thirsty, feed and refresh them, and thus assure them of our good will and desire to overcome evil with good. In short, we ought to do good, commending ourselves to every man's and woman's conscience, and, according to the law of Christ, do unto others as we would wish them to do unto us" (Irvin B. Horst, trans., *Mennonite Confession of Faith*, 33). Various translations of the Dordrecht Confession are available; Horst's is the most accurate. On nineteenth-century Mennonite objections to posting no trespassing notices, see Jacob W. Stauffer, *Stauffer's Geschicht-Büchlein von der sogenannten Mennonisten Gemeinde*, 87—88. But note that Stauffer's argument presupposes that most (Old) Mennonites did not share his opposition.

40. In 1905 Lewis J. Heatwole estimated the number of Mennonite households in Virginia to be about 350 in the 1860s. See Lewis J. Heatwole, "The Virginia Conference," 207. Later, however, Heatwole estimated there were 400 Mennonite families in Virginia when the war began. Heatwole wrote a number of manuscripts with considerable repetition, the contents of which were published in a number of places; his typed manuscripts are found in the Lewis J. Heatwole Collection, I-MS-1, MSHLA. From the number of Mennonite communicants served by bishop Jacob Hildebrand in the spring of 1861, as reported in his diary, there were a total of 368

adult baptized members in three congregations (Hildebrand in Augusta County; Pike and Dry River in Rockingham County). Hence, the number 400 families may not be far off the mark because Hildebrand did not include all congregations in Rockingham.

41. Christina Herr to "Cousin Sarah" and, in the same letter, J. & B. Herr to J[acob] & C[atherine] Nold, undated, apparently written in 1864; Jacob Nold Collection, Hist Mss. 1-873, MCA-G.

1. Politics and Peoplehood in a Restless Republic

1. Hopkins, "Uneasy Neighbors: Germans and Blacks in Nineteenth-Century Lancaster County," 74–75, quotes from the original *Der Lancaster Correspondent* letter; Ruth, *The Earth Is the Lord's*, 402–403, quotes from the subsequent English-language reprinting of the letter and the governor's response, in *Intelligencer and Weekly Advertiser*, 30 July 1800. McKean was a Jeffersonian Republican, as were the two papers in which the letter appeared. Mennonites tended to support the Federalists, so the letter and its response were overtures across a partisan divide. McKean, who had been chief justice on the Pennsylvania Supreme Court in 1777–99, had upheld the wartime limitations on nonresistants' political rights—restrictions that appeared to have been overturned in the new 1790 state constitution.

2. See MacMaster, with Horst and Ulle, *Conscience in Crisis*, 209–10, and 165–74, for context.

3. MacMaster, *Land, Piety, Peoplehood*, 262–64.

4. A succinct overview of antebellum Mennonite views of American government is Theron F. Schlabach, *Peace, Faith, Nation*, 141–54. One of the few primary sources that speaks directly to these issues is Christian Burkholder, *Useful and Edifying Address to the Young. . . .*, 179–257. The 1804 German original edition is *Nützliche und Erbauliche Anrede an die Jugend, von der wahren Busse, von dem Selig-machenden Glauben an Jesu Christo, und der reinen Worte Gottes, und der reinen übergab der Seelen, an die Hand Gottes: Vorgestellt in Frag und Antwort* ([Ephrata, Pa.?]: s.n.).

5. This assumption did not necessarily mean that Mennonites and Amish believed nonresistance was not God's will for all people—but only that many Christians refused to submit to Christ's teaching in all things. If pressed into argument, some nonresistants could be quite sharp in their rebuke of those who discounted the centrality of peace. When a Maryland farmer criticized Mennonite nonresistance on the grounds that it mistakenly focused on incidental themes ("gnats," he metaphorically called them), rather than on the major elements ("camels") of the gospel, Mennonite Peter S. Hartman, who had fled Virginia rather than fight, retorted: "If you call going to war and killing your fellow man a gnat, I certainly would hate to

see your camel." Hartman's memory of the exchange is in Brunk, ed., *Life of Peter S. Hartman*, 70.

6. Although they shared a number of similarities, Quakers differed from Anabaptists groups in significant ways. First, Quaker theology engaged active participation in the affairs of this world and hoped for the reformation of human society in this age. Quakers were active in antislavery efforts—in contrast to Mennonites and Amish, who prohibited slavery but were not political abolitionists. In addition, Quaker thought placed more of an accent on individual conscience as an ethical guide. As a result, some Quakers were much less willing to negotiate with state authorities and more confrontational (rather than separatist) in their relations with government. At the same time, the Friends' emphasis on personal conscience also meant that individual Quakers were more often able to interpret a righteous cause—such as emancipation—as one worth taking up arms for as faithful Quakers. Thus, some Quakers ended up fighting in the Civil War as an expression of, rather than a rejection of, their faith.

Closer to Mennonite and Amish peace theology were the German Baptist Brethren, or "Dunkers," who were heirs of eighteenth-century European pietists who had been influenced by Anabaptist ideals. Since Dunkers had immigrated to Pennsylvania in the 1700s at about the same time as the Mennonites and settled in many of the same areas, Dunkers, Mennonites, and Amish were neighbors in Pennsylvania, Maryland, Virginia, and parts of the Midwest. Their penchant for plainness and a nonresistant stance mirrored Mennonite nonresistance more than Quaker activist pacifism.

7. Jesse Beitler, a Chester County, Pennsylvania, (Old) Mennonite minister, lost an arm in a farming accident in 1853, after which his neighbors were "very kind to him and elected him to township office from that time until his death" in 1863; Beitler would rather have been a farmer, but public service was an acceptable alternative. See Fretz, *A Genealogical Record of the Descendants of Jacob Beidler*, 209. At the same time, other wealthy Mennonites, such as Mathias Pannebecker Jr. of Montgomery County, "Farmer John" Landis of Lancaster County, or Joseph Snively of Franklin County, apparently pursued politics for its own sake.

8. CVB, 12 Nov. 1862.

9. Godschalk, *A Family Record and Other Matters*, 109–10. Recent Mennonite reflection on the place of conscience in peace theology and political philosophy is found in John Richard Burkholder, "For Conscience' Sake? Examining a Commonplace," 250–57.

10. Documentation from the War of 1812 is sparse, but apparently in some local jurisdictions during that war, those with "conscientious scruples" could hire a man who was not enrolled in the militia as a substitute rather than opting out through

payment of the equivalency tax. See the example near Canton, Stark County, Ohio, of John Rowland who paid $100 for a militia substitute in the War of 1812, in Swope, "Columbiana County, Ohio, Mennonites and the Ohio State Militia," 7.

11. Lewis J. Heatwole, "The Virginia Conference," 207. Heatwole believed the equivalency was $0.50 per drill. However, much earlier, in 1817, it was more like $1.00 per drill (Joseph K. Ruebush Collection, II-MS-8, MSHLA).

12. "Fairfield Township Journal of the Trustees Minutes," for the years 1844−46, provided by Wilmer D. Swope, Leetonia, Ohio. Other Midwestern states, including Indiana, Illinois, and Iowa, had similar laws of equivalency fines for men with consciences against fighting. See Wherry, *Conscientious Objection*, 1:39−40.

13. Abraham Kurtz Account Book, in possession of Ada Beam, Morgantown, Pa.

14. Watson, *Liberty and Power: The Politics of Jacksonian America*.

15. Holt, *The Rise and Fall of the American Whig Party*.

16. Carwardine, *Evangelicals and Politics in Antebellum America*, 4 and 274, classifies Mennonites as apolitical pietists who did not involve themselves in any partisan activity. Such an assessment seems to be based on assumed theological categories rather than on documentary evidence. Discussion of the range of Protestant evangelicals' reactions to antebellum politics (pp. 5−30) focuses on British-rooted denominations. Mennonites and Amish may not have felt a Christian responsibility for the success of the republic, which was more common in Calvinist and some Methodist circles, but many were active in politics for their own reasons.

17. Wokeck, "The Flow and the Composition of German Immigration to Philadelphia."

18. Fogleman treats this region in the eighteenth century in *Hopeful Journeys*; see also Purvis, "Patterns of Ethnic Settlement in Late-Eighteenth-Century Pennsylvania." Although "Dutch" is today often considered a misnomer—a corruption of the word *Deutsch*—it was, according to the *Oxford English Dictionary*, the proper eighteenth-century English term for Rhine Valley inhabitants to the Swiss border. Thus, eighteenth-century British officials spoke of "Dutch" and "Switzer" immigrants, meaning (in today's English) Germans and Swiss. The English spoke of "Hollanders" or "Holland Dutch" to refer to the people group today commonly known as "Dutch." See Don Yoder, "Palatine, Hessian, Dutchman," 107−29.

19. For more examples, see Nolt, "Finding a Context for Mennonite History."

20. Nolt, *Foreigners in Their Own Land*.

21. Examples and analysis of Mennonite and Amish political involvement and public service in the early nineteenth century is found in Ruth, *Maintaining the Right Fellowship*, 188, 218−20, 225, 237−39, 337; Ruth, *The Earth Is the Lord's*, 402−404, 415, 481−82, 503−504, 532; Burdge and Horst, *Building on the Gospel Foundation*, 198−202, 224−25; and Kauffman, *Mifflin County Amish and Mennonite*

Story, 141–49. There is a wealth of additional anecdotal evidence in genealogies, e.g., Fretz, *A Brief History of Bishop Henry Funck,* 419. See also the translated text of a remarkable broadside from September 1812, in which an anonymous writer (perhaps Amish minister Christian Zook Jr.?) urged Mennonites, Dunkers, and Amish to vote for the "peace-ticket" in the upcoming presidential election so as to end the War of 1812. See Luthy, trans. and ed., "An Important Pennsylvania Broadside of 1812," 2–4.

22. Tradition says Zook politely declined to show interest in the governorship. Yet he did serve as local auditor nine times, as township supervisor three times, as assessor once, as election inspector once, as school director twice, and as secretary for the county Whig Party. See Kauffman, *Mifflin County Amish and Mennonite Story,* 146–47.

23. Washington County, Maryland, (Old) Mennonite minister John Welty left the church or was expelled (sources vary) after voters elected him to the Maryland legislature as a Whig representative. It seems that Welty's being a minister, rather than his being a Mennonite, was the problem in his case. See also Burdge and Horst, *Building on the Gospel Foundation,* 225, for comment on the incompatibility of public and churchly office holding. As the sources in note 21 above indicate, some antebellum Pennsylvania German Mennonite commentators criticized voting, political activity, and public office-holding on the part of other Mennonites. However, these were minority voices who sooner or later found themselves outside their regional Mennonite mainstream, such as John Herr and his Reformed Mennonite Church after 1812, or Jacob Stauffer and his Pike Mennonite Church after 1845. The bitterness with which these critics complained suggests something of their minority position.

24. Kenneth W. Keller, "Cultural Conflict in Early-Nineteenth-Century Pennsylvania Politics," 509–30, describes some of the ethnic and political dynamics of the time and place.

25. Wust, *Virginia Germans,* 23, 27–57, 93–108, 133, 152–85; and essays in Koons and Hofstra, eds., *After the Backcountry,* such as McCleary, "Forging a Regional Identity," 92–110; or Ridner, "Status, Culture, and the Structural World in the Valley of Pennsylvania," 77–91. See also Christian B. Keller, "Pennsylvania and Virginia Germans During the Civil War."

26. Longenecker, *Shenandoah Religion,* is a cogent analysis that gives attention to Dunker and Mennonite marginality in politics, economics, and religion. Ayers, *In the Presence of Mine Enemies,* 16–31, describes Augusta County, Virginia.

27. "Church Record," kept by bishop Jacob Hildebrand, JHC. An 1861 diary of Hildebrand is also in English. By 1860 Virginia Conference minutes were also kept in English. Already in the 1830s, noted Virginia Mennonite publisher and music teacher Joseph Funk was busy issuing English print materials and holding singing

schools in English for fellow church members (and others) in the Shenandoah Valley. Brunk, *History of the Mennonites in Virginia*, 1:9–109, 144–56, describes antebellum Mennonite life.

28. Simmons and Sorrells, "Slave Hire and the Development of Slavery in Augusta County, Virginia," provides much detail on how elite values of honor and social hierarchy transformed even the once-egalitarian evangelical churches of the lower classes, while Longenecker, *Shenandoah Religion*, explores both adjustment and resistance to these values on the part of Valley Mennonites and Dunkers (see esp. 113–52 on slavery). See also Wust, *Virginia Germans*, 121–28 (on slavery) and 129–52 (on churches).

29. Lehman, "The Coffmans at 'Mannheim' on Wenger Mill Road and the Slave Trade," 2–6. See Wust, *Virginia Germans*, 109–20, on German outsiderhood and Virginia politics.

30. Swierenge, "The Settlement of the Old Northwest."

31. See, e.g., HCF, 23 Oct. 1862. On February 21, 1861, the HCF's editor, James A. Estill, published Jefferson Davis' inaugural address. Then, on March 7, he printed Lincoln's inaugural—beside a biographical sketch of Davis Estes, *A Goodly Heritage*, 48.

32. On Reeser, see Willard H. Smith, *Mennonites in Illinois*, 417. Interestingly, the two Republican ballots Reeser's granddaughter claimed he cast were for Lincoln in 1860 and 1864. While this is certainly possible, there was strong popular incentive—especially in Illinois—to claim, after the fact, that one had voted for Lincoln. In any case, the larger pattern is more significant than the possible 1860s exceptions. For Yoder, see "Speech of Hon. S. S. Yoder of Ohio, Tariff Reform and Pensions," before the House of Representatives, 8 Oct. 1888, "Speech, Article, and Book File," SSYP.

33. Estes, *A Goodly Heritage*, 47–48; and Estes, *Living Stones*, 83–85.

34. Christian Farni to Abraham Lincoln, 17 Aug. 1859, Robert Todd Lincoln Collection, microfilm reel 4, Library of Congress. For context and background, see Nolt, "Christian Farni and Abraham Lincoln"; and Nolt, "The Rise and Fall of an Amish Distillery."

35. Levine, *Half Slave and Half Free*, and Holt, *The Fate of Their Country*.

36. Gienapp, *Origins of the Republican Party*; Foner, *Free Soil, Free Labor, and Free Men*; Anbinder, *Nativism and Slavery*.

37. For eastern Pennsylvania, see note 22. Other examples included Jonas Roth, son of Mennonite bishop Abraham Roth, who was said to have been a Democrat until the outbreak of the war in 1861, when he became a Republican; see *History of Cumberland and Adams Counties, Pennsylvania*, 386, 554. In Somerset County, Mennonites around Jacob's Creek became involved politically, first with old-line Whigs,

then with the Republican party and the Union cause; see Levi Miller, "The Growth and Decline of Mennonites Near Scottdale, Pennsylvania," 8–10.

38. Risser correspondence, 30 March 1857 and 4 Jan. 1858, trans. Elizabeth Horsch Bender, Early Mennonite Correspondence and Papers, Hist Mss. 1-10, MCA-G.

39. Johannes Risser, "Enthält das alte Testament, das heilige Wort Gottes, eine Lehre oder nur einen entfernten Grund, welcher zu Gunsten unserer Sklaverei im Süden spricht?" 12; and "Abschaffung der Sklaverei," 20. On 24 August 1865, Risser wrote that he had penned an essay on Genesis 9:20–27, disputing the widely held American belief that God's curse of Noah's son Ham justified human slavery. On the contemporary strength of the arguments Risser was fighting, see Haynes, *Noah's Curse.*

40. Johannes Risser (1787–1867) was a minister in Friedelsheim, Palatinate Mennonite church from 1825–32, then immigrated to Ashland County, Ohio, in 1833 and served as a Mennonite preacher there until 1838, when he resigned for reasons no longer evident. See his entry in *ME,* 4:341; and a brief biographical sketch by Joe Springer, "Johannes Risser," *MHB* 37 (October 1976), 2–3, which highlights his post-1844 years and union church connections.

41. Of all arrivals between 1700 and 1775 to the British "thirteen colonies" that would become the United States, 47 percent were slaves, 9 percent were convicts sentenced to labor, 18 percent were indentured servants or redemptioners, and 26 percent were free labor (Fogleman, "From Slaves, Convicts, and Servants to Free Passengers," 44).

42. Nash, "From 1688 to 1788: Slavery and Freedom in Pennsylvania," 32–35. For an example of a Pennsylvania German-speaking African-American slave, see Gudehus, "Journey to America," 247.

43. Some did pay transit for so-called "redemptioners"—German immigrants who could not afford the trans-Atlantic fare and traded work for passage—but they apparently rejected hereditary, race-based slavery. The redemptioner system differed in an important way from traditional indentured servitude. Indentured servants arrived in North America with contracts stipulating fixed terms of work; only the contract price was negotiable. Redemptioners, in contrast, arrived with a fixed price for passage and then negotiated the terms and work conditions. Unfree labor originating in the British Isles tended to be indentured servants, while the redemptioner system was used with coerced labor from German-speaking Europe. See Fogleman, "From Slaves, Convicts, and Servants to Free Passengers," 51–56.

44. Moulton, ed., *Journal and Major Essays of John Woolman,* 73–74 (entry from sixth month, 1757); and "John Hunt's Diary," 28–29 (entry for 1781, 9th month, 23rd day).

45. Baptist Association minutes, quoted in MacMaster, *Land, Piety, Peoplehood*, 220.

46. UCWE, 2:69, reporting testimony Brenneman gave in 1877.

47. The details of this situation and the unanswered questions it raises are presented carefully in Burdge and Horst, *Building on the Gospel Foundation*, 221–23.

48. This 1688 Germantown, Pennsylvania, anti-slavery petition was the first formal protest against human bondage offered by white Americans. Written to a Quaker meeting, the petition was signed by four Quakers, three of whom were converts from Mennonitism. See Nash, "From 1688 to 1788," 27–37; and Ruth, *Maintaining the Right Fellowship*, 70–71.

49. Randall M. Miller, "Introduction," 4–7, in *States of Progress*; Tully, "Patterns of Slaveholding in Colonial Pennsylvania." Longenecker, "The Narrow Path: Antislavery, Plainness, and the Mainstream," makes a similar point for the Shenandoah Valley.

50. *The Confession of Faith of the Christians Known by the Name of Mennonites*, 419.

51. Slaughter, *Bloody Dawn*.

52. Longenecker, "The Narrow Path." On slavery and Germans more generally, see Wust, *Virginia Germans*, 121–28.

53. There are some oral traditions regarding Mennonite-owned houses being used in the Underground Railroad. These stories, which connect to little or no contemporary documentation, are often difficult to confirm. In general, it seems that very few Mennonites were active participants in the Underground Railroad. But see valuable anecdotes and balanced discussion related to escaped slaves in Ruth, *The Earth Is the Lord's*, 538–40.

54. Soderlund, *Quakers and Slavery*. Owen Ireland has discovered that Pennsylvania German legislators of all religious traditions were typically not abolitionists, even though they had almost no direct vested interest in maintaining the institution. Ireland credits this stance to their cultural bias against dramatic social change and instability (Ireland, "Germans Against Abolition"). Ruth, *Maintaining the Right Fellowship*, 218–19, and Burdge and Horst, *Building on the Gospel Foundation*, 225, describe Mennonite roles in Pennsylvania's 1837–38 debate over African-American voting rights. Bucks County Mennonite Abraham O. Fretz was narrowly elected county commissioner with the support of 39 black voters, whose ballots a judge later ruled invalid, forcing Fretz from office. The state constitutional convention then debated wording to guarantee black franchise—wording Mennonite delegates Mathias Pannebecker supported and Joseph Snively opposed. The amendment lost, and racial limitations on voting became explicit in the 1838 constitution.

55. The transfer of loyalties from the Whig to Republican parties may not have happened everywhere, but it certainly did in places such as Pennsylvania, where the majority of Mennonites lived, making it demographically significant.

56. Harry Rexrode letter, 10 July 1865, Box 1, Significant Individual Collections, I-MS-21. Rexrode said he experienced some criticism in Indiana "on account of our southern birth by some unruly abolitionists that have negro on the brain, honest & respectable people did not persecute us at all [O]ur church & the Amish church are the only two churches that did not preach negro in this county during the war." But later he blasts the "humbug of southern slavery," giving the impression that he opposed the institution of slavery but was no supporter of abolition or racial equality.

57. Liechty and Lehman, "From Yankee to Nonresistant," 205–209, provides helpful background.

58. Ruth, *Maintaining the Right Fellowship*, 282–83, 307, 320. The Hunsicker family had sided with John H. Oberholtzer's progressive Mennonite movement in 1847, but by 1851 they had left that group too. Nevertheless, for years the Hunsickers considered themselves Mennonites. The Hunsickers not only organized Freeland Seminary for men but also, in 1852, helped establish Pennsylvania Female College, the first college for women in the state. These institutions eventually evolved into Ursinus College, Collegeville, Pennsylvania, which affiliated with the [German] Reformed Church in the United States.

59. John F. Funk diaries, JFFC. A few times Funk even attended Democratic rallies.

60. Jacob Funk to John F. Funk, 11 June 1861, JFFC.

61. A. K. Funk to John F. Funk, 8 Sept. 1860, JFFC.

62. F. R. Hunsicker to John F. Funk, 2 June 1860 and 12 Sept. 1860, JFFC.

63. William Thompson to John F. Funk, 24 May 1860 and 6 July 1860, JFFC. Funk had penned a remarkably strident antislavery piece in October 1856 for a Pennsylvania paper (likely the BCI); see John F. Funk, "More Border Ruffianism."

64. Most Northern Mennonites and Amish fit the cultural and economic voter profiles described in Gienapp, "Who Voted for Lincoln?" 50–97, although one suspects that most so-called Swiss Mennonites, recent immigrants in Wayne and Allen counties, Ohio, and Adams and Wells counties, Indiana, were Democratic. Other Mennonites and Amish in heavily Democratic Holmes County, Ohio, or in parts of Iowa and Illinois may have voted against Lincoln too. (See further discussion in chapter 5.) On the religious appeal of Republicanism to native-born Northern Protestants, see Carwardine, *Evangelicals and Politics*, 279–318. Hamm, *Transformation of American Quakerism*, 61–62, reports strong Quaker support for Republicanism in 1860 (with a few exceptions, 61 and 101).

65. Quotes in McPherson, *Battle Cry of Freedom*, 243.

66. Ibid., 251–54.

67. Rable, *Confederate Republic*, 20–63, details the politics of secession and the establishment of the Confederate States of America. On the role of religious lead-

ers in the cause of secession, see Wyatt-Brown, "Church, Honor, and Secession," 89–109.

68. Johannsen, *Stephen A. Douglas*, 858–68, citing *Chicago Tribune*, 2 May 1861. Because John F. Funk's diary for 1861 skips about four months, from an entry on Tuesday, 22 April to an entry on Saturday, 10 August, we do not know if he attended the bipartisan rally Douglas addressed. Christian B. Keller discovered that the German-language press in eastern Pennsylvania was not uniformly anti-Confederate until Fort Sumter, at which point Democratic papers all swung behind the Union. To the degree that eastern Pennsylvania Mennonites and Amish read the German-language press, they would have found no equivocal editorial voices after April 1861. See C. B. Keller, "The Reaction of Eastern Pennsylvania's German Press to the Secession Crisis."

2. Our Country Is at War

1. J. F. Funk to A. K. Funk, 8 July 1861, JFFC.

2. J. F. Funk diary, 15, 17, 18, and 21 April 1861, JFFC.

3. Jacob Funk to John F. Funk, 28 April 1861, JFFC.

4. A. K. Funk to J. F. Funk, 20 May and 11 June 1861, JFFC; MacMaster, with Horst and Ulle, *Conscience in Crisis*.

5. Jacob Funk to J. F. Funk, 11 June 1861, JFFC.

6. By 1861 Virginia's Mennonite churches—all (Old) Mennonite—were organized into three circuits, or districts, two in Rockingham County and one in Augusta. John Geil served as bishop in the Northern District in Rockingham. Martin Burkholder was bishop of the Middle District, which covered western and southern Rockingham, until he died, in December 1860, at age 43. Ordained in his place in July 1861 was 39-year-old Samuel Coffman. Bishop Jacob Hildebrand served the Southern District (Augusta County). Recently discovered documents provide new detail on Augusta County Mennonites that were not available to earlier historians—see "Church Record," apparently kept by bishop Jacob Hildebrand, and bishop Jacob Hildebrand Diary, 1861, JHC; and church trustee (and later deacon) Jacob R. Hildebrand's journal and other papers in Jacob R. Hildebrand Collection, I-MS-58, MSHLA.

7. RR, 15 Feb. 1861.

8. Crofts, *Reluctant Confederates*, describes the resistance to secession in the Shenandoah Valley and the swift swing in public opinion following Lincoln's call for troops.

9. SS, 8 Jan. 1861. Ayers, *In the Presence of Mine Enemies*, 86–89, 97–107, 119–29, 133–40, details the debate over secession in Augusta County.

10. SS, 22 Jan. 1861.

11. RR, 4 Feb. 1861.

12. Ayers, *In the Presence of Mine Enemies*, 119–29, 133–40.

13. Donald, *Lincoln*, 290; Ayers, *In the Presence of Mine Enemies*, 130–32. McPherson, *Battle Cry of Freedom*, 271–73.

14. McPherson, *Battle Cry of Freedom*, 278–80.

15. Ayers, *In the Presence of Mine Enemies*, 126, 138. Coffman was of Mennonite ancestry and was a slave owner; see Lehman, "The Coffmans at 'Mannheim.'" Later, some convention delegates who had voted against secession changed their votes to give Virginia's secession decision a larger majority (103 to 46), but delegates from Augusta and Rockingham counties did not.

16. SS, 16 April 1861; RR, 12 Apr. 1861.

17. SS, 23 April 1861.

18. SS, 21 May 1861.

19. RR, 17 May 1861.

20. "Church Record" and Bishop Jacob Hildebrand diary for 1861, JHC; *Minutes of the Virginia Mennonite Conference*, v, 4. The minutes record actions passed and not necessarily the general course or content of discussion. Perhaps leaders discussed secession and the referendum but deliberately avoided mention of them in the minutes. Apparently, no sessions of the Virginia Mennonite Conference were held for the remainder of 1861 and all of 1862. The next conference was April 1863.

21. Jacob Hildebrand diaries, 23 May 1861, JHC. With the Augusta County bishop changing his loyalties to the Confederacy, one might expect the same from others in his congregations, and Jacob R. Hildebrand, the bishop's first cousin, kept a journal that recorded his pro-Confederate bias.

22. RR, 17 May and 24 May 1861; SS, 28 May 1861. State-wide, the vote was 128,884 in favor and 32,134 opposed. Most of the opposition centered in thirty-five western counties where voters opposed secession by a margin of three to one, portending these counties' eventual separation to form West Virginia.

23. Bishop Jacob Hildebrand diaries, 13 June 1861, JHC. This fast day was the first of ten that Confederate President Jefferson Davis proclaimed during the war. Bishop Hildebrand's diaries for 1862–65 are not extant (if he kept any), but his 1861 diary explicitly records his church observing the two days of prayer and fasting Davis called in 1861, this one in June and a second on 15 November ("fast day proclaimed by Davis. We had preaching at church"). The bishop's 1861 diary also reveal that Hildebrand had held a special preaching service on January 4 because U.S. President James Buchanan had designated it a national day of prayer and fasting. On Davis's and Abraham Lincoln's use of national days of fasting, see Stout, *Upon the Altar of the Nation*, 48, 475 n. 5

24. After the war, many Rockingham Mennonites filed for reimbursement of lost property on the basis of having been consistent Union men active in their sym-

pathies to the North. See the discussion in chapter 11, and documentation in the massive transcription and publication project *Unionists and the Civil War Experience in the Shenandoah Valley* (UCWE).

25. Horst, *Mennonites in the Confederacy*, 26−27. Horst based his conclusion on research in postwar Claims Commissions applications; his findings are confirmed and more completely documented in UCWE.

26. Voting was not by secret ballot. See, e.g., the testimony in UCWE, 1:80−82, reproducing John Gangwer Claim No. 8996.

27. UCWE, 3:812, reproducing John Brunk Claim No. 21856. Under similar duress, Emanuel Suter also voted for secession; see letter from Congressman Charles T. O'Mallery to Emanuel Suter, Emanuel and Elizabeth Suter Collection, I-MS-31, MSHLA; and UCWE, 3:743, 747, 769, reproducing Emanuel Suter Claim No. 8336.

28. UCWE, 2:269, reproducing Jacob Wenger Claim No. 15912.

29. Horst, *Mennonites in the Confederacy*, 26.

30. UCWE, 2:339, reproducing Jacob Geil Claim No. 21844.

31. Claims Commission, Abraham Shank, No. 9738, microfilm in MSHLA.

32. Claims Commission, Samuel Shank, No. 9739, microfilm in MSHLA.

33. LDEE, 19 June 1861. See Lehman, "Conflicting Loyalties of the Christian Citizen," for more detail.

34. LI, 25 June 1861. The *Express* then retracted parts of its original story, acknowledging that the Mennonites of Strasburg had not held a "convention," but rather their usual preparatory meeting prior to their semiannual communion service.

35. LDEE, 29 June 1861.

36. LDEE, 2 July 1861.

37. LEH, 17 July 1861.

38. LEH, 24 July 1861.

39. LEH, 7 and 14 Aug. 1861.

40. LEH, 21 Aug. 1861.

41. Stampp, *And the War Came*, 288−95. See Ziegler, *Advocates of Peace in Antebellum America*, 149−76, for a detailed and nuanced discussion of the collapse of the peace movement; and Curran, *Soldiers of Peace*, on the tiny remnant of the movement that survived.

42. Quoted in Ruth, *Maintaining the Right Fellowship*, 317. Davis lost his life in the war. His remains lie buried in the Providence Mennonite Church cemetery, Collegeville, Pa.

43. Ibid., 318−19. The problem of identifying Mennonite or Amish names on military lists may be illustrated with the Stauffer/Stover surname. Richard E. Stauffer has published a genealogy, *Stauffer-Stouffer-Stover and Related Families*, in which he claims that 120 men by that name served in the Civil War. A hundred of

these were from Pennsylvania, many in areas that had Mennonite communities. A dozen or more of that name in the declining Mennonite community close to Scottdale, Pennsylvania, probably were not Mennonite. However, from the long list of Lancaster County, Pennsylvania, Stauffers, it is possible that upwards of a dozen or more were from Mennonite homes.

44. As reported many years later in "Up and Down Montgomery County," NTH, 13 April 1936. See also Lehman, "Conflicting Loyalties of the Christian Citizen," 2.

45. LG, 18 and 25 April 1861; BCI, 23 April 1861; LDEE, 13 and 19 June 1861.

46. Jacob S. Funk [Jr.] to J. F. Funk, 8 Dec. 1861, JFFC.

47. WCD, 6 June 1861; HCF, 2 May 1861.

48. HCF, 2 May and 9 May 1861.

49. "Life of Captain Ezra Yoder: Farmer, Teacher, Soldier, Doctor, Preacher, Salvationist," The War Cry, [Salvation Army newspaper], 17 Sept. 1887, 14; Lehman, Creative Congregationalism, 86−87. Yoder, a nephew of Oak Grove Amish Mennonite bishop John K. Yoder, stayed in the service only a short time due to a disability he developed. He returned home but soon got into a quarrel with his church and was excommunicated. Later he moved to Kansas and eventually joined the Salvation Army.

50. Albert, History of the Forty-Fifth Regiment, 446, 450, 454; Kauffman, Mifflin County Amish and Mennonite Story, 141.

51. HCF, 25 April 1861. It is not known with certainty that the families from which Hostetler, Troyer, and Miller came were Amish, but their names suggest they were.

52. HCF, 2 May 1861.

53. OR, Series III, v. 1, 70−73.

54. News stories in HCF, 23 May 1861; WCD, 6 June 1861.

55. OR, Series III, v. 1, 311−21.

56. Trefousse, Thaddeus Stevens, 106−15. The quotation comes from Catton, The Coming Fury, 423−24. For a contemporary appraisal, see Samuel M. Schmucker, A History of the Civil War in the United States (1862), 166.

57. J. F. Funk diary, 10 Aug. 1861, JFFC.

58. A. K. Funk to J. F. Funk, 3 Nov. 1861, JFFC. Samuel later moved to California, became a prominent attorney for the Southern Pacific Railroad, and converted to Catholicism.

59. Jonathan Fly to J. F. Funk, 28 Dec. 1861, JFFC.

60. CVB, 4 Sept. 1861, 10; and 27 Nov. 1861, 34; J. F. Funk diary, 15 Sept. 1861, JFFC. Funk's admission of spending Sundays at the post office may surprise modern readers unaware that U.S. post offices operated seven days a week in the eighteenth and nineteenth centuries. Around the time of the Civil War, the Post

Office Department allowed some post offices in smaller towns and rural areas to close on Sunday, but until 1912 offices in larger towns and cities remained open for business every day of the week. Post offices often served as clearinghouses for local and national news, as patrons read and exchanged newspapers delivered from other parts of the country and shared news contained in letters from other states. Indeed, the fact that post office lobbies attracted so many men on Sunday mornings and thus kept them away from religious services was a major concern of Christian activists who tried, unsuccessfully, to get post offices to close on Sundays. See John, "Taking Sabbatianism Seriously."

61. J. F. Funk diary, 26 Sept. 1861, and various entries around this time.

62. W. R. Moody, *Life of Dwight L. Moody*, 81–85.

63. "Wayne Co., Ohio, in 1861," *MHB* 34 (April 1973), 4–5.

64. Jacob and Maria Landes, Upper Salford Township, Montgomery County, Pa., 3 Feb. 1862, to Tobias and Magdalena Kolb, Breslau, Waterloo County, Canada, Early Mennonite Correspondence and Papers, 1708–1901, Hist. Mss. 1-10, MCA-G.

65. Donald, *Lincoln*, 328–33.

3. Conscription, Combat, and Virginia's "War of Self-Defense"

1. L. J. Heatwole mss., "Trials and Privations of the Church During the Great Civil War," L. J. Heatwole Collection, MSHLA.

2. Coffman, *His Name Was John*, 26, based on the memory of the author's grandfather, John S. Coffman (1848–99), who was present at this church service.

3. RR, 5 July 1861.

4. Apparently it was well known that some Mennonites had voted for the secession resolution, which is not surprising in a day when ballots were not secret.

5. RR, 5 July 1861.

6. RR, 9 Aug. 1861.

7. L. J. Heatwole mss., "A Brief History of the Mennonite Congregations in Virginia and West Virginia," 5, L. J. Heatwole Collection, MSHLA; Coffman, *His Name Was John*, 26–27.

8. Brunk, ed., *Life of Peter S. Hartman*, 51; UCWE, 2:268–69, reproducing Jacob Wenger Claim No. 15912; Heatwole mss., "Brief History of the Mennonite Congregations," 6.

9. Samuel L. Horst, *Mennonites in the Confederacy*, 38. Individual cases were typically more complex than can be summarized here. For example, after Henry Rhodes was drafted in June 1861, his employer hired a substitute for him, but some officers notified Rhodes that he was liable again. When he objected, he was assigned to be a teamster, but a month into this teamster work he deserted and hid until spring

1862, when commutation became a possibility; see UCWE, 1:273, reproducing Henry L. Rhodes Claim No. 21836.

10. Heatwole mss., "Brief History of the Mennonite Congregations," 6.

11. UCWE, 3:532, reproducing Michael Shank Claim No. 19059; Brunk, ed., *Life of Peter S. Hartman*, 51–53; L. J. Heatwole Collection, MSHLA; Heatwole, "The Virginia Conference," in Hartzler and Kauffman, *Mennonite Church History*, 207–208; S. L. Horst, *Mennonites in the Confederacy*, chap. 3, cites other men.

12. Hildebrand, *A Mennonite Journal, 1862–1865*, xi, 59; Driver, *52nd Virginia Infantry*, 120.

13. Church Record Book, JHC.

14. It is not entirely clear what Hildebrand meant in this case, unless Eavers left for annual militia day drill and was soon home again. At this point the referendum had not been held yet on Virginia joining the Confederacy.

15. Church Record Book, JHC, 21 April 1861 entry. Hildebrand's other hired hand was Joel Y. Wheeler, who joined the Mennonite church on April 28 and who later figured in an unusual Mennonite petition to Virginia Gov. John Letcher. According to that document, in mid-summer, Wheeler had "volunteerd in this County and Joined a Company under Capt. William Long, stationed at Staunton." On Monday, August 5, 1861, the bishop noted in his diary that he sent a petition to the governor. He had asked the governor to intervene and allow Wheeler a sixty-day furlough to help run Hildebrand's threshing rig, after which, the bishop promised, Wheeler would "again report himself for duty." The petition has 36 signatures, "the undersigned neighbors of Mr. Hildebrand [who] certify that in our opinion it would be a great inconvinience to the neighbour-hood should Mr. Wheeler go into service." A number of the signatories were Mennonites, including Peter J. Shumaker, a Hildebrand Church minister; John Grove, the deacon; David Kennedy, son-in-law of the bishop; and the bishop's elderly father, Jacob Hildebrand Sr. Co-author James O. Lehman secured a copy of the petition from Archives Research Services, The Library of Virginia, Richmond, Va., and now located in JHC.

16. Joseph H. Wenger, *History of the Descendants of Abraham Beery*, 56. The entry for Joseph W. Grove simply says, "died single in the Union army." This statement is curious, for his fellow Augusta Countians were Confederates. Perhaps he died in a Union prison.

17. Huffer and Purdy, comps., "Civil War Soldiers Buried in Augusta County, VA, Cemeteries." Those who might not have been Mennonites are Thomas Cox, Elias Hanger, John Henne, and Abraham and David Matthews. Driver, *52nd Virginia*, 115, 125.

18. J. H. Langhorne to his mother, 12 Jan. 1862, quoted in McPherson, *Battle Cry of Freedom*, 429.

19. Quoted in Rable, *Confederate Republic*, 141. The most detailed narrative of

the legal recognition of conscientious objection in the Confederacy is still Edward Needles Wright, *Conscientious Objection in the Civil War* (1931), 91–120, although its focus is largely on the actions and reactions of North Carolina Quakers. (Friends in North Carolina were especially active, and their story is intriguing because their state, unlike Virginia, began the war with no constitutional acknowledgement of conscientious scruples against bearing arms, not to mention specific provisions for such sentiment and practice.) For succinct discussions of the draft and exemption in the Civil War South, set in a broader political context, see Davis, *Look Away!* 226–28, 238; and Emory M. Thomas, *The Confederate Nation*, 152–55.

20. Horst, *Mennonites in the Confederacy*, 65–69, outlines the events. The relevant section of the 29 March 1862 Virginia statute is reproduced in Horst, *Mennonites in the Confederacy*, 70, quoting from *Acts of the General Assembly of the State of Virginia, 1861–62*, 50–51.

21. OR, Series I, v. 12, pt. 3, 835.

22. OR, Series I, v. 12, pt. 3, 841; Special Order to Lieutenant Colonel J. R. Jones, quoted in Horst, *Mennonites in the Confederacy*, 35.

23. Most Mennonite teamsters seem to have deserted when they had opportunity, e.g., UCWE, 2:268–69, reproducing Jacob Wenger Claim No. 15912.

24. SS, 15 April 1862. Also *Richmond Whig*, 15 April 1862.

25. L. J. Heatwole, manuscripts, MSHLA; Horst, *Mennonites in the Confederacy*, 56–61.

26. UCWE, 2:348, testimony from Col. Algernon S. Gray in Jacob Geil Claim No. 21844.

27. Brunk, ed., *Life of Peter S. Hartman*, 59; Horst, *Mennonites in the Confederacy*, 70–71.

28. Horst, *Mennonites in the Confederacy*, 50–56; two of those initially captured, Mennonite Peter Blosser and Dunker David Miller, escaped before the entire group arrived in Richmond. A more dramatic account of the trip to Richmond had the captured men herded into a railroad boxcar and "given the night to decide" whether to join the Confederate army or "be shot in the morning." The men prayed and sang through the night, in this telling, and "decided that they would not fight" (Joseph Walton Diaries, vol. 13, p. 148, Quaker Collection, Haverford College, Haverford, Pa.). Walton heard this story from eastern Pennsylvania Mennonites.

29. Hildebrand, *A Mennonite Journal*, 6 (20 Mar. 1862).

30. Neely, *Southern Rights*, 80–86, 89–91.

31. OR, Series II, v. 3, 835, 837. After the war, some Mennonites whose horses the Confederates had pressed into commissary service insisted that they had given their animals unwillingly, notwithstanding the nominal payment they had received in Confederate currency; see, e.g., UCWE, 3:591; reproducing Peter Blosser Claims Nos. 16500 and 21853.

32. Three days later, Baxter says, he received word that the Confederate Congress had passed a law on March 29, allowing exemption upon payment of $500 and being taxed two percent of their property. Baxter then reiterated his recommendation that the men be discharged if they took the oath of allegiance. Baxter's comment on loyalties to the South are of interest because other sources emphasize the men's unionism. Another report indicates that twenty-seven of the men were willing to join "Stonewall" Jackson's brigade as teamsters, among them J. Showalter, Jacob Nieswander, Manasses Heatwole, Henry M. Wanger, Rush Rhodes, Isaac Suter and Jacob Wanger; see Letters Received, Confederate Secretary of War, 444-B-1862, Record Group 109, National Archives, Washington, D.C., quoted in Horst, *Mennonites in the Confederacy*, 53–54, 122.

33. Dunker Benjamin Funk, quoting Gray in Sanger and Hays, *The Olive Branch of Peace*, 73.

34. Wright, *Conscientious Objection in the Civil War*, 101–106; and Horst, *Mennonites in the Confederacy*, 80–82, detail the legislative steps and reproduce several petitions and excerpts from *Public Laws of the Confederate States of America. Confederate Statutes at Large*, 1862–1864, chap. 45, 77–79. Wright and Horst also describe the Quaker pamphlets and Joseph Funk's translation of the Mennonites' Dordrecht Confession of Faith, which petitioners provided to the legislature. The non-creedal Dunkers had no formal confessional writings and so endorsed the Mennonite documents. It is not clear what group the Confederate Congress had in mind when, on October 3, it added "Nazarenes" to the list of exempt churches. Wright, *Conscientious Objectors in the Civil War*, 6–7, speculates on the group's identity but offers no solid evidence. A different possibility is that "Nazarenes" was a local name for one of the many Southern restorationist churches (associated with Alexander Campbell, Tolbert Fanning, David Lipscomb, and others) that more often were known as Disciples of Christ or Churches of Christ. Many of these restorationists were pacifist.

35. Driver, *52nd Virginia*, 120. Heatwole was absent without leave from 8 May to 26 Sept. 1862 and from 28 July to 13 Oct. 1863, with his desertion listed officially on the latter date at Clarksburg, West Virginia. Heatwole was in Company F; Benjamin Hildebrand was in Company A.

36. Horst, *Mennonites in the Confederacy*, 73.

37. Ibid., 39–40.

38. UCWE, 2:340, reproducing Jacob Geil Claim No. 21844; Horst, *Mennonites in the Confederacy*, 39, citing Abraham Blosser source from 1888.

39. McPherson, *Battle Cry of Freedom*, 429–32. Toward the end of 1864, Confederate conscription was failing, for all practical purposes, due to exhaustion over the war, too many exemptions, and the rising argument about arming slaves. By that time, many military and civilian leaders "were ready to abandon the Bureau of Con-

scription." See Albert B. Moore, *Conscription and Conflict in the Confederacy*, 332–39; and Bruce Levine, *Confederate Emancipation*.

40. Samuel S. Wenger, ed., *The Wenger Book*, 226, says that Samuel's brother David served in the military, but Samuel, in his claim for reimbursement of property damage, says that he had no near relative in either army (UCWE, 3:618–25, reproducing Samuel Coffman Claim No. 9519). Samuel Coffman's Claims Commission report indicates that he moved to Rockingham County from Greenbrier County in 1846. Greenbrier became a part of West Virginia in 1863.

41. UCWE, 3:619, 625; and Brunk, *History of the Mennonites in Virginia*, 1:164.

42. Heatwole enlisted 22 June 1861 and deserted 12 Aug. 1862. Reidenbaugh, *33rd Virginia Infantry*, 124; Heatwole, *The Burning*, 137–38; Horst, *Mennonites in the Confederacy*, 125.

43. For more on Parret, see Burdge and Horst, *Building on the Gospel Foundation*, 277–82.

44. Murphy, *10th Virginia Infantry*, 172. Shank was a prisoner of war at Chancellorsville but was paroled and then exchanged in October 1863. He was captured again at Fisher's Hill.

45. Samuel A. Rhodes, "The Rebellion, the Cause of My Traveling Adventures to the North," Significant Individual Collections, I-MS-21, MSHLA. It appears that he wrote the journal sometime after the earliest events transpired. Rhodes's diary also appears in an edited form as Samuel L. Horst, ed., "The Journal of a Refugee."

46. Hildebrand, *A Mennonite Journal*. Regrettably, the journal only covers 6 March to 14 June 1862 and 26 July 1863 to 13 May 1865. The published journal is easily followed chronologically, so further documentation is omitted hereafter.

47. This may have been the senior deacon at the Hildebrand Church, whose name was John Grove and whose son, Abraham J., was also in the Confederate army.

48. The Valley Campaign lasted roughly from May 8 to June 9. See Tanner, *Stonewall in the Valley*. Military historians still consider this campaign significant, as evidenced by the recent scholarly debate represented in Gallagher, ed., *The Shenandoah Valley Campaign of 1862*.

49. A few days later, Hildebrand's journal fell silent for over a year; if he kept a journal during that time, it has not been found.

50. Brunk, ed., *Life of Peter S. Hartman*, 62–64. Note that Hartman's memories, recorded well after the events described, include several chronological points of confusion. He tells of learning of Ashby's 1862 death in a story that comes after his recounting Maj. Gen. David Hunter's 1864 raid on Lexington.

51. Whanger, "*The Trail of Agony*," 9–44. Whanger reports the oral tradition that David Whanger was ordained, but recent research raises some question whether he was a minister; see Lehman, "Greenbrier County, West Virginia." Soldiers David

and Joseph Whanger were cousins-once-removed to Rockingham County, Virginia, Mennonite bishop Samuel Coffman.

52. Whanger, "*The Trail of Agony*," 34, 43.

4. Negotiation and Notoriety in Pennsylvania

1. Geary, *We Need Men*, 10–11, 22.

2. Ibid., 3–21. Already on August 9 and September 5, 1861, *LDEE* had warned that if volunteers came too slowly, the federal government might have to resort to a draft, so Mennonite readers in some places may have been aware of such a possibility.

3. Letter Books, Gov. Morton, 1861–67 Collection, L1456, Archives Division, Indiana Commission on Public Records, Indianapolis, Ind.; McPherson, *Battle Cry of Freedom*, 447–48, 461–77, 490–94; Geary, *We Need Men*, 8.

4. E. B. Long, with B. Long, *The Civil War, Day by Day*, 230–34, 242; McPherson, *Battle Cry of Freedom*, 471–72, 485; Grimsley, *The Hard Hand of War*, 120–41.

5. Geary, *We Need Men*, 22–31.

6. OR, Series III, v. 2, 333–335 carries the full text of General Orders No. 99, from Adj. Gen. Lorenzo Thomas of the War Department.

7. Geary, *We Need Men*, 32–48, details the challenges of putting the 1862 militia draft into practice.

8. Ibid., 35–36; Jacob Beidler to Jacob Nold, 26 Oct. 1862 (trans. Elizabeth Bender), Jacob Nold Collection, Hist. Mss. 1-442, MCA-G. The John Z. Gehman diary contains a 23 Oct. 1862 entry saying, "On the 21st John and Andreas Mack went to Harrisburg"—John Ziegler Gehman Diary, 1829–1882 (trans. Raymond E. Hollenbach, 1965), Mennonite Heritage Center Archives, Harleysville, Pa.; Andreas Mack probably refers to Andrew S. Mack (1836–1917). See also John C. Wenger, *History of the Mennonites of the Franconia Conference*, 281.

9. I. G. Musser, "How About Voting?" *GH* 5 (3 Oct. 1912), 429.

10. COD-1862.

11. "One Hundred Years Ago," *Mennonite Research Journal* 6 (January 1965), 6. Original 14 Sept. 1862 letter to Henry and Magdalena Detweiler located at Mennonite Heritage Center Archives, Harleysville, Pa.

12. BCI, 19 Aug. 1862.

13. No date or documentation is given on the page of questions, but the handwriting, when compared to several letters written by Boyd, appears to be his handwriting. General Correspondence, 1793–1935, Series 19–29, Box 16, AGR.

14. Criticisms appear in Thomas Evans to William M. Meredith, 9 mo. 16th, 1862; and Chas. Harthorne to Wm. M. Meredith, 17 Sept. 1862, both in General Correspondence, 1793–1935, Series 19.29, Box 16, AGR; and Thomas Evans to

Governor A. G. Curtin, 8 mo. 30th, 1862, General Correspondence, 1793–1935, Series 19.29, Box 15, AGR. The authors are indebted to Jonathan Stayer, Head, Reference Section, Pennsylvania State Archives, for providing numerous documents relating to the 1862 state militia draft.

15. Isaac Kulp and John Berge, Skippackville, to Andrew Curtin, 24 Sept. 1862; Wm. N. Clemmer to Andrew G. Curtin, Sept. 22, 1862, both in General Correspondence, 1793–1935, Series 19.29, Box 16, AGR. Clemmer noted that others "holding our views have been exempted" in neighboring counties.

16. James Boyd to Eli Slifer, 20 Sept. 1862, General Correspondence, 1793–1935, Series 19.29, Box 16, AGR. Boyd's remarks about the peace churches indicate that he was not well acquainted with Mennonites, Schwenkfelders, and Dunkers. He also said that large numbers of Quakers were boycotting application for exemption because they were unhappy with his disposition of their cases.

17. A. K. M'Clure, per A. G. Curtin, to James Boyd, 21 Oct. 1862, Abraham Harley Cassel Collection, MS-20, Archives, Juniata College, Juniata, Pa.

18. Jacob Beidler to Jacob Nold, 26 Oct. 1862, Jacob Nold Collection, Hist. Mss. 1-442, MCA-G.

19. Ruth, *Maintaining the Right Fellowship*, 327.

20. "One Hundred Years Ago," *Mennonite Research Journal* 6 (January 1965), 6.

21. CVB, 29 Oct. and 12 Nov. 1862.

22. Eastern District Minutes of "First Thursday of October," 1863, Mennonite Heritage Center Archives, Harleysville, Pa. See also minutes for 2 Oct. 1862.

23. Eastern District Minutes of "First Thursday of October," 1863, stress the importance of "loyal support of our civil authorities" and insist that ministers admonish against any "rebellion spirit."

24. OR, Series III, v. 2, 316, 329; Sterling, "Civil War Draft Resistance," 87.

25. An unusual Republican exception was *Lancaster Examiner & Herald*, Lancaster, Pa., which criticized the draft for actually putting only a "handful of men" into service. It estimated that "every drafted man who enters the service will have cost nearly one thousand dollars, so large have the expenses been" (*LEH*, 19 Nov. 1862).

26. VS15-5, Schwenkfelder Historical Library, Pennsburg, Pa.; Ruth, *Maintaining the Right Fellowship*, 322.

27. OR, Series III, v. 2, 280–82; Sterling, "Civil War Draft Resistance," 69.

28. NR, 18 Oct. 1862; and *HFP*, 21 Oct. 1862.

29. *Bauernfreund & Demokrat* (Pennsburg and Sumneytown, Pa.), 11 Nov. 1862. This issue in possession of I. Clarence Kulp, Vernfield, Pa.; COD-1862.

30. *HFP*, 18 and 25 Nov. 1862.

31. In January 1863, the Pennsylvania Senate asked for a report on how many men from each county had actually claimed exemption for reasons of conscience; M'Clure, supplied the information. See ND, 3 March 1863.

32. Ibid.

33. Kauffman, *Mifflin County Amish and Mennonite Story*, 138. See p. 369 for the complete list of 117 names.

34. LG, 22 October 1862.

35. LG, 8 October 1862.

36. However, surviving draft records suggest only a total of 1,580 men. *LEH*, 22 and 29 Oct. 1862; *LDEE*, 17 Nov. 1862.

37. "Enrollment of Citizens," Books 1–8 (books 3 and 7 are missing), Lancaster County Historical Society Library, Lancaster, Pa. We assumed that many men with common Mennonite names were from Mennonite families. With such a large list, it is not possible to identify with certainty each name.

38. *Reading Adler*, Reading, Pa., 21 and 28 Oct. 1862; *Berks & Schuylkill Journal*, Reading, Pa., 21 Oct. 1862; *Daily Times*, Reading, Pa., 21 Nov. 1862; *FB*, 22 Oct. 1862. Likewise, Chester County's comprehensive draft record book, located at Chester County Historical Society Library, in West Chester, and listing names, occupations, and disposition of cases, includes only a few among the 200 exemptions for conscience that suggest even possible Mennonite connections. Most Chester County men of conscience were Quakers.

39. *York Gazette*, York, Pa., 12 Aug. 1862.

40. Prowell, *History of York County Pennsylvania*, 533. This source also names David S. Whitmer as being a Democrat, which was unusual. Nineteenth-century Pennsylvania county histories invariably name Mennonites as Republicans.

41. "Affidavits of Disability, 1862," Spruance Library, Doylestown, Pa. In 1979 the documents had not been opened in such a long time that some ink particles fell off, suggesting that they had been untouched for more than a century. Several typed pages of names from these affidavits are in the files of James O. Lehman, Harrisonburg, Va.

42. McPherson, *Battle Cry of Freedom*, 603 (although McPherson's discussion is set in the context of 1863, the background applies here). Illustrating the popularity of substitution in general in the 1862 Pennsylvania draft is the fact that of the 1,580 names conscripted in Lancaster County that fall, 582 got substitutes. *LDEE*, 17 Nov. 1862.

43. PDT, 11 Nov. 1862; *LDEE*, 12, 17, and 18 Nov. 1862. See also comments in ND, 25 Aug., 1 Sept., and 15 Dec. 1863. See also PDT, 16 Oct. and 4 Nov. 1862; PAU, 25 Nov. 1862.

44. Paton Yoder, *Eine Würzel*, 34.

45. John Ziegler Gehman Diary, Mennonite Heritage Center Archives, Harleysville, Pa.

46. Ruth, *Maintaining the Right Fellowship*, 319, 328, 334–35.

47. *History of Cumberland and Adams Counties*, 386, 554. Tobias Kauffman, of

Reformed Mennonite parentage, served in the military, was promoted to colonel, and for a time was a prisoner of war at the infamous Libby Prison.

48. Burkhart, "The Diller Mennonite Church," 246–47; and Conway, *History of Cumberland County*, 129–30. Mennonite families settling in the county before the war are named in Weaver, *Mennonites of Lancaster Conference*, 232–47.

49. Steffen, "The Civil War and the Wayne County Mennonites."

50. FRT, 3 Sept. 1862 and later issues. Rowe, *A Sketch of the 126th Regiment*, 61, 67, 71–72, 80–81, 85.

51. Burdge and Horst, *Building on the Gospel Foundation*, 226–27. Pages 233–37 detail Franklin County Mennonites and the 1862 militia draft.

52. In some places, the Amish and Mennonite presence was simply too small to render many generalizations. Juniata, Perry, and Snyder counties had small Mennonite communities. Few newspapers survive, and other records are sparse, but of the seventeen Juniata men who filed conscientious objector depositions, all but two are believed to have been Mennonite or Amish, and apparently the October draft did not strike them. A few others believed to have been Mennonite secured substitutes. During the war, Rebecca A. Lauver, of Perry County, remarked that the "draft hit some very hard," and named Daniel Auker and Isaac Winey. Snyder County had a large draft but only eight men had filed depositions of conscience. Militia draft records have not survived for Huntingdon, Blair, Centre, and Clearfield counties, but Mennonites in those places were very few. See COD-1862; Rebecca A. Lauver, Millerstown, Perry County, Pa. to Nancy and John Burkholder, 25 Oct. [1862?], located at the Mennonite Historical Center, Richfield, Pa.; "Veterans Serving in Snyder County Units But Buried Elsewhere," a typed manuscript compiled by Grave Registration Co., 1935, Snyder County Historical Society Library, Middleburg, Pa.; J. N. Durr, "History of the Mennonite Church in Morrison's Cove," GH 20 (10 Nov. 1927), 714–15, for a small handful of Mennonite names. Blair County had 73 depositions of conscience, most of them Dunkers or River Brethren.

53. The face of Abraham Overholt still survives on the label of Old Overholt whiskey (now produced in Kentucky). It was not unusual for Mennonites and Amish at the time to operate distilleries, nor was drinking alcoholic beverages uncommon, since the practice had been brought from Europe.

54. Levi Miller, "The Growth and Decline of Mennonites near Scottdale, Pennsylvania." Two of distiller Abraham Overholt's grand-nephews, the twin sons of Mennonite bishop John D. Overholt, are said to have begged their father for permission to enlist. He first forbade them, but because of their insistence, was "forced to consent" in the summer of 1862. John S. R. Overholt rose to the rank of corporal by March 1865; his brother, Aaron S. R. Overholt, to the rank of sergeant. Family patriotism was such that young Abe Overholt, grandson of patriarch Abraham, was photographed as a boy wearing a child-sized uniform. Two other grandsons of

Abraham Overholt who enlisted were John O. Tintsman and Henry O. Tintsman. Abraham Overholt, son of Jacob D. and Mary (Freed) Overholt, a nephew of the bishop, was killed in the war. Another nephew of the bishop, John Overholt, son of Henry D. and Elizabeth (Sherrick) Overholt, died of typhoid at Nashville, Tennessee. Christian S. Overholt (son of distiller Abraham) sent his nephew by marriage as a substitute and promised him three years of college after the war. See Sandow, ed., "*Remember Your Friend Until Death*," 8–15. Two other grand-nephews of the aged businessman were Henry Durstine, who was killed in the battle of Petersburg, and Henry C. Durstine, who lost an arm in the war; see Winifred Erb Paul, "Genealogical Chart on Several Families," copy in possession of James O. Lehman, Harrisonburg, Va.

55. George D. Albert, ed., *History of the County of Westmoreland, Pennsylvania*, 689.

56. "Somerset County," ME, 4:574; Thomas Irvin Maust II, "The Glades Amish of Brothersvalley," in *The Berlin Area, which Includes Berlin Borough* . . . (Berlin, Pa.: Berlin Area Historical Society, 1977), 130; Richard B. Yoder, "Nonresistance Among the Peace Churches of Southern Somerset County," 14.

57. OR, I, v. 37, pt. 1, 131–33, 305; *History of Bedford, Somerset and Fulton Counties*, 566A. See also Ivan J. Miller, *History of the Conservative Mennonite Conference*, 37.

58. Blackburn, *History of Bedford and Somerset Counties Pennsylvania*, 3:118, 120. Benedict and Sarah (Miller) Yoder's son, Samuel B., from Stony Creek Township, enlisted in the 42nd Regiment and was wounded at Gettysburg.

59. Drafted Men and Substitutes, 1862, General Correspondence, 1793–1935, Series 19.29, Box 16, AGR. See also *History of Bedford, Somerset and Fulton Counties*, 131–33, 145, 153–54.

In southern Somerset County, around Springs and Salisbury, church communities straddled state lines into Garrett (at that time Allegheny) County, Maryland, and Preston County, Virginia (now West Virginia). Allegheny had no Union draft in 1862 because it had already furnished 1,463 volunteers—even though its quota was only 872. Yet among the list of soldiers are names common among the Amish and Mennonites; see Lowdermilk, *History of Cumberland, Maryland*, 406–407; "Garrett County and the Civil War," *The Glades Star* 3 (June 1961), 97; and 3 (June 1962), 175.

60. Richard B. Yoder, "Nonresistance Among the Peace Churches," 19. Reported to Yoder in January 1959 by Lilly Hostetler, Myersdale, Pa., who was an aged daughter of Christian Hostetler. In 1959 she held her father's discharge papers.

61. Ibid., 20–21. In the 1950s, Jonas's daughter, Magie Rotomer, claimed that "during the Civil War Mennonites were not as much opposed to war as today."

62. Telephone interview by Alta Schrock, Granstville, Md., with Ellis Shoe-

maker, 4 Jan. 1982, and reported to co-author James O. Lehman by Schrock. Shoemaker was a grandson of John Folk.

63. Interview by James O. Lehman with Ivan J. Miller, Grantsville, Md., 4 Jan. 1982.

64. They included Michael and Jacob Hochstetler, William Maust, Christian T. and Jacob T. Livingood, John Tressler, Jeremiah J. Folk, Amos and Abraham Thomas, Samuel Gneagy, and Jeremiah Hershberger. Jeremiah Folk obtained a substitute. Michael and Jacob Hochstetler, John Tressler, Samuel Gneagy, and Jeremiah Hershberger were discharged upon receiving conscientious objector status. William Maust and Jacob T. Livingood reportedly did not show when drafted. Probably the son of Mennonites, Livingood had likely not joined the church but was working near the present town of St. Paul for a wealthy man named Wilhelms. Oral tradition held that Livingood was drafted twice, but both times Wilhelms bought substitutes for him, "a little favor which took him seven years to repay." When Livengood was drafted a third time, Wilhelms declined and Livingood went into hiding. He first hid beneath the trapdoor in the kitchen, which his wife covered with carpet. He also hid in a small cave near the foot of Mount David. Silas Tressler and others carried food to him, but in the winter sometimes for weeks they could not visit him because of the tracks they would leave. See Alta Schrock, "The Story of Jakie's Cave," *The Casselman Chronicle* 1 (Autumn 1961), 8; and Richard B. Yoder, "Nonresistance Among the Peace Churches," citing a handwritten account by Mrs. John Folk and Samuel H. Livengood, grandchildren of Jacob T. Livengood.

65. Jonas Kauffman was the son of Jonas and Rachel (Blough) Kauffman. See Storey, *History of Cambria County Pennsylvania*, 2:256; 3:196, 575.

66. Storey, *History of Cambria County*, 3:196, 418–19, 575; Gable, *History of Cambria County Pennsylvania*, 2:990–91. Another veteran was Noah Weaver.

67. See also reports in *Democrat and Sentinel*, Ebensburg, Pa., 15 Oct. 1862; and *Cambria Tribune*, 24 Oct. 1862.

68. *Cambria Tribune*, Johnstown, Pa., 19 Sept. 1862.

69. An example of such a complaint from Lebanon County, in the southeastern Pennsylvania German region, is Adam Grittinger to Eli Slifer, 13 Sept. 1862, General Correspondence, 1793–1935, Series 19.29, Box 16, AGR.

70. DD, 9 and 16 Sept. 1862.

71. BCI, 14 Oct. 1862.

72. BCI, 28 Oct. 1862.

73. DD, 4 and 18 Nov. 1862. The *Democrat* made a doubtful statement that conscientious people were switching their vote to the Democrats because of the inconsistency of voting for war and refusing to help fight it.

74. LI, 28 Oct. and 11 Nov. 1862.

75. Ibid.

76. *LEH*, 27 Aug., 17 Sept., and 29 Oct. 1862.

77. *LDEE*, 15 Sept. 1862.

78. *LDEE*, 3 Oct. 1862.

79. "Locofoco" was a derogatory label for members of the Democratic Party. The term became associated first with a New York faction of the party in 1834 when, during a Tammany Hall meeting, someone tried to adjourn the session by putting out the lights, at which point those who wished to continue the proceedings used "locofoco" (i.e., easy striking) matches to rekindle the lights and continue the meeting.

80. *LG*, 3 Sept. 1862.

81. *The True Democrat*, quoted in Kauffman, *Mifflin County Amish and Mennonite Story*, 142.

82. *LG*, 10 Sept. 1862. That statement, indeed, seems to be true. Kauffman, *Mifflin County Amish and Mennonite Story*, 140, found no evidence of a single case of a Mifflin County Amish draftee hiring a substitute.

83. *LG*, 17 Sept. 1862.

84. *LG*, 5 Nov. 1862.

85. *LG*, 22 Oct. 1862.

86. *LDEE*, 3 Oct. 1862. If the paper is correct that already 500 men had signed the certificates by that time, it appears that not all the certificates are extant anymore.

87. *HFP*, 21 Oct. 1862. Unfortunately for the editor, that year the Democratic candidate won; see *Der Neutralist und allgemeine Neuigkeits-Bote*, Skippackville, Pa., October 1862.

88. *LDE*, 30 Aug. 1862. A few other Pennsylvania newspapers also ran the story: *FB*, 1 Oct. 1862, repeated the same story, crediting the *Lancaster Volksfreund*, who, *FB* said, picked it up from *LDE*. The story also appeared on a printed broadside; see Rempel Smucker, "War, Government, and Mennonites."

5. Patterns of Peace and Patriotism in the Midwest

1. Eli J. Hochstedler, Kokomo, Howard County, Ind. to Samuel S. Yoder, Holmes County, Ohio, 6 Oct. 1862, Family Correspondence, SSYP.

2. On Iowa, see Wright, *Conscientious Objectors*, 51–52; on Illinois, see OR, Series III, v. 2, 337.

3. *Union Press*, Bryan, Ohio, 1 Aug. 1862.

4. David Tod Papers, 1862–1864, Collection 306, Box 2, Library/Archives Division, Ohio Historical Society, Columbus, Ohio. At that point, regrettably, the two-page letter ended, the last page apparently having been lost. No clue has been found as to who authored the letter. A few days later, Millersburg attorney and

former Holmes County Democratic member of Congress Daniel P. Leadbetter communicated a somewhat similar message to Tod: that the Amish would make poor soldiers and that it would be better to extract an equivalency fee from them than to force their induction.

5. OR, Series III, v. 2, 650, 662, 693, 704. In late July, Tod had proposed exempting from any potential draft those who made a "substantial donation" to the military fund or hired a substitute. For context, see Geary, *We Need Men*, 36–37; and Fisher, "Groping Toward Victory."

6. OR, Series III, v. 2, 587–90. Exchanges between Governor Morton and C. P. Buckingham are also located in L1456, pp. 284–91, "Correspondence Documents & Reports of Governor Oliver P. Morton," Gov. Morton 1861–67 Collection, Archives Division, Indiana Commission on Public Records, Indianapolis, Ind.

7. For the minutes of these meetings, held annually 1862–78 (except 1877), see Yoder and Estes, *Proceedings of the Amish Ministers' Meetings*. The 1862 meeting was held in the barn of Samuel and Lydia (Schmucker) Schrock. The lone reference to the war during the war itself was in the 1863 minutes, when the meeting was held in Mifflin County, Pennsylvania.

8. Lehman, *Sonnenberg: A Haven and a Heritage*, 79–88; Lehman, *Creative Congregationalism: A History of the Oak Grove Mennonite Church*, 64–67.

9. WR, 5 June and 10, 17, 24, and 31 July 1862.

10. Lehman, *Sonnenberg*, 20–25. We know of no other congregation that held a special meeting for the purpose of discussing the threatening draft or the "sad state of the country." Co-author Lehman and his wife are natives of this congregation. His great-great-grandparents came to America in 1840; her grandfathers came as teenagers in the 1870–80 era, partially to escape European militarism.

11. David Tod Papers, 1862–1864. See Appendix A for the full text of the petition.

12. Lehman, *Sonnenberg*, 89–95. Lehman did not have access to this document when he wrote *Sonnenberg*. Extensive research has verified that none of the Sonnenberg men went to war. The petition was not written by either of the signatories who were unable to compose an English document of this quality. Most likely, Ulrich Welty, a school teacher from the congregation, drafted the petition, perhaps with the help of his brother Christian, based on the congregation meeting. Ulrich often served as a liaison between the Swiss congregation and local English officials.

13. David Tod Papers, 1862–1864. Frederick Grätz wrote the petition, but it carried the signatures of bishop Christian Suter and ministers Johannes C. Lugibuhl, Johannes Moser, and Peter Schumacher.

14. Part of Jacob Nold's worry about the coming draft may have been due to incorrect information. After the draft was over, he wrote Johannes Gross about

the "considerable anxiety" regarding the information he received prior to the draft that men of conscience would not be permitted to pay a commutation fee. Jacob and Catharina Nold to Johannes Gross and wife, Columbiana, Ohio, 3 Nov. 1862, Mennonite Heritage Center Archives, Harleysville, Pa.

15. Ibid.

16. Jacob Kolb to Jacob Nold, 19 August 1862 (trans. Elizabeth Bender), Jacob Nold Collection, Hist Mss. 1-873, MCA-G.

17. "A Civil War Petition to President Lincoln," *MHB* 34 (October 1973), 2–3. Original in Jacob Nold Collection, Hist Mss. 1–873, MCA-G. The petition was discovered in eastern Ohio in 1973.

18. Although he had relatives in Virginia, Brenneman likely was only superficially acquainted with Virginia Mennonites' wartime experience and apparently did not know that some of them had voted for secession and a few supported the Confederacy.

19. Perhaps this statement simply reflected Brenneman's greater familiarity with the situation in his home state, though the bishop was well-traveled throughout the Midwest and may have been speaking comparatively from anecdotal evidence. In any case, the general order from the War Department on August 8, 1862 (and elaborated on the 11th and again on the 13th) did direct police in any "town, city, or district" to arrest and imprison anyone who was engaged "by act, speech, or writing" in discouraging volunteer enlistment, or to give "aid and comfort to the enemy," or in any other way encourage disloyalty to the United States. It further prohibited men liable for the draft from leaving their state until after the draft was completed. *OR*, Series III, v. 2, 321–22.

20. "Cover Letter to Petition" *MHB* 34 (October 1973), 3. The letter was dated August 21 and the original is located in the Jacob Nold Collection, Hist Mss. 1-873, MCA-G.

21. *History of Allen County, Ohio*, 732–33. Father Yost had died in 1849; Anna (Hochstetler) then married Tobias Miller.

22. A few young men from Amish families in Holmes County went to war. Three of Jeptha T. Miller's sons went, and two of them, Tobias and Stephen, were killed the same day, July 10, 1863. Their brother Isaac served as an aide to Ulysses S. Grant. Tradition says that he is "the young man with a thin mustache standing in the background in photos of General Grant and General Lee sitting at a small table during Lee's surrender at Appomattox"; see Lou Witman, "Grandfather Aided Gen. Grant," *Elkhart Truth*, 1 July 1992, B2.

23. German Township had the largest quota (77) of men to be drafted. Not far behind were Walnutcreek (56) and Paint (55) townships. See RDMO, which is arranged by county and includes names, township of residence, regiment assigned,

names of substitutes, exemptions (such as physical disability), and other comments, such as "Paid $200." On May 17, 1993, Leroy Beachy, Berlin, Ohio, provided church identification for these men.

24. Lehman, *Growth Amidst Struggle*, 61–62. Peter Longenecker Jr.'s sons were David, John, William, Joseph, and Peter. Their first cousin, Isaac Longenecker, enlisted early in the war and served nearly four years. Forty-four letters that Isaac Longenecker wrote to his brother-in-law, J. F. Lenz, are located in the archives of the U.S. Military History Institute, Army War College, Carlisle, Pa. Peter III, youngest son of Peter Jr., was only 15 when the war began. His grave marker in the Longenecker Mennonite Church cemetery indicates he served in the military. Other soldiers from this church included Noah Landis, Aaron Mumaw, Abraham Rohrer, Martin Moyer, Jacob S. Haun, Joseph Kolb (who went as a substitute in 1864), Jacob A. Lantz, Samuel Culp (who died Feb. 11, 1864, at Camp Todd in Washington, D.C.), and George L. Shutt.

25. Lehman, *Growth Amidst Struggle*, 24, 38, 62. Henry Newcomer, likely not a Mennonite, is included on the list because he sent Joseph Longenecker, son of Mennonite parents Peter and Elizabeth (Shank) Longenecker Jr. (and grandson of the bishop and founder of the Longenecker/Kolb Mennonite congregation), as a substitute. Newcomer had married Malinda King and lived on the farm just north of the Mennonite church. He was a son of Uriah Newcomer, a local Republican and unsuccessful candidate for the state legislature. Uriah's father was son of a Mennonite minister in Fayette County, Pennsylvania.

26. Falb, *Fruits of Diversity*, 18–19, 98, 116; Frey, *Grandpa's Gone*; Schmutz, *History of the 102d Regiment*, 58; *Hardesty's Historical and Geographical Encyclopedia*. Jonas and Isaac were the sons of Jonas and Catharine (Dill) Huntsberger, who had migrated to Wayne County from Cumberland County, Pennsylvania. Jonas was captured on September 24, 1864, held as prisoner at Athens, Alabama, and approved for exchange on April 22, 1865. He died five days later, when the transport ship on which he had been placed, the *Sultana*, exploded on the Mississippi River near Memphis. Isaac's brother-in-law, Benjamin F. Kurtz, also entered the military and died in the service on April 16, 1863, at Millikens Bend. See Steffen, "The Civil War and the Wayne County Mennonites," 1–2.

27. Lehman, *Sonnenberg*, 88–95. Several men with surnames virtually identical to those found at Sonnenberg have turned up, namely, John Tschantz, Friederich Nussbaum, and George Nussbaumer ("Soldiers Discharge Record," Wayne County Administration Building, Wooster, Ohio). They seemed to have come from Mt. Eaton, which had a Swiss Reformed Church, or from the Winesburg Reformed and Lutheran Church, where some similar names occurred. These names illustrate the need for identifying "Mennonite names" with great care. The names of those contributing money to the Military Committee between August 20, 1862, and January

3, 1863, appeared on the front page of the WCD, 26 Feb. 1863. Coauthor James O. Lehman compared the names against Sonnenberg church records—records that were much more complete than for most other Mennonite congregations at the time.

28. Curiously, the names of senior bishop Ulrich Sommer and deacon Abraham Tschantz do not appear.

29. Lehman *Creative Congregationalism*, 57−59.

30. Two of the Chester men sought exemption in the 1862 draft, one by paying the fee and the other by obtaining a substitute. The Chippewa Swiss (later Crown Hill Mennonite) people seemed less affected by the war. Several paid commutation fees when drafted, but only a little money went to the military committee, and we know of none serving in the military. One questionable source claims that John C. Steiner, a son of one of the ministers, "took an active part in furnishing men from Milton Township." The questionable source is the *Commemorative Biographical Record of Wayne County, Ohio* (Chicago: J. N. Beers & Co., 1889), 50, quoted in Lehman, *Crosswinds: From Switzerland to Crown Hill*, 26−27; Jacob Stoll of the Reformed Mennonite Church obtained a substitute.

31. James O. Lehman interview with John L. Steiner, Mediapolis, Iowa, 21 July 1978; Wiegand, comp., *Steiner Family Record*, 12−13, 76−77, 182−84.

32. RDMO, 1862. An extra issue of WR on October 9, 1862, listed the names of the drafted men. That source has a few variations from the official Record of Drafted Militia.

33. Stark County was also home to the diminishing Rowland Mennonite Church in Canton, made up of people from Pennsylvania and Maryland, who found the city encroaching on them by the time of the war (Stoltzfus, *Mennonites of the Ohio and Eastern Conference*, 49).

34. Unusually, the 1862 "Record of Drafted Militia" for one Jacob Kreider, age 44, says simply that he was discharged for being "conscientious." A few from this area joined the military.

35. Elmer S. Yoder, *From Das Buchenland to The Beech*, 42, 112.

36. RDMO, 1862. Among those paying the $200 equivalency were Jacob Brechbill, Christian Hoover, Henry Hackman, Peter E. Stoufer, Michael Stonacker, Abraham and Jacob Snyder, and Jacob Stauffer. Those purchasing substitutes included names such as Blough, Buchtel, Bender, Bowers, Hoover, Hartman, Lentz, Miller, Newcomer, Roland, Stauffer, and Stoner. Volunteers to the 16th, 76th, or 115th Ohio Infantry were Christian Bowers, Jacob P. Bixler, David Gahman, Daniel Martin, Jacob S. Miller, and Jacob Rhodes. Elmer Yoder, local historian of the Stark County Amish community, says records are too obscure to be certain which names were of Amish church members and which were sons of members.

37. Samuel Hage, Washington County, Iowa, to Samuel Mast, 15 June 1862. Samuel Mast Collection, Hist Mss. 1-346, MCA-G. Hage was ordained deacon

for the church eventually known as the Eicher Amish, and after 1893 as the Eicher Emmanuel Mennonite Church. In 1880 Hage left this church to help organize a more revivalist-oriented Mennonite Brethren in Christ congregation (now known as the Missionary Church).

38. HCF estimated that from half to "probably three-fourths" of the population were Amish in those townships ("The Amish," HCF, 4 Sept. 1862).

39. The HCR believed that some Amish did vote, chiding that, if they were going to refuse to fight, they should also refrain from voting (HCR, 9 Oct. 1862). The Holmes County Mennonite vote, concentrated in Paint Township, tended to be Republican, but it was too small to be of electoral significance.

40. Election results from HCF, 12 Sept. 1861 and 23 Oct. 1862:

Townships	1860		1861		1862	
	Democrat	Republican	Democrat	Republican	Democrat	Republican
German	160	42	185	23	250	1
Berlin	121	76	110	75	125	48
Walnutcreek	115	39	104	22	191	1
Paint	224	76	202	63	238	41
Saltcreek	202	123	189	105	186	73
Total	822	356	790	288	990	164

41. HCF, 9 Oct., 23 Oct., 6 Nov. 1862. See HCR response in 6 Nov. 1862.

42. The Democrat's margin was smaller (2,980 to 2,208) than in Holmes County, but in largely Mennonite and Amish townships the spread was wider. See also WR, 23 Oct. 1862.

Township	Democrat George Bliss	Republican Martin Welker
Paint	207	49
Sugar Creek	197	122
Chippewa	253	109
Milton	156	80
Green	149	143
East Union	187	106

43. Lehman, Sonnenberg, 94, reporting the author's interview with Menno Zuercher, Dalton, Ohio, 29 June 1967. Apparently few Sonnenberg Swiss appreciated the vocal minority of deacon Peter P. Lehman, and Ulrich and Christian Welty, who supported abolition. It is probably not coincidental that the Weltys

and Lehman left Wayne County soon after the war, despite the fact that Christian Welty had by then also become a Sonnenberg deacon.

44. HCF, 2 Oct. 1862; Lehman, *Growth Amidst Struggle*, 26. It should be noted that at Winesburg, in Paint Township, there were other German-speaking residents, particularly the members of the Lutheran and Reformed union church.

45. HCR, 9 Oct. 1862.

46. HCF, 9 Oct. 1862; HCR, 6 Nov. 1862.

47. RDMO.

48. Jacob and Catharina Nold, Columbiana, Ohio, to Johannes Gross and wife, 3 Nov. 1862, Jacob Nold Collection, Hist Mss. 1-873, MCA-G (Abraham Nold was one of eleven Columbiana County Mennonites drafted); Jacob Nold and wife Catharine, Columbiana, Ohio, to Johanas Gross and Wife, 18 Oct. 1863 (trans. Noah G. Good), Wilmer Reinford Collection, Hist Mss 1-280, MCA-G; RDMO.

49. *Mac-a-Cheek Press*, 8 Aug. 1862. They include John B. Yoder ($20), John K. Hartzler ($5), John H. Kenagy ($15), Peter Troyer ($2), John D. Yoder ($10), D. C. Yoder ($5), Eli Yoder ($10), and Peter Lantz ($5). This paper was published from several different addresses during its run; during the Civil War it was published at Bellefontaine, Ohio.

50. *Urbana Citizen and Gazette*, 25 April 1861; 31 July 1862; 12 March 1863. Included are Benj. Yoder and John E. Mast ($2 each), J. K. Mast, Jacob Zook, Samuel Yoder, J. R. King, C. S. King, John Zook, Jos. N. Kauffman ($5 each), Joel Hartzler, John Mast, C. Kauffman, Noah Troyer, Jacob Yoder, Lemuel Weaver, David King ($10 each), John C. Yoder, J. Troyer ($20 each), Isaac Mast ($30), and Christian Yoder ($40).

51. RDMO.

52. *Press and Leader*, Bryan, Ohio, 13 Nov. 1862. This was a Republican paper.

53. A fire in July 1864 destroyed the courthouse and its records; see *Weekly Democrat*, Bryan, Ohio, 21 July 1864. Orland Grieser, local historian of the area, found very little on the war era, except the local tradition that "many of the young men left for the army during this era." Grieser named the following as going to war but was uncertain if all were Amish: Dan Burkholder, Abe Baer, Harris Wise, Unas Baer, Benjamin Brenneman, J. F. King, and Samuel and Andrew Baer. Orland Grieser Records, Grant M. Stoltzfus Collection, II-MS-29, MSHLA. An undocumented and undated story from this community, recorded by early Mennonite historian C. Henry Smith, tells that a "company of Amish had assembled for the purpose of securing exemptions" and were "attacked by a mob of men who had been less fortunate in obtaining exemptions" (Smith, *Mennonites of America*, 315). Smith does not indicate a year.

54. Four men from German Township—Christian Ricksicker, John Recklaw,

Joseph Stutesman, and Michall Webber—were discharged as "conscientious" with no indication of their paying the $200 fee. No information is listed on the Joseph Rupp and Peter Guyman cases. Recklaw and Webber were not familiar Amish names in this area.

55. Records in Militia Enrollment Book, Elkhart Co., 1862. (999.18), Elkhart County Historical Society, Bristol, Ind.; L723, "Drafted Men 1862, No. 1," Adjutant General's Office, Archives, Indiana State Library.

56. GT, 11 Sept. 1862; Peddycord, *History of the Seventy-Fourth Regiment*, 51–53, 67, 79–80.

57. Records in Militia Enrollment Book, Elkhart Co., 1862 (999.18), Elkhart County Historical Society, Bristol, Ind. In June 1861 Thomas Nunemaker and several other Elkhart County Mennonites had joined more than 150 neighbors in signing a petition protesting the county commissioners' "appropriating the sum of $800 to defray the expenses of outfitting for a company of volunteers." However, the petition does not indicate that peace principles were involved in the remonstrance; fiscal restraint seems to have been the petitioners' sole motivation. See "Remonstrance of Citizens of Elkhart [County], June 6, 1861," 77.16.187 Commissioners Papers, 1861, June (d), Civil War Volunteers, Elkhart County Historical Society, Bristol, Ind.

58. Nonetheless, according to the GD, the October 6 draft passed off quietly in Elkhart County, as it published the names drawn from the various townships and specifically separated the names of the "conscientious exempts" who were expected to pay $200 each. See GD, 8 Oct. 1862.

59. Order Book of Naturalization #1, located in Adams County, Ind., courthouse. For details on these Swiss Mennonite and Amish families, their immigration, and settlement, see Habegger and Adams, *The Swiss of Adams and Wells Counties, Indiana.*

60. DE on October 9 listed men from French Township who were "conscientiously opposed to bearing arms," including: Peter Kloppenstine, Jacob Meyer, Nicholas Stucky, John Zimmerman, Christian Augsberger, Jacob Lichty, Christian Roth, Christian Schwartz, Nicholas Rich, Christian Aschliman, Christian Zimmerman, Jacob P. Moser, John Bixler, and Jacob Lehman. From the townships of Wabash, Monroe, and Hartford appeared Christian, Abram P., and Peter E. Springer; John, Abraham, and John P. Lugibill; John Newschbaum; Jacob Richer; Peter Moser; Christian Ausberger; Joseph Wise; and two Peter Lichtys. The militia enrollment for Harrison Township in Wells County uses the phrase "Says he is conscientiously opposed to bearing Arms" after listing enrollees' ages and occupations. The following names are believed to be Mennonites: David Bombgarner; Benjamin and Daniel Bomgarner; John and Peter Steffen; and John, Christian, Peter, and Ulric Garver. See Militia Enrollment Sheets for Wells County, Harrison Township, L699, Box

24, Archives, Indiana State Library. Enrollers rarely took the unusual step of noting church affiliation, but they did so in the townships of Erwin and Monroe, where altogether they listed 100 Dunkers and Quakers taking the conscientious position. See Militia Enrollment Record, listed on cards in L706, Box 10, in the Archives of Indiana State Library.

61. DE, 13 Nov. 1862. Details reported in 1869, when W. H. H. Terrell issued an eight-volume *Report of the Adjutant General* concerning that state's participation in the Civil War. See Terrell, *Indiana in the War of the Rebellion*, 53–55.

62. Siddall had argued that since the national quota assigned to Indiana in proportion to the whole number of militia was 40 percent, then 40 percent of those who signed the enrollment as having conscientious scruples should be drafted and forced to pay $200 each, regardless of how many men the draft actually required. Records in Militia Enrollment Book, Elkhart Co., 1862. (999.18), Elkhart County Historical Society, Bristol, Ind., confirm and illustrate this curious interpretation that 40 percent of those enrolled as men of conscience pay the fee, even if the draft called for a much smaller number of men. So too does discussion in Eli J. Hochstedler, Kokomo, Ind. to Samuel S. Yoder, Holmes County, Ohio, 6 Oct. 1862, Family Correspondence, SSYP.

63. Local newspapers, though using the story for their respective partisan purposes, confirm Terrell's report. In early January 1863, Governor Morton gave a major message, presenting "a comprehensive and intelligent outline" of how the draft had proceeded. GD, in a long column entitled "The 'Conscientious' Tax," gave detail on the governor's extensive explanation of the issue, then criticized his handling of it. See GD, 28 Jan. 1863; and GT, 15 Jan. 1863. *The Elkhart Review*, Elkhart, Ind., 17 Jan. 1863, published similar conclusions. Other details are in GD, 4 Feb. 1863. State records may be found in Drawer 107, Folder 77, "State Paymaster's Report," Archives, Indiana State Library. No other state gave such a refund.

64. Terrell, *Indiana in the War of Rebellion*, 50–51.

65. "The Amish," HCF, 4 Sept. 1862.

66. See McPherson, *For Cause and Comrades*, for a highly nuanced explanation of the role of ideology and principled patriotism in the motivation of enlistees and draftees.

67. Samuel Hage, Washington County, Iowa, to Samuel Mast, 15 June 1862. Samuel Mast Collection, Hist Mss. 1-346, MCA-G.

68. Although those born abroad were somewhat under-represented in the Federal forces, they did comprise 25 percent of Unionists in uniform. McPherson, *Battle Cry of Freedom*, 606–607, and n. 31, summarizes secondary literature on this point.

69. E. G. Kaufman, *General Conference Mennonite Pioneers*, 271.

70. John D. Thiesen, North Newton, Kans., letter to James O. Lehman, 4 June

1991. One settlement of recent (1832–54) Amish Mennonite immigrants was located, not in the Midwest, but in Lewis County, New York. Only two men from this community, Joseph Leyendecker and John Yousey, joined the military; see Yousey, *Strangers and Pilgrims*, 39, 67.

71. Sprunger, *The First Hundred Years*, 14; supplemented with information from Karen Adams, Berne (Ind.) Public Library, 18 Aug. 2005.

72. *The Past and Present of Woodford County, Illinois*, 340;

73. Estes, *A Goodly Heritage*, 50–51.

74. Weber, *Centennial History of Mennonites*, 110; Estes, *Living Stones*, 84–85.

75. *History of Peoria County Illinois*, 641; and *Biographical Album of Peoria County, Illinois*, 384–85.

76. Amish Mennonite volunteers from the region continued to step forward in 1863 and 1864; see correspondence from Steven R. Estes, 1 Oct. 1982, and 11 Jan. 1983. Estes cites information from "A Record of Soldiers Discharges," Vol. I, Woodford County Clerk and Recorder's Office, Eureka, Ill., and several volumes of J. N. Reece, *Report of the Adjutant General of the State of Illinois* (Springfield, Ill.: Adjutant General, 1901), and makes further identification of Amish and Mennonite men from his research in several genealogies and published works; see also W. H. Smith, *Mennonites in Illinois*, 346; and *Portrait and Biographical Record of Tazewell and Mason Counties, Illinois*, 377.

77. Barnett, *History of the Twenty-Second Regiment, Iowa Volunteer Infantry*, 130; "Emanuel Hochstetler Writes to Peter Swartzendruber in 1862," Iowa Mennonite Historical Society *Reflections* 5 (Summer 1991), 3–4; Reschly, *Amish on the Iowa Prairie*, 96–114; Melvin Gingerich, *Mennonites in Iowa*, 147, 385.

78. For more on this theme, see McPherson, *For Cause and Comrades*, 6, 13, 25–26, 31, 76–78. See also Mitchell, "Soldiering, Manhood, and Coming of Age," 46, 50.

79. E. J. Hochstedler to S. S. Yoder, 27 Sept. 1862, Family Correspondence, SSYP.

80. Levi Eash, Middlebury, Lagrange Co., Ind. to Samuel S. Yoder, 2 March 1862, SSYP.

81. See Family Correspondence, 1861–64, SSYP.

82. Noah and Moses enlisted by October 1861, in the 51st Ohio.

83. N. W. Yoder to S. S. Yoder, Nashville, Ten., 16 May 1862, SSYP. His comments do not make it clear whether it was the community in general or the Amish (or both) that treated the family badly because they were poverty stricken.

84. C. Y. Yoder to Samuel Yoder, 16 Jan. 1863; Noah W. Yoder to David Tod, Governor of Ohio, n.d., SSYP.

85. N. W. Yoder to S. S. Yoder, 14 Nov. 1861, Camp Dennison, Ohio; N. W. Yoder to S. S. Yoder, 21 Dec. 1861, Camp Wickliffe, New Haven, Ky., N. W. Yo-

der to S. S. Yoder, Nashville, Ten., 26 April and 30 Aug. 1862; Catherine Yoder to S. S., 10 Nov. 1862, all in SSYP.

86. M. F. Yoder to S. S. Yoder, Camp Wickliffe, Ky., 9 and 26 Jan. and 9 Feb. 1862, SSYP.

87. "Artical of agreement [sic] between S. S. Yoder and Directors of district No. 4, Berlin Twp., Holmes Co., O."; J. T. Yoder to N. W. [Yoder], 10 Oct. 1862. Jacob studied at Smithville High School to be a teacher; see Jacob T. Yoder to N. W. Yoder, 17 Sept. 1862. Catherine Y. Yoder, wife of Noah, revealed Jacob's plan to sell himself as a substitute in a letter to S. S. [Yoder], on 10 Nov. 1862; all in SSYP.

88. Moses T. Yoder to S. S. [Yoder], 16 May 1863, SSYP.

89. N. W. Yoder to S. S. Yoder, 4, 15, 17, and 18 July 1864, SSYP.

6. The Fighting Comes North

1. Guelzo, *Lincoln's Emancipation Proclamation*, treats these developments in detail and shows Lincoln's commitment to pushing emancipation despite a thicket of political realities. Berlin et al., *Slaves No More*, 1–76, provides helpful context.

2. Donald, *Lincoln*, 366–69. Helpful primary sources appear in the collection Johnson, ed., *Abraham Lincoln, Slavery, and the Civil War*.

3. Jones, *Abraham Lincoln and a New Birth of Freedom*.

4. Ayers, *In the Presence of Mine Enemies*, 166–68, 216–19, 237–40, presents the lively debate in Franklin County, Pennsylvania, over emancipation—an example of discussion that was part of the public environment in one northern Mennonite community.

5. Quoted in Burdge and Horst, *Building on the Gospel Foundation*, 226. Originals located as Henry Shank, Putnam Co., Ohio, to Frederick Shank, Leitersburg, Md., 7 Jan. 1863, f. 12, Clarence E. Shank Collection, MHACV; and Jonas Shank, Putnam Co., Ohio, to Frederick Shank, Leitersburg, Md., 1 Mar. 1863, Box 7, f. 5, J. Irvin Lehman Collection, MHACV.

6. Yoder and Estes, *Proceedings of the Amish Ministers' Meetings*, 36–37. In typical Amish fashion, the meetings disregarded political boundaries and included Canadian Amish churches as well.

7. At age 79, Catherine (Horst) Hunsecker vividly remembered events from her teenage years as she narrated them to her grandnephew, Levi Horst, who translated them and had them published as Catherine Hunsecker, "Civil War Reminiscences," in the *Christian Monitor*.

8. Interestingly, however, Northern Mennonites' support of the Union did not draw on civil religion themes, but followed two-kingdom theological logic that appreciated government without sanctifying it. There is virtually no record of Northern Mennonites or Amish observing the three national days of fasting called by

President Lincoln. The rare exceptions are a diary entry of Reformed Mennonite Jacob Stouffer, Chambersburg, Pennsylvania, for 26 September 1861, and a letter from Mennonite minister Jacob Kolb, Cambria County, Pennsylvania, noting that his church would observe Lincoln's designation of April 30, 1863, as a day of prayer and fasting. See Green, ed., *Pages from a Diary*, 17; and Jacob Kolb to Jacob Nold Jr., 27 Apr. 1863, Jacob Nold Collection, Hist. Mss. 1-442, MCA-G.

9. Peter Eshleman, Washington Co., Md., to Jacob Nold, Columbiana, Ohio, 8 Apr. 1862 (trans. Peter Hoover), Jacob Nold Collection, Hist. Mss. 1-442, MCA-G.

10. OR, Ser. I, v. 19, pt. 2, 601–602; on this campaign, see McPherson, *Crossroads of Freedom: Antietam*, 73–131.

11. Green, ed., *Pages from a Diary*, 18; *Herald and Free Press*, Norristown, Pa., 16 Sept. 1862. Curtin's alarm over the lack of defense forces for Pennsylvania coincided, ironically, with a U.S. War Department message of September 8—just two days after the Confederate occupation of Frederick, Maryland—that informed all "U. S. marshals, military commandants, provost- marshals, police officers, [and] sheriffs," that recruitment was strong enough that it was no longer necessary to stringently enforce the 1862 conscription orders (OR, Ser. III, v. 2, 525–26). Given Lee's advance into Maryland, however, President Lincoln endorsed Curtin's call for volunteers for "home defense and protection" and promised that the federal government would accept up to 50,000 of them formally into Union service and pay them "to the extent that they can be armed, equipped, and usefully employed" (OR, Series III, v. 2, 538–39, 563).

12. LDEE, 4 Sept. 1862; 8 Sept. 1862.

13. LDEE, 13 Sept. 1862; 30 Aug. 1862. See also criticisms in 15 Oct. 1862 and 3 Oct. 1862.

14. Burdge and Horst, *Building on the Gospel Foundation*, 237–38.

15. Ibid., 60 n.78, on Lesher's war damage claim application.

16. Green, ed., *Pages from a Diary*, 18.

17. The Mumma meetinghouse—immortalized in the post-battle photograph of Matthew Brady's protégé, Alexander Gardner, served from 1852 to 1921 as one of the meeting places for the Manor German Baptist Brethren circuit outside Hagerstown. See *Brethren Encyclopedia*, 1:41, 2:787.

18. McPherson, *Crossroads of Freedom*, 3, 177 n.56.

19. Green, ed., *Pages from a Diary*, 18–19.

20. Ayers, *In the Presence of Mine Enemies*, 322–31.

21. OR, Series I, v. 19, pt. 2, 52–55; Green, ed., *Pages from a Diary*, 19–20; Burdge and Horst, *Building on the Gospel Foundation*, 241, lists the names of fourteen Mennonites and eight Reformed Mennonites who applied for compensation in 1863 to the state of Pennsylvania for horses lost to Stuart's October 1862 raid.

22. Donald, *Lincoln*, 373–83; McPherson, *Crossroads of Freedom*, 138–56. On soldiers' responses to the Proclamation, see an analysis of their letters in McPherson, *For Cause and Comrades*, 117–30. A letter from the front lines by Mennonite-reared soldier John Longenecker and published in *HCR*, 3 Mar. 1863, illustrates Union troops' willingness to embrace abolition as a means to more quickly win the war. For how the Proclamation fit a Northern military strategy evolving from conciliation to "hard war," see Grimsley, *Hard Hand of War*, 120–41.

23. Pease and Randall, eds., *Diary of Orville Hickman Browning*, 1:600, entry for 18 Dec. 1862.

24. Geary, *We Need Men*, 52.

25. John King to John Gross, 24 Jan. 1863, MHCA, Harleysville, Pa. The quotation is a free rendition of King's extremely poor English.

26. Mary Elizabeth Yoder, "Amish Settlers and the Civil War," 26.

27. Maust, *Descendants of Jacob Swartzentruber*, 12–13. Versions of this story place it in 1863 or 1864—though the earlier date is more likely, given troop movements in the area.

28. M. E. Yoder, "Amish Settlers and the Civil War," 26–27; M. Marie and Paul H. Yoder, *The Daniel Beachy Family of Aurora, West Virginia*, 223. Another account of this event says the traveling party included a woman, Anna Thomas—information and name included in an interview by Alta Schrock, Grantsville, Md., with Kate Hershberger. Coauthor James O. Lehman, in turn, interviewed Schrock and reviewed her interview files on 4 Jan. 1982.

29. Luthy, *Amish in America*, 491; M. M. and P. H. Yoder, *Daniel Beachy Family*, 223; OR, v. 25, Part I, 105, 107, 117, 132–34.

30. Fellman, *Inside War*; Bright, "The McNeill Rangers: A Study in Confederate Guerrilla Warfare."

31. Erb, *South Central Frontiers*, 45; Luthy, *Amish in America*, 241–42. Christian Raber is said to have been called as a witness for the soldier's court-martial (which acquitted him).

32. This was General Order No. 11, covering Jackson, Cass, Bates, and some of Vernon counties; see Castel, "Order No. 11 and the Civil War on the Border."

33. It is hard to square this piece of family tradition with accounts of how General Order No. 11 functioned.

34. Erb, *South Central Frontiers*, 46–47; Iona Schrock, "Celebration of 125 Years of Mennonites in Cass County, Missouri," *South Central Conference Messenger* 44 (Sept./Oct. 1991), 5–6. See also "The Sycamore Grove Mennonite Church," *MHB* 28 (July 1967), 717. "History of the Bethel Church, Cass County, Missouri," *MHB* 13 (April 1952), 3, says that Christian P. Yoder "employed a Negro with an ox to bring Mrs. [Solomon] Yoder and children to Independence." Violence from Missouri spilled into the Davis County, Iowa, Amish Mennonite settlement in October

1864, when Confederate partisans from Missouri, dressed as Union soldiers, raided southeastern Iowa, looting homes and taking hostages. Pillaged Amish farms were those of Daniel and Christian Swartzendruver and Jeremiah Miller; see Melvin Gingerich, *Mennonites in Iowa*, 62–64.

35. McPherson, *Battle Cry of Freedom*, 646–51.

36. Alexander et al., *Southern Revenge*, 69–73; Green, ed., *Pages from a Diary*, 21.

37. Hess, *By the Grace of God*, 135, 137–38. Burdge and Horst, *Building on the Gospel Foundation*, 245, and 761, n. 96, cites archival records on Heatwole's Confederate service.

38. Coddington, *Gettysburg Campaign*, 153–79; Ayers, *In the Presence of Mine Enemies*, 396–412. A first-person account from a Mennonite perspective is Henry B. Hege, Marion, Pa. to Henry G. Hege, Lancaster Co., Pa., 12 July 1863, Civil War file, MHACV (copy supplied to the authors by Edsel Burdge Jr.). Copies of this letter have been duplicated and circulated in various communities; one is located in Harry A. Brunk Collection, I-MS-13, MSHLA, and it was published in Conrad, *Conococheague*.

39. OR, Series I, v. 27, pt. 3, 942–943; Coddington, "Prelude to Gettysburg."

40. Hunsecker, "Civil War Reminiscences."

41. Green, ed., *Pages from a Diary*, 21. After the war, sixty-four household heads (47 Mennonite and 17 Reformed Mennonite) filed damage claims with the state of Pennsylvania for losses at the hands of Confederate requisitioners; see Burdge and Horst, *Building on the Gospel Foundation*, 250 and 762, n.121, for archival citations. Another first-person account is that of Reformed Mennonite Elizabeth (Fuss) Leidig. She vividly recollected the "harrowing experience, of two long days duration," recorded in Jacob A. Hoffman, *The Leidig Family* (Hagerstown, Md.: n.p., 1960), no pagination; copy located at the Washington County (Md.) Public Library.

42. Henry B. Hege, Marion, Pa. to Henry G. Hege, Lancaster County, Pa., 12 July 1863.

43. This was Isaac Strite, a Franklin County Dunker; see Robinson and Strite, *History and Genealogical Records of the Strites*, 737–38.

44. Hunsecker, "Civil War Reminiscences," 407, remembered that Confederates threatened her father, Levi, in front of his family, with execution if he did not hand over his horses. Since Horst had sent his horses away for safe keeping in advance of the army, he did not know where they were and could not procure them. When the soldiers did locate several colts and a horse at an adjoining tenant house, they left without harming Levi.

45. "Deacon Michael Hege's Church Record Book." Much later Hege composed a 24-stanza German poem narrating these events. An English translation, with forced meter and rhyme, by Harvey S. Reiff, appeared as "God's Help in Trouble," *Gospel Witness* 2 (Dec. 5, 1906), 575. Various copies of German and English print-

ings of the poem are located in MSHLA. A more literal translation into English by Peter Hoover is included in its entirety in Burdge and Horst, *Building on the Gospel Foundation*, 248–49.

46. This transcription was included in "A Letter from Canada," *HT*, Dec. 1864, 80, by David Sherk of Berlin (now Kitchener), Ontario, who said he heard the story and copied the inscription while visiting Franklin County, Pennsylvania, in November 1864. A few family stories also point to respectful behavior on the part of Lee's troops. See, e.g., Jacob and Elizabeth (Lesher) Grove's claim that Confederates "behaved themselves as men should" and that they did not commit the "horribly repugnant crimes" the Groves had expected, in Samuel Grove Sollenberger and Grace Hege, *Jacob Grove and Elizabeth Lesher Grove Family* (S.l.; n.d.); copy located at the Washington County (Md.) Public Library.

47. Hunsecker, "Civil War Reminiscences," 406; Henry B. Hege, Marion, Pa. to Henry G. Hege, Lancaster Co., Pa., 12 July 1863.

48. E.g., Hunsecker, "Civil War Reminiscences," 407: of Union soldiers "we were not so much afraid." The Horsts supplied Union men with food, on occasion; father Levi took "nearly whole churnfuls of buttermilk over to the camps at once."

49. On the morning of Thursday, June 25 Gen. Ewell had vacated his headquarters at the Franklin hotel in Chambersburg and moved to the Mennonite meetinghouse north of town. Later, he turned the church building over to Lt. Gen. Longstreet for his use as a headquarters—see Hoke, *The Great Invasion of 1863*, 153–55.

50. Early's orders were to possess the Wrightsville-Columbia Bridge, cross into Lancaster County, and divide his army into two parts. One would "cut the Pennsylvania Central Railroad, march upon Lancaster, lay that town under contribution, and then attack Harrisburg in the rear," while the other part attacked the capital city from the front. See OR, Series I, v. 27, pt. 2, 467.

51. *New York Times*, 16 June 1863; OR, Series I, v. 27, pt. 3, 68–69, 112–13, 136–37, 145, 174–75; PDT, 23 June 1863.

52. Spotts, *They Called It Strasburg*, 32; LDEE, 16, 23, 26, and 27 June 1863; and Heisey, "Lancaster In The Gettysburg Campaign."

53. Ruth, *The Earth Is the Lord's*, 566. Christian F. Charles (1847–1935), who was later (1898) ordained deacon for the Mount Joy (Pa.) Mennonite congregation, is coauthor Steven M. Nolt's great-great grandfather.

54. Ruth, *The Earth Is the Lord's*, 566–67. Ruth also cites a contemporary diary mentioning the number of civilian refugees from York County who flooded into Lancaster County, no doubt heightening locals' sense of anxiety.

55. *New York Times*, July 2, 1863.

56. LDEE, 23 June 1863.

57. OR, Series I, v. 27, pt. 2, 466.

58. OR, Series I, v. 27, pt. 2, 443, 466–67, 491–93, 498; McSherry, "The Defense of Columbia," 136, 150–51.

59. LDEE, 30 June 1863; PDT, 30 June 1863; and quotes in McSherry, "The Defense of Columbia," 142–50. The militia first attempted to drop one of the bridge's spans, thereby blocking Confederate crossing without destroying the entire bridge structure; when this strategy proved impossible, they opted for burning the bridge—see OR, Series I, v. 27, pt. 2, 277–79. In 1868 a new bridge was built on the old piers; until then, commerce across the Susquehanna River was inconvenienced. The old bridge had been owned by the Columbia Bank, which tried, unsuccessfully, to recover some of its loss from the Pennsylvania Claims Commission for wartime losses.

60. OR, Series I, v. 27, pt., 467.

61. Kraybill and Zimmerman, History of a John Graybill Family, 670. Sarah Graybill Seaman (1847–1946) recounted this story to a reporter in Kansas, where she lived as an adult.

62. McPherson, Hallowed Ground, provides a concise overview of the battle.

63. OR, Series I, v. 27, pt. 1, 175.

64. Gambone, Life of General Samuel K. Zook; Zook, "A Biographical Sketch of Samuel K. Zook"; Reed, "Montgomery County's 'Bivouac of the Dead,'" 56–57; HFP, 12 April 1864; and H. F. Gingerich and R. W. Kreider, Amish and Amish Mennonite Genealogies, 548, 550, 555. The Amish settlement in Chester County disbanded in the 1830s; some of Zook's childhood years were spent in neighboring Montgomery County; see Mook, "An Early Amish Colony." Apparently, at some point, Zook had begun using the Polish military hero's name Kosciusko as a middle name in place of Kurtz, the Amish surname that had been his given middle name.

65. Foote, The Civil War: A Narrative, 580–95.

66. OR, Series I, v. 27, pt. 3, 966–67. Estimates of the number of Confederate wounded vary, but all agree that Lee's official report of 12,700 wounded is too low; the numbers here come from McPherson, Hallowed Ground, 131–34. More detail on the retreat is contained in Schildt, Roads from Gettysburg; and Hoke, Great Invasion, 477–507.

67. Henry B. Hege, Marion, Pa. to Henry G. Hege, Lancaster County, Pa., 12 July 1863.

68. Burdge and Horst, Building on the Gospel Foundation, 251.

69. McPherson, Battle Cry of Freedom, 663–666.

70. Here, and in the paragraphs that follow, Peter Nissley, Marietta, Lancaster Co., Pa. to John F. Funk, 6 Aug. 1863, JFFC.

7. Thaddeus Stevens and Pennsylvania Mennonite Politics

1. Hoke, *Great Invasion of 1863*, 107. See p. 171, where Confederate Maj. Gen. Jubal Early, who led the burners, wrote to J. Fraise Richard, on May 7, 1886, that Early ordered the burning of Stevens' ironworks on June 26 because "in some speeches in Congress, Mr. Stevens had exhibited a most vindictive spirit toward the people of the South."

2. From March 1843 to February 1933, the Congressional district was contiguous with the borders of Lancaster County.

3. The best biography of Stevens is Trefousse, *Thaddeus Stevens*.

4. Hamm, *Transformation of American Quakerism*, 61, reports a similar relationship between Quakers in Indiana and Radical Republican (and religiously Unitarian) George W. Julian, though a few traditionalist Quakers criticized this alliance.

5. Some references to the seriousness of the situation are found in OR, Series III, v. 3, 37, 55.

6. McPherson, *Battle Cry of Freedom*, 600–605.

7. Geary, *We Need Men*, 49–64, discusses the politics of passing this 1863 legislation; see p. 58 for comment on winter weather.

8. OR, Series III, v. 3, 35–36.

9. *Congressional Globe*, 37th Cong., 34d Sess., 994 (1863); Geary, *We Need Men*, 55–56.

10. McPherson, *Battle Cry of Freedom*, 603.

11. *Congressional Globe*, 37th Cong., 34d Sess., 994 (1863).

12. Wright, *Conscientious Objectors in the Civil War*, 65–68.

13. Geary, *We Need Men*, 60–61. Democrats, with the exception of William E. Lehman of Philadelphia, opposed it; see *New York Times*, 26 and 27 Feb. 1863.

14. LDEE, Lancaster, Pa., 12 March 1863.

15. In the three 1864 drafts the procedure was a bit different. Each district received a quota adjusted by the number of those already volunteered and then had 50 days either to raise the difference with more volunteers or to resort to a draft.

16. Jacob and Maria Landes, 6 May 1863, to Tobias and Magdalena Kolb, Waterloo County, Canada, Early Mennonite Correspondence and Papers, 1708–1901, Hist. Mss. 1–10, MCA-G.

17. Mahlon Yardley to James B. Fry, 30 Sept. and 6 Oct. 1863, complained of Bucks County draftees going to Canada. See Entry 2932, "Register of Applicants for Exemption Service, June 1863-February 1865," 2 vols., RG 110, 6th District records (although they likely belong in the 5th District records), Part IV, National Archives, Washington, D.C. On 1862 skedaddlers from the Franconia-Lower Salford area, see Ruth, *Maintaining the Right Fellowship*, 322. On failure to report and draft evaders more generally, see Geary, *We Need Men*, 99–102.

18. "Register of Applicants for Exemption Service, June 1863-February 1865," 2 vols. RG 110, Entry 3035, 9th District of Pennsylvania, Part IV. National Archives, Washington, D.C.; OR, Series III, v. 3, 794.

19. Exhaustive genealogical work would confirm many names, but certainly not every one.

20. LEH, 29 July 1863.

21. LI, 28 July 1863.

22. LG, 1 July 1863.

23. LG, 22 July, 5 and 26 Aug., 7 and 14 Oct. 1863; Kauffman, *Mifflin County Amish and Mennonite Story*, 138–40.

24. Kauffman, *Mifflin County Amish and Mennonite Story*, 141.

25. LG, 16 Sept., 21 and 28 Oct. 1863.

26. Seyfert, "A Page of Lancaster County History," 112–13. For a primary source account, see BCI, 14 April 1863. Hoover, *Enemies in the Rear*, is a somewhat fictionalized rendering. Although Hoover thought of the Knights as a Pennsylvania Dutch movement (see p. 21), he was aware of no Mennonite involvement.

27. *Address of Dr. William Wetherill to the Citizens of Lower Providence Township, Montgomery County* (Norristown: Republican Office, 1863), 1–7. A detailed discussion of the Union Leagues in urban areas is chapter 4 of Lawson, *Patriot Fires*.

28. Whiteman, *Gentlemen in Crisis*, 16; "Publications Distribution, Union League of Philadelphia," Record in the Archives of the Union League, Philadelphia, Pa.

29. *Weekly Express*, Lancaster, Pa., 30 May 1863.

30. HFP, 10 Feb. 1863.

31. Ruth, *Maintaining the Right Fellowship*, 322. Joining the Union League from Lower Salford were Henry H. Derstine, Samuel Swartley, Isaac Landis, and John M. Kulp.

32. LDEE, 5 Oct. 1863. The partisan paper may have inflated the attendance. Democrats had held a rally in Lancaster on September 17 at which the LI claimed an attendance of 10,000. Traditional Mennonite names in the list of Democratic county representatives are very sparse, but a few crop up: Christian Erb, Jacob Brubaker, Henry Kurtz, Benjamin Eby, Martin Kendig, and Christian Herr. See LI, 22 Sept. 1863.

33. LEH, 7 Oct. 1863; Robertson, "The Idealist as Opportunist."

34. HFP, 16 Oct. 1863.

35. BCI, 6 Oct. 1863.

36. Jacob S. Funk to John F. Funk, 19 Oct. 1863, JFFC.

37. Sterling, "Civil War Draft Resistance in the Middle West," 283–86.

38. Peter Levine, "Draft Evasion in the North During the Civil War," 816.

39. Cook, *Armies of the Streets*. The July 13–16, 1863, New York City draft riots killed eleven African Americans, eight soldiers, two policemen, and eighty-four

rioters. Troops fresh from the battle of Gettysburg quelled the unrest, which saw largely poorer, Democratic, Irish mobs attack drafting offices, African Americans, white Republican businesses and businessmen, and street cleaning and dock loading equipment that was blamed for throwing laborers out of work. Rioters also burned the Colored Orphan Asylum. What passed for a draft riot in Lancaster, Pa., occurred on July 15, when rumors circulated that the draft would resume the next day. Some "Dutch women" of the "German element" in Lancaster city reportedly formed a "mob" to stop the draft wheel. Democratic mayor George Sanderson called extra police. A reporter on hand said that when the doors opened the next day, the crowd rushed in and the women "commenced a screaming and yelling which almost deafened us" (*LDEE*, 14 and 16 July 1863).

40. Geary, "Civil War Conscription in the North."

41. E.g., *LI*, 28 July 1864.

42. McPherson, *Battle Cry of Freedom*, 448. After all the exemptions and deductions, the rate stood at 3 percent up to $10,000 and 5 percent beyond that amount.

43. For a listing see Lehman, "Duties of the Mennonite Citizen," 18–20. The *LDEE* published the lists in February 1865.

44. Interestingly, only a relatively small number of Amish or Mennonites appear on such tax lists elsewhere—though a few show up. An Amishman known as "rich Isaac Kauffman," reputed to be the "wealthiest man in Somerset County," was said to have been worth $250,000 upon his death in 1884, three years after he had distributed $100,000 among his children; see *Johnstown Tribune*, 10 Mar. 1865; and Luthy, *Amish in America*, 410. On Mifflin County income tax lists, see Kauffman, *Mifflin County Amish and Mennonite Story*, 174–75. See also comments from Columbiana County, Ohio, in the next chapter.

45. And of course it was not only the Amish and Mennonites who tried to avoid the draft. Many in the general population did too. See story in *FB*, 19 Aug. 1863.

46. Other congregations had similar programs. Johannes Gross explained a number of these efforts to Jacob Nold in Johannes Gross to Jacob Nold, 1 Nov. 1863, Jacob Nold Collection, Hist Mss. 1-873, MCA-G. See another example (though without indication of place or exact date) in "A Mutual Aid Plan from the Civil War Era," *MHB* 34 (October 1973), 4; original located at MCA-G.

47. Eastern District Minutes, early October 1863, Mennonite Heritage Center Archives, Harleysville, Pa.

48. *LDEE*, 2 Nov. 1862.

49. *LDEE*, 17 Dec. 1862; and *LI*, 23 Dec. 1862; *LDEE*, 15 Jan. 1863. The Dorcas Society also received $20 from the "Hon. James Buchanan."

50. Kauffman, *Mifflin County Amish and Mennonite Story*, 143–44, quotes from various September to December 1862 papers.

51. They were not alone; Catholic orders such as the Benedictine Order of Monks in Westmoreland County, Pennsylvania, and the Order of the Holy Cross at Notre Dame, Indiana, also requested total exemption. OR, Series III, v. 3, 333–36; 341–5; 844–45.

52. *The Friend* 37 (Seventh-Day, Eighth Month 27, 1864), 413. Stanton proposed that commutation fees go into a fund to assist former slaves, but the Friends rejected any coerced contributions. See Wright, *Conscientious Objectors in the Civil War*, 72–74, quoting from the Minutes of the Meeting for Sufferings of Indiana Yearly Meeting, 12 mo. 22, 1863, 333–34.

53. OR, Series III, v. 3, 1173; Geary, *We Need Men*, 109–10.

54. Capt. Freedley, of the 6th District in eastern Pennsylvania noted the ruling with a document entitled "Quakers, when Drafted to be put on Parole till Called for." Despite the title, the wording of the document certainly could have been interpreted as applying more broadly than to the Quakers. See George D. Ruggles to Major C. C. Gilbert, A. A. [Acting Assistant] Provost Marshal General, Philadelphia, Pa. In Group #2935, Record Group 110, National Archives. In December 1863, draft officials for District 5 (which included Bucks County) recorded in their minutes this new directive but said nothing about its implementation. Group #2915, Proceedings of the Board of Enrollment May 1863–Dec. 1864, 5th District, Part IV, Record Group 110, National Archives, Washington, D.C. There were many incidents reported by Friends of officials paroling drafted objectors; see *The Friend* 38 (Seventh-Day, Tenth Month 29, 1864), 71. Also see Wright, *Conscientious Objectors in the Civil War*, 86–88.

55. *Congressional Globe*, 38th Cong., 1st Sess., 229 (1864). Other commentary appears in OR, Series III, v. 3, 1175–77; and *Congressional Globe*, 38th Cong., 1st Sess., 255 (1864).

56. Presented to Congress on January 11, 1864, Jacob Leatherman et al., and Rev. Isaac Overholtzer et al. (Bucks County, Pa.) to Senate and House of Representatives, [Jan. 1864], HR38A-H1.1, House Committee on Military Affairs and the Militia, Record Group 46, National Archives, Washington, D.C.; see Ruth, *Maintaining the Right Fellowship*, 335.

57. The designation "River Brethren" was in common usage until the Civil War. "The military draft instituted by the Union Government then created the necessity for the Brethren to register in Washington as a nonresistant organization. After counseling about the matter, they decided to register as 'Brethren in Christ.'"—Wittlinger, *Quest for Piety and Obedience*, 27.

58. Manuscripts dated 14 Dec. 1863 and 9 Feb. 1864, in possession of Wilmer Reinford, Creamery, Pa.

59. Ibid.

60. Jacob S. Engel to "Honerable T. Stevens," 4 Jan. 1864, Thaddeus Stevens Papers, General Correspondence, Box 2, Manuscript Division, Library of Congress.

61. Spangler feared that any prepared document from Stevens' office would be filled with jargon—the "chirography would be all latin to them"—so that it would be best for Spangler to prepare a document with the help of a local attorney acquaintance.

62. James Nile to Hon. T. Stevens, 11 Dec. 1863, Thaddeus Stevens Papers, General Correspondence, Box 2, Manuscript Division, Library of Congress.

63. *Congressional Globe*, 38th Cong., 1st Sess., 579 (1864). Wright, *Conscientious Objectors in the Civil War*, 81–83; Geary, *We Need Men*, 116–50, details the debates over repealing the commutation fee.

64. OR, Series III, v. 4, 131. The idea of hospital service may have come from Maj. Gen. John Dix, commander of New York City forces. He had assigned Quakers to hospital duty and recommended it for all nonresistants; see OR, Series III, v. 3, 922.

65. *The Friend* 3 (Third Month 5, 1864), 215. But see chap. 8, n. 29, for one exception.

66. George Eyster to James B. Fry, in #3333, "Letters Sent May 1863–Nov. 1865," 4 vols., Part IV, 16th District, Record Group 110, National Archives, Washington, D.C.

67. Blackburn, *History of Bedford and Somerset Counties Pennsylvania*, 492.

68. Geary, *We Need Men*, 134–35, and 78–86, provides data for the entire country, illustrating the heavy use of commutation fees and substitutes; *Congressional Globe*, 38th Cong., 1st Sess., 2909 (1864).

69. Geary, *We Need Men*, 136–38; OR, Series III, v. 4, 473 (General Orders No. 224). In February 1864, Congress had retained commutation but reduced its effective exemption coverage to a single draft; if called in a future draft, those who had paid the commutation fee would again be liable for the fee, a substitute, or bodily service. Now in July, Congress did away with commutation entirely except for those with scruples.

70. George Eyster to James B. Fry, 2 Nov. 1864, in #3336, Box 47, Pennsylvania Western Division, 16th District, Record Group 110, National Archives, Washington, D.C. In mid-November, Eyster responded to an inquiry from Maj. A. B. Sharp regarding the practice of commutation, explaining that "our practice has been in every case to hold the party to strict proof . . . that first he is a member of a denomination and that he is in his conscience opposed to bearing arms; second that the rules and articles of faith and practice of that denomination prohibit him from bearing arms; and in addition the oath of two respectable citizens that they know his statement to be true and that his deportment has been uniformly consistent with

his declaration. The persons who were allowed to pay commutation were 'Quakers, Seventh Day Baptists, German Baptists or Tunkers and Amish.' All are old sects. The Amish live in Somerset County only a few being found in Bedford." See Eyster to Maj. A. B. Sharp, 15 Nov. 1864.

71. I. M. Hay, Salisbury, Pa. to Eyster, 17 March 1865.

72. *Johnstown Democrat*, 9 March 1865; 6 April 1865.

73. *LI*, 28 July and 4 Aug. 1864.

74. Donald, *Lincoln*, 527–30; Wilson, "McClellan's Changing Views on the Peace Plank."

75. *LI*, 20 Sept. 1864.

76. Perhaps the author was familiar with the arguments posed a few months earlier by Reformed Mennonite Daniel Musser, discussed below.

77. *LI*, 27 Oct. 1864.

78. Ibid. For contrast, See Stout, *Upon the Altar of the Nation*, 386–92, on evangelical Protestants' use of religious arguments to support Lincoln.

79. *LI*, 10 Nov. 1864.

80. Just before the election, *LDEE* published a defense of "The Non-Combatant Vote" (5 Nov. 1864) by quoting from the *Friends Review* of Philadelphia, in a manner that served as a reply to the attacks in the *LI*.

81. "Lancaster County and the Civil War," *MHB* 35 (April 1974), 4. Weber was writing to his cousin, Samuel Weber, of Waterloo Township, Upper Canada, on 10 Jan. 1865. In 1868 John Weber moved to Elkhart County, Indiana. When the Old Order Mennonite church emerged there in 1872, Weber affiliated with that group.

82. Jno. Naille to Hon. T. Stevens, 14 Oct. 1864, Thaddeus Stevens Papers, General Correspondence, Box 2, Manuscript Division, Library of Congress.

83. Robertson, "Idealist as Opportunist," 90–91. Lehman, "Duties of the Mennonite Citizen," 14–15, gives voting statistics for all jurisdictions.

84. McClellan won majorities in some counties with Mennonites or Amish residents, including Adams, Berks, Bucks, Cumberland, Juniata, Mifflin, Montgomery, Somerset, Westmoreland, and York; but in these areas the Mennonites and Amish were too small in number to influence the vote much. See Shankman, *Pennsylvania Antiwar Movement*, 199–201.

85. Daniel Musser, *Non-Resistance Asserted*, 32. The essay "Non-Resistance Asserted" comprises pp. 5–46, while "No Concord between Christ and Belial" makes up pp. 47–74. The themes of both pieces are similar and obviously related, though the first essay focuses more explicitly on the application of peace principles, while the second centers more on ecclesiology. One of the essay's interesting sections (37–38), from a modern perspective, is Musser's critique of Christian legitimation of the American Revolution and of Revolutionary heroes.

86. Ibid., 5−6.

87. Ibid., 9.

88. Ibid., 32−33. Of course, the nineteenth-century reality was that immigrants did posses political power, influence, and legal (including property) rights; and in many jurisdictions they could vote before securing actual citizenship. On antebellum nativist ideology, see Knobel, "America for the Americans," 1−39, 88−154.

89. Musser, Non-Resistance Asserted, 32−33, 42−44.

90. Ibid., 33−35, 40−41.

91. Levi Miller, "Daniel Musser and Leo Tolstoy."

8. Did Jesus Christ Teach Men to War?

1. Jacob Nold and wife Catharine, Columbiana, Ohio, to Johannes Gross and wife, 18 Oct. 1863 (trans. Noah G. Good), Wilmer Reinford Collection, Hist Mss 1-280, MCA-G.

2. Ibid.

3. Letter from J. Longenecker to his sister, Lydia, Murfreesboro, Tenn., June 1863, personal papers of Worth N. Yoder, Elkhart, Ind.

4. McPherson, For Cause and Comrades, 142−46, 176−77; for broader context, see Klement, Lincoln's Critics.

5. HCR, 26 March and 9 Apr. 1863. Other soldiers complained about home news. See I. N. R. Crawford (23rd Ohio Regt.), A. H. Tuttle (16th), H. H. Eberhart (120th), C. Kelser (23rd), John J. Jack (8th), W. H. Anderson (80th), Frederick Shine (80th), and J. W. Fox (102nd), HCR, 2, 9, 16, and 23 April, and 4 June 1863.

6. Bluffton Banner, Bluffton, Ind., 6 Mar. 1863.

7. Sterling, "Civil War Draft Resistance in the Middle West," 236.

8. The 52-line poem reflects Mennonite and Amish theology, with the exception of a couple of lines near the end that seem to question paying taxes.

9. Holliday, "Relief for Soldiers' Families in Ohio," 99.

10. WR, 16 July 1863; Salem Republican, Salem, Ohio, 29 July 1863. Morgan's five-day ride through Indiana had instilled a great deal of fear there too; see GT, 18 June 1863. On Morgan, see Ramage, Rebel Raider.

11. Mahoning Herald, 18 Sept. 1863.

12. WR, 3 Mar. and 20 May 1864.

13. E.g., John D. Miller, J. C. Kurtz, Martin Winger, Christian Roth, and Christian Weaver. Data in this paragraph from #4837, "Proceedings of the Board of Enrollment May 1863−Jan. 1865," and #4840, "Descriptive Book of Drafted Men, May-Oct. 1864," Record Group 110, National Archives, Washington, D.C.

14. E.g., David Miller, Daniel Gingerich, Jonas Stutzman, Daniel Raber, Jacob Farmwalt, Christian Farmwalt, and Levi J. Stahl (ibid.).

15. *General and Local Laws . . . of the State of Ohio*, v. 61 (Columbus: Richard Nevins, 1864), 110–26. See also Fisher, "Groping toward Victory," 37–38.

16. HCF, 7 and 14 July 1864. On August 4, the WR also warned Wayne countians about the $4.00 fee to pay by August 15 "for non-performance of military duty"; see WR, 10, 20, and 26 May, 9 June, 4 Aug. 1864.

17. Fulton County Militia Records, 1864, located at Northwest Ohio—Great Lakes Research Center, Bowling Green State University, Bowling Green, Ohio.

18. E.g., GT, 5 Mar. 1863.

19. Joseph Stoll, ed., "An Amishman's Diary—1864," *Family Life*, September 1969, 38.

20. DE, 27 June, 25 July, 7 Nov. 1863. The editor may not have been aware of it, but more than forty Swiss Mennonites and a few Amishmen had already taken out their naturalization papers in the late 1850s, not long after their arrival. See "Order Book of Naturalization," Adams County Courthouse, Decatur, Ind.

21. Marie Diller Brown, "Biography of Bishop Henry Egly," 6. Brown cites several sources at the end of her two-and-a-half-page essay, including three print sources and an oral interview. None of the print sources that she cites include reference to Egly's being drafted or to his commutation, suggesting that Brown got the information from the family interview source. That this story was passed on into the 1960s, even after Egly's churches no longer stressed nonresistance, suggests its veracity rather than its being an attempt to harmonize the founder's life with his church's 1960s practice. The nature of oral tradition may also explain Brown's reporting his paying $250 when the commutation fee was actually $300.

22. Sterling, "Civil War Resistance in the Middle West," 248–49.

23. On the rise in substitute cost, see Geary, *We Need Men*, 140–50.

24. North, "Bishop David Burkholder."

25. Melvin Gingerich, *Mennonites in Iowa*, 64. This story may be based on a corrupted oral tradition; unless Baughman was not yet baptized—rather unlikely for one old enough to own a farm—he more likely used the money to pay the commutation fee rather than hire a substitute. However, family memory that he hired a substitute cannot be discounted. Historian Gingerich cites the *Report of the Adjutant General of Iowa, January 11, 1864 to January 1, 1865* to indicate that another Davis County Amishman—and one each from Henry and Johnson counties—were stricken from enrollment lists because they were not citizens.

26. Weber, *Centennial History of the Mennonites of Illinois*, 110. Weber names John Smith as one of those paying the fee; Estes, *Living Stones*, 84–85.

27. Certificate located at Heritage Historical Library, Aylmer, Ontario, Canada.

28. "Civil War CO Documents," MHB 34 (April 1973), 6. The original documents, notices, and receipts are located in Samuel D. Guengerich (1836–1929) Collection, Hist. Mss. 1-2, MCA-G. See also J. F. Swartzendruber, "Grandfather's

Wedding Present," a one-page story by Swartzendruber written in September 1990, regarding his grandfather, S. D. Guengerich, in the same collection. After paying the $300 commutation fee in Pennsylvania, Guengerich and his wife left for their home in Iowa. See Guengerich's obituary in "Kalona News Supplement," *Kalona News*, Kalona, Iowa, Jan. 17, 1929; and Luthy, "Amish in the Civil War," 17.

29. HT 2 (19 Mar. 1865), 19.

30. Troyer et al., *Mennonite Church History of Howard and Miami Counties, Indiana*, 60.

31. Lehman, *Crosswinds*, 27.

32. DE, 5, 21, and 28 Mar. 1863. Adams County had voted strongly Democratic in the fall elections—1,477 votes to 432 for the Republicans. Perhaps the Swiss Mennonites were also part of the area's Democratic support since, in French Township with its numerous Mennonites, the vote was 94 to 6; see DE, 9 and 23 Oct., 13 Nov. 1862.

33. Sterling, "Civil War Draft Resistance in the Middle West," 236.

34. HCF, 26 Apr. 1863. The editor was a master at sarcasm and at mixing biblical imagery with his politics. See, e.g., the 31-verse parody that began, "In the second year of the reign of King Abraham" in the land "over which David the Yankee [Ohio governor David Tod] beareth rule . . ." HCF, 26 Feb. 1863.

35. The facts surrounding this resistance are hard to sort out because the event has become encrusted with myth and legend. W. E. Farver collected considerable documentation, including records of court deliberations, compiled by Gilbert G. Fites between 1945 and 1957. One of the better sources seems to be D. W. Garber, *The Holmes County Rebellion* (S.l.: Pub. by author, 1967), which is based partly upon three articles he wrote for the *Mansfield News Journal* in 1962. His sources included upwards of 20 stories in various Ohio newspapers and 15 books and journal articles, including material from OR, Series I, v. 23, pt. 1. Another source is Catherine Taylor Cline, *A History of the Killbuck Area*, ed. Cheryl Anderson Gallion ([Killbuck, Ohio: C. T. Cline], 1976), though Cline quotes largely and freely from Garber.

36. OR, Series I, v. 23, pt. 1, 395–97; OR, Series III, v. 3, 349–50; HCR, 25 June 1863, 2 July 1863; Garber, *Holmes County Rebellion*, 6–10. Garber does not know of any deaths; he mentions several wounded and names seven "rebels" taken prisoner. See also Erv Schlabach, *A Century and a Half with the Mennonites at Walnut Creek*, 17, quoting *Ohio State Journal*, 22 June 1863; "The Excitement in Ohio," *New York Times*, 26 June 1863; and *Der Neutralist and Allgemeine Neuigkeits-Bote*, 30 June 1863.

37. Abraham Rohrer to Jacob Nold, 22 June 1863, Jacob Nold Collection, Hist. Mss. 1–442, MCA-G. See also, Lehman, *Growth Amidst Struggle*, 59–65. In Holmes County's Knox Township, the next township north of where the "Fort Fizzle"

fracas occurred, lived Mennonite Abraham S. Oberholtzer and his family, who had migrated there from eastern Pennsylvania many years before this. The children married non-Mennonites, and the Oberholtzers and some of their children were buried in the Lutheran cemetery near Nashville. See Elisha S. Loomis, *Some Account of Jacob Oberholtzer*, 91.

38. "Three Civil War Letters from Ohio to Maryland," 12. The three letters are in the Clarence E. Shank Collection, MHACV.

39. Klement, *Limits of Dissent*.

40. HCF, 17 Sept., 8 and 15 Oct. 1863.

41. HCF, 22 Oct. 1863; WCD, 22 Oct., 5 Nov. 1863; *Ohio Democrat*, New Philadelphia, Ohio, 6 Nov. 1863.

42. Ohio counties with large Mennonites and Amish populations:

County	Brough	Vallandigham
Allen	1,745	1,958
Holmes	1,140	2,545
Putnam	989	1,534
Wayne	3,008	3,116

43. Election results in northern Indiana that fall in townships with significant Amish and Mennonite populations were inconclusive enough that voting patterns are not apparent. As a whole, Republicans won Elkhart County by a narrow majority of 200 votes. Clinton and Locke townships went strongly Democratic, while the townships of Middlebury, Harrison, Olive, and Benton went Republican; GD, 24 Sept., 8, 14, and 28 Oct. 1863.

44. John M. Brenneman to Peter Nissley, 9 Nov. 1864, Peter Nissley Collection, Hist. Mss. 1-293 SC, MCA-G.

45. This evolution is traced in detail in Liechty and Lehman, "From Yankee to Nonresistant"; pp. 243–44 document his family's and friends' surprise at his change.

46. E.g., CVB, 6 Aug. 1862.

47. John F. Funk diary, 22 Aug. 1862, JFFC.

48. John F. Funk to Jacob Funk, 17 Oct. 1862, JFFC.

49. John F. Funk diary, 11 Jan. 1863, but written on pages marked 29 Nov.–1 Dec. 1862, JFFC.

50. Brock, *Pacifism in the United States*, 787, quoting an unspecified Funk manuscript "Notebook." In the 1960s, when Brock worked in JFFC, the voluminous materials were not fully catalogued and not individually numbered. It has been difficult to identify which of the dozens of lengthy notebooks contain this quotation.

51. Mennonites from Pennsylvania first moved to this northern Illinois community in 1852 and a church was organized in 1858.

52. Liechty and Lehman, "From Yankee to Nonresistant," 239–40; Peter Nissley to John F. Funk, 22 Aug. 1863, JFFC.

53. John F. Funk, *Warfare: Its Evils, Our Duty*.

54. Ibid., 5, 9, 15.

55. Umble, "The Fairfield, Ohio, Background of the Allen County, Ohio, Mennonite Settlement"; Lehman, *Seedbed for Leadership*.

56. For example, another daughter of Henry and Rachel Stemen married Josiah Kesler, who left his wife and five children to enlist in September 1864, only to be killed three months later at Nashville. Already in the summer of 1861, the Stemens had four grandsons in the army. David Brenneman, son of Jacob, enlisted on August 12, 1862, to serve in the 118th Ohio for nearly three years. Peter and Mary (Blosser) Stemen had two sons, John and Christian, in the war. Samuel P. Stemen, son of Christian Steman, was in the 51st Ohio National Guard, having enlisted on 8 September 1863. Bishop Brenneman also had relatives at Winesburg, Ohio, in Holmes County where he sometimes did bishop work. There he knew of young men from Mennonite homes going into military service. See *History of the Stemen Family* (Fort Wayne: Pub. privately, 1881), 7–8; Lehman, *Seedbed for Leadership*, 14–16; *A Portrait and Biographical Record of Allen and Putnam Counties, Ohio*, 212, 365, 496, 498. The Allen County, Ohio, "Roll of Honor" includes other names of men who may have had Mennonite connections (e.g., Christian Bender, who died in Andersonville prison; J. R. Brenneman, Isaac Lehman, several Moyers, B. F. Sherrick, and several more Stemen young men); see *Hardesty's Historical and Geographical Encyclopedia*. There were, of course, also some church members in Brenneman's area who sought exemption. In November 1864, Brenneman sighed with relief that another draft was over in two townships where "brethren" resided and that among the many draftees, "thanks be to God, every Brother came off clear"—John M. Brenneman to Peter Nissley, 9 Nov. 1864, Peter Nissley Collection, Hist. Mss. 1-293 SC, MCA-G.

57. John M. Brenneman to John F. Funk, 28 July 1863, JFFC.

58. [John M. Brenneman], *Christianity and War*. The address was later translated into German and published as *Das Christenthum und der Krieg: Eine Predigt, Die Leiden der Christen darstellend, . . . Von einem Diener der Mennoniten-Gemeinschaft* (Lancaster, Pa.: Gedruckt für die Verleger von Johann Bär's Söhnen, 1864).

59. [Brenneman], *Christianity and War*, 14–18, 31, 41.

60. Ibid., 48–50.

61. John M. Brenneman to John F. Funk, 28 July 1863; and 12 Aug. 1863, JFFC.

62. J.[ohn] F. F[unk], "Conference Meeting in Elkhart Co., Ind.," *HT* 1 (Nov. 1864), 71–72; Johns et al., eds., *Minutes of the Indiana-Michigan Mennonite Conference, 1864–1929*, 8.

63. "An Amish Bishop's Conference Epistle of 1865," 222–29.

64. Ibid.

65. In 1867 Funk moved to Elkhart, Ind., and the *HT* was issued from there until it ceased publication in 1908; the German *Herold der Wahrheit* ceased publication in 1901.

66. John F. Funk, "Shall We Have a Religious Paper?"; John M. Brenneman, "Ought We To Have a Religious Paper?"; "Peace Be with You All that are in Christ Jesus," *HT* 1 (January 1864), 1–4.

67. J. M. B., "Kriegs-Lied," *Herold der Wahrheit* 1 (January 1864), 2.

68. J. M. B., "Be Ye All of One Mind," *HT* 1 (May 1864), 1–3.

69. "The Draft," *HT* 1 (August 1864), 50.

70. "Non-Resistance," *HT* 1 (August 1864), 51, describing Daniel Musser, *Non-Resistance Asserted* (1864). Funk was "highly pleased with the contents," which "contains my own views on this subject throughout."

71. [John F. Funk editorial], "A Serious Consideration," *HT* 2 (January 1865), 6–7.

72. J. M. C. [John M. Christophel], "Preventing the Draft," *HT* 2 (March 1865), 21.

73. From Manheim, Pennsylvania came a letter commenting on the Civil War as a spiritual test. See C. F. H. "The Holy Warfare," *HT* 1 (November 1864), 74.

74. "Letter from Bro. Landis, recently of Va." and "A Letter, Lancaster Co., Pa., Nov. 19th '64," *HT* 1 (December 1864), 81–83.

9. Resistance and Revenge in Virginia

1. For snapshots of the Confederacy "at full tide" in 1863, and on inflation and economic trouble, see Davis, *Look Away!* 199–201, 212–14, 254–58; and Thomas, *Confederate Nation*, 215–44. On inflation in Augusta County, Virginia, in particular, see Hildebrand, *Mennonite Journal*, 32 (6 Feb. 1864). On the April 1863 Richmond bread riot, see Chesson, "Harlots or Heroines?"

2. Hildebrand, *Mennonite Journal*, 35 (14 Mar. 1864). See also 19 (11 and 18 Sept. 1863) for examples of tax-in-kind impressment. Davis, *Look Away!* 201, 286–91; Thomas, *Confederate Nation*, 196, 264.

3. UCWE, 1:294, reproducing Estate of John Rhodes Claim No. 16949; and 2:313, reproducing David C. Brenneman Claim No. 9123; R. J. Heatwole, "Reminiscences of War Days," 444. Brunk, ed., *Life of Peter S. Hartman*, 60–61, describes

the impressments of the Hartmans' horses and wagon, and young Peter's accompanying them to Staunton.

4. RR, 31 July 1863, says Mennonites gave eleven barrels of flour plus bacon to "poor and needy families of Confederate solders living at the head of Brock's Gap." On hunger and refugees, see Davis, *Look Away!* 210−12, 292−98; on short food supplies in Augusta County by winter 1863, see Ayers, *In the Presence of Mine Enemies*, 333−34.

5. Bleak as this picture was, the Confederacy still enjoyed great confidence among white Virginians; see Gallagher, *Confederate War*.

6. Included in the record for each man is his age, height, complexion, hair and eye color, occupation, and whether he is Mennonite or a Dunker. No other government record with this much detail has been located elsewhere. Regrettably, no such record has been found for Augusta County, Virginia.

7. Horst, *Mennonites in the Confederacy*, 85−86 (including *Richmond Daily Examiner* quotation); Wright, *Conscientious Objectors in the Civil War*, 108−10.

8. Richardson, ed., *Compilation of the Messages and Papers of the Confederacy*, 1:370.

9. Wright, *Conscientious Objectors*, 112.

10. Horst, *Mennonites in the Confederacy*, 89.

11. R. J. Heatwole, "A Civil War Story," 7.

12. R. J. Heatwole, "Reminiscences of War Days," 444−45. The story of Henry G. Brunk's flight, as told by Brunk's granddaughter, Ethel Estella Cooprider Erb, is *Story of Grandmother Heatwole-Brunk-Cooprider*, 18−25.

13. R. J. Heatwole, "Civil War Story," 3−4; Erb, *Story of Grandmother*, 18−25.

14. Handwritten minutes from the April 1864 Virginia Mennonite Conference session, three contemporary copies, reporting virtually identical wording: those of deacons Jacob Geil ("Jacob Geil Book," Significant Individual Collections, I-MS-21) and Frederick A. Rodes (Frederick A. Rodes Collection, I-MS-5), and that of bishop Jacob Hildebrand (Jacob Hildebrand Collection, I-MS-3), all in MSHLA. (Note that Brunk, *History of the Mennonites in Virginia*, 185, is inaccurate in saying these were 1860 conference actions.) Although by Virginia standards relatively few residents of Rockingham and Augusta counties owned slaves, hiring slave labor was common; see Simmons and Sorrells, "Slave Hire and the Development of Slavery in Augusta County, Virginia."

15. "To Our German Friends," RR, 26 Feb. 1864; "We Have Been Informed" and "To the Farmers of Augusta, Rockingham, and Shenandoah," RR, 4 Mar. 1864.

16. "Our German Friends," RR, 11 Mar. 1864; "For the Register," RR, 18 Mar. 1864; "For the Register," RR 1 Apr. 1864; and "To Those Who Are Exempt on Religious Grounds," RR, 12 Aug. 1864. On Confederate economic woes and tax

policy at this time, see Thomas, *Confederate Nation*, 197–200; and Davis, *Look Away!* 199–201, 377–81.

17. Benjamin Funk, *Life and Labors of Elder John Kline*, 479–80; R. M. Zigler, "Elder John Kline—Churchman." The names of those who killed Kline were known in the community but never publicly acknowledged, and no one was brought to trial for the murder. One of the men, surnamed Showalter, was of Mennonite descent and is buried in the cemetery of the Trissels Mennonite Church near Broadway. One strand of local lore says that after Kline was knocked off his horse by the first shots, Showalter shot him at close range.

18. RR, 24 June 1864, as reproduced in Sappington, *Brethren in the New Nation*, 393–94. These pages and p. 395 reproduce contemporary documents related to Kline's murder. On the general rise of lawlessness and vigilantism in the Confederacy as the war persisted, see Davis, *Look Away!* 163–88.

19. Jacob Hildebrand, "Letter from Virginia," HT 2 (July 1865), 53.

20. Shannon W. Swortzel, "Bishop Jacob Hildreband, Jr.," Unpublished paper, n.d., 29, MSHLA. (Swortzel is a descendant of Hildebrand.) Brunk, *History of Mennonites in Virginia*, 1:408, states that Hildebrand owned about a thousand acres.

21. Jacob Hildebrand to Samuel Coffman, 26 Dec. 1862, quoted in Brunk, *History of Mennonites in Virginia*, 1:165–66. The location of the original letters is no longer known.

22. Ibid., 10 Jan. 1863. Hildebrand's actions had long diverged from those of his fellow Virginia bishops. For example, on November 6, 1861, Hildebrand's diary had noted, "I was at Waynesboro at lechion I votet for [Jefferson] Davis"; see Jacob Hildebrand diaries, JHC. Hildebrand was correct that Shenandoah Valley Dunker leaders had, in fact, planned a special thanksgiving day in response to the Confederate Congress's extension of conscientious exemption; see D. H. Zigler, *History of the Brethren in Virginia*, 122–23.

23. Samuel Hildebrand to "Dear Father," 5 Jan. 1863, JHC.

24. J. Hildebrand, Hermitage, Augusta, Va. to "Dear Son," 19 Mar. 1863, JHC.

25. See Hildebrand, *Mennonite Journal*, 78 n. 9, for elaboration of "Home Guards" and "Raid Guards." Some men volunteered for their state's Home Guard on the assumption that state governments could not order such units to leave their home state, and thus they could serve the military cause while remaining close to home and away from major engagements. Since there was always battlefield action in Virginia, such reasoning was likely less common among those signing up for the Home Guard here.

26. Jacob Hildebrand, Hermitage [Va.] to "Dear Son," 22 Sept. 1863, JHC.

27. E.g., Hildebrand, *Mennonite Journal*, 20 (28 Sept. 1863).

28. Ibid., 33 (22 Feb. 1864); 18 (25 Aug. 1863).

29. Ibid., 42 (18 May 1864).

30. Ibid., 19 (5 Sept. 1984); 22–23 (various Oct. 1864); 26 (1 Nov. 1863); and 28 (20–23 Dec. 1864).

31. Brunk, *History of Mennonites in Virginia*, 1:409; "Materials From Family Bible," JHC. Bishop Hildebrand had intended to ordain a minister and two deacons in the Southern District and collected nominations for all three offices, but in the end—for reasons no longer known—ordained only the deacons and not a minister. Significantly, Jacob R. Hildebrand's name was on the nominee list for both minister and deacon, suggesting the regard with which his fellow church members held him. The five nominations to the ministerial candidate list were Jacob Harshbarger, Jacob Kegey, Jacob R. Hildebrand, Solomon Peters, and Joel Y. Wheeler. Wheeler was the same man who at one time had worked as bishop Hildebrand's threshing rig manager but who had enlisted for military service two-and-a-half years earlier.

32. The eight men nominated for deacon were Isaac Harshbarger, Rudolph Kegey, David Kennedy, Albert Freed, Jacob Landes, John Landes, Abraham Kindig, and Jacob R. Hildebrand. (Kennedy, who had joined the church in spring 1861, had enlisted in the 52nd Virginia Infantry in early October 1862, but was absent without leave in late November 1862; see Driver, *52nd Virginia*, 125.) On December 25, 1863, bishop Hildebrand oversaw the selection of two deacons by using a method of drawing lots. This method was a common nineteenth-century (Old) Mennonite and Amish Mennonite mechanism for choosing leaders. Church members first nominated candidates for leadership posts, and then the candidates themselves drew lots to see which of them would be ordained—thus, it was believed, placing the final selection in the hands of God. The actual process of drawing lots involved the prearrangement of a set of identical books (usually hymn books), one per candidate, and with a slip of paper in one of the books. After the bishop preached a sermon on the responsibility of church leaders and offered a lengthy prayer, each candidate chose a book, and the one who found a slip of paper in his book was immediately ordained. In this case, since two deacons positions were to be filled, two books contained slips of paper. The two men who drew these books and were ordained deacons for the Southern District of the Virginia Mennonite Conference were Jacob Landes and Jacob R. Hildebrand.

33. Hildebrand, *Mennonite Journal*, 28 (25 Dec. 1863). The entry also modestly noted that "there were two Deacons ordained in the Menonite church today." Later, in 1870, Jacob R. Hidebrand was ordained minister in the Southern District, in which capacity he served until his death in 1908.

34. Ibid., 29–43; esp. 39 (8 Apr. 1864) and 40 (29–30 April 1864). The Augusta County Mennonites had also observed President Davis' declared days of prayer on June 13 and November 15, 1861 (Bishop Jacob Hildebrand Diary, 1861, JHC), May 16, 1862, and August 20, 1863 (J. R. Hildebrand, *Mennonite Journal*, 11, 17). Raised in a Baptist home, educated in Roman Catholic schools, and mar-

ried twice to Episcopalians, Jefferson Davis was knowledgeable about religion but claimed no deep personal faith until the first major crisis of the Confederacy in spring 1862. He was then baptized and confirmed on May 6, 1862, in the Episcopal Church and began taking religion very seriously. Several days later he called another national day of prayer. His speeches cast the Confederacy in the scheme of God's will, and his personal conversation suggested a firm reliance on divine providence. See Cooper, *Jefferson Davis, American*, 262, 387–89, 545, 548.

35. Hildebrand, *Mennonite Journal*, 33 (16 Feb. and 22 Feb. 1864); 40 (16 April 1864); 47 (29 July 1864).

36. Brunk, ed., *Life of Peter S. Hartman*, 60–63. Note that Hartman's memories, recorded many years after the events described, include several chronological errors. He mistakenly dates Maj. Gen. David Hunter's raid on Lexington as 1863 instead of 1864, and says Hunter engaged "Stonewall" Jackson. Jackson was killed in 1863, but Hunter did encounter Jackson's former corps, now commanded by Lt. Gen. Jubal Early.

37. "Extract from a Letter," HT 1 (Nov. 1964), 73. Letter dated 19 Oct. 1864.

38. This and other entries quoted in Burdge and Horst, *Building on the Gospel Foundation*, 258.

39. Hunsecker, "Civil War Reminiscences."

40. Hoke, *Reminiscences of the War*, 48–53; Alexander et al., *Southern Revenge*, 93–104.

41. Alexander et al., *Southern Revenge*, 120–27; Slingluff, "The Burning of Chambersburg."

42. Hunsecker, "Civil War Reminiscences," 407.

43. Ibid.

44. Burdge and Horst, *Building on the Gospel Foundation*, 259; Ruth, *Maintaining the Right Fellowship*, 334.

45. McPherson, *Battle Cry of Freedom*, 756–58.

10. Burning the Shenandoah Valley

1. J. R. Hildebrand, *A Mennonite Journal*, 33, 42, 44. Note that pp. 64–71 reproduce service records of Benjamin, Gideon, and Michael Hildebrand.

2. As part of the campaign for Atlanta, Union Brig. Gen. William T. Sherman ordered a disastrous attack on Confederate forces at Kennesaw Mountain, June 27, 1864. One Northern soldier who survived the battle, Abraham H. Landis, was a son of the Butler County, Ohio, Mennonite community. Returning home, Landis named his next son (b. 1866) after the battle: Kenesaw Mountain Landis. "Ken" Landis later became a noted federal judge and, in 1920, the first Commissioner of

Major League Baseball. Judge Landis retained some curiosity about his Mennonite ancestry; see Nolt, "The Baseball Commissioner and the Mennonites."

3. McPherson, *Battle Cry of Freedom*, 718–24, 756–61.

4. Ibid., 758; OR, Series I, v. 37, pt. 2, 558.

5. OR, Series I, v. 37, pt. 2, 301; OR, Series I, v. 40, pt. 3, 223. Grant's order appeared in enough dispatches that the message certainly was clear as to what Sheridan was to do.

6. OR, Series I, v. 37, pt. 2, 328–29.

7. OR, Series I, v. 38, pt. 1, 18–19.

8. Lehman, *Lindale's Song*, 17–18. Wenger later lost several barns and a mill to Sheridan's burning, though he was able to recover and rebuild later, drawing in part on his sizable 1,600-acre landholdings. Documents detailing Wenger's property losses (Claim No. 9778) appear in *UCWE*, 2:425–72. Wenger's claim to never have supported the Confederacy was disallowed and his claim denied.

9. Grimsley, *Hard Hand of War*, 142–70, charts this evolving policy and Grant's role. Stout, *Upon the Altar of the Nation*, discusses the evolution of Northern tactics under the rubric of "total war"; e.g., xv–xvi, 139–43, 185–93, 259–62, 381.

10. Gallagher, ed., *Struggle for the Shenandoah*, 1. There is no scarcity of books on the Valley Campaign; John L. Heatwole, *The Burning: Sheridan in the Shenandoah Valley* (1998) is the most detailed. A recent biography of Sheridan is Roy Morris Jr., *Sheridan: The Life and Wars of General Phil Sheridan* (1992).

11. Brunk, ed., *Life of Peter S. Hartman*, 64–66.

12. Hildebrand, *A Mennonite Journal*, 43–44. Grove was likely the son of deacon John Grove.

13. Ibid., 44–47 (5 June–8 Aug. 1864).

14. Ibid., 51.

15. OR, Series I, v. 43, pt. 1, 917.

16. Document in possession of Martha Shank Whissen, Broadway, Va., and shown to coauthor James O. Lehman by Janet Shank, Broadway, Va., on 22 Feb. 1991. This copy of the order from Sheridan is probably not the original but a copy made to give Samuel Shank some claim for reimbursement on house, barn, and crops.

17. OR, Series I, v. 43, pt. 2, 202; J. L. Heatwole, *The Burning*, 43.

18. J. L. Heatwole, *The Burning*, 44.

19. Hildebrand, *A Mennonite Journal*, 52.

20. Gallagher, ed., *Struggle for the Shenandoah*, 44–56.

21. Morris, *Sheridan*, 202.

22. The most famous of these was Early's surprise attack on October 19 in what became the Battle of Cedar Creek. Sheridan had gone to Washington for a com-

manders' conference, but he returned just in time to rally his retreating troops and eventually claim what became a legendary victory.

23. Hildebrand, *A Mennonite Journal*, 51 (25 Aug.–2 Sept. 1864). Samuel M. Miller had been raised in the Dunker church.

24. Ibid., 52.

25. McCordick, *The Civil War Letters (1862–1865) of Private Henry Kauffman*, 87–88. Stout, *Upon the Altar of the Nation*, 379–85.

26. OR, Series I, v. 43, part 2, 249–50.

27. Grimsley, *Hard Hand of War*, 168. Note that Grimsley places Sheridan's actions and those of his troops in a context of hard war that was not without limits; see 167–86 for a discussion of the calculated combination of destruction *and restraint* that marked this campaign—a nuanced view not found in every account of the 1864 Valley campaign.

28. Leonard, *Above the Battle*, 18, citing Harold D. Lasswell, *Propaganda Technique in the World War* (New York: A. A. Knopf, 1927), 83. OR, I, v. 43, pt. 1, 573–85, 610–15, detail Confederate resistance to Sheridan's march down the valley.

29. OR, I, v. 43, pt. 2, 307–308.

30. Sheridan, *Personal Memoirs*, 1:488.

31. J. L. Heatwole, *The Burning*, 89.

32. Ibid., 91; Jubal A. Early, "Winchester, Fisher's Hill, and Cedar Creek," in Johnson and Buel, eds., *Battles and Leaders of the Civil War*, 4:525.

33. OR, Series I, v. 43, pt. 2, 220.

34. Taylor, *With Sheridan Up the Shenandoah Valley*, 430–39.

35. J. L. Heatwole, *The Burning*, 94.

36. Grimsley, *Hard Hand of War*, 183, quotations and discussion of the place of the earlier burning of Chambersburg in inciting revenge.

37. William T. Patterson diary, 4 October 1864, Ohio Historical Society, Columbus, Ohio.

38. Wayland, *A History of Rockingham County, Virginia*, 149–50, quoting the written memory of Col. T. Tschappat of the 116th Ohio. Today there is a small memorial in Dayton honoring Wildes.

39. W. T. Patterson diary, 4 October 1864. See also Heatwole, *The Burning*, 103–105. Much later, Sheridan, in *Personal Memoirs*, 2:52, simply said that after a few houses were burned, he rescinded the order.

40. Heatwole, *The Burning*, 96–97.

41. Ibid., 109–10.

42. It is unclear whether the Coffman barn was burned. Coffman, *His Name Was John*, 48–49; coauthor James O. Lehman interview with David Coffman (a great-grandson of the bishop), Harrisonburg, Va., 15 June 1995. David Coffman said he heard that the soldiers were bribed to save the barn; he claims the story to have been

verified by Abraham Blosser, who got the story from Samuel Coffman. Heatwole, *The Burning*, 110, as well as L. J. Heatwole manuscripts, MSHLA, claim that the barn was burned. Perhaps the two events occurred at different times. UCWE 3: 615–25, Samuel Coffman Claim No. 9519, does not mention the barn having been destroyed.

43. At that time the Weavers meetinghouse stood on the north side of the road.

44. This log home has been relocated to the CrossRoads: Valley Brethren-Mennonite Heritage Center complex, Harrisonburg, Va.

45. UCWE, 3:575–84, reproducing Noah C. Wenger Claim No. 15531; Wayland, *Virginia Valley Records*, 194.

46. HT 1 (December 1864), 81–82.

47. UCWE, 3:571–52, reproducing Benjamin Wenger Claim No. 9525. Wenger's recorded property losses of $2,737 were among the higher claims in Rockingham County. After the war they rebuilt and eventually prospered again.

48. HT 1 (December 1864), 82–83.

49. Horst, *Mennonites in the Confederacy*, 102, quoting L. J. Heatwole manuscripts at MSHLA.

50. Brunk, ed., *Life of Peter S. Hartman*, 64–65.

51. J. L. Heatwole, *The Burning*, 165.

52. Grimsley, *Hard Hand of War*, 186, quoting Roger Hannaford in Stephen Z. Starr, *The Union Cavalry in the Civil War* (Baton Rouge: Louisiana State University Press, 1979–85), 2:302.

53. Morris, *Sheridan*, 233.

54. OR, Series I, v. 43, pt. 2, 307–308. It is curious that Sheridan reported it that way on October 7, not mentioning that Dayton had been spared.

55. OR, Series I, v. 43, pt. 2, 348.

56. Flinn, *Campaigning with Banks in Louisiana*, 235–37.

57. *Richmond Whig* quoted in Greeley, *American Conflict*, 2:611.

58. Horst, *Mennonites in the Confederacy*, 106, quoting L. J. Heatwole manuscripts at MSHLA.

59. OR, Series I, v. 43, pt. 2, 308. Peter S. Hartman said much later that there were 1,600 wagons; it is unclear where Hartman drew his figure. For a Confederate perspective, see OR, Series I, v. 43, pt. 1, 578.

60. Brunk, ed., *Life of Peter S. Hartman*, 65–67.

61. Emanuel Suter diary, Emanuel and Elizabeth Suter Collection, I-MS-31, MSHLA; Suter, *Memories of Yesteryear*, 43.

62. Brunk, ed., *Life of Peter S. Hartman*, 68–71.

63. LDEE, 18 Oct. 1864.

64. DD, 1 Nov. 1864.

65. *Der Neutralist und Allgemeine Neuigkeits-Bote*, 8 Nov. 1864.

66. In Holmes County, Ohio, four months after Sheridan's systematic destruction ended, readers got a hint of trauma in Virginia, but the item was buried inside the local news and was deeply flawed, reporting merely that "a party of 125 of Sheridan's cavalry went up the Shenandoah valley on a scouting expedition, and were principally gobbled up by a part of [Confederate guerilla fighter John Singleton] Moseby's men"; HCF, 23 Feb. 1865.

67. RR, 11 Nov. 1864. After the war, Pennsylvania Amishman Jonathan Hartzler visited Virginia and wrote that few Northerners could imagine the scope and scale of destruction still visible in the Shenandoah Valley; see Jonathan K. Hartzler, "A Visit to the Shenandoah Valley," HT 4 (July 1867), 106.

68. McPherson, *Battle Cry of Freedom*, 772–78.

69. OR, Series I, v. 43, pt. 1, 37.

70. OR, Series I, v. 43, pt. 2, 830–831.

71. Hildebrand, *A Mennonite Journal*, 52–53.

72. Ibid., 55.

73. McPherson, *Battle Cry of Freedom*, 822–24.

74. Early's forces "broke and ran, leaving behind sixteen hundred captured comrades, eleven pieces of artillery, two hundred ambulances, and seventeen blood-red flags." See Morris, *Sheridan*, 238; Hildebrand, *A Mennonite Journal*, 56–57.

75. Hildebrand, *A Mennonite Journal*, 56–57.

76. McPherson, *Battle Cry of Freedom*, 845–46; E. B. Long, with Barbara Long, *The Civil War, Day by Day*, 663–64.

77. Hildebrand, *A Mennonite Journal*, 57. On September 28, 1863, Benjamin Hildebrand had been elected a 2nd Lieutenant, and he was commanding three companies at the time of Appomattox.

78. W. G. Shaver to J. R. Hildebrand, 22 June 1865. The letter was recently located between the pages of the Hildebrand English family Bible, which, along with other Hildebrand material, is located in JHC.

79. Jacob Hildebrand, "Church Record Book," JHC.

80. Hildebrand, *A Mennonite Journal*, 57.

11. Reconstructed Nation, Reconstructed Peoplehood

1. Jacob D. Guengerich diary, quoted in Raber, "Jacob D. Guengerich," 101–105.

2. Holmes, "'Such Is the Price We Pay'"; Frederickson, *Inner Civil War*.

3. Paton Yoder, *Eine Würzel*, 33–34. See an example of Mennonites hiking across farm fields to watch the train pass, in Ruth, *The Earth Is the Lord's*, 574.

4. Brunk, ed., *Life of Peter S. Hartman*, 72.

5. LI, 3 May 1865; HCF, 20 and 27 Apr. 1865; Chesebrough, *No Sorrow Like*

Our Sorrow; Guelzo, *Abraham Lincoln: Redeemer President*, 439–63; Stout, *Upon the Altar of the Nation*, 448–56.

6. "Death of President Lincoln," HT 2 (May 1865), 38.

7. Trefousse, *Andrew Johnson*.

8. The best history of "Reconstruction"—the dozen years (1865–77) that followed the war—remains Eric Foner's *Reconstruction: America's Unfinished Revolution* (1988). See also Trefousse, *Thaddeus Stevens*, 161–223. See LI, 12 Apr. 1865, for text of a speech Stevens gave at the Lancaster, Pennsylvania, courthouse on African-American civil rights.

9. Rable, *But There Was No Peace*.

10. See various case studies in Cimbala and Miller, eds., *The Freedmen's Bureau and Reconstruction*.

11. S. L. Horst, ed., *The Fire of Liberty in Their Hearts: The Diary of Jacob E. Yoder*.

12. Ibid., xii–xiv.

13. Ibid., xv–xx.

14. Ibid., 31–33.

15. Ibid., 3, 8.

16. Ibid., xx–xxiv, 54–138.

17. Ibid., xxix–xxxii. At a July 1877 mass meeting, the Lynchburg African-American community petitioned the school board to appoint Yoder principal because he "has the confidence of both parents and children." Yoder married a fellow Freedmen's Bureau teacher, Anna Whitaker, who had come to Virginia from Connecticut under the Baptist Home Mission Board. The couple joined a Lynchburg Baptist church. When Yoder died in 1905, his memorial service was held at a Black Baptist church.

18. Theron F. Schlabach, *Gospel Versus Gospel*, 20, 74–78, 100, 106, 233, 247–62; Swartz, "'Mista Mid-Nights'"; Guy F. Hershberger, "Mennonites and the Current Race Issue: Observations, Reflections, and Recommendations Following a Visitation to Southern Mennonite Churches, July-August 1963, with a Review of Historical Background," Committee on Economic and Social Concerns Collection, 1-3-7, MCA-G; Bush, *Two Kingdoms, Two Loyalties*, 210–17. While the *Herald of Truth* did not print articles condoning racism, its critiques of racism, racial violence, or segregation were few; but see HT 1 (Feb. 1864), 7; 26 (15 Nov. 1889), 341–43; 27 (1 Mar. 1890), 74–75; 27 (1 Apr. 1890), 106; 28 (1 July 1891), 206; and 32 (1 Apr. 1895), 106–107. See also the appraisal in Berry, "Mennonites, African Americans, the U.S. Constitution and the Problem of Assimilation."

19. Blight, *Race and Reunion*.

20. Emanuel Suter to "Much esteemed and most affectionate Father," 17 June 1865, Emanuel and Elizabeth Suter Collection, I-MS-31, MSHLA; see also Suter, *Memories of Yesteryear*, 31.

21. The impact of the Civil War on the shaping and reshaping of national, regional, and ethnic identities is, of course, a much larger story. For a sample of the literature, see Lawson, *Patriot Fires*; Christian B. Keller, "Germans in Civil War-Era Pennsylvania"; and Gaines, *Ghosts of the Confederacy*.

22. Thomas J. Brown, *The Public Art of Civil War Commemoration*; Blight, *Race and Reunion*.

23. An 1888 Civil War monument in Somerset, Pennsylvania, honors men from Somerset County who served in the war. Those known or believed to have Mennonite or Amish connections are: David Miller, Samuel Miller, George W. Stahl, Isaac Yoder, Adam Hochstetler, Solomon Berkey, John A. Miller, John Berkey, Jacob A. Berkey, John Kennel, Martin Hoover, John Harshberger, John M. Kauffman, George Mishler, Ephraim Harshberger, Samuel Kuhns, Tobias Miller, Francis Weaver, Christian Burkholder, Noah Miller, John Miller, Joseph Berkey, Christian Berkey, John Yoder, George Mishler.

24. Grossman, *On Killing*, 21–25, 249–61; Richard M. Brown, *No Duty to Retreat*, 31–36. Holmes quotes from Juhnke and Hunter, *The Missing Peace*, 123, citing "Harvard College in the War," 25 June 1884, in *The Mind and Faith of Justice Holmes: His Speeches, Essays, Letters, and Judicial Opinions*, ed. Max Lerner (New York: Modern Library, 1943), 23.

25. Estes, *A Goodly Heritage*, 51.

26. Schneck enlisted in Evansville, Indiana, joining the 60th Indiana on February 1, 1862. Eventually Schneck attended seminary and was pastor at a number of Reformed Church in the U.S. congregations, including Emanuel Reformed, near Bluffton, Ohio. Schneck was always reluctant to talk about his war experiences, even to close acquaintances. Everyone knew he had suffered in prison and assumed he had been a Confederate prisoner, never knowing that he had been court-martialed for desertion from the Union army and had spent time in hard labor in a Union prison. He had deserted at Indianapolis on November 28, 1862. Nearly two years later he was found at Lima, Ohio; arrested and court-martialed at Thibodaux, Louisiana; and sentenced to three years at Fort Jefferson, Florida. See letter from Bertha Goetsch, Cleveland, Ohio, 21 May 1981, and photocopies of the war records she obtained from Military Service Records, National Archives, Washington, D.C. in August 1974. Goetsch, whose parents were married by Schneck and spoke highly of him, tried to locate family and friends of Schneck. When she received his war record, she was greatly surprised and distressed to learn that he had been a deserter, not a Confederate prisoner. Coauthor James O. Lehman exchanged a series of letters with Mrs. Goetsch in the early 1980s, interviewed her on 16 Nov. 1982, and has copies of government records relating to Schneck.

27. *History of Allen County, Ohio*, 732–33.

28. See the very different presentations of Buchwalter in Falb, *Fruits of Diversity*,

22, 32, and 44; and Frey, *Grandpa's Gone*. Frey includes military-themed family photos and stories that Buchwalter enthusiastically passed on to his children and a 1918 Memorial Day ribbon that bore Buchwalter's face. Falb describes Buchwalter as a respected member of the congregation whom the larger Ohio Mennonite Conference sent as a delegate with a peace message to the state's governor during the Spanish-American War. Primary sources for these aspects of Buchwalter's life include HT 35 (1 July 1898), 198, where Ohio Conference sent Buchwalter, David Rudy, and C. B. Brenneman to present a statement on nonresistance to the governor.

29. Yoder, *Eine Würzel*, 34. Interestingly, Stoltzfus's wife's sister and brother-in-law had a son in 1864 whom they named Ulysses Grant Neuhauser! Another story that critiqued the substitution system is found in Lehman, *Sonnenberg*, 90.

30. Krehbiel, *Prairie Pioneer*, 21, 43–44; Susanna Amalia Krehbiel autobiography in manuscript form, Susanna Amalia Krehbiel Collection, Hist. Mss. 1-551 SC, MCA-G.

31. E.g., Brunk, ed., *Life of Peter S. Hartman*, 51. UCWE, 2:18 n. 48, traces a different version of this sort of story. Versions of such non-shooter stories also appear in the postwar Claim Commission testimonies, e.g., UCWE, 3:532, reproducing Michael Shank Claim No. 19059.

32. Ruth, *The Earth Is the Lord's*, 563–64, quoting Quaker journal of Joseph Elkinton, Friends' Historical Library, Swarthmore, Pa. Ethical questions sometimes combined contemporary military and civilian experiences, such as the letters that discussed nonresistance on the battlefield in relation to self-defense in the case of a May 1865 murder in a Sonnenberg, Ohio, Swiss Mennonite family. See Lehman, *Sonnenberg, A Haven and a Heritage*, 94.

33. Klingberg, "The Southern Claims Commission." See also the helpful introductory essays by Emmert F. Bittinger in each volume of UCWE. This series, representing countless hours on the part of editors Norman R. Wenger and David S. Rodes, provides access to annotated transcriptions of Southern Claims Commission records from the National Archives.

34. Congress established Southern Claims Commission, composed of three leading Northern politicians, in 1871; a staff of twenty-nine delegated commissioners worked regionally to collect local testimony. The Commission functioned until 1880, after which unresolved claims and appeals of earlier denials were processed by the U.S. Court of Claims. To file a claim, claimants had to be American citizens who lived in a seceding state, and be able to present evidence that they were loyal to the United States during the entire war and that their property losses were a result of confiscation by Union troops for use by the Union army (and not just battle damage). The names of all claimants were published locally, calling attention to their unionist claims, which invited neighbors to testify against them. Claims could be

denied if the claimant was shown to have rendered any aid to the Confederacy or had voted for secession. Nationally, 22,298 claims (worth over $60 million) were filed; Virginia had the second largest number of claims, with 2,930. The Commission allowed less than 9 percent of the total amounts claimed.

35. The sample consisting of UCWE, vols. 1–3, shows that about 32 percent of Dunker claims and 40 percent of Mennonite claims were allowed.

36. E.g., UCWE, 2:70, reproducing Mary Brenneman Claim No. 16503, where Brenneman admitted that she "felt very bad when I heard of the slaughter and suffering of men on either side," even though she hastened to add that "we were glad when the Union cause prospered as well when the rebellion was put down"; or UCWE, 3:446, reproducing Gabriel D. Heatwole Claim No. 8857, in which commissioners rejected Heatwole's loyalty claim because they believed his wartime actions stemmed from his religious opposition to war in general and not because of "strong Union principles."

37. UCWE, 2:425–71, reproducing Isaac Wenger Claim No. 9778.

38. UCWE, 1:171–73, 298; 3:588, 593–94, 597, 601, 605, 610, 639–40, 650, 812–13.

39. Cf. Brunk, *Life of Peter S. Hartman*, 45–73 (from the late 1920s), with Hartman's 1875 testimony to the Claims Commission, UCW, 3:663–65. See also the material in Brunk's *History of the Mennonites in Virginia*, 1:167–77.

40. Estes, *Living Stones*, 86. For context, see Silber, "Intemperate Men, Spiteful Women, and Jefferson Davis," 625–32.

41. On wartime and postwar prosperity in the North, see the case study Quigley, *Second Founding*. Cronon, *Nature's Metropolis*, 87–90, 125–28, 175, 238, 295, 302; and 311; Sensenig, comp., *The "Sensineys" of America*, 95.

42. I. G. Musser, "What About Voting?" GH 5 (3 Oct. 1912), 428.

43. Ibid.

44. Burkholder, *Be Not Conformed to This World*, 59–73.

45. BCI, 4 Apr. 1865. Several other newspapers had also picked up on these resolutions: *Germantown Telegraph*, 29 Mar. 1865; DD, 4 Apr. 1865; HFP, 23 Mar. 1865.

46. On this group, see Burdge, "The Prosperity of Zion in This Place," 13–15, 18–19.

47. BCI, 2 May 1865.

48. Jacob Hildebrand, "Letter from Virginia" and "Another from the Same," HT 2 (July 1865), 53; Jacob Hildebrand, "From Virginia," HT 5 (January 1868), 9.

49. Niebuhr, *Christ and Culture*. For more discussion of this denomination- and identity-building program, see Nolt, "A 'Two-Kingdom' People in a World of Multiple Identities."

50. Juhnke, *A People of Two Kingdoms*. The phrase "apolitical logic" does not im-

ply that Midwestern (Old) Mennonites and Amish Mennonites never engaged in partisan politics, since anecdotal evidence shows that they did. Rather, their leaders consistently interpreted such activity as a deeply troubling contradiction for peace people, e.g., *Report of the Eastern* [primarily Ohio] *Amish Mennonite Conference*, (S.l., 1898), 11; Johns et al., eds., *Minutes of the Indiana-Michigan Mennonite Conference*, 1864–1929, 25–26, reporting Indiana (Old) Mennonite minutes for 1876. In contrast, eastern Pennsylvania leaders, although not valuing politics, do not appear to have seen it as profoundly threatening to nonresistants' place in society or to Mennonite identity.

51. Urry, *Mennonites, Politics, and Peoplehood*. Emphasizing the impact of the war on U.S. history can obscure international context; see Winks, *Canada and the United States*, for the significance of the Civil War in defining Canadian national identity.

52. Harding, "The Christian and the Race Question," 521, 524–25. Harding was associate pastor at Chicago's Woodlawn Mennonite Church, 1957–1961, and led Mennonite Central Committee's Atlanta voluntary service unit, 1961–1964.

References

Archive and Manuscript Collections

Adams County Courthouse, Decatur, Ind.
  "Order Book of Naturalization."
Chester County Historical Society Library, West Chester, Pa.
Elkhart County Historical Society, Bristol, Ind.
  Commissioners Papers, 1861 (77.16.187).
  Militia Enrollment Book, Elkhart Co., 1862 (999.18).
Great Lakes Research Center, Bowling Green State University, Bowling Green, Ohio.
  Fulton County, Ohio Militia Records, 1864.
Haverford College Archives, Haverford, Pa.
  Quaker Collection, Quaker Journals and Diaries.
Heritage Historical Library, Aylmer, Ont.
Indiana Commission on Public Records Archives Division, Indianapolis.
  Letter Books, Gov. Morton 1861–67 Collection, L1456.
Indiana State Library Archives, Indianapolis.
  Drafted Men 1862, No. 1, Adjutant General's Office, L723.
  Militia Enrollment Record.
  Militia Enrollment Sheets for Wells County, Harrison Township, L699, Box 24.
  State Paymaster's Report, Drawer 107, Folder 77.
Juniata College Archives, Huntington, Pa.
  Abraham Harley Cassel Collection, MS-20.
Lancaster County Historical Society Library and Archives, Lancaster, Pa.
Library of Congress
  Robert Todd Lincoln Papers.

Samuel S. Yoder Papers.

Thaddeus Stevens Papers.

Menno Simons Historical Library and Archives, Harrisonburg, Va.

Emanuel and Elizabeth Suter Collection, I-MS-31.

Frederick A. Rodes Collection, I-MS-5.

Grant M. Stoltzfus Collection, II-MS-29.

Harry A. Brunk Collection, I-MS-13.

Jacob Hildebrand Collection, I-MS-3.

Jacob R. Hildebrand Collection, I-MS-58.

Joseph K. Ruebush Collection, II-MS-8.

Lewis J. Heatwole Collection, I-MS-1.

Significant Individual Collections, I-MS-21.

Mennonite Church USA Archives, Goshen, Ind.

Committee on Economic and Social Concerns Collection, 1-3-7.

Early Mennonite Correspondence and Papers, 1708–1901, Hist. Mss. 1-10.

Jacob Nold Collection, Hist. Mss. 1–873.

John F. Funk Collection, Hist. Mss. 1-1.

Peter Nissley Collection, Hist. Mss. 1-293 SC.

Samuel D. Guengerich Collection, Hist Mss. 1-2.

Samuel Mast Collection, Hist. Mss. 1-346.

Susanna Amalia Krehbiel Collection, Hist. Mss. 1-551 SC.

Wilmer Reinford Collection, Hist. Mss. 1-280.

Mennonite Heritage Center Archives, Harleysville, Pa.

Eastern District Mennonite Conference Minutes.

John Ziegler Gehman Diary, 1829–1882.

Johannes Gross Collection.

Mennonite Historical Archive of the Cumberland Valley, Chambersburg, Pa.

Civil War file.

Clarence E. Shank Collection.

J. Irvin Lehman Collection.

Mennonite Historical Center, Richfield, Pa.

The Library of Virginia, Richmond, Va.

National Archives, Washington, D.C.

Correspondence, Major C. C. Gilbert A. A. [Acting Assistant] Provost Marshal General, Philadelphia, Pa., RG 110, Entry 2935, Provost Marshal Records, Civil War, Division of Military Records.

Letters Sent May 1863–Nov. 1865, 4 vols., 16th District of Pennsylvania, Part IV, RG110, Entry 3333, Provost Marshal Records, Civil War, Division of Military Records.

Presented to Congress on January 11, 1864, Jacob Leatherman, et al., and Rev. Jacob Overholtzer, et al. (Bucks County, Pa.) to Senate and House of Representatives, [Jan. 1864], HR38A-H1.1, House Committee on Military Affairs and the Militia, RG 46.

Proceedings of the Board of Enrollment, May 1863–Dec. 1864, 5th District of Pennsylvania, Part IV, RG 110, Entry 2915, Provost Marshal Records, Civil War, Division of Military Records.

Register of Applicants for Exemption Service, June 1863–February 1865. 2 vols. 9th District of Pennsylvania, Part IV, RG 110, Entry 3035, Provost Marshal Records, Civil War, Division of Military Records.

Ohio Historical Center, Columbus, Ohio

Record of Drafted Militia in 1862, Series 89.

Ohio Historical Society, Library/Archives Division, Columbus, Ohio.

David Tod Papers, 1862–1864, Collection 306.

Pennsylvania State Archives, Harrisburg, Pa.

Civil War Muster Rolls and Related Records, 1861–1866. Series 19.11, Office of the Adjutant General, Department of Military Affairs.

Conscientious Objector Depositions, 1862. Series 19.15, Office of the Adjutant General, Department of Military Affairs.

General Correspondence, 1793–1935. Series 19.29, Office of the Adjutant General, Department of Military Affairs.

Private Papers of Ada Beam, Morgantown, Pa.

Private Papers of Bertha Goetsch, Cleveland, Ohio

Private Papers of Wilmer Reinford, Creamery, Pa.

Private Papers of Wilmer Swope, Leetonia, Ohio.

Private Papers of Alta Schrock, Grantsville, Md.

Private Papers of Martha Shank Whissen, Broadway, Va.

Private Papers of Worth N. Yoder, Elkhart, Ind.

Schwenkfelder Historical Library, Pennsburg, Pa.

Snyder County Historical Society Library, Middleburg, Pa.

Spruance Library, Doylestown, Pa.

Affidavits of Disability, 1862.

U. S. Military History Institute, Army War College, Carlisle, Pa.

Union League Archives, Philadelphia, Pa.

Wayne County Administration Building, Wooster, Ohio

Soldiers Discharge Record.

Woodford County Clerk and Recorder's Office, Eureka, Illinois

Record of Soldiers Discharges, vol. I.

Newspapers

Bauernfreund & Demokrat, Pennsburg and Sumneytown, Pa

Berks & Schuylkill Journal, Reading, Pa.

Bluffton Banner, Bluffton, Ind.

Bucks County Intelligencer, Doylestown, Pa.

Cambria Tribune, Johnstown, Pa.

Chicago Tribune, Chicago, Ill.

Das Christliche Volks-Blatt, Milford Square, Pa.

Congressional Globe, Washington, D.C.

The Daily Times, Reading, Pa.

Decatur Eagle, Decatur, Ind.

Democrat and Sentinel, Ebensburg, Pa.

Doylestown Democrat, Doylestown, Pa

The Elkhart Review, Elkhart, Ind.,

Elkhart Truth, Elkhart, Ind.

Franklin Repository and Transcript, Chambersburg, Pa.

Der Friedens-Bote, Allentown, Pa.

The Friend, Richmond, Ind.

Goshen Democrat, Goshen, Ind.

Goshen Times, Goshen, Ind.

Harrisburg Daily Telegraph, Harrisburg, Pa.

Herald and Free Press, Norristown, Pa.

Herald of Truth, Chicago, Ill.

Holmes County Farmer, Millersburg, Ohio

Holmes County Republican, Millersburg, Ohio

Johnstown Tribune, Johnstown, Pa.

The Kalona News, Kalona, Iowa

Lancaster Daily Evening Express, Lancaster, Pa.

Lancaster Examiner & Herald, Lancaster, Pa.

Lancaster Intelligencer, Lancaster, Pa.

Lancaster Volksfreund, Lancaster, Pa.

Lewistown Gazette, Lewistown, Pa.

Mac-a-Cheek Press, Bellefontaine, Ohio

Mahoning Herald, Youngstown, Ohio

National Defender, Norristown, Pa

Der Neutralist und allgemeine Neuigkeits-Bote, Skippackville, Pa.

New York Times, New York, N.Y.

Norristown Republican, Norristown, Pa.

Norristown Times Herald, Norristown, Pa.

Ohio Democrat, New Philadelphia, Ohio.

Patriot & Union, Harrisburg, Pa.

Pennsylvania Daily Telegraph, Harrisburg, Pa.

Press and Leader, Bryan, Ohio

Reading Adler, Reading, Pa.

Richmond Whig, Richmond, Va.

Rockingham Register, Harrisonburg, Va.

Salem Republican, Salem, Ohio

Staunton Spectator, Staunton, Va.

Union Press, Bryan, Ohio.

Urbana Citizen and Gazette, Urbana, Ohio.

Wayne County Democrat, Wooster, Ohio.

Weekly Express, Lancaster, Pa.

Wooster Republican, Wooster, Ohio

York Gazette, York, Pa.

Books, Articles, and Theses

Aamodt, Terrie D. *Righteous Armies, Holy Causes: Apocalyptic Imagery and the Civil War.* Macon, Ga.: Mercer University Press, 2002.

Address of Dr. William Wetherill to the Citizens of Lower Providence Township, Montgomery County. Norristown, Pa.: Republican Office, 1863.

Albert, Allen D. *History of the Forty-Fifth Regiment, Pennsylvania Veteran Volunteer Infantry, 1861–1865.* Williamsport, Pa.: Grit Publishing Co., 1912.

Albert, George Dallas. ed., *History of the County of Westmoreland, Pennsylvania, with Biographical Sketches.* Philadelphia: L. H. Everts and Co., 1882.

Alexander, Ted, et al. *Southern Revenge: Civil War History of Chambersburg, Pennsylvania.* Shippensburg, Pa.: White Mane, 1989.

"An Amish Bishop's Conference Epistle of 1865." Trans. and ed. Harold S. Bender. *Mennonite Quarterly Review* 20 (July 1946): 222–29.

Anbinder, Tyler. *Nativism and Slavery: The Northern Know Nothings and the Politics of the 1850s.* New York: Oxford University Press, 1992.

Armstrong, Warren B. *For Courageous Fighting and Confident Dying: Union Chaplains in the Civil War.* Lawrence: University Press of Kansas, 1998.

Ayers, Edward L. *In the Presence of Mine Enemies: War in the Heart of America, 1859–1863.* New York: W. W. Norton, 2003.

Barnett, Simeon. *History of the Twenty-Second Regiment, Iowa Volunteer Infantry, Assault on Vicksburg.* Iowa City: N. H. Brainerd, 1865.

Benedict, David. *A General History of the Baptist Denomination in America and Other Parts of the World.* New York: Lewis Colby and Co., 1848.

Berlin, Ira, et al., *Slaves No More: Three Essays on Emancipation and the Civil War* (New York: Cambridge University Press, 1992)

Berry, Lee Roy, Jr. "Mennonites, African Americans, the U.S. Constitution and the Problem of Assimilation," *Mennonite Quarterly Review* 80 (July 2006): 337–70.

Biographical Album of Peoria County, Illinois. Chicago: Biographical Publishing Co., 1890.

Blackburn, E. Howard. *History of Bedford and Somerset Counties Pennsylvania, with Genealogical and Personal History.* 3 vols. New York: Lewis Pub. Co., 1906.

Blight, David W. *Race and Reunion: The Civil War in American Memory.* Cambridge, Mass.: Harvard University Press, 2001.

Bowman, Rufus D. *The Church of the Brethren and War 1708–1941.* Elgin, Ill.: Brethren Publishing House, 1944.

[Brenneman, John M.]. *Christianity and War: A Sermon Setting Forth the Suffering of Christians, . . . by a Minister of the Old Mennonite Church.* Chicago: Chas. Hess, 1863.

Brethren Encyclopedia. 3 vols. Philadelphia: Brethren Encyclopedia, Inc., 1983.

Bright, Simeon Miller. "The McNeill Rangers: A Study in Confederate Guerrilla Warfare." *West Virginia History* 12 (July 1951): 338–87.

Brock, Peter. *Freedom from War: Nonsectarian Pacifism, 1814–1914.* Toronto: University of Toronto Press, 1991.

———. *Freedom from Violence: Sectarian Nonresistance from the Middle Ages to the Great War.* Toronto: University of Toronto Press, 1991.

———. *Pacifism in the United States: From the Colonial Era to the First World War.* Princeton: Princeton University Press, 1968.

———. *The Quaker Peace Testimony, 1660–1914.* Syracuse, N.Y.: Syracuse University Press, 1990.

Brown, Marie Diller. "Biography of Bishop Henry Egly, Founder of Our Church in 1865." *Evangelical Mennonite*, 15 March 1965, 6.

Brown, Richard Maxwell. *No Duty to Retreat: Violence and Values in American History and Society.* New York: Oxford University Press, 1991.

Brown, Thomas J. *The Public Art of Civil War Commemoration: A Brief History with Documents.* Boston: Bedford/St.Martin's, 2004.

Brunk, Harry A. *History of the Mennonites in Virginia.* Vol. 1: 1727–1900. Staunton, Va.: McClure Printing Co., 1959.

———. ed., *Life of Peter S. Hartman, Including his Lecture "Reminiscences of the Civil War" and Articles by the Hartman Family.* Harrisonburg, Va.: Hartman Family, 1937.

Burdge, Edsel B., Jr. "The Prosperity of Zion in This Place: Mennonites in Germantown, 1790–1876." *Pennsylvania Mennonite Heritage* 7 (January 1984): 9–20.

Burdge, Edsel, Jr., and Samuel L. Horst. *Building on the Gospel Foundation: The Mennonites of Franklin County, Pennsylvania, and Washington County, Maryland, 1730–1970.* Scottdale, Pa.: Herald Press, 2004.

Burkhart, J. Paul. "The Diller Mennonite Church, Newville, Pa." *Christian Monitor* 14 (August 1927): 246–47.

Burkholder, Christian. *Useful and Edifying Address to the Young . . . ,* 179–257. Bound in *Christian Spiritual Conversation on Saving Faith, for the Young, in Questions and Answers . . .* Lancaster, Pa.: John Baer and Sons, 1857.

Burkholder, Roy S. *Be Not Conformed to This World: A Narrative History of the Weaverland Mennonites, 1900–1975.* Morgantown, Pa.: Masthof Press, 1997.

Burkholder, John Richard. "For Conscience' Sake? Examining a Commonplace." In *The Measure of My Days: Engaging the Life and Thought of John L. Ruth,* eds. Reuben Z. Miller and Joseph S. Miller, 250–57. Telford, Pa.: Cascadia Publishing House, 2004.

Bush, Perry. *Two Kingdoms, Two Loyalties: Mennonite Pacifism in Modern America.* Baltimore: Johns Hopkins University Press, 1998.

Butler, Jon. *Awash in a Sea of Faith: Christianizing the American People.* Cambridge, Mass.: Harvard University Press, 1990.

Carwardine, Richard J. *Evangelicals and Politics in Antebellum America.* New Haven, Conn.: Yale University Press, 1993.

———. "Methodists, Politics and the Coming of the Civil War." In *Methodism and the Shaping of American Culture,* eds. Nathan O. Hatch and John H. Wigger, 309–42. Nashville: Kingswood Books, 2001.

Castel, Albert. "Order No. 11 and the Civil War on the Border." *Missouri Historical Review* 57 (Oct. 1962): 357–68.

Catton, Bruce. *The Coming Fury.* Garden City, N.Y.: Doubleday, 1961.

Chamberlain, Daniel R. "First Pure, Then Peaceable: The Position of the Wesleyan Methodist Church on War and Peace from its Founding to the Civil War." In *Within the Perfection of Christ: Essays on Peace and the Nature of the Church,* ed. Terry L. Brensinger and E. Morris Sider, 217–30. Nappanee, Ind.: Evangel Press, 1990.

Chesebrough, David B. *Clergy Dissent in the Old South, 1830–1865.* Carbondale: Southern Illinois University Press, 1996.

———. *"God Ordained This War": Sermons on the Sectional Crisis, 1830–1865.* Columbia: University of South Carolina Press, 1991.

———. *No Sorrow Like Our Sorrow: Northern Protestant Ministers and the Assassination of Lincoln.* Kent, Ohio: Kent State University Press, 1994.

Chesson, Michael. "Harlots or Heroines? A New Look at the Richmond Bread Riot." *Virginia Magazine of History and Biography* 92 (April 1984): 131–75.

Cimbala, Paul A., and Randall Miller, eds. *The Freedmen's Bureau and Reconstruction: Reconsiderations.* New York: Fordham University Press, 1999.

Coddington, Edwin B. *The Gettysburg Campaign: A Study in Command.* New York: Scribner's, 1968.

———. "Prelude to Gettysburg: The Confederates Plunder Pennsylvania." *Pennsylvania History* 30 (April 1963): 123–31.

Coffman, Barbara F. *His Name Was John: The Life Story of an Early Mennonite Leader.* Scottdale, Pa.: Herald Press, 1964.

Commemorative Biographical Record of Wayne County, Ohio. Chicago: J. N. Beers & Co., 1889.

The Confession of Faith of the Christians Known by the Name of Mennonites . . . Winchester, Va.: Robinson and Hollis, 1837.

Conrad, W. P. *Conococheague: A History of the Greencastle-Antrim Community, 1736–1971.* Greencastle: Greencastle-Antrim School District, 1971.

Conway, Wing. *History of Cumberland County Pennsylvania.* Philadelphia: James D. Scott, 1879.

Cook, Adrian. *Armies of the Streets: The New York City Draft Riots of 1863.* Lexington: University Press of Kentucky, 1974.

Cooper, William J., Jr., *Jefferson Davis, American.* New York: Alfred A. Knopf, 2000.

Crofts, Daniel W. *Reluctant Confederates: Upper South Unionists in the Secession Crisis.* Chapel Hill: University of North Carolina Press, 1989.

Cronon, William. *Nature's Metropolis: Chicago and the Great West.* New York: W. W. Norton, 1991.

Curran, Thomas F. *Soldiers of Peace: Civil War Pacifism and the Postwar Radical Peace Movement.* New York: Fordham University Press, 2003.

Currey, Cecil B. "The Devolution of Quaker Pacifism: A Kansas Case Study, 1860–1955." *Kansas History* 6 (Summer 1983): 120–33.

Davis, William C. *Look Away! A History of the Confederate States of America.* New York: Free Press, 2002.

"Deacon Michael Hege's Church Record Book." *Conococheague Mennonist* 1 (July 1993): 8–12.

Diner, Hasia R. *A Time for Gathering: The Second Migration, 1820–1880.* Baltimore: Johns Hopkins University Press, 1992.

Driver, Robert J., Jr. *52nd Virginia Infantry.* Lynchburg, Va.: H. E. Howard, Inc., 1986.

Donald, David Herbert. *Lincoln.* New York: Simon and Schuster, 1995.

Durnbaugh, Donald F. *Fruit of the Vine: A History of the Brethren, 1708–1995.* Elgin, Ill.: Brethren Press, 1997.

Durr, J. N. "History of the Mennonite Church in Morrison's Cove." *Gospel Herald* 20, 10 November 1927, 714–15.

"Emanuel Hochstetler Writes to Peter Swartzendruber in 1862." Iowa Mennonite Historical Society *Reflections* 5 (Summer 1991): 3–4.

Erb, Ethel Estella Cooprider. *Story of Grandmother Heatwole-Brunk-Cooprider.* Hesston, Kans.: Book and Bible Room, [1944].

Erb, Paul. *South Central Frontiers: A History of the South Central Mennonite Conference.* Scottdale, Pa.: Herald Press, 1974.

Estes, Steven R. *A Goodly Heritage: A History of the North Danvers Mennonite Church.* Danvers, Ill.: North Danvers Mennonite Church, 1982.

———. *Living Stones: A History of the Metamora Mennonite Church.* Metamora, Ill.: Metamora Mennonite Church, 1984.

Falb, Timothy R. *Fruits of Diversity: Martins Mennonite Church and Pleasant View Mennonite Church, 1834–1984.* Orrville, Ohio: Martins and Pleasant View Mennonite Churches, 1984.

Faust, Drew Gilpin. "Christian Soldiers: The Meaning of Revivalism in the Confederate Army." *Journal of Southern History* 53 (February 1987): 63–90.

———. *The Creation of Confederate Nationalism: Ideology and Identity in the Civil War South.* Baton Rouge: Louisiana State University Press, 1988.

———. *Mothers of Invention: Women of the Slaveholding South in the Civil War.* Chapel Hill: University of North Carolina Press, 1996.

Fellman, Michael. *Inside War: The Guerrilla Conflict in Missouri During the American Civil War.* New York: Oxford University Press, 1989.

Fisher, Noel. "Groping Toward Victory: Ohio's Administration of the Civil War." *Ohio History* 105 (Winter-Spring 1996): 25–45.

Flinn, Frank M. *Campaigning with Banks in Louisiana, '63 and '64, and with Sheridan in the Shenandoah Valley in '64 and '65,* 2nd ed. Boston: W. B. Clarke and Co., 1889.

Fogleman, Aaron S. "From Slaves, Convicts, and Servants to Free Passengers: The Transformation of Immigration in the Era of the American Revolution." *Journal of American History* 85 (June 1998): 43–76.

———. *Hopeful Journeys: German Immigration, Settlement, and Political Culture in Colonial America, 1717–1775.* Philadelphia: University of Pennsylvania Press, 1996.

Foner, Eric. *Free Soil, Free Labor, and Free Men: The Ideology of the Republican Party before the Civil War.* New York: Oxford University Press, 1970.

———. *Reconstruction: America's Unfinished Revolution.* New York: Harper and Row, 1988.

———.*Slavery, the Civil War, and Reconstruction: The New American History, Revised and Expanded.* Washington, D.C.: American Historical Association, 1997.

Foote, Shelby. *The Civil War: A Narrative. Fredericksburg to Meridian.* New York: Random House, 1963.

Fox-Genovese, Elizabeth, and Eugene D. Genovese. "The Divine Sanction of Social Order: Religious Foundations of the Southern Slaveholders' World View." *Journal of the American Academy of Religion* 55 (Summer 1987): 211–33.

Fredrickson, George M. "The Coming of the Lord: Northern Protestant Clergy and the Civil War Crisis." In *Religion and the American Civil War*, eds. Randall M. Miller, Harry S. Stout, and Charles Reagan Wilson, 110–130. New York: Oxford University Press, 1998.

———.*The Inner Civil War: Northern Intellectuals and the Crisis of the Union.* New York: Harper and Row, 1965.

Freehling, William W. *The South vs. the South: How Anti-Confederate Southerners Shaped the Course of the Civil War.* New York: Oxford University Press, 2001.

Friedman, Leon. "Conscription and the Constitution: The Original Understanding." *Michigan Law Review* 67 (June 1969): 1493–552.

Fretz, A. J. *A Brief History of Bishop Henry Funck and Other Funk Pioneers.* Elkhart, Ind.: Mennonite Publishing Co., 1899.

———.*A Genealogical Record of the Descendants of Jacob Beidler of Lower Milford Township, Bucks Co., Pa.* Milton, N.J.: A. J. Fretz, 1903.

Frey, Jerry. *Grandpa's Gone: The Adventures of Daniel Buchwalter in the Western Army, 1862–1865.* Shippensburg, Pa.: Burd Street Press, 1998.

Funk, Benjamin. *The Life and Labors of Elder John Kline, the Martyr Missionary; Collated from his Diary.* Elgin, Ill.: Brethren Pub. House, 1900.

Funk, John F. *Warfare: Its Evils, Our Duty.* Chicago: Chas. Hess, 1863.

———. "More Border Ruffianism." *Mennonite Historical Bulletin* 34 (April 1973): 2–3.

Gable, John E. *History of Cambria County Pennsylvania.* 2 vols. Topeka [Kans.]: Historical Pub. Co., 1926.

Gaines, Foster M. *Ghosts of the Confederacy: Defeat, the Lost Cause, and the Emergence of the New South, 1865–1913.* New York: Oxford University Press, 1987.

Gallagher, Gary W. *The Confederate War: How Popular Will, Nationalism, and Military Strategy Could Not Stave off Defeat.* Cambridge, Mass.: Harvard University Press, 1997.

———, ed. *Struggle for the Shenandoah: Essays on the 1864 Valley Campaign.* Kent: Kent State University Press, 1991.

———,ed. *The Shenandoah Valley Campaign of 1862.* Chapel Hill: University of North Carolina Press, 2003.

Gambone, A. M. *The Life of General Samuel K. Zook: Another Forgotten Union Hero*. Baltimore: Butternut and Blue, 1996.

Garber, D. W. *The Holmes County Rebellion*. Pub. by author, 1967.

Geary, James W. "Civil War Conscription in the North: A Historiographic Review." *Civil War History* 32 (September 1986): 208–28.

———. *We Need Men: The Union Draft in the Civil War*. DeKalb: Northern Illinois University Press, 1991.

General and Local Laws . . . of the State of Ohio, v. 61. Columbus: Richard Nevins, 1864.

Gienapp, William E. *The Origins of the Republican Party, 1852–1856*. New York: Oxford University Press, 1987.

———. "Who Voted for Lincoln?" In *Abraham Lincoln and the American Political Tradition*, ed. John L. Thomas, 50–97. Amherst, Mass.: University of Massachusetts Press, 1986.

Gingerich, Hugh F., and Rachel W. Kreider, comps. *Amish and Amish Mennonite Genealogies*. Gordonville, Pa.: Pequea Publishers, 1986.

Gingerich, Melvin. *The Mennonites in Iowa*. Iowa City, Iowa: State Historical Society of Iowa, 1939.

Goen, C. C. *Broken Churches, Broken Nation: Denominational Schism and the Coming of the Civil War*. Macon, Ga.: Mercer University Press, 1985.

Godschalk, Abraham. *A Family Record and Other Matters*. Harrisburg, Pa.: United Evangelical Press, 1912.

Goldfield, David. *Still Fighting the Civil War: The American South and Southern History*. Baton Rouge: Louisiana State University Press, 2002.

Gratz, Delbert L. *Bernese Anabaptists and their American Descendants*. Scottdale, Pa.: Herald Press, 1953.

Greeley, Horace. *The American Conflict: A History of the Great Rebellion in the United States of America, 1860–65*. 2 vols. Hartford, Conn.: O. D. Case, 1867.

Green, Helen Binkley, ed., *Pages from a Diary, 1843–1880: Excerpts from the Diaries of Jacob Stouffer and Eliza Ryder Stouffer*. Hagerstown, Md.: Helen B. Green, 1966.

Grimsley, Mark. *The Hard Hand of War: Union Military Policy Toward Southern Civilians, 1861–1865*. New York: Cambridge University Press, 1995.

Grossman, David. *On Killing: The Psychological Cost of Learning to Kill in War and Society*. Boston: Little, Brown, and Co., 1995.

Gudehus, Jonas Heinrich. "Journey to America." In *Ebbes fer Alle—Ebber Ebbes fer Dich: Something for Everyone—Something for You*, ed. Albert F. Buffington, trans. Larry M. Neff, 173–329. Breinigsville, Pa.: Pennsylvania German Society, 1980.

Guelzo, Allen C. *Abraham Lincoln: Redeemer President*. Grand Rapids, Mich.: Wm. B. Eerdmans, 1999.

———. *Lincoln's Emancipation Proclamation: The End of Slavery in America*. New York: Simon and Schuster, 2004.

Habegger, David L., and Karen C. Adams. *The Swiss of Adams and Wells Counties, Indiana, 1838–1862*. Fort Wayne: D. L. Habegger, 2002.

Hamm, Thomas D. *The Transformation of American Quakerism: Orthodox Friends, 1800–1907*. Bloomington: Indiana University Press, 1988.

Hardesty's Historical and Geographical Encyclopedia, Illustrated: Containing . . . Special Military History of Ohio. New York: H. H. Hardesty & Co., 1885.

Harding, Vincent. "The Christian and the Race Question." In *The Lordship of Christ: Proceedings of the Seventh Mennonite World Conference, August 1–7, 1962, Kitchener, Ontario*, ed. C. J. Dyck, 520–25. Elkhart, Ind.: Mennonite World Conference, 1963.

Hatch, Nathan O. *The Democratization of American Christianity*. New Haven, Conn.: Yale University Press, 1989.

Haynes, Stephen R. *Noah's Curse: The Biblical Justification of American Slavery*. New York: Oxford University Press, 2002.

Heatwole, John L. *The Burning: Sheridan in the Shenandoah Valley*. Charlottesville, Va.: Rockbridge Publishing, 1998.

Heatwole, Lewis J. "The Virginia Conference." In *Mennonite Church History*, ed. J. S. Hartzler and Daniel Kauffman, 198–224. Scottdale, Pa.: Mennonite Book and Tract Society, 1905.

Heatwole, R. J. "A Civil War Story." *Mennonite Historical Bulletin* 9 (January 1948): 3–4.

———. "Reminiscences of War Days." *Gospel Herald* 4, 12 October 1911, 444.

Heisey, M. Luther. "Lancaster in the Gettysburg Campaign." *Papers Read Before the Lancaster County Historical Society* 43 (No. 2, 1939): 58–63.

Hess, Nancy B. *By the Grace of God*. Harrisonburg, Va.: Hess Book Co., 1979.

Heyrman, Christine Leigh. *Southern Cross: The Beginnings of the Bible Belt*. Chapel Hill: University of North Carolina Press, 1997.

Hildebrand, Jacob R. *A Mennonite Journal, 1862–1865: A Father's Account of the Civil War in the Shenandoah Valley*, ed. John R. Hildebrand. Shippensburg, Pa.: Burd Street Press, 1996.

Hill, Samuel S. "Religion and the Results of the Civil War." In *Religion and the American Civil War*, ed. Randall M. Miller, Harry S. Stout, and Charles Reagan Wilson, 360–77. New York: Oxford University Press, 1998.

History of Allen County, Ohio. Chicago: Warner, Beers & Co., 1885.

History of Bedford, Somerset and Fulton Counties, Pennsylvania. Chicago: Waterman, Watkins & Co., 1884.

History of Cumberland and Adams Counties, Pennsylvania. Chicago: Warner, Beers & Co., 1886.

The History of Peoria County Illinois. Chicago: Johnson & Company, 1880.

Hoffman, Jacob A. *The Leidig Family.* Hagerstown, Md.: n.p., 1960.

Hoke, Jacob. *Reminiscences of the War; or Incidents which Transpired in and about Chambersburg, during the War of the Rebellion.* Chambersburg, Pa.: M. A. Foltz, 1884.

———. *The Great Invasion of 1863; or, General Lee in Pennsylvania.* Dayton, Ohio: W. J. Shuey, 1887.

Holliday, Joseph E. "Relief for Soldiers' Families in Ohio During the Civil War." *Ohio History* 71 (July 1962): 97–112.

Holmes, Amy E. "'Such Is the Price We Pay': American Widows and the Civil War Pension System." In *Toward a Social History of the American Civil War*, ed. Maris Vinovskis, 171–95. Cambridge: Cambridge University Press, 1990.

Holt, Michael F. *The Fate of Their Country: Politicians, Slavery Extension, and the Coming of the Civil War.* New York: Hill and Wang, 2004.

———. *The Rise and Fall of the American Whig Party, Jacksonian Politics and the Onset of the Civil War.* New York: Oxford University Press, 1999.

Hoover, Francis T. *Enemies in the Rear: or a Golden Circle Squared.* Boston: Arena Publishing Co., 1894.

Hopkins, Leroy T. "Uneasy Neighbors: Germans and Blacks in Nineteenth-Century Lancaster County." In *States of Progress: Germans and Blacks in America over 300 Years*, ed. Randall M. Miller, 72–88. Philadelphia: German Society of Pennsylvania, 1989.

Horst, Irvin B., trans., *Mennonite Confession of Faith.* Lancaster, Pa.: Lancaster Mennonite Historical Society, 1988.

Horst, Samuel L., ed. "The Journal of a Refugee." *Mennonite Quarterly Review* 54 (October 1980): 280–304.

———. *Mennonites in the Confederacy: A Study in Civil War Pacifism.* Scottdale, Pa.: Herald Press, 1967.

———, ed. *The Fire of Liberty in Their Hearts: The Diary of Jacob E. Yoder of the Freedmen's Bureau School, Lynchburg, Virginia, 1866–1870.* Richmond, Va.: The Library of Virginia, 1996.

Huffer, Donna, and Ken Purdy, comps. "Civil War Soldiers Buried in Augusta County, VA, Cemeteries." Typed manuscript located in the Staunton Public Library, Staunton, Va.

Hughes, Richard T. *Myths America Lives By.* Urbana: University of Illinois Press, 2003.

Hunsecker, Catharine. "Civil War Reminiscences." *Christian Monitor* 16 (January 1924): 406–407.

Ireland, Owen S. "Germans Against Abolition: A Minority's View of Slavery in Revolutionary Pennsylvania." *Journal of Interdisciplinary History* 3, no. 4 (1973): 685–706.

"John Hunt's Diary." *Proceedings of the New Jersey Historical Society* 53 (January 1935): 26–43.

John, Richard. "Taking Sabbatianism Seriously: The Postal System, the Sabbath, and the Transformation of American Political Culture." *Journal of the Early Republic* 10 (Winter 1990): 517–67.

Johannsen, Robert W. *Stephen A. Douglas.* New York: Oxford University Press, 1973.

Johns, Ira S., et al., eds. *Minutes of the Indiana-Michigan Mennonite Conference, 1864–1929, Compiled by Order of Conference.* Scottdale, Pa.: Mennonite Publishing House, [1929?].

Johnson, Curtis D. *Redeeming America: Evangelicals and the Road to Civil War.* Chicago: Ivan R. Dee, 1993.

Johnson, Michael P., ed., *Abraham Lincoln, Slavery, and the Civil War: Selected Writings and Speeches.* Boston: Bedford/St.Martin's, 2001.

Johnson, Robert U., and Clarence C. Buel. *Battles and Leaders of the Civil War.* 4 vols. New York: Century Co., 1887–1888.

Jones, Howard. *Abraham Lincoln and a New Birth of Freedom: The Union and Slavery in the Diplomacy of the Civil War.* Lincoln, Neb.: University of Nebraska Press, 1999.

Juhnke, James C. *A People of Two Kingdoms: The Political Acculturation of the Kansas Mennonites.* Newton, Kans.: Faith and Life Press, 1975.

Juhnke, James C., and Carol M. Hunter. *The Missing Peace: The Search for Nonviolent Alternatives in United States History,* 2nd ed. Kitchener, Ont.: Pandora Press, 2004.

Kauffman, S. Duane. *Mifflin County Amish and Mennonite Story: 1791–1991.* Belleville: Mifflin County Mennonite Historical Society, 1991.

Kaufman, Edmund G. *General Conference Mennonite Pioneers.* Newton: Bethel College, 1973.

Keller, Christian B. "Germans in Civil War–Era Pennsylvania: Ethnic Identity and the Problem of Americanization." Ph.D. diss., Pennsylvania State University, 2001.

———."Pennsylvania and Virginia Germans During the Civil War: A Brief History and Comparative Analysis." *Virginia Magazine of History and Biography* 109 (Spring 2001): 37–86.

———."The Reaction of Eastern Pennsylvania's German Press to the Secession Crisis: Compromise or Conflict?" *Yearbook of German-American Studies* 34 (Winter 1999): 35–61.

Keller, Kenneth W. "Cultural Conflict in Early Nineteenth-Century Pennsylvania Politics." *Pennsylvania Magazine of History and Biography* 110 (October 1986): 509–30.

Klement, Frank L. *Lincoln's Critics: The Copperheads of the North*. Shippensburg, Pa.: White Mane Books, 1999.

———. *The Limits of Dissent: Clement L. Vallandigham and the Civil War*. Lexington: University Press of Kentucky, 1970.

Klingberg, Frank W. "The Southern Claims Commission: A Postwar Agency in Operation." *Mississippi Valley Historical Review* 32 (Sept. 1945): 195–214.

Knight, George R. "Adventism and Military Service: Individual Conscience in Ethical Tension." In *Proclaim Peace: Christian Pacifism from Unexpected Quarters*, eds. Theron F. Schlabach and Richard T. Hughes, 157–71. Urbana: University of Illinois Press, 1997.

Knobel, Dale T. *"America For the Americans": The Nativist Movement in the United States*. New York: Twayne Publishers, 1996.

Koons, Kenneth E., and Warren R. Hofstra, eds. *After the Backcountry: Rural Life in the Great Valley of Virginia, 1800–1900*. Knoxville: University of Tennessee Press, 2000.

Kraybill, Spencer L., and Noah L. Zimmerman. *History of a John Graybill Family in America, 1681–1981*, 2nd ed. Baltimore: Gateway Press, 1982.

Krehbiel, Christian. *Prairie Pioneer: The Christian Krehbiel Story*. Newton, Kans.: Faith and Life Press, 1961.

Kselman, Thomas A., ed. *Belief in History: Innovative Approaches to European and American Religion*. Notre Dame, Ind.: University of Notre Dame Press, 1991.

"Lancaster County and the Civil War." *Mennonite Historical Bulletin* 35 (April 1974): 4.

Lawson, Melinda. *Patriot Fires: Forging a New American Nationalism in the Civil War North*. Lawrence: University Press of Kansas, 2002.

Lehman, James O. *A Century of Grace: In the Community and Around the World*. Pandora, Ohio: Grace Mennonite Church, 2004.

———. "The Coffmans at 'Mannheim' on Wenger Mill Road and the Slave Trade." *Shenandoah Mennonite Historian* 12 (Autumn 2005): 2–6.

———. "Conflicting Loyalties of the Christian Citizen: Lancaster Mennonites and the Early Civil War Era." *Pennsylvania Mennonite Heritage* 7 (April 1984): 2–15.

———. *Creative Congregationalism: A History of the Oak Grove Mennonite Church in Wayne County, Ohio*. Smithville, Ohio: Oak Grove Mennonite Church, 1978.

———. *Crosswinds: From Switzerland to Crown Hill*. Rittman, Ohio: Crown Hill Mennonite Church, 1975.

———. "Duties of the Mennonite Citizen: Controversy in the Lancaster Press Late in the Civil War." *Pennsylvania Mennonite Heritage* 7 (July 1984): 5–20.

———. "Greenbrier County, West Virginia, Home of an Early Mennonite Community and Church Where Mennonitism Failed to Survive." *Shenandoah Mennonite Historian* 13 (Summer 2006): 1–6, 8.

———. *Growth Amidst Struggle: A Sesquicentennial History of the Longenecker Mennonite Church.* Winesburg, Ohio: Longenecker Mennonite Church, 1980.

———. *Lindale's Song: A Century of Harmony, Growth and Fellowship, 1898 to 1998.* Harrisonburg, Va.: Lindale Mennonite Church, 1998.

———. *Salem's First Century: Worship and Witness.* Kidron, Ohio: Salem Mennonite Church, 1986.

———. *Seedbed for Leadership: A Centennial History of the Pike Mennonite Church.* Elida, Ohio: Pike Mennonite Church, 1974.

———. *Sonnenberg, A Haven and a Heritage: A Sesquicentennial History of the Swiss Mennonite Community of Southeastern Wayne County, Ohio.* Kidron, Ohio: Kidron Community Council, 1969.

Leonard, Thomas C. *Above the Battle: War-Making in America From Appomattox to Versailles.* New York: Oxford University Press, 1978.

Levine, Bruce. *Confederate Emancipation: Southern Plans to Free and Arm Slaves during the Civil War.* New York: Oxford University Press, 2005.

———. *Half Slave and Half Free: The Roots of Civil War,* Rev. ed. New York: Hill and Wang, 2005.

Levine, Peter. "Draft Evasion in the North During the Civil War, 1863–1865." *Journal of American History* 67 (March 1981): 816–34.

Liechty, Joseph, and James O. Lehman. "From Yankee to Nonresistant: John F. Funk's Chicago Years, 1857–1865." *Mennonite Quarterly Review* 59 (July 1985): 205–209.

Long, E. B., with Barbara Long, *The Civil War, Day by Day: An Almanac, 1861–1865.* New York: Doubleday, 1971.

Longenecker, Stephen L. *Shenandoah Religion: Outsiders and the Mainstream, 1716–1865.* Waco, Tex.: Baylor University Press, 2002.

———. "The Narrow Path: Anti-slavery, Plainness, and the Mainstream." In *After the Backcountry: Rural Life in the Great Valley of Virginia, 1800–1900,* eds. Kenneth E. Koons and Warren R. Hofstra, 185–193. Knoxville: University of Tennessee Press, 2000.

Loomis, Elisha S. *Some Account of Jacob Oberholtzer.* Cleveland: Pub. by author, 1931.

Lowdermilk, Will H. *History of Cumberland, Maryland.* Reprint. Baltimore: Regional Publishing Co., 1976.

Luthy, David. *The Amish in America: Settlements that Failed, 1840–1960.* Aylmer, Ont.: Pathway Publishers, 1986.

———. "Amish and the Civil War." *Family Life* 29 (March 1996): 16–20.

———, trans. and ed. "An Important Pennsylvania Broadside of 1812." *Pennsylvania Mennonite Heritage* 7 (July 1984): 2–4.

MacMaster, Richard K. *Land, Piety, Peoplehood: The Establishment of Mennonite Communities in America, 1683–1790.* Scottdale, Pa.: Herald Press, 1985.

MacMaster, Richard K., with Samuel L. Horst and Robert F. Ulle, *Conscience in Crisis: Mennonites and Other Peace Churches in America, 1739–1789.* Scottdale, Pa.: Herald Press, 1979.

Maust, Alvin L. and Edna (Miller). *Descendants of Jacob Swartzentruber.* Meyersdale, Pa.: Authors, 1980.

McCleary, Ann E. "Forging a Regional Identity: Development of Rural Vernacular Architecture in the Central Shenandoah Valley, 1790–1850." In *After the Backcountry: Rural Life in the Great Valley of Virginia, 1800–1900*, eds. Kenneth E. Koons and Warren R. Hofstra, 92–110. Knoxville: University of Tennessee Press, 2000.

McCordick, David. *The Civil War Letters (1862–1865) of Private Henry Kauffman.* Lewiston: Edwin Mellen Press, 1991.

McKivigan, John R. *The War Against Proslavery Religion: Abolitionism and the Northern Churches, 1830–1865.* Ithaca, N.Y.: Cornell University Press, 1984.

McKivigan, John R. and Mitchell Snay, eds. *Religion and the Antebellum Debate over Slavery.* Athens: University of Georgia Press, 1998.

McPherson, James M. *Battle Cry of Freedom: The Civil War Era.* New York: Oxford University Press, 1988.

———. *Crossroads of Freedom: Antietam.* New York: Oxford University Press, 2002.

———. *For Cause and Comrades: Why Men Fought in the Civil War.* New York: Oxford University Press, 1997.

———. *Hallowed Ground: A Walk at Gettysburg.* New York: Crown, 2003.

McSherry, Patrick M. "The Defense of Columbia, June 1863." *Journal of the Lancaster County Historical Society* 84 (1981): 136, 150–51.

Mennonite Encyclopedia, vols. 1–4. Scottdale, Pa.: Mennonite Publishing House, 1955–1959; vol. 5. Scottdale, Pa.: Herald Press, 1990.

Miller, Ivan J. *History of the Conservative Mennonite Conference 1910–1985.* Grantsville: Ivan J. and Della Miller, 1985.

Miller, Levi. "Daniel Musser and Leo Tolstoy." *Mennonite Historical Bulletin* 54 (April 1993): 1–7.

———. "The Growth and Decline of Mennonites Near Scottdale, Pennsylvania: 1790–1890." *Pennsylvania Mennonite Heritage* 13 (Oct. 1990): 2–15.

Miller, Randall M. "Catholic Religion, Irish Ethnicity, and the Civil War." In *Religion and the American Civil War*, ed. Randall M. Miller, Harry S. Stout, and Charles Reagan Wilson, 261–96. New York: Oxford University Pres, 1998.

———. "Introduction." In *States of Progress: Germans and Blacks in America over 300 Years*, ed. Randall M. Miller, 4–7. Philadelphia: German Society of Pennsylvania, 1989.

Miller, Randall M., Harry S. Stout, and Charles Reagan Wilson, eds., *Religion and the American Civil War*. New York: Oxford University Pres, 1998.

Minutes of the Virginia Mennonite Conference. Harrisonburg: Virginia Mennonite Conference, 1939.

Mitchell, Reid. "Christian Soldiers? Perfecting the Confederacy." In *Religion and the American Civil War*, ed. Randall M. Miller, Harry S. Stout, and Charles Reagan Wilson, 297–309. New York: Oxford University Pres, 1998.

———. "Soldiering, Manhood, and Coming of Age: A Northern Volunteer." In *Divided Houses: Gender and the Civil War*, eds. Catherine Clinton and Nina Silber. New York: Oxford University Press, 1992.

———. *The Vacant Chair: The Northern Soldier Leaves Home*. New York: Oxford University Press, 1993.

Moody, William R. *The Life of Dwight L. Moody, by His Son*. New York: Fleming H. Revell, 1900.

Mook, Maurice A. "An Early Amish Colony in Chester County, Pennsylvania." *Mennonite Historical Bulletin* 16 (July 1955): 1–3.

Moore, Albert Burton. *Conscription and Conflict in the Confederacy*. New York: Macmillan, 1924.

Moore, R. Laurence *Religious Outsiders and the Making of Americans*. New York: Oxford University Press, 1986.

Moorehead, James H. *American Apocalypse: Yankee Protestants and the Civil War, 1860–1869*. New Haven, Conn.: Yale University Press, 1978.

Morris, Roy, Jr. *Sheridan: The Life and Wars of General Phil Sheridan*. New York: Crown Publishers, 1992.

Moulton, Phillips P., ed. *The Journal and Major Essays of John Woolman*. New York: Oxford University Press, 1971.

Murphy, Terrence V. *10th Virginia Infantry*. Lynchburg, Va.: H. E. Howard, Inc., 1989.

Musser, Daniel. *Non-Resistance Asserted: or The Kingdom of Christ and the Kingdom of This World Separated, and No Concord Between Christ and Belial. In Two Parts*. Lancaster, Pa.: Elias Barr & Co., Publishers, 1864.

Musser, I. G. "What About Voting?" *Gospel Herald* 5 (3 October 1912), 428–29.

"A Mutual Aid Plan From the Civil War Era." *Mennonite Historical Bulletin* 34 (October 1973): 4.

Nash, Gary B. "From 1688 to 1788: Slavery and Freedom in Pennsylvania." In *States of Progress: Germans and Blacks in America over 300 Years*, ed. Randall M. Miller, 27–37. Philadelphia: The German Society of Pennsylvania, 1989.

Neely, Mark E., Jr. *Southern Rights: Political Prisoners and the Myth of Confederate Constitutionalism*. Charlottesville: University Press of Virginia, 1999.

Nelson, Jacquelyn S. *Indiana Quakers Confront the Civil War*. Indianapolis: Indiana Historical Society, 1991.

Niebuhr, H. Richard. *Christ and Culture*. New York: Harper and Row, 1951.

Noll, Mark A. *America's God: From Jonathan Edwards to Abraham Lincoln*. New York: Oxford University Press, 2002.

———. *The Civil War as a Theological Crisis*. Chapel Hill: University of North Carolina Press, 2006.

Nolt, Steven M. "The Baseball Commissioner and the Mennonites." *Mennonite Historical Bulletin* 62 (July 2001): 4–5.

———. "Christian Farni and Abraham Lincoln: Legal Advice and the Election of 1860." *Illinois Mennonite Heritage* 23 (March 1996): 1, 13–14.

———. "Finding a Context for Mennonite History: Pennsylvania German Ethnicity and the (Old) Mennonite Experience." *Pennsylvania Mennonite Heritage* 21 (October 1998): 2–14.

———. *Foreigners in Their Own Land: Pennsylvania Germans in the Early Republic*. University Park: Pennsylvania State University Press, 2002.

———. *A History of the Amish*, rev. ed. Intercourse, Pa.: Good Books, 2003.

———. "The Rise and Fall of an Amish Distillery: Economic Networks and Entrepreneurial Risk on the Illinois Frontier." *Illinois Mennonite Heritage* 22 (September 1995): 45, 53–63; and (December 1995): 65, 75–79.

———. "A 'Two-Kingdom' People in a World of Multiple Identities: Religion, Ethnicity, and American Mennonites." *Mennonite Quarterly Review* 73 (July 1999): 485–502.

North, Homer F. "Bishop David Burkholder." *Gospel Herald* 27 (Dec. 6, 1934), 767.

Nosworthy, Brent. *The Bloody Crucible of Courage: Fighting Methods and Combat Experience of the Civil War*. New York: Carroll & Graf, 2003.

Paludan, Philip Shaw. *"A People's Contest": The Union and the Civil War, 1861–1865*. Lawrence: University Press of Kansas, 1996.

———. "Religion and the American Civil War." In *Religion and the American Civil War*, ed. Randall M. Miller, Harry S. Stout, and Charles Reagan Wilson. New York: Oxford University Press, 1998.

The Past and Present of Woodford County, Illinois. Chicago: Wm. LeBaron & Co., 1878.

Pease, Theodore C., and James G. Randall, eds. *The Diary of Orville Hickman Browning*. 2 vols. Springfield, Ill.: Illinois State Historical Library, 1925–1933.

Peddycord, Will F. *History of the Seventy-Fourth Regiment Indiana Volunteers, Infantry: A Three Years' Organization.* Warsaw, Ind.: Smith Printing, 1913.

A Portrait and Biographical Record of Allen and Putnam Counties, Ohio. Chicago: A. W. Bowen & Co., 1896.

Portrait and Biographical Record of Tazewell and Mason Counties, Illinois. Chicago: Biographical Publishing Co., 1894.

Prowell, George R. *History of York County Pennsylvania.* Vol. 2. Chicago: J. H. Beers & Co., 1907.

Purvis, Thomas L. "Patterns of Ethnic Settlement in Late Eighteenth-Century Pennsylvania." *Western Pennsylvania Historical Magazine* 70 (April 1987): 107–22.

Quigley, David. *Second Founding: New York City, Reconstruction, and the Making of American Democracy.* New York: Hill and Wang, 2004.

Rable, George C. *But There Was No Peace: The Role of Violence in the Politics of Reconstruction.* Athens: University of Georgia Press, 1984.

——. *The Confederate Republic: A Revolution Against Politics.* Chapel Hill: University of North Carolina Press, 1994.

Raber, Merrill and Boots (Esch), comps. and eds. "Jacob D. Guengerich: A Remarkable Pioneer Who Moved to Iowa in 1846." *Mennonite Family History* 15 (July 1996): 101–105.

Raboteau, Albert J. *Slave Religion: The "Invisible Institution" in the Antebellum South.* New York: Oxford University Press, 1978.

Ramage, James A. *Rebel Raider: The Life of General John Hunt Morgan.* Lexington: University Press of Kentucky, 1986.

Reece, J. N. *Report of the Adjutant General of the State of Illinois.* Springfield, Ill.: Adjutant General, 1901.

Reed, John F. "Montgomery County's 'Bivouac of the Dead.'" *Bulletin of the Historical Society of Montgomery County* 13 (1961): 49–64.

Reidenbaugh, Lowell. *33rd Virginia Infantry.* Lynchburg, Va.: H. E. Howard, Inc., 1987.

Rempel Smucker, David J. "War, Government, and Mennonites: A Broadside of the Civil War Period." *Pennsylvania Mennonite Heritage* 26 (April 2003): 13–16.

Reschly, Steven D. *The Amish on the Iowa Prairie, 1840–1910.* Baltimore: Johns Hopkins University Press, 2000.

Richardson, James D., ed. *A Compilation of the Messages and Papers of the Confederacy, Including the Diplomatic Correspondence, 1861–1865.* 2 vols. Nashville, Tenn.: United States Publishing, 1906.

Ridner, Judith "Status, Culture, and the Structural World in the Valley of Pennsylvania." In *After the Backcountry: Rural Life in the Great Valley of Virginia,*

1800–1900, eds. Kenneth E. Koons and Warren R. Hofstra, 77–91. Knoxville: University of Tennessee Press, 2000.

Risser, Johannes. "Abschaffung der Sklaverei," Das Christliche Volks-Blatt 6, 2 October 1861, 20.

———. "Enthält das alte Testament, das heilige Wort Gottes, eine Lehre oder nur einen entfernten Grund, welcher zu Gunsten unserer Sklaverei im Süden spricht?" Das Christliche Volks-Blatt 6, 4 September 1861, 12.

Robertson, Andrew. "The Idealist as Opportunist: An Analysis of Thaddeus Stevens' Support in Lancaster County, 1843–1866." Journal of the Lancaster County Historical Society, 84 (Easter 1980): 80–86.

Robinson, Carl F., and Amos W. Strite, The History and Genealogical Records of the Strites and Allied Families. Hagerstown, Md.: Amos Strite, 1963.

Rowe, D. W. A Sketch of the 126th Regiment, Pennsylvania Volunteers. . . . Chambersburg, Pa.: Cook and Hays Publishers, 1869.

Russell, R. R. "Development of Conscientious Objector Recognition in the United States." George Washington Law Review 20 (March 1952): 409–48.

Russo, Paul G. "The Conscientious Objector in American Law." Religion in Life 10 (Summer 1941): 333–45.

Ruth, John L. Maintaining the Right Fellowship: A Narrative Account of Life in the Oldest Mennonite Community in North America. Scottdale, Pa.: Herald Press, 1984.

———. The Earth Is the Lord's A Narrative History of the Lancaster Mennonite Conference. Scottdale, Pa.: Herald Press, 2001.

Sandow, Robert M. ed., "Remember Your Friend Until Death": A Collection of Civil War Letters From the West Overton Archives. West Overton, Pa.: West Overton Museums, n.d.

Sanger, Samuel F., and Daniel Hays. The Olive Branch of Peace and Good Will to Men: Anti-War History of the Brethren and Mennonites, the Peace People of the South, During the Civil War 1861–1865. Elgin, Ill.: Brethren Publishing House, 1907.

Sappington, Roger E. The Brethren in the New Nation: A Source Book on the Development of the Church of the Brethren, 1785–1865. Elgin, Ill.: Brethren Press, 1976.

Schildt, John W. Roads from Gettysburg. Shippensburg, Pa.: Burd Street Press, 1998.

Schlabach, Erv. A Century and a Half With the Mennonites at Walnut Creek. Walnut Creek, Ohio: Walnut Creek Mennonite Church, 1978.

Schlabach, Theron F. Gospel Versus Gospel: Mission and the Mennonite Church, 1863–1944. Scottdale, Pa.: Herald Press, 1980.

———. Peace, Faith, Nation: Mennonites and Amish in Nineteenth-Century America. Scottdale, Pa.: Herald Press, 1988.

Schmucker, Samuel M. A History of the Civil War in the United States, with a Preliminary View of Its Causes. . . . Philadelphia: Bradley & Co., 1862.

Schmutz, George S. *History of the 102d Regiment, O.V.I.* [Wooster, Ohio]: G. S. Schmutz, 1907.

Schrock, Iona. "Celebration of 125 Years of Mennonites in Cass County, Missouri." *South Central Conference Messenger* 44 (Sept./Oct. 1991): 5–6.

Scott, Stephen E. *An Introduction to Old Order and Conservative Mennonite Groups.* Intercourse, Pa.: Good Books, 1996.

Sensenig, Barton, comp. *The "Sensineys" of America (Senseny, Sensenig, Sensenich, Senseney).* Philadelphia: Lyon and Armor, 1943.

Seyfert, A. G. "A Page of Lancaster County History, During Civil War Times." *Papers Read Before the Lancaster County Historical Society* 31, no. 8 (1927): 111–17.

Shankman, Arnold M. *The Pennsylvania Antiwar Movement, 1861–1865.* Rutherford, N.J.: Farleigh Dickinson University Press, 1980.

Shattuck, Gardiner H., Jr., *A Shield and a Hiding Place: The Religious Life of the Civil War Armies.* Macon, Ga.: Mercer University Press, 1999.

Sheridan, Philip H. *Personal Memoirs of P. H. Sheridan, General, United States Army,* 2 vols. New York: Charles L. Webster & Co., 1891.

Silber, Nina. "Intemperate Men, Spiteful Women, and Jefferson Davis: Northern Views of the Defeated South," *American Quarterly* 41 (December 1989): 614–35.

Simmons, J. Susanne, and Nancy T. Sorrells, "Slave Hire and the Development of Slavery in Augusta County, Virginia," In *After the Backcountry: Rural Life in the Great Valley of Virginia, 1800–1900,* eds. Kenneth E. Koons, and Warren R. Hofstra, 169–84. Knoxville: University of Tennessee Press, 2000.

Slaughter, Thomas P. *Bloody Dawn: The Christiana Riot and Racial Violence in the Antebellum North.* New York: Oxford University Press, 1991.

Slingluff, Fielder C. "The Burning of Chambersburg," *The Pennsylvania-German* 10 (July 1909): 323–30.

Smith, C. Henry. *The Mennonites of America.* Goshen: Author, 1909.

Smith, Willard H. *Mennonites in Illinois.* Scottdale, Pa.: Herald Press, 1983.

Snay, Mitchell. *Gospel of Disunion: Religion and Separatism in the Antebellum South.* New York: Cambridge University Press, 1993.

Snyder, C. Arnold. *Anabaptist History and Theology: An Introduction.* Kitchener, Ont.: Pandora Press, 1995.

Soderlund, Jean R. *Quakers and Slavery: A Divided Spirit.* Princeton, N.J.: Princeton University Press, 1985.

Sollenberger, Samuel Grove, and Grace Hege. *Jacob Grove and Elizabeth Lesher Grove Family* (S.l.; n.d.).

Spotts, Charles D. *They Called It Strasburg (18th and 19th Centuries).* Lancaster, Pa.: Schaff Library, 1968 [published as Community Historians Annual, v. 7].

Springer, Joe. "Johannes Risser." *Mennonite Historical Bulletin* 37 (October 1976): 2–3.

Sprunger, Eva F. *The First Hundred Years: A History of the Mennonite Church in Adams County, Indiana, 1838–1938*. Berne, Ind.: n.p., 1938.

Stampp, Kenneth M. *And the War Came: The North and the Secession Crisis, 1860–1861*. Baton Rouge: Louisiana State University Press, 1950.

Starr, Stephen Z. *The Union Cavalry in the Civil War*, 3 vols. Baton Rouge: Louisiana State University Press, 1979–85.

Stauffer, Jacob W. *Stauffer's Geschicht-Büchlein von der sogenannten Mennonisten Gemeinde . . . durch J. St. Geschrieben im Jahr 1850*. Lancaster, Pa.: Johann Bär und Söhnen, 1855.

Stauffer, Richard E. *Stauffer-Stouffer-Stover and Related Families*. Old Zionsville, Pa.: R. E. Stauffer, 1977.

Steffen, Dorcas. "The Civil War and the Wayne County Mennonites." *Mennonite Historical Bulletin* 26 (July 1965): 1–3.

Sterling, Robert E. "Civil War Draft Resistance in the Middle West." Ph.D. diss., Northern Illinois University, 1974.

Stoll, Joseph, ed. "An Amishman's Diary—1864." *Family Life* 2 (September 1969): 34–39.

Stoltzfus, Grant M. *Mennonites of the Ohio and Eastern Conference*. Scottdale: Herald Press, 1969.

Storey, Henry Wilson. *History of Cambria County Pennsylvania*. vols. 2 and 3. New York: Lewis Publishing Co., 1907.

Stout, Harry S. *Upon the Altar of the Nation: A Moral History of the Civil War*. New York: Viking, 2006.

Suter, Mary E. *Memories of Yesteryear: A History of the Suter Family*. Waynesboro, Va.: Charles F. McClung, Printer, 1959.

Swartz, David R. "'Mista Mid-Nights': Mennonites and Race in Mississippi." *Mennonite Quarterly Review* 78 (October 2004): 469–502.

Swierenge, Robert P. "The Settlement of the Old Northwest: Ethnic Pluralism in a Featureless Plain." *Journal of the Early Republic* 9 (Spring 1989): 73–105.

Swope, Wilmer D. "Columbiana County, Ohio, Mennonites and the Ohio State Militia." *Mennonite Historical Bulletin* 23 (July 1962): 7.

Swortzel, Shannon W. "Bishop Jacob Hildreband, Jr." Unpublished paper, n.d., in Menno Simons Historical Library and Archives.

Tanner, Robert G. *Stonewall in the Valley: Thomas J. "Stonewall" Jackson's Shenandoah Valley Campaign, Spring 1862*. Garden City, N.Y.: Doubleday, 1976.

Taylor, James E. *With Sheridan Up the Shenandoah Valley in 1864: Leaves From a Special Artist's Sketch Book and Diary*. Cleveland: Western Reserve Historical Society, 1989.

Terrell, W. H. H. *Indiana in the War of the Rebellion: Report of the Adjutant General.* Reprint of vol. 1. Indianapolis: Indiana Historical Bureau, 1960.

Thomas, Emory M. *The Confederate Nation: 1861–1865.* New York: Harper and Row, 1979.

"Three Civil War Letters from Ohio to Maryland." *Conococheague Mennonist* 3 (January 1995): 9–12.

Trefousse, Hans L. *Andrew Johnson: A Biography.* New York: W. W. Norton, 1989.

———. *Thaddeus Stevens: Nineteenth-century Egalitarian.* Chapel Hill: University of North Carolina Press, 1997.

Troyer, Glenn L., et al. *Mennonite Church History of Howard and Miami Counties, Indiana.* Scottdale, Pa.: Mennonite Publishing House, 1916.

Tully, Alan. "Patterns of Slaveholding in Colonial Pennsylvania: Chester and Lancaster Counties, 1729–1758." *Journal of Social History* 6 (Spring 1973): 284–305.

Umble, John S. "The Fairfield, Ohio, Background of the Allen County, Ohio, Mennonite Settlement, 1799–1860." *Mennonite Quarterly Review* 6 (January 1932): 5–29.

Unionists and the Civil War Experience in the Shenandoah Valley. 3 vols. Comp. by Norman R. Wenger and David S. Rodes; ed. Emmert F. Bittinger. Harrisonburg, Va.: Valley Brethren-Mennonite Heritage Center and Valley Research Associates, 2003–2005.

Urry, James. *Mennonites, Politics, and Peoplehood: Europe-Russia-Canada, 1525–1980.* Winnipeg: University of Manitoba Press, 2006.

War of the Rebellion: A Compilation of the Official Records of the Union and Confederate Armies. 128 vols. Washington, D.C.: Government Printing Office, 1880–1901.

Watson, Harry L. *Liberty and Power: The Politics of Jacksonian America.* New York: Hill and Wang, 1990.

Wayland, John W. *A History of Rockingham County, Virginia.* Dayton, Va.: Ruebush-Elkins Co., 1912.

———. *Virginia Valley Records: Genealogical and Historical Materials of Rockingham County, Virginia, and Related Regions.* Strasburg, Va.: Shenandoah Publishing House, 1930.

Weaver, J. Denny. *Becoming Anabaptist: The Origin and Significance of Sixteenth-Century Anabaptism,* 2nd ed. Scottdale, Pa.: Herald Press, 2005.

Weber, Harry F. *Centennial History of the Mennonites of Illinois, 1829–1929.* Goshen, Ind.: Mennonite Historical Society, 1931.

Wenger, John C. *History of the Mennonites of the Franconia Conference.* Telford, Pa.: Franconia Mennonite Historical Society, 1937.

Wenger, Joseph H. *History of the Descendants of Abraham Beery.* Reprint. Kokomo, Ind.: Selby Publishing, 1989.

Wenger, Samuel S., ed. *The Wenger Book: A Foundation Book of American Wengers.* Lancaster, Pa.: Pennsylvania German Heritage History, 1978.

Whanger, Thomas Richard. *"The Trail of Agony": The Arduous Civil War Journey of David Whanger.* Pittsburgh: Pub. by author, 1993.

Wherry, Neal M. *Conscientious Objection.* Special Monograph No. 11, 2 vols. Washington, D.C.: Government Printing Office, 1950.

Whiteman, Maxwell. *Gentlemen in Crisis: The First Century of the Union League of Philadelphia 1862–1963.* Philadelphia: Union League, 1975.

Wiegand, Martha Steiner, comp. *Steiner Family Record, 1720–1978: The Ancestry and Posterity of John and Anna (Steiner) Steiner.* Morning Sun, Iowa.: M. S. Wiegand, 1978.

Wilson, Charles R. "McClellan's Changing Views on the Peace Plank of 1864." *American Historical Review* 38 (April 1933): 498–505.

Winks, Robin W. *Canada and the United States: The Civil War Years.* Baltimore: Johns Hopkins University Press, 1960.

Wittlinger, Carlton O. *Quest for Piety and Obedience: The Story of the Brethren in Christ.* Nappanee, Ind.: Evangel Press, 1978.

Wokeck, Marianne. "The Flow and the Composition of German Immigration to Philadelphia, 1727–1775." *Pennsylvania Magazine of History and Biography* 105 (July 1981): 249–78.

Woodworth, Steven E. *While God is Marching On: The Religious World of Civil War Soldiers.* Lawrence: University Press of Kansas, 2001.

Wright, Edward Needles. *Conscientious Objectors in the Civil War.* Philadelphia: University of Pennsylvania Press, 1931.

Wust, Klaus. *The Virginia Germans.* Charlottesville: University Press of Virginia, 1969.

Wyatt-Brown, Bertram. "Church, Honor, and Secession." In *Religion and the American Civil War,* ed. Randall M. Miller, Harry S. Stout, and Charles Reagan Wilson, 89–109. New York: Oxford University Press, 1998.

Yoder, Don. "Palatine, Hessian, Dutchman: Three Images of the German in America." In *Ebbes fer Alle—Ebber Ebbes fer Dich: Something for Everyone—Something for You,* ed. Albert F. Buffington, 107–29. Breinigsville, Pa.: The Pennsylvania German Society, 1980.

Yoder, Elmer S. *From Das Buchenland to The Beech.* Louisville, Ohio: Beech Mennonite Church, 1991.

Yoder, Mary Elizabeth. "Amish Settlers and the Civil War." *Family Life* 4 (March 1971): 26–28.

Yoder, M. Marie, and Paul H. *The Daniel Beachy Family of Aurora, West Virginia: Their Lineage and Life Stories.* Grantsville, Md.: M. M. and P. H. Yoder, 1995.

Yoder, Paton. *Eine Würzel: Tennessee John Stoltzfus.* Lititz, Pa.: Sutter House, 1979.

———. *Tradition and Transition: Amish Mennonites and Old Order Amish, 1800–1900.* Scottdale, Pa.: Herald Press, 1991.

Yoder, Paton, and Steven R. Estes, trans. and eds. *Proceedings of the Amish Ministers' Meetings, 1862–1878.* Goshen, Ind.: Mennonite Historical Society, 1999.

Yoder, Richard B. "Nonresistance Among the Peace Church of Southern Somerset County, Pennsylvania During the Civil War." Unpublished paper, filed in Mennonite Historical Library, Goshen, Ind., 1959.

Yousey, Arlene. *Strangers and Pilgrims: History of Lewis County Mennonites.* Croghan, N.Y.: Arlene Yousey, 1987.

Ziegler, Valarie H. *The Advocates of Peace in Antebellum America.* Bloomington: Indiana University Press, 1992.

Zigler, D. H. *A History of the Brethren in Virginia.* Elgin, Ill.: Brethren Publishing House, 1908.

Zigler, Robert M. "Elder John Kline—Churchman." *Brethren Life and Thought* 9 (Summer 1964): 3–20.

Zook, Douglas D., Jr. "A Biographical Sketch of Samuel K. Zook." *Bulletin of the Historical Society of Montgomery County* 23 (Spring 1982): 94–123.

Index

The Authors

James O. Lehman is director emeritus of libraries at Eastern Mennonite University, Harrisonburg, Virginia, and is the author of nine congregational and community histories as well as a book on twentieth-century Mennonite revivalism.

Steven M. Nolt is a professor of history at Goshen College, Goshen, Indiana. His books include *Plain Diversity: Amish Cultures and Identities* (2007) and *Amish Enterprise: From Plows to Profits* (2nd ed., 2004), both published by the Johns Hopkins University Press.

Calvin Redekop, Stephen C. Ainlay, and Robert Siemens, *Mennonite Entrepreneurs*

Benjamin W. Redekop and Calvin W. Redekop, eds. *Power, Authority, and the Anabaptist Tradition*

Steven D. Reschly, *The Amish on the Iowa Prairie, 1840 to 1910*

Kimberly D. Schmidt, Diane Zimmerman Umble, and Steven D. Reschly, *Strangers at Home: Amish and Mennonite Women in History*

Diane Zimmerman Umble, *Holding the Line: The Telephone in Old Order Mennonite and Amish Life*

David Weaver-Zercher, *The Amish in the American Imagination*